SO, WHAT'S YOUR POINT ?

Finding *The* Plot in a Chart Your Own Adventure Culture

Fran Sciacca

HANDS
of HUR

Hands of Hur, Inc.
4725 Caldwell Mill Road
Birmingham, AL 35243-3056
www.handsofhur.org

Cover and interior design: geoffsciacca design; www.geoffsciacca.com

ISBN-10: 0985967609
ISBN-13: 978-0-9859676-0-4

Printed in China

P   10   9   8   7   6   5   4   3   2   1

Y   20   19   18   17   16   15   14   13   12

Εγώ σε ἐδόξασα ἐπὶ τῆς γῆς τὸ ἔργον τελειώσας ὃ δέδωκάς μοι ἵνα ποιήσω.

Ιωάννης 17·4

Endorsements

As a student in one of Fran Sciacca's first classes, I was the beneficiary of his passion and zeal for seeing students renewed by the Gospel—not just salvation from our sins and a free pass to heaven, but the height, depth, breadth and glory of the Story of redemption. Now, thirty years later, his passion burns more brightly. *So, What's Your Point?* is a realistic and honest portrait of the mess we live in, but also a beautiful painting of God's loving mercy for his creatures. As he did in my life so long ago, Fran's work continues to give hope and a mission to those who will listen.

Elisabeth Maxwell Ryken
First Lady, Wheaton College

If you are content with our culture, comfortable with the North American church scene, and confident that if you die Jesus will applaud you for having invested your time, goods, talents, and spiritual gifts for His glory, then you will not like this book. Nevertheless, you should read it. On the other hand, if you see much in yourself and the Christian culture around you that needs to be transformed by Jesus Christ, read this book because it might help you get closer to true North on your spiritual compass. Fran Sciacca is a modern day Jeremiah. He will not make his readers comfortable, but he needs to be heard.

Lyle Dorsett, Ph.D.
Author and Billy Graham Professor of Evangelism
Beeson Divinity School

Like a master craftsman, Fran has woven together the elements of God's great redemptive story. *So, What's Your Point?* is clear, concise, and compelling. A great service to the Body of Christ, helping us understand our role in The Story.

Dana L Thomas
COO/Executive Director
Kids Across America

Like most of my generation I am weary of the therapeutic theology and snake-oil spirituality that has dominated much of the evangelical landscape over the last thirty years. The primary message to us has been that the Christian life is ultimately all about us as individuals. But I believe that many of us have found the life of being a moralistic narcissist wanting and empty. Our hunger to get out in the world, and in the words of my father, be "shalom restorers" is only increasing. In my opinion, *So, What's Your Point?* provides a fresh and invigorating understanding of our biblical identity. It unearths the long-lost plot of the faith and provides fresh marching orders on how Christ's followers can join Him in bringing grace and peace to a sin-strangled world. If the readers of this book will absorb these prophetic words and put them into action then I have great hope for the future of America and the American Church.

Ben Sciacca
Urban Youth Worker, and Author

Fran Sciacca brings decades of observation, study, and teaching to its proper culmination in a compelling, refreshingly authentic read. One of the book's most important contributions to a society desperately seeking "what's my point?" is the challenge that true purpose can only be found in design and that meaningful adventure comes when we quit chasing our own dreams and instead chase the dreams of God. This work is an outstanding read and a gift and wake up call to the Church.

MariBeth Poor
Minister to Young Marrieds and Young Professionals
Mountain Top Community Church

Zeal with knowledge; passion with humility...Fran Sciacca has delivered an honest and Biblically driven critique of where many of us in the American church have lost our way...shooting 'pointless' arrows into targets that were never on God's radar to begin with. Read at your own risk, and pray to God to be part of the solution...which will be your "point."

Matt Letourneau
Atlanta City Director
The Navigators

Fran Sciacca's *So, What's Your Point?* is truly timely, deeply and convincingly biblical. A prophet's voice—self-cheated and at peril are those who ignore it; savingly located are those who heed it.

Walter J. Schultz, Ph.D.
Professor of Philosophy
Northwestern College

I have made a decision over the past few years to read less, but reread more of the books that challenge me to change. *So, What's Your Point?* is now on that list. I will repeatedly revisit this book and encourage my children to do the same.
Carl Lynn
Executive Director
Restoration Academy

It's difficult the isolate one genre to describe this important book. It's a perceptive and incisive *social analysis*—particularly of American, and more pointedly Evangelical, cultural values. Sciacca writes out of his considerable research and wide-ranging personal experiences to analyze and critique important developments since the pivotal 1960's. But more, he shows convincingly the impact of these developments on the church that has sadly come to mirror the culture in a multitude of ways. The book is also *self-help*, if there can be a best sense of that genre. That is, Sciacca seeks to help followers of Christ come to embrace and live out their God-designed identity, not on the basis of the values and messages the culture champions and sells so effectively. But the book is also a *biblical theology*—and Sciacca is careful to tell the full story of the Bible, what some call the "Grand Narrative." If Christians understand who they are and what God's redemptive program in the world entails, they will fine their own mission and real fulfillment, though probably not the "American Dream"! This book will provoke a crisis: do we really want what God wants or do we want what we want? Do we define the goal of life in terms of American values, or God's call? Sciacca is bold, in the pattern of God's prophets, telling God's life-giving message in a day of great crisis. And, to be sure, Sciacca knows the ins and outs of that crisis in the lives of real people after a lifetime of teaching students and speaking widely, not to mention his own life story. Sciacca's writing is gripping, alive, and engaging; he's clearly an accomplished communicator. My fear is that those who most need to read and heed his message won't bother to read the book, or that we read the book and dismiss its wakeup call. But if we do, we will live much diminished lives. Sciacca gives Christians a prescription and a mandate for lives worth living, ones that truly fulfill the mission of God for this world.
William W. Klein, Ph.D.
Professor of New Testament
Denver Seminary

Table of Contents

A Word To The Rising Generation

My generation is a curious one. On one hand, I have great hope for us. There is a robust enthusiasm to infuse our sin-saturated culture with life. Many of us are passionate about using our talents, treasures, and strength to spread the gospel. This involves entering the workforce, but also moving into broken and gritty communities as missionaries.

It's not unusual for us to move into the hood or raise support to pursue overseas mission work. We are active, and unlike many generations that preceded us, we are not satisfied with making regular church attendance our primary expression for following Jesus. Nor do we find it adequate to merely make "check cutting" and tithe our primary means of supporting missions. I believe that we've chosen what some have termed "incarnational" ministry as our chief way of showing a sin-strangled world the Savior. We aren't satisfied with Jesus merely meeting our needs and christening our vocations and families with His blessing. Many of us are convinced that He's calling us to participate in a larger story - His Story. And we want to be a part.

Unfortunately, I have also found in my generation an epidemic of short-term commitment. Any roots that we put down are shallow at best. We are distracted. Flippant. Easily offended. Few are willing to stay the course and go the distance when adversity shows up (or a better opportunity presents itself). There is always the proverbial "greener grass," and so what we're doing "now" is really just a setup to position us for what we're going to do eventually. I have dubbed us the "tumbleweed generation" because like the uprooted desert vegetation, we are prone to blow through jobs, churches, ministry "callings" and even marriages with great flippancy and frequency. Consequently, for many, our legacy will be as transient as footprints along the shoreline of the beach.

I would challenge the quality of our depth and mettle as well. Much of our substantive thinking has been reduced to glib Tweets and insipid Facebook status updates. We champion and amuse ourselves with the trivial. Craving community, we've found the ethereal social network to suffice for relationships and even as a means of disciple-making. It's not unusual for us to throw the white wires in our ears and tune out the world - fully immersed in our playlists and podcasts. Our skin is thin, and we struggle with confrontation, and so much of our self-worth hinges on the praise or criticism of others. When our feelings get hurt, we tend to sulk and cower, or rant like spoiled children. We need to be noticed and appreciated.

Much of our condition exists because my generation is plot-starved. Sometimes, we are plot-jaded. The primary brand of Christianity that was passed on to us as children, espoused the idea that Jesus was chiefly interested in saving us from hell, making us better people, and being a big part of whatever *we* chose to do in life. At the outset this plan sounded quite pleasant - mainly because it was all about us. It was sanctified narcissism. But after having tried this brand of Christianity, most of us found it wanting. After gorging at the spiritual all-you-can eat buffet line we came away feeling bloated, overindulged, and spiritually constipated. The brand of Christianity that we received largely failed.

Even so, some of us stayed with the plot and are now adult versions of the "me-myself-and-Jesus Christianity" that was peddled to us as kids. Others have abandoned the faith altogether and adopted a non-religious view (hence the "nones") or have even embraced atheism as an alternative. And still there are many of us who know that there has to be more - that there has to be a genuine plot to the story of our lives. We yearn to believe that Jesus has something for us to do. To be. To become.

Now in our twenties and thirties the proverbial baton is being passed into our hands. And whether we're ready or not, it's becoming our race to run and our war to fight. I think that deep within us we have the goods as far as our internal makeup, but we're missing a concise course of action. And, our maverick mentality needs a serious makeover. Our identity is somewhat fragmented. Like confused characters in a cinematic event, some of us have forgotten and lost our lines. And, we aren't connected to the rest of the "cast." Others of us are still searching for the script. It's for these reasons that I asked my dad to write this book. If you come to love this book as I have, then you can shake my hand. If you don't, then lay the blame on me. For several years, I begged and cajoled my father to put this message into print. And, I wasn't alone. Now I'm grateful that he gave in and that this book exists. I pursued him on this because I firmly believe that the truths borne on these pages are revolutionary even though they are ancient. I sincerely believe that they can be a lighthouse for those of us who feel adrift and are yearning to find out who we are and where we fit into what Jesus is doing in this ever-darkening world. If my generation (or any reader for that matter) will take heed to the warnings, embrace the instruction, and immerse themselves in the plot that Christ has set out for us then I have great hope for us and for the efficacy of the Church to join Jesus in reaching the lost.

Ben Sciacca
Birmingham, AL
September 2012

A Word From The Retiring Generation

"God is acting according to his plans for his purposes in Christ Jesus."

This is the very present, fundamental, dynamic reality underlying all things. Everything will be made right. A day is coming when all things will finally be as they were meant to be. Nothing can prevent it. Redemption accomplished and applied will issue ultimately in every redeemed persons' intimate fellowship with God on the earth. Out of his inexhaustible fullness of riches in Christ, God will himself be everything to every created being. The earth will be thoroughly saturated with peace and justice—forever. Those who do not belong to Jesus will be excluded forever. Are you in? Do you want in? Before you answer, you should know that it doesn't make any difference, because either way you—and everything else—are involved in God's comprehensive purposes that will be brought to pass.

Disturbing and astonishing as it may seem, this truth is not so vivid in the minds of American Christians. Just when and why the sense that only the historical progression of God's purposeful actions gives structure and meaning to all things began to diminish or fade in the collective conscious of God's people is a question for scholars. My point is that God keeps raising up those who present it again. In 1739 pastor Jonathan Edwards began a series of sermons recounting that same history, calling the collection of sermons a "History of the Work of Redemption." For decades in the last century, professor James Hatch taught a course at Columbia Bible College and Seminary titled "Progress of Redemption." Tracing the history, influences and differences of all those who held that the Bible is primarily a narrative record of God's redemptive purpose may be worthy of a doctoral dissertation. That is not my concern. Rather, given the gravity of what is at stake, God seems always to raise up people of obvious stature—people who have tasted and fully understand the effects of sin and suffering and the struggle of faith—God faithfully enables these servants to speak to his people with clarity, passion, truth, and gravity. They remind us that we are part of a much, much bigger story than we realize and to exhort us not to waste our lives, but to live them deliberately and faithfully as followers of Jesus.

Using the literary metaphors of story and drama, Fran Sciacca presents this truth in ways that enlighten, encourage, challenge, yea—even at times offend. But, these have always been the range of effects the words of the prophets have had on those who hear. There is an urgency in his writing that sets aside the often tedious and unconvincing qualifications that accompany the writings of academics and of those who are too careful in advancing their own agenda. God's people are so easily distracted from their identity, design and purpose that are borne out of this Story that begins before Eden and ends with earth being filled with the knowledge of the glory of the Lord. Stern warnings and stinging criticisms served up with unmistakable love are always in order. Faithful are the wounds of a prophet.

When Jonathan Edwards was asked to assume the presidency of the College of New Jersey (later to be renamed Princeton University) he begged off, explaining that, "My heart is so much in these studies, that I cannot find it in my heart to be willing to put myself into an incapacity to pursue them any more." Edwards never brought his History of the Work of Redemption to completion. In a similar way, this book springs from Sciacca's heart for the church. I found myself reading it like any other book. It was an inanimate object that I was paying attention to. But soon that changed. It absorbed me, swallowed me, and located me within its message. It may occur to the reader that Sciacca's use of the expression, "The Story" and his referring to the stages of God's acting as though they were "Acts" in a play is an accommodation to the postmodern skepticism regarding the truthfulness of any historical report. (James Hatch used the same metaphor long before narrative theology took on its current flavor.) The reader soon discerns that Sciacca never prostrates himself to the spirit of the times. Rather, the idea of a drama structure by "Acts" and "Scenes" is a helpful literary device used by a skillful teacher to speak the plain truth.

They say that one should always begin reading a book with the last paragraph. Listen to the last two sentences of Sciacca's work: "What remains is for you to determine whether you've been trying to find a role for Jesus in your own Chart Your Own Adventure, or find your place in His. This is really the only choice you have. And, it's the only one that matters. Choose well." It is no coincidence if you think you hear an echo of Joshua's voice across the millennia. When Joshua was about to die, he gathered the people of Israel together. At that meeting he accounted for their collective identity and their present circumstances by "locating them" (so to speak) historically in God's purposeful actions beginning with God's promises to Abraham given some 600 years earlier. Joshua's speech may be the first, publically-given, or communal confession of faith recorded in scripture. Some 800 years after Joshua, Ezra repeats the account beginning again from Abraham and locating the Jews of the restoration from the Babylonian captivity in God's redeeming actions. Some 500 years after Ezra's speech and after the death and resurrection of Jesus the Christ and the outpouring of God's Spirit in the redeemed, Peter, Stephen, and Paul all account for things by retelling a history beginning with God's promises to Abraham. In his letter to the Galatian Christians, Paul explains, "Christ redeemed us so that in Christ Jesus the blessing of Abraham might come to the Gentiles, so that we might receive the promised Spirit through faith." What these confessions have in common is that they recount the mighty acts of God as he fulfills his purposes according to his promise to Abraham. To put it another way, the public confessions of faith recorded in scripture all begin with Abraham and recount "the mighty acts of God"—who acts according to his plans for his purposes in Christ. The people of God owe their being, their identity, their significance, their present circumstances, and their eternal destiny to God's purposeful actions in Christ.

Fran Sciacca, standing in and extending the several thousand-year tradition going back at least to Joshua, is a twenty-first century prophet led by grace. In his hands, the familiar doctrines of sin, salvation, and spirituality are faithfully restated in a series of seven concepts: Christians are Adamic, Adopted, Abrahamic, Apprentices who are Alien Ambassadors and Advocates to a world lying under the oppression of things that, "are *not* as they're supposed to be." Let anyone who has ears to hear this prophet and who for whatever reason is distracted or deeply discouraged—let that person decisively and deliberately take every thought captive to the fact that one's Identity, Design, and Purpose are meant for Shalom. Choose. Take up your bed and walk. Work, for the Day is at hand.

Walter Schultz, Ph.D.
Roseville, MN
August 2012

Preface *(or...why I wrote this book)*

As a man in his sixties, I am properly schooled *and* experienced regarding the immediate danger of criticism in which I place myself, by comparing anything I've ever done to the labor of childbirth. Stronger men than I have been dismantled in dialogue with, or in the presence of women, by carelessly comparing or contrasting childbirth to something they have endured. Having coached my wife through three natural childbirth deliveries—the last of which was a set of twins with a breach caveat thrown in by God—I'm no stranger to the pain, although I'm no veteran of it either. However, as I've pondered how to begin this book, I am continually drawn back to the metaphor of labor and delivery; the whole birthing experience.

Nearly a quarter of a century ago, I set out to write a book on behalf of a generation that was in their late teens. I was actually recruited to write this book. Now, that generation is in its twenties and thirties. Some are even in their forties. That book was a rather audacious appeal to my own generation—the Baby Boomers—for us to put on our big boy pants and admit complicity, even responsibility, for the spiritual demise of the American flavor of Western Christianity. I labored in that book to validate the assertion that the Sixties was a decade that altered the cultural landscape of the US permanently. The Church in America had been in bed with the culture for at least two decades. I made the claim that we had become slightly more than a marginally moral, mirror-image of the larger culture. Replete with our own industries to one another, our own magazines, entertainment, schools, and franchises, We had slowly, like the proverbial frog in the kettle, become our own subculture instead of a counter-culture. For many of us, faith was more a product of democracy and Wall Street than the Scriptures. The book was titled, *Generation at Risk: What Legacy Are Baby Boomers Leaving Their Kids.*

In the metaphor of parenting, *Generation* was a stillbirth. The publisher solemnly announced to me that the book was officially *out* of print three months before it was *in* print. A decision had been made to curtail the publishing arm of the organization to focus its efforts and budget on its central calling—evangelism. It was a wise and reasonable decision for them, and one that I've come to admire as an older man. Nonetheless, then, I was stunned. Without trying to hijack the birthing metaphor too much, it was akin to a final doctor's visit just before delivery, in which you discover your long-awaited child is no longer living. *Generation* was put on the auction block. Another well-known publisher bought the rights to the book, but because of a complex mixture of circumstances, *Generation* suffered a second death. I returned to teaching, and writing dropped off my radar.

That was nearly twenty-five years ago. In the ensuing two decades, I immersed myself in the students who populated my classrooms day in and day out. I listened. I watched. I learned. And I realized that the things I was so passionate about earlier—the ideas that had woven themselves into the tapestry of *Generation*—were coming to pass before my eyes. The "generation at risk" had become the generation at hand. I adjusted my teaching to focus on what I believed was vital for the spiritual health of the twenty-first century Church. These new passions congealed into a corpus of material I had so internalized that it became difficult for me and any who knew me, to distinguish between the two.

In 2005, I left the formal classroom for an informal one, and founded Hands of Hur, a ministry to existing ministries through teaching and resources. My commitment to remain a diminutive and obscure blip on the Kingdom radar seemed safe. However, about five years ago, while at a lake house owned by a younger man for whom I have the highest regard, a heated debate broke out between us regarding *his* conviction that I had a "responsibility" to write for the next generation. He insisted, in no tender terms, that I "owed" it to his children and my own grandchildren, to leave some textual legacy of the heart and soul of what had become signature teaching and talking points for me. I wasn't interested. I told him I'd already tried that. He wasn't persuaded by my arguments. Instead, he laid a challenge on the table: Had I ever considered that the whole purpose of my life was somehow related to what I would leave, more than what I said while living? I patronized his spirituality, but dismissed his admonishment. He was only forty. What did he know?

Since that conversation, almost imperceptibly, I have slowly been led back to the rising generation. This time through the teaching and training of collegiate ministers and the students they serve. My wife Jill and I are now deeply engaged in helping the current generation of campus ministry workers understand the secular and Church cultures, the effects of technology on spirituality, and God's grand drama called the gospel. Their interest and enthusiasm energized me. It all culminated in the fall of 2011 when, on two occasions, I addressed nearly 1,000 college students from 25 secular college campuses. I had sought to distill my greatest passions into three 1-hour messages, knowing I would leave much under-explained, and ever more totally untouched. Yet, I found myself working on these messages months in advance, something very foreign to my intense, "just-in-time" production mindset. The title of the message series was, "So, What's Your Point?"

So, here I am again, giving birth to another book I hadn't planned to conceive. It may turn out that this is the book God had been shaping within me all along. The obvious difference is that instead of writing on *behalf* of the generation at risk, I now find myself writing *to* them. Therefore, this book, while surely suitable for any modern believer or seeker, regardless of age, it has a special application for that demographic.

My own generation, with the final shore in sight, is focused on the harbor ahead. How, when, and where our own story will end. Our lives are not yet over, but our options are increasingly diminished. End of life and health care issues, physical limitations, and the sheer energy requirement for relocation, make dramatic life-change choices retreat into the realm of unlikelihood. For some of us, there comes a point in life when we can't awaken from the American Dream, even if we want to. And, in fairness to my own generation I need to express to those *not* facing that final shore, a few words of encouragement. God is also expanding the number of older believers who deeply desire to do all *they* can to empower and equip the rising generation to do all that *they* can to enlarge the Kingdom of God. Wherever it leads them.

However, the generation that is coming of age shows signs of a profound and genuine spiritual awakening. This revitalization is characterized by radical commitments to mobility, simplicity, authenticity, and a longing for community as a context to explore all the above. They, unlike us, have barely "left the dock," if at all, and their lives are open to redirection, reimagination, and the kinds of choices rigorous commitment to the gospel requires. If the "generation at risk" has become the "generation at hand," I would be honored to contribute to the conversation God appears to be initiating with them, regarding His plans for His people.

It's daunting to me, as a man in his sixties, to believe I can speak with relevance and authority to those half my age. But, it may well turn out that we are again on the steps of the church in Wittenberg.[1] If I can contribute a line or two to the theses God is penning to the modern Church, it will be enough.

---

1 There were certainly a multitude of factors and individuals responsible for what we now collectively call, "The Protestant Reformation." However, it is common to ascribe the Reformation's birth or early momentum to the posting of 95 theses by Martin Luther on the door of the Castle Church in Wittenberg, Germany on May 31, 1517. Europe and world history were changed forever as a result of the events that unfurled from that point on. One of the clarion cries of the Reformers was, *"Ecclesia semper reformanda est,"* the Church is always to be reformed. Perhaps God will grant us a new era again.

Prolegomena

Introduction — *Robert and Rehoboam*

Maybe it's just a coincidence, but then again, maybe it's not that at the 2012 Digital-Life-Design conference in Munich, there was an 18 year age-span between the opening and closing keynote speakers. Viviane Reding, the European Commission's vice-president for justice, and Sheryl Sandberg, the chief operating officer for Facebook, are nearly half a generation apart in age. Harry Truman was the president when Reding was born. Sandberg, however, was born roughly 2 weeks after Woodstock in 1969. Generational differences have always existed, but perhaps at no other time in history have they been more significant. It is profound, even iconic, that the 72 hour conference opened with a 60-year-old European woman, professionally dressed, speaking from a printed manuscript, standing politely behind a podium. But, it ended with an attractive, youthful, American in "business casual" attire, meandering casually across the platform with a behind-the-ear headset, queuing her remarks via multiple screens and a handheld remote. The former spoke of caution, the latter of freedom, in the digital age. Facebook's Sandberg extolled the value of the "wisdom of friends," over the "wisdom of the crowd." Her unspoken assumption; of course, is that one's friends are wise. And most likely, "friends" in this context is a synonym for peers. This pithy proverb of the digital era is really just a mashup of sorts, an error in reasoning thirty-five centuries old. And, the consequences of an unexamined infatuation with this mentality, will likely produce the same devastation it did then.

I am especially sensitive to this line of thinking, because I was both participant and spectator during the decade of its most recent prior and lasting manifestation—the Sixties.[1] It was to this era that scholar Paul Johnson, in his landmark book, *Modern Times*, gave the chilling label, "America's Suicide

---

1 For a fuller discussion of this era, what led up to it and flowed from it, see *Generation At Risk: What Legacy Are Baby-Boomers Leaving Their Kids*, by Fran Sciacca.

Attempt."[1] You couldn't have convinced any of us that *we* were trying to kill America or us. We were convinced America was trying to kill anyone with a dissenting voice. Crosby, Stills, Nash, and Young's haunting lyrics, *"Tin soldiers and Nixon coming, we're finally on our own. This summer I hear the drumming. Four dead in Ohio."*[2] reminded us that the National Guard still had all the guns. By the decade's end, we had "drunk the Kool-Aid," regarding the moral imperative of what we were doing, a full decade before the Jonestown massacre would put that phrase in the dictionary. We were confident that song titles like, *All You Need Is Love, You've Got a Friend,* and *We're Coming to Strawberry Fields Forever,* were as axiomatic as the geometry we had learned as children. And more significantly, we had followed the political advice of a young, itinerant minstrel from the Mesabi Iron Range in Minnesota, named Robert Zimmerman. His migration to New York, and subsequent name change to Bob Dylan catapulted him into the role of spokesman for the era. His ideology became ours too, thanks to the comparatively narrow-band phenomenon known as radio. Free speech and free enterprise had gotten in bed just when the youth culture had aged from *Rebel Without A Cause* to *Easy Rider.*[3] Rock 'n Roll was the Internet then, promoting cohesion and autonomy, as well as music and mayhem.

Dylan's inclusion in the 1999 TIME magazine's "100 Most Important People of the Century," demonstrates the broad and long half-life this musical prophet has had in American culture. Of special importance to me, as I begin this book, is the pathos he captured and catapulted in his 1964 release, a song that described and defined the era:

> *Come mothers and fathers*
> *Throughout the land*
> *And don't criticize*
> *What you can't understand*
> *Your sons and your daughters*
> *Are beyond your command*
> *Your old road is rapidly agin'*
> *Please get out of the new one*
> *If you can't lend your hand*
> *For the times they are a-changin'*[4]

Whether Dylan realized it, he endorsed the kind of thinking and decision-

1 cf. Paul Johnson. *Modern Times: The World from the Twenties to the Eighties.* New York: Harper & Row, 1983.

2 These lyrics are from CSN&Y's single, *Ohio,* a song protesting the death of four Kent State University students at the hands of the National Guard on May 4, 1970. This event was a monumental boost to the antipathy and the counterculture's dissatisfaction with America.

3 These two movies served as summary statements of sorts, for the ideological longings of the children of the Fifties and the Sixties. James Dean's role in *Rebel Without a Cause* became a lightening rod for a generation of youth who were starting to "feel" and believe it was okay to talk about your feelings. Peter Fonda's role in *Easy Rider* as the representative for the free-wheeling, harmony-seeking Sixties generation, proved to be as naive as he was hopeful.

4 *The Times, They Are a Changin'.* Copyright © 1963, 1964 by Warner Bros. Inc.; renewed 1991, 1992 by Special Rider Music. All rights reserved. (Citation under the Fair Use Clause, Title 17, Chapter 1, § 107 of the U.S. Code.)

making that wrecked havoc in the ancient Middle East, and is enjoying a resurgence in the twenty-first century. Many, if not most of my generation, in one fashion or another, ingested this ideology. That is, that the "wisdom of friends," is better than the "wisdom of the crowd"; especially if the "crowd" is one generation removed. For us, this was the parent culture.

Unfortunately, this polarization between the "wisdom of friends" and the "wisdom of the crowd" is a perennial problem, not merely an ancient one. Like tectonic plates, generations seem to clash, especially over what should be permanent and what should be transient. Whether it's clothing, cuisine, character, or truth itself, generational agreement has always been an agony. However, until recently, generational differences were also quarantined in a sense, insulated by geographical distances. That is, the sheer space between like-minded, similarly-aged groups, negated the possibility of a cohesive identity or solidarity congealing. There was no such thing as "crowd-sourcing," the "hive mind," or the "Like" button. That all changed, irreversibly, in the early 90's with the birth of the world-wide-web. Since that time, or shortly thereafter, in the words of journalist Thomas Friedman, the world became "flat."[1] I would edit Friedman's metaphor slightly by adding that although it is "flat," it is surely not "level." There is a highpoint in the current technological topography, a place from which everything seems to flow *downstream*. With the advent of Web 2.0 and the Mordor-like spread of what has become the transparent matrix of social-networking, a digital benevolent oligarchy has emerged, concentrated in Silicon Valley. A sort of Technorati. They seem to be "nice," but also hold all the guns because they have all the skill, innovation, bandwidth, and data. It is no exaggeration to say that information is the new currency, the new "oil."[2] But, most of those who populate this Technorati who hold much of the "new money" (as well as stockpiles of the "old money"), could be my children. And, at the end of the day, in the real world, I am *not* in their circle when they speak of "the wisdom of friends." Neither, I suspect, is Viviane Reding part of the "wisdom of friends" in Sheryl Sandberg's mind as she crafts her vision for a world in which Facebook's 90% penetration of some countries is the new normal. And this is true, regardless if their names are among the list of "friends" on each other's Facebook wall.

A reasonable question should be emerging in your minds about now. What do Bob Dylan, Facebook, and Israel in the tenth century BC have in common? I believe the commonality is more than tangential. It is monumental. One of the wisest men on record was the son of someone who in America, would make for a wonderful biography. His great-great-grandmother was a Canaanite whore,

---

1 Friedman's book, *The World Is Flat*, is build on the confluence of a number of factors in a "perfect storm" that has yielded an irreversible globalization of economies, politics, and societies. At the heart of it all, is information and communications technology.

2 In fact, this was a central theme both keynote speakers referenced at the 2012 DLD conference in Munich. Ironically, this is not a new idea, even though it is a new reality. Twenty years earlier, the notion that "information" would be a form of currency and power was the malevolent driving force in the movie, *Sneakers*.

and his great-grandmother's racial heritage was an embarrassment to her husband's village. This wise man's father had been chosen to be the second king of what would soon be the nation of Israel. His name was David. His story is amazing, and competes with anything ever spawned in the City of Angels. And David's legendary son, via a rather disappointing tryst-become-marriage, became the archetype Renaissance Man, 2,300 years before da Vinci. A skilled architect, songwriter, poet, botanist, and a supremely astute philosopher and theologian, "Solomon" is an iconic summary of Ancient Middle Eastern wisdom.[1] He and his family also stand forever as a monument to how much life can change in a single generation. Solomon's wisdom seems undisputed. His public relations acumen, however, left much to be desired. Viewed as a tyrant by the populace for his near extortion of money and labor, the news of his death created a hiatus of sorts among the people of his realm. Would *his* son, Rehoboam, continue his father's public policy of "higher taxes," or would he be cut from a different cloth? Would he value people more than progress, and the beauty of humanity more than the beauty of stone?

Rehoboam began well. His first challenge came from a unified populace: *"Your father made our yoke heavy. Now therefore lighten the hard service of your father and his heavy yoke on us, and we will serve you."* In response, he asked for three days of contemplation.[2] He then sought "the wisdom of the crowd." In this case, the men who had surrounded the previous king, his father. He gathered his father's advisors, and sought their counsel. Their response was immediate and unanimous:

> Then King Rehoboam took counsel with the old men, who had stood before Solomon his father while he was yet alive, saying, "How do you advise me to answer this people?" And they said to him, "If you will be a servant to this people today and serve them, and speak good words to them when you answer them, then they will be your servants forever."   **–1 Kings 12:6, 7**

What transpired next in this narrative is chilling in its consequences, and yet familiar in its details. Rehoboam sought the "wisdom of friends," those who had grown up with him (peers) and "stood before him" (on his payroll). Seeing the glimmer of unlimited opportunity at a young age—having an Angel Investor for your startup, if you will—their counsel turned out to be the polar opposite of those who through age and experience, had seen the result of an oppressive monarchy for four decades. Rehoboam "Liked" the "wisdom of friends," which turned out to be a blistering promise of "Solomon on Steroids":

> And the young men who had grown up with him said to him, "Thus shall you speak to this people who said to you, 'Your father made our yoke heavy, but you lighten it for

---

1 It is interesting to note that the description of him in the Hebrew Bible sets him up as the "gold standard" by which wisdom is measured: *"And God gave Solomon wisdom and understanding beyond measure, and breadth of mind like the sand on the seashore, so that Solomon's wisdom surpassed the wisdom of all the people of the east and all the wisdom of Egypt. For he was wiser than all other men,...And people of all nations came to hear the wisdom of Solomon, and from all the kings of the earth, who had heard of his wisdom."* 1 Kings 4:29-30, 34

2 cf. 1 Kings 12:4, 5

us,' thus shall you say to them, 'My little finger is thicker than my father's thighs. And now, whereas my father laid on you a heavy yoke, I will add to your yoke. My father disciplined you with whips, but I will discipline you with scorpions.'"
–1 Kings 12:10, 11

The immediate result of his short-sightedness was the split of a united kingdom into Israel and Judah, a distinction that remained for nearly a millennium, and generated a history more known for apostasy and wickedness than truth and beauty.[1] Subsequently, Israel in the North, became a synonym for idolatry and rebellion. Not a single righteous king would sit on its throne, and names like Ahab and Jezebel would enter the narrative only to be enshrined in infamy. The ruthless Assyrians would extinguish what little light remained in the North in 722 BC. The southern kingdom of Judah too, though punctuated with bright spots like King Josiah, followed the path to anarchy and was eventually battered and taken by Babylon. The choices facing young King Rehoboam had consequences that endured long after him. The future is always contained in the present. In a very real way, without knowing it, we choose for our grandchildren. Sometimes, those who've lived long enough to see the present unfold into the future and understand this, are best suited to provide insight to those whose sight has a limited horizon. The point here is not that Rehoboam should have *ignored* the "wisdom of friends," and blindly embraced the "wisdom of the crowd." Rather, his greatest error was in choosing one and disregarding or dismissing the other.

Several years ago, when our middle son was completing his MFA in Graphic Design, he had an idea for nurturing racial healing on his campus. The 50-year anniversary of Brown vs. Board of Education[2] was approaching, and in the Deep South, that landmark decision had repercussions that were still reverberating. Geoff made a series of posters and tabletop-tents that reminded the students in this Louisiana college of the anniversary *and* the fact that they were now voluntarily segregating themselves in the campus lunchroom. After stretching a piece of duct tape down the middle of the lunchroom and dragging several tables into the "neutral zone," he challenged them to "meet in the middle" one day during that week. He and his girlfriend essentially ate alone that day. Only a few joined them "in the middle." The white students ate on their "side" of the lunchroom, and the blacks on theirs. Although the law had taken down the dividing wall of hostility a half century earlier, the students chose to polarize themselves day after day. Living in the middle is sometimes a sign of laxity, sometimes a sign of bigotry. But, when it comes to the "wisdom of the crowd"

---

1 (This is 1 KIngs 12 thru 2 Kings 25 in our Bibles) In the Old Testament, the prophet was more important than the king. The king's role was to lead God's people in covenant faithfulness. The prophet, on the other hand, was to speak to the king on behalf of God, *especially when he neglected or refused to follow God*. It is noteworthy that the role of the prophet veritably exploded after Rehoboam's folly. Of the 167 occurrences of "prophet" in the Old Testament, only 30 of them appear prior to 1 Kings 12, the record of his decision to follow the "wisdom of friends."

2 As a result of this landmark Supreme Court decision in 1954, it was deemed unconstitutional for states to establish separate public schools based on ethnicity (i.e. segregation).

versus the "wisdom of friends," the middle might be a good place to land.

Rehoboam and Robert Zimmerman have something in common. Rehoboam and his "friends" also seemed to believe that "the times they are a changin,'" and that the older generation should either get on board, or get off the dock. He and Zimmerman both advocated a cultural platform that was generationally defined and existentially driven. Whether it's called the "wisdom of friends" or "Rehoboam's Folly," it's a dangerous choice to polarize generations when determining which direction and at what speed the world should be driven. But, this sword cuts both ways! Many of my own generation only seek the counsel of our children when the digital clock our the DVD player is flashing "12:00" after a power outage. There is also a need for us to understand and appreciate the immense spiritual and social capital residing in the rising generation. A provocative modern caricature of the beauty and power of this type of multi-generational synergism is the 2007 film, *Live Free or Die Hard*. In the film, a luddite, yet efficient cop (Bruce Willis) finds himself unexpectedly and unintentionally wedded vocationally to a youthful, high-tech Jedi (Justin Long). Their reluctant yet amazing convergence of analog and digital approaches to life not only rivets you to the screen, it brings resolution to the plot.

A renegade first century Galilean, whose age also landed him somewhere between generations, isolated the real issue:

> And the Pharisees and Sadducees came, and to test him they asked for him to show them a sign from heaven. He answered them, "When it is evening, you say, 'It will be fair weather, for the sky is red.' And in the morning, 'It will be stormy today, for the sky is red and threatening.' You know how to interpret the appearance of the sky, but you cannot interpret the signs of the times."   **–Matthew 16:1-3**

Jesus' perennial struggle with the adult generation of his day was that they just didn't get it. They were so locked into the "old" that they were blind to the "new." In fact, the "new" was so foreign, frightening, and threatening to them, and their own perspective so rigid, embracing the "new" would *destroy* their whole worldview.[1] The remarkable middle ground that Jesus offers, and is indeed available today, is found in a single brief statement he made to a small group in Galilee:

> And he said to them, "Therefore every scribe who has been trained for the kingdom of heaven is like a master of a house, who brings out of his treasure what is new and what is old.   **–Matthew 13:52**

The word "old" here is *palaios*, a word whose meaning carries within it the notion of "ancient." Jesus told first century seekers that those who really "get it," are those who value and embrace both the "new," and the "ancient." Unfortunately for us as 21st century Christians, we seem to either have both feet in the "new," and are so sexy that we're *irreverent*, or we have both feet in the "old," (*not* the ancient), and thus are *irrelevant* to the point of invisibility. Being rooted

---

1 Jesus used the metaphor of "new wine" and "old wineskins" to illustrate this dilemma. There simply was no way to simultaneously hold on to their presuppositions about the Kingdom of God *and* embrace the teaching of Jesus. Their theology wasn't merely wrong, it was too small (cf. Matt. 9:17).

in the "ancient," yet free to step into the "new" is the modern antidote to falling prey to Robert and Rehoboam on one hand, and the Pharisees and Sadducees on the other. And I want to suggest to you that though "old school" is often something that needs a proper funeral, "ancient school" is not. My desire in the pages that follow is that, unlike God's people in Judah, you *will* heed the voice of Yahweh spoken 26 centuries ago through the prophet Jeremiah:

> Thus says the LORD: "Stand by the roads, and look, and ask for the ancient paths, where the good way is; and walk in it, and find rest for your souls. But they said, 'We will not walk in it.' –**Jeremiah 6:16**

My appeal to you then, as we begin this journey *backwards* to the "ancient paths" to find our way *forward* in a Chart Your Own Adventure (CYOA) culture, is that despite which demographic you find yourself a resident—the rising or retiring generation—you would be willing to ask for the ancient paths, seek the good way, and by walking in it, submit yourself to the One Story of the One God. My commitment is to steer you onto those paths. Because I'm in the last lap of my life, the time is short, and the stakes are high. This book is being self-published, so I am answerable only to God for what lies between its covers. I'm going to be honest, prophetic, and passionate. It's too late for me to dance gracefully around provocative points for fear of offending. I surely don't desire to offend. But, I also refuse to dance. It's time for those of us who claim the name of Jesus, to perform an audit of our own spirituality. If you're not willing to do this, then I suggest you close the book and go play golf or Angry Birds, depending on your age. However, if you are willing to step out, not knowing where it might lead, well...make sure your seats and trays are in the upright and locked position.

We're In Middle Earth, Dorothy, Not Kansas

In the 1939 classic, *The Wizard of Oz,* Dorothy (played by a very young Judy Garland), leans over to her tiny canine companion upon entering the majestic city of Oz, and says *"Toto, I've a feeling we're not in Kansas any more."* For those of us old enough to recall hearing those words emanate from the tiny black and white TVs in our living room, we could never have imagined a day when that statement would be a national confession. More recently, Galadriel's lament, *"The world is changed. I feel it in the water. I feel it in the earth. I smell it in the air. Much that once was, is lost, for none now live who remember it,"* which opens the 2001 screen version of Tolkien's epic trilogy, has become a requiem of sorts, for us living a half century later. At least for those of us who've been paying attention. But how many are? Paying attention that is. The good news is, the number is growing. The bad news...they're almost exclusively *outside* the family of believers.[1]

Less than 40 years ago, one of the founders of a major firm in the computer industry announced without hesitation, *"There is no reason for any individual to have a computer in their home."*[2] Obviously, he never envisioned a day when millions would have computers in their *pockets*, or worse, as quasi-appendages! Since the recent meteoric and geometric trajectory of technological innovation, change has become the only constant. Unfortunately, because of the dizzying rate at which it is occurring, we have become numb to the tectonic-level, trans-

---

1 Even a brief perusal of the bibliography at the end of this book will reveal a startling absence of Christian authors when it comes to the topic of social changes instigated and/or nurtured by innovation and invention in the arenas of communication and informational technologies. You might also be interested in the messages on this topic that I have delivered to collegians and pastors (see: www.handsofhur.org/Audio.html)

2 This statement is attributed to Ken Olson, one of the founders of Digital Equipment Corporation. (see: http://www.snopes.com/quotes/kenolsen.asp)

parent transformations occurring around us,[1] and *in us.*[2] And, if this book purports to be a journey to discover our "point" or purpose, it would be prudent to have an informed understanding of the stage upon which we find ourselves—America in the twenty-first century. Things have "changed," but *how* have they changed, and to what degree? Because I'm neither a historian nor the son of one, what follows will surely be broad strokes with a large brush on a small canvas. But, I believe it will suffice, as I simply want this chapter to set the table for what follows.

The Spiritual Landscape Has Changed

America has always boasted that we have open arms and borders (although recently the word "borders" is as volatile as "Communist" was in the 50's!). I am a second generation child, born of Sicilian immigrants. My grandparents' names are in the records on Ellis Island a half mile from the Statue of Liberty. Emma Lazarus' poem on the base of that statue, is a historic *call* for diversity, especially to those who are poor and broken. My ancestors, and those of my wife heeded that call. Recently, there has been no end to the rhetoric and dialogue about quotas and qualifications for crossing our borders. But, while all the talking was taking place, an amazing shift quietly occurred; much of it via humanitarian efforts to refugees on one hand, and an eagerness for diversity in our universities on the other. America's religious landscape shifted. My grandmother would not recognize it. Interestingly however, neither would many of my contemporaries. She, because she knew her surroundings. They, because they don't. And that's a significant distinction. Consider the following:

Although each of the following bullet points is not alarming in itself, collectively, they paint a portrait of American religious life that has an eerie consonance with Galadriel's comments above. The world *has* changed. At least the little patch of it known as the US.

- There are more Buddhists in the U.S. than Muslims (0.7% vs 0.6%).[3]
- There are as many Muslims in the U.S. as Jehovah's Witnesses.[4]
- Most American Buddhists were born here; most American Hindus and Muslims were not.[5]
- Those calling themselves "Christian" have fallen on average 10% since

---

1 The size and significance of both the number and degree of changes is exacerbated by the speed at which they are occurring *and* the relative transparency in which it is happening. Rex Miller's book, *The Millennium Matrix* (2004) sought to draw the Church out of the dark and into the arena of the new public square. Phyllis Tickle's book, *The Great Emergence* is an excellent historical study on the massive shifts within Christianity that have appeared in roughly 500 year intervals. She sees the present as one of them. I would concur.

2 The late Neil Postman warned us of our need to look beyond the promises made by the purveyors of technology regarding what it will "do for us," to the larger questions never asked, such as: "What will it do *to me?*" "What will it demand *of me?*" and "What will it take *from* me?"

3 *Pew Religious Landscape Survey*, 2007.

4 Ibid.

5 Ibid.

1990 (from 86% to 76%).[1]

- 25% of those 18 and older have "no religious affiliation"; this number has *doubled* since those in this group were children.[2]
- Only 4% of 18-25 year olds listed "becoming more spiritual" as their most important goal in life.[3]

When I came to faith on the college campus in the late 60's—a generation ago—in the midst of a heavy cloud of Marxism and cannabis, there was intense interest in the spiritual. It was common to have "all-nighters" of meaningful dialogue about God, not just the Vietnam War and Civil Rights. Not so today. Mark Silk, professor of religion and public life at Trinity College in Hartford, Connecticut puts it bluntly, *"The real dirty little secret of religiosity in America is that there are so many people for whom spiritual interest, thinking about ultimate questions, is minimal."*[4] This is consistent with the findings of the results of a survey of nearly 300,000 college freshman conducted by the American Council on Education each year.[5] The survey results have nearly inverted since the Sixties regarding the big questions of purpose versus personal comfort.

"A very important goal is to be well-off financially."
  1966 = 43%   1982 = 71%   2008 = 74%
"A very important goal is to develop a meaningful philosophy of life."
  1966 = 84%   1982 = 43%   2008 = 51%

Some of this, no doubt, is the consequence of the natural trajectory of the human race since Adam's rebellion.[6] However, I believe an equally culpable perpetrator is the American Church herself. Unfortunately, since the Sixties collapsed, we have simultaneously withdrawn from the public square *and* created a caricature of Christianity that resembles biblical faith less and less. Researcher Christian Smith apparently believes we have, in some ways, become our own worst enemy:

> It's not so much that U.S. Christianity is being secularized. Rather more subtly, Christianity is either degenerating into a pathetic version of itself, or more significantly, Christianity is actively being colonized and displaced by a quite different religious faith.[7]

Without falling prey to being simplistic, I think one can almost chart our

1 *The American Religious Identification Survey,* 2008 (http://www.americanreligionsurvey-aris.org/)

2 *The Pew Religious Landscape Survey,* 2007 (http://religions.pewforum.org/) and *The American Religious Identification Survey,* 2008 (http://www.americanreligionsurvey-aris.org/) This demographic has been labeled "the Nones" by some. Hemant Mehta, who blogs as the Friendly Atheist, calls them the "apatheists."

3 *Pew Research Center Report,* 2007 (http://people-press.org/report/300/a-portrait-of-generation-next)

4 The Birmingham News, 1/14/12, "Losing Our Religion," by Cathy Lynn-Grossman, Religious News Service.

5 Results from various years of the survey (national scores and specific scores for Oklahoma State University) are available here: http://uat.okstate.edu/index.php?option=com_content&view=article&id=34

6 Genesis 3 records the refusal of Adam and Eve to honor God's one prohibition, that they stay away from the one tree in the garden that belonged exclusively to Him. Their total disregard of this request in light of the One who made it, can only be understood in terms of rebellion. The fruit of their decision is seen every day, in every way people refuse to kneel and confess, "You are God. I am not."

7 See pages 117-181 of Christian Smith, and Melinda Lundquist Denton. *Soul Searching: The Religious and Spiritual Lives of American Teenagers.* (Oxford: Oxford University Press, 2005).

migration from authenticity to paucity by decade.

In the church culture of the Sixties, "Christian" was an assumed synonym for an "American." Christianity and Democracy were presumed to be inseparable. (These unfortunate associations are still alive, but shows signs of languishing.)[1] This genre of patriotic spirituality was a distinct carryover from the complacency of the Fifties, in which a worldview solidified that was colored more by the flag than the Bible. It explains why a dear friend and fellow "hippie" who had come to faith after an engaging inner struggle with a variety of competing ideologies, was ejected from a Baptist church near our campus when he walked in one Sunday morning. He was dressed as he always was—suede jacket with fringes, knee-high moccasins, and a leather hat with feathers. Two deacons, one on each arm, escorted him to the door with the words, "Your kind is not welcome here." Our "kind" was distinguished by our clothing and hair, obviously not our hearts. But, the counterculture was anti-American, and therefore in the minds of the status-quo Americanized Church, anti-Christian. Most of us in the counterculture were, I suspect, some threat to the American way of life. But, we were no threat to the gospel. I believe the Church, as an institution, lost much of its credibility with the rising generation during that decade through a perceived, or perhaps real, attitude of self-righteousness.

The Seventies seemed to be a decade of seeking to regain that lost credibility. It was a season of intense interest in apologetics and the Christian mind. Books by Francis Schaeffer, Os Guinness, Josh McDowell, James Warwick Montgomery, and others began to pour out of Christian publishing houses. Schaeffer was passionate about helping the Christian Church regain its credibility by demonstrating that a Christian can have a satisfied mind, not just a warm heart. He surely shaped *my* thinking and many of those of my ilk. But, the 70s was also a period of incredible accommodation to culture. In the words of one observer, *"Alas, in leaning over to speak to the modern world, we had fallen in."*[2] There seemed to be a campaign to convince the watching world that they should take us seriously. The mistake, I believe, was laboring to convince them that Christians were "just as good at everything" as they were. Christian day school enrollment exploded; Christian industries (music, clothing, publishing) burgeoned, and being "born-again" became a household word.[3] The "Dove Awards," a Christian version of the Grammys, was birthed by the Gospel Music Association at this same time. Country rock singer Kris Kristofferson headed-up an all-star cast for Explo '72, a conference sponsored by Campus Crusade for Christ, and hailed as a Christian Woodstock. Kristofferson's best-selling hit, *Why Me, Lord?* no doubt made him an obvious choice. It was a season when impressing the secu-

---

1 See: Gabe Lyons, *The Next Christians: The Good News About the End of Christian America*. New York: Doubleday Religion, 2010.

2 Stanley Hauerwas and William H. Willimon, *Resident Aliens* (Nashville: Abingdom, 1989), 27.

3 Chuck Colson's best-seller, *Born Again*, was released in 1976. Jimmy Carter is credited with being the first "born again" President in the same era.

lar culture became the "point." An unfortunate byproduct was the formation of a distinct and very visible Christian subculture. One that was, under close examination, a mirror image of the larger culture. And, like the previous decade, there was enormous collateral damage, though it was largely unperceived by Christians. We quietly traded a distinct *biblical* identity as individuals, and corporately as a community of faith, for a subcultural one. We began to see ourselves in *contrast* to the culture instead of in *comparison* with Scripture. It should come as no surprise that the 80s became a decade of Christian narcissism. They were an intense season of "focus," but tragically, it was primarily on ourselves.

A 1980's edition of *Current Christian Books* listed nearly 500 titles that began with, *How To...* Books promising sexual fulfillment in marriage, foolproof parenting, success in business, and personal happiness were commonplace. I joked back then that I was waiting for the book, *How To Lead Your Pet To Christ*. Fortunately, I failed in that prediction! Professional Christian counseling services sprang up everywhere, as we sought to find, nurture, and heal our inner selves. It would be no exaggeration to say that in the 80s the American Church fell in love with itself. The consequences were numerous and significant, but one stands out among the rest: A near complete loss of cultural influence and concern. But, that would soon change, or at least at attempt would be made to do so. As if waking up from a hangover in which one had left his home unlocked, we seemed to suddenly notice that the culture had continued moving in its normal trajectory away from God. Why this realization dawned with such force, I'm not sure. But, it hit all the hot buttons within American evangelicalism simultaneously.

The 90s became a decade defined by our attempts to retrieve what secular culture had "stolen" from us while we were partying on the rooftop of perceived popularity. Thanks to the rhetoric of several prominent Christian leaders, we wound up being "at war" with the culture. Christian activism was the theme of radio and TV talk shows, conferences, and books. And about the time Jerry Falwell's Moral Majority was retreating into obscurity, several other Christian activist groups were emerging to replace it. The "Culture Wars" became a lightening rod for Christian passion. The clarion call was for us to reclaim what had been taken from us as Americans, and as Christians. Having lived through those years in the Mecca of popular evangelicalism, I think it would be more honest to admit that the Seventies were less a time of "stealing" than it was of "surrendering." When you're wrapped up in yourself, you become a very small package indeed. I think it's significant that Roe vs. Wade was decided roughly six months within the performance of Kristofferson at Explo '72. Were we *really* paying attention to the culture in the 70s and 80s? Jesus said that the strong man's house couldn't be plundered unless he was tied up. I suspect that the plundering of "traditional values" happened because we *were* tied up, but not by someone else. We were "tied up" with our busyness and distracted, worshipping at the shrine of Self, in the name of Christ.

The thing that was relinquished during this period was a sense of *mission*. The Church came to believe its purpose was to redeem culture; to restore it to an original Constitutional condition. In the process, the mandate to be ambassadors of Yahweh, committed to reconciling sinners, fell out of our spiritual backpack somewhere along the journey. And, if we are honest, the way of life we had come to love because of our preoccupation with ourselves in the 80s, was what was threatened more than the Kingdom of God. Those we found ourselves "at war" with, were the very ones to whom we were sent. In our zeal to heal ourselves, we had become poisoned by distraction. A commitment to issues replaced a burden for individuals. Politics had become more important than people. Leonard Sweet summarized our condition clearly, *"The greatest sin of the Church today is not any sin of commission or sin of omission, but the sin of no mission."*[1]

By this time, it should become apparent why the word "missional" is currently on the radar of many thoughtful Christian leaders and the agendas of most Christian organizations. I am deeply encouraged by the rising number of churches planting other churches, and the growing sensitivity to the need to have a reason, a purpose, for existing. And in an America whose spiritual landscape has been reordered by religious diversity and atrophy, learning to think "missionally" might be a good thing. But, if it turns out to be the next hot thing for God's people, then being "missional" might be an attempt to fill a void *within*, not responding to a call from without.[2] This is especially plausible if more than just our religious landscape has shifted.

Our Inner Landscape Has Changed

The eighth century BC prophet Isaiah, speaking on behalf of Yahweh, made a jarring pronouncement:

> For by people of strange lips and with a foreign tongue the LORD will speak to this people, to whom he has said, "This is rest; give rest to the weary; and this is repose"; yet they would not hear. And the word of the LORD will be to them precept upon precept, precept upon precept, line upon line, line upon line, here a little, there a little, that they may go, and fall backward, and be broken, and snared, and taken.
>
> –Isaiah 28:11-13

Yahweh informs His covenant people that He will soon address them from *outside* the community of faith. In addition, the sobering context of this imaginary dialogue between Israel and Yahweh, is one of judgment. Because of Israel's refusal to be attentive to the word of Yahweh revealed through their own prophets, He would address them through people who have no regard for either Him or His Word. I do not believe I'm over-extending the truth of this passage when I say one thing seems clear: when God resorts to addressing His people from *outside* the covenant community, they are far from Him. When

---

1 Leonard Sweet, *Carpe Mañana: Is Your Church Ready to Seize Tomorrow?* (Grand Rapids, Mich: Zondervan, 2001), 27.

2 (4/5/12) The word "missional" scored nearly 2 million hits on Google.

the prophetic voice is missing from God's people, either by refusal to speak or refusal to listen, we are flirting with judgment. And unfortunately, most of the thoughtful assessment of the deeper shifts occurring around us, is coming from researchers and writers in the secular world. There is a comparative silence from within our own ranks. And, to up that ante even more, their assessment of what's happening to us collectively, is rather monolithic in its volume and consistency. This is important to me because the American expression of Christianity has modeled the culture more than molded it. The "voices in the street" regarding the tectonic shifts in our inner landscape, in describing culture, are therefore indirectly addressing the Church. And, the "voices" seems to be echoing the same four observations. Mind you, these are *not* theologians!

Mirror Mirror...

Generation Me had no need to reincarnate ourselves;[1] we were born into a world that already celebrated the individual. The self-focus that blossomed in the 1970s became mundane and commonplace over the next two decades, and GenMe accepts it like a fish accepts water. If Boomers were making their way in the uncharted world of the self, GenMe has printed step-by-step directions from Yahoo! Maps—and most of the time we don't even need them, since the culture of the self is our hometown. We don't have to join groups or talk of journeys, because we're already there. We don't need to 'polish' the self, as [Tom] Wolfe said, because we take for granted that it's already shiny. We don't need to look inward, we already know what we will find. Since we were small children, we were taught to put ourselves first. That just the way the world works—why dwell on it? Let's go to the mall.[2]

Unfortunately, the Christian world and remnants of the secular educational machine are still operating under the assumption that self esteem is a prerequisite to altruism; that we must learn to love ourselves *before* we can truly love others,[3] or be successful in school, for that matter. In fairness to the origin of this sentiment, it is true that there *is* a longing deep within each of us to understand ourselves. But alas, what we think *of* ourselves is an ocean removed from how we *see* ourselves, the subject of the next chapter. Regardless, being labeled "narcissistic" is surely no compliment to anyone, believer or unbeliever. And what's worse, the voices from outside the Church are *also* informing us of something that is antithetical to the notion of being in touch with God, our perennial boast as Christians.

---

1 This is a reference to a previous quote, *"We are the first generation to reincarnate ourselves in our own lifetime.",* a statement 60s Yippie radical attributes to a friend in his book, *Growing (Up) at Thirty-Seven.*

2 Jean M. Twenge. *Generation Me: Why Today's Young Americans Are More Confident, Assertive, Entitled—and More Miserable Than Ever Before.* (New York: Free Press, 2006), 49.

3 (April 2012) A search on Christianbook.com's website yielded nearly 650 titles/products related to the subject of "self-esteem." A revised edition of James Dobson's 1974 best-seller, *Hide or Seek* was released in 2010 under the title, *Building Confidence in Your Child.* Joel Olsteen's 2007 New York Times best seller, *Become a Better You,* has sold over 1.5 million copies. But, perhaps the most sobering epiphany was granted to the California Task Force to Promote Self-Esteem. In a recent study they discovered, much to their dismay, that *"American students consistently have higher self-esteem but lower reading and math scores than students from other industrialized countries."* (see: www.http://dineshdsouza.com/articles/feelinggood.html)

Wide But Not Deep

The second assessment coming from "the voices in the street" has to do with a documented atrophy in a key item on our résumé as humans—the ability to utilize our rationality. Even for Darwinians, humans stand higher than the rest of the air-breathers on the planet by virtue of our ability to employ sustained engagement, both with our minds and our emotions. Sadly, the jury is weighing in that Americans as a rule—which means Christians as well—are becoming increasingly "shallow," both intellectually and emotionally! The charge of being wrapped up in ourselves was hard enough to face. How much more the claim that the package itself is small, and shrinking?

Nicolas Carr, in *The Shallows: What the Internet is Doing to Our Brains,* a riveting and believable analysis of the physiological and emotional cost we are paying to be tethered to our gadgets, believes at the end of the day, we are being diminished as people:

> What both enthusiast and skeptic miss is what McLuhan[1] saw: that in the long run a medium's content matters less than the medium itself in influencing how we think and act. As our window into the world, and onto ourselves, a popular medium molds what we see and how we see it—and eventually, if we use it enough, it changes who we are, as individuals and as a society....Media work their magic, or their mischief, on the nervous system itself.[2]

Carr's research is both compelling and sobering. The very idea that my brain is remapping itself based on the *kind* of activity I engage in while using keyboards and smartphones, is more than eery, it's frightening. Those laboring in the world of secondary education have substantiated his findings. Their students talk about the task of reading long narratives using adjectives that are fitting of marathon runners: discomfort, pain, even fatigue. Maggie Jackson, a very sensitive and thorough journalist, has arrived at very similar conclusions about whether we're creating our electronic gadgets, or if they're recreating us in their own image; one that is linear instead of nuanced:

> So who are we becoming as we play God to the machine and face the future of sharing our earth with mechanical creatures that we can create, love, and nurture? This question is entangled in another way with the fate of the machine. Put simply, as machines seemingly become more human, we are becoming in many ways more like our machines. Our evolutionary calling cards are shifting quietly from Homo sapiens to post-human, with the tick of a pacemaker, whir of a brain implant, rush of an attention-enhancement pill, or the beat from a chip-implanted arm as we passed through security. This physical fusion with the machine empowers us and yet risks narrowing us in ways that may be hard to imagine.[3]

---

1 Carr is referring to Marshal McLuhan's 1964 landmark work, *Understanding Media: The Extension of Man,* in which he sought to alert us to the impact technology was having. "The medium is the message," perhaps McLuhan's most memorable concept, is derived from this book. It is significant to me, that the book is still in print, after nearly fifty years. He. like the late Neil Postman, were unheeded prophets, in my opinion.

2 Nicholas G. Carr, *The Shallows: What the Internet Is Doing to Our Brains.* (New York: W.W. Norton, 2010), 3.

3 Maggie Jackson. *Distracted: The Erosion of Attention and the Coming Dark Age.* (Amherst, N.Y.: Prometheus Books, 2008), 197.

The long human journey from an oral culture to a digital culture—with stopping off points as a print culture, and a broadcast culture—has been intoxicating and spectacular. Unfortunately, we seem to have gotten turned around in the process and are retracing our steps, according to some experts, instead of progressing. Among the growing din of voices is Jaron Lanier, father of virtual reality technology and a true "insider" to digital culture. The title of his "manifesto" is itself an abbreviated paradigm: *You Are Not a Gadget*. Lanier, Jackson, Carr and others[1] are describing the human race in ways that are beyond embarrassing. They are insulting. But, that's not the "bad news." The bad news is they are right. But, my contention—one that I'll seek to unpack in the rest of this book—is that they haven't got it right *enough*. Things are much worse than they propose because *we* are more than they suppose. It's a good thing to tell people that they are not a "gadget," but it's not instructive unless you help them see what they *are*. Lanier's lament is genuine:

> But the challenge on the table now is unlike previous ones. The new designs on the verge of being locked in, the web 2.0 designs,[2] actively demand that people define themselves downward. It's one thing to launch a limited conception of music or time into the contest for what philosophical idea will be locked in. It is another to do that with the very idea of what it is to be a person.[3]

Sadly, his solution, although reasonable to a postmodern mind, is impotent. In a society that has excluded God from conversations about cultural disintegration (*and* one in which Christians are mostly silent), the burden to create lasting solutions will always rest on the shoulders of the very ones in need. And, our refusal to fall into nihilism on one hand, and a blind Nietzschean optimism on the other, seems to leave us orphans in time, hoping in hope itself:

> One of our essential hopes in the early days of the digital revolution was that a connected world would create more opportunities for personal advancement for everyone.... During the past decade and a half, since the debut of the web, even during the best years of the economic boom times, the middle class in United States declined. Wealth was ever more concentrated. I'm not saying this is the fault of the net, but if we digital technologists are supposed to be providing a cure, we aren't doing it fast enough. If we can't reformulate digital ideals before our appointment with destiny, we will have failed to bring about a better world. Instead we will usher in a dark age in which everything human is devalued.[4]

I concur that we are indeed becoming "shallow," "narrow," and "defining

---

1 The list of contributors to the discussion is long and varied. And the combination of the number and variety of people speaking into our "de-evolution" as humans, in my opinion, lends tremendous credibility to the assertion. Sherry Turkle's TED talk, "Alone Together," is a classic example of a "prophetic voice" coming to us from *outside* the community of faith (see http://www.ted.com/talks/sherry_turkle_alone_together.html)

2 "Web 2.0" is used as a demarcation of sorts in online technology's timeline. It refers to the move from "Web 1.0" characterized by searching and retrieving data and information, to near total interactivity in one's online experience (e.g., "Like" buttons, "Rate" buttons, blogging, comments, first-person reviews, etc. The internet is now perceived as something each of us is *creating*, not merely using (i.e., Web 2.0).

3 Jaron Lanier. *You Are Not a Gadget: A Manifesto*. (New York: Alfred A. Knopf, 2010), 19.

4 Ibid., 82.

ourselves downward." I also subscribe to the notion that we have an "appointment with destiny," and a responsibility to preserve and nurture a sense of nobility among people. But, I disagree with what has caused this trajectory for humanity, and what is required for a remedial redirection. There is inherent emotive power in words like "ideals," "destiny," and a "better world." They are excellent words. Their value; however, hinges forever on the meaning ascribed to Lanier's final noun, "human." But before we get to that, I want to say without equivocation that I am grateful for these voices, and they need to be taken very seriously. They are, I believe, the voice of Yahweh Himself, speaking into a world that has gone further east of Eden. Unfortunately for us, the vast majority of those getting it right in their descriptions of our demise, get it wrong in their prescriptions for correction. So, while I applaud and thank them for the thoroughness of their work, I am forced to part ways when it comes to a regimen for recovery.

Reality's Address Has Changed

A third warning coming to us from these "voices in the street" is the stepchild of "shallowness," and a temptress to narcissism's folly. Some believe we are becoming a race that prefers the virtual to the real to such an extent that we are on the cusp of renorming what exactly "real" is, *and* that we prefer to "live" there. Over half a century ago, in his critique, *An Essay on Man*, Ernst Cassirer made an astute observation about people and their growing obsession with a visually rich new technology called television: *"Physical reality seems to recede in proportion as man's symbolic activity advances. Instead of dealing with the things themselves, man is in a sense constantly dealing with himself..."*[1] He saw people receding from the world around them, spiraling further inward, fueled in their imaginations by a script not their own. This has a near déjà vu sense to it when we listen to modern social critics such as Chris Hedges, whose seminal work, *Empire of Illusion: The End of Literacy and the Triumph of Spectacle* explores the notion that the image-laden "virtual" is the new narcotic:

> The more we sever ourselves from a literate, print-based world, a world of complexity and nuance, a world of ideas, for one informed by comforting, reassuring images, fantasies, slogans, celebrities, and a lust for violence, the more we are destined to implode. As the collapse continues and our suffering mounts, we yearn, like World Wrestling Entertainment fans, or those who confuse pornography with love, for the comfort, reassurance, and beauty of illusion. The illusion makes us feel good. It is its own reality....The worse reality becomes, the less a beleaguered population wants to hear about it, and the more it distracts itself with squalid pseudo-events of celebrity breakdowns, gossip, and trivia....More than the the the divides of race, class, or gender, more than rural or urban, believer or nonbeliever, red state or blue state, our culture has been carved up into radically distinct, unbridgeable, and antagonistic entities that no longer speak the same language and cannot communicate.[2]

---

1 Quoted in *Amusing Ourselves to Death*, by Neil Postman (New York: Penguin Books, 1986), 10.

2 Chris Hedges. *Empire of Illusion: The End of Literacy and the Triumph of Spectacle*. (New York: Nation Books, 2009), 190.

Maggie Jackson, also writing in our own day about the internet, speaks of this same drift toward narcissistic atrophy of our personhood:

> Do we yearn for such a voracious virtual connectivity that others become optional and conversation fades into a lost art? For efficiency's sake, do we split focus so finely that we thrust ourselves in a culture of loss threads? Untethered, have we detached from not only the soil but the sensual richness of our physical selves?[1]

Later, Jackson warns of the inevitable solitude that is the fruit of trying to be everywhere at once: *"Lose the will to focus deeply, to point the compass of our lives firmly in one another's direction, and we become islands."*[2] Her counsel, though profoundly true, is not new. A first century Roman stoic warned of the inevitable void that is the fruit of seeking to be larger than oneself: *"To be everywhere is to be nowhere."*[3] But then again, Seneca didn't have a Twitter feed!

The consensus of the "voices in the street," in conjunction with the fact that nearly one out of ten people of Earth is on Facebook, seems to suggest we are in danger of becoming two-dimensional people in love with 3-D movies. And, I believe we are. On that lovely note, I'd like to suggest a way forward. And, the road to the future goes through the past. The ancient past. But before we begin that journey, we need to spend some time exploring why we seem to be walking in circles, searching for the road itself.

---

1 Jackson, *Distracted*, 215.

2 Ibid., 241

3 Seneca the Younger, *Epistulae Morales*, II, 2.

Pushing Koheleth's Chain

Disillusion is the child of illusion. Often, the things that disappoint us most in the end, we had wrong from the beginning. This was certainly true about us Baby Boomers in our anticipation of the fruit of the counterculture's dissent. We believed in magic. Woodstock had galvanized our hopes for change. The theme song from the rock musical, *Hair,* had both hypnotized and caricatured us. When the 5th Dimension sang, *"We're coming to the Age of Aquarius...harmony and understanding, sympathy and trust abounding, no more falsehoods or derisions..."* we believed them. But it never arrived, this Age of Aquarius. Instead, in less than half a decade, the Beatles changed their tune from, *All Ya' Need Is Love* to *Live And Let Die.*[1] For songwriters like Carole King, Pete Townsend, and others, disillusion became the ambiance of the early seventies.[2] But that's because illusion was its parent. We had it wrong from the beginning. We discovered the hard way that Jesus' blistering reprisal of the Pharisees self-righteousness— *"why do you see the speck that is in your brother's eye, but do not notice the log in your own eye?"* —had come to land on us. *We* were what was wrong with America as much anyone. That realization, conscious or not, launched my generation into a despair as palpable as the heavy Alabama humidity in August.

But, the relationship between disillusion and illusion has a wider application than my own past. It stands as both warning and exposition for much of the current abandonment of faith and marriage that has become the signature

---

1 The Beatles' song, *All You Need Is Love,* was first performed live at an event known as "Our World," hailed as the world's first live global link. The message was intended for all nations. *All You Need Is Love* seemed like the perfect song to unite the world under a slogan that seemed tailored for the pathos of that era. Unfortunately, "love" wasn't all the *Beatles* needed. The group began the proceedings leading to its dismantling in 1970, a process that was to drag on for half a decade. McCartney was no longer with the Beatles when he penned the lyrics to *Live and Let Die,* the theme song to a 1973 James Bond movie of the same name. He was touring with a group known as Paul McCartney & Wings.

2 For a more detailed discussion on this dramatic loss of hope evidenced in popular music, see *Generation at Risk: What Legacy Are Baby-Boomers Leaving Their Kids?,* s 67–83.

dogma of the rising generation.[1] If one has an *illusory* understanding on what it means to enter and maintain a relationship with anyone, God included, then *disillusionment* is a short distance on the road ahead. And because we surely bear the imprint of the culture the voices in the street have described, it is relatively certain that the burrs of narcissism, shallowness, and escapism have attached themselves to us on our journey. If this is indeed the case, then it is also likely that we will approach all relationships (including one with God) from the perspective of self-gratification and immediacy, instead of sacrifice and longevity. It's also unlikely that we will be able to assign a hierarchy of value to any of our relationships. Rather, we will find ourselves living our lives as a series of status updates, flipping through relationships like the touchscreen on a smartphone, instead of intentionally and reflectively. Life will begin to resemble a patchwork quilt rather than a tapestry; colorful patterns without continuity, and in the end lacking true beauty and purpose. And, most importantly, there will be little patience and surely no appreciation for inconvenience, difficulty, and disappointment—the necessary fabric of mature relationships in a world that is real rather than virtual.

I believe this illusory view of life in general and Christianity in particular, is at the heart of the current migration of the rising generation away from costly relationships, of which marriage, church, and authentic faith are preeminent expressions. Either through ignorance or anemic teaching, many have come to believe both marriage and Christianity have to do with *their* fulfillment, and therefore should be characterized by the presence of happiness and the absence of pain. And many also believe that thanks to the wisdom provided by Google, skills in cooking, parenting, sexual fulfillment, and a life of meaning are two or three screen taps away. There is enough truth in this line of thinking to be compelling, but without an enlarged and informed understanding of who we are, and why we're alive, both marriage and faith will degenerate into sources of a discouragement of the grandest variety. When life of the real kind introduces—what statistically is inevitable for us—wrenching pain and disappointment, an illusory image of God or a spouse will shatter like mishandled china; and even more so the institutions that contain both, church and marriage. In the end, we will find ourselves without strength, without hope, and frequently angry and feeling cheated. Disillusionment is another word for it. But, the cause usually *does not lie* with our spouse or with God, but with our expectations—the fruit of an illusory image of both. I suppose in an ironic way, the illusory and the virtual have this in common: both can be sources of pleasure when life is smooth but are worthless in time of need. For instance, if I need a kidney, I'd be best not to contact someone who's a doctor in Second Life, or is advertising one on Craig's

---

1 *"The hot religion statistical trend of recent decades was the rise of the "Nones"—the people who checked "no religious identity" on the American Religious Identification Survey—who leapt from 8% in 1990 to 15% in 2008. The "So What's" appear to be a growing secular subset. The Pew Forum on Religion and Public Life's Landscape Survey dug into the Nones to discover that nearly half said they believed "nothing in particular."* (Taken from: The Birmingham News, 1/14/12, "Losing Our Religion," by Cathy Lynn-Grossman, Religious News Service)

List! And equally, I shouldn't "defriend" God if I'm the one whose kidney is failing. Unfortunately, after decades of the, *"God loves you and has a wonderful plan for your life"* version of Christianity, there's no place for failed kidneys; or the loss of a job or death of a child, for that matter. But most importantly, the "wonderful plan" edition of the gospel as it is popularly presented—and appealing as it has become—has *no place in the Scriptures,* or the life of a believer, as we'll see in the rest of this book.

The same is true of marriage. Illusory views of marriage are the stepchildren of illusory views of humanity. (I'll seek to unpack this idea in detail in Part II.) I'm not referring to having an illusory perspective on a *spouse* that is exposed through the rigors of marriage. I am referring to an illusory (i.e. anemic) understanding of what it means to be human, period. That includes me *and* my spouse. Unfortunately, though the Church has labored for two thousand years to forge a responsible and accurate *theology* (doctrine of God), we have done a miserable job at forging a clear *anthropology* (doctrine of humanity). And at the end of the day, I think the latter is more important than the former.

We enter marriage and a host of other relationships (work, neighborhoods, church, etc.) with a profound ignorance regarding who and what we are, what to expect, and how it all fits together. This is evidenced daily by how quickly we are disappointed, angered, and disgusted...by others! And, honesty demands that I admit that those same three emotions must also be felt, from time to time by others...toward me. The speed at which we change or abandon relationships, testifies either to our own ignorance, or our immaturity, or both. We become disillusioned with people because we have an illusory understanding of what "people" are. Getting this straight—"who am I?" —will be similar to the final few turns of the lenses during an eye exam. It will put nearly everything else into focus. But, like an eye exam, we have a few other *"which is better, 1 or 2?"* adjustments to make.

This idea of understanding "who I am" is vital for more than avoiding disillusionment; it is a prerequisite to finding fulfillment, because fulfillment is the fruit of following design, not following desire. When something does what it was designed to do, its purpose is fulfilled. And this is as true of people as it is space shuttles. Conversely, when things are used in ways that defy their design, they typically break. And frequently, the people misusing them are hurt in the process. C. S. Lewis cautioned on the crucial danger of disregarding this principle, *"When we want to be something other than the thing God wants us to be, we must be wanting what, in fact, will not make us happy."*[1] Lewis correctly assumed that what God "wanted" us to be, He has also *designed* us to be. It is safe to say that God intends for us to live in a fashion that honors our design. Unfortunately for us, it is something we rarely choose to do. This becomes complicated further by our anemic biblical anthropology. If we're really not sure of who and what we are, how can we "want to be" what we do not know we *should* be? Not

---

1 C. S. Lewis, *The Problem of Pain.* (San Francisco: HarperSanFrancisco, 2001), 46.

knowing, when it comes to this issue, is the result of either not being told, or not asking. For many Christians of the American variety, it's both.

Don't Ask, Don't Tell

One of the byproducts of aging is the gradual aggregation of perceptions that weave themselves into conventional wisdom. After six decades, based on what I've seen, heard, and done myself, I've come to realize that as a whole, we Christians have an annoying reputation for "having all the answers." It appears we've developed an erroneous self-confidence, thinking that because we possess the Truth, we must also have all the "answers"—at least the important ones! Or worse, we boast that we have answered questions that it turns out no one is really asking. This air of certainty without humility is correctly perceived as arrogance by the watching world. Maybe our fear or refusal to periodically confess, "I don't know," drives us to be talking, when in many cases we should be listening. Or at least asking questions, something we Christians as a whole, apparently are not known for. However, even having the "right" answers is only important if one is asking the right questions in the first place, something those *outside* the faith are no better at than we are.

Thirty centuries ago, a brilliant thinker and writer decided to tell God to take a long hike off a short pier. Well, not exactly, but in effect that's how it turned out. He was determined to find a formula for meaning and purpose that didn't include God in the equation. He was looking for an answer to the question, *"So, what's the point?"* He followed his ideology down many predictable roads: hedonism, materialism, intellectualism, sensuality, and a few others. Fortunately for us, he kept a journal of sorts, a kind of ancient "blog" I suppose, as it ended up going viral. The salient quality of this journal—known to Jews as Koheleth (the Preacher)[1] and as Ecclesiastes to Christians—is the centrality of questions. In the 222 verses of this poetic journal, there are 32 questions. Good questions on timeless topics such as: the value of work, the nature of love, the purpose of life, the certainty of death and what to do between it and birth, wisdom and folly, and others. Wonderful, thoughtful exploration of the kinds of questions for which everyone should be seeking answers. Though this journey was long and convoluted, his journal was short, and linear, about 11 pages. The author's adventures are varied, yet his conclusions are not. Our existential explorer discovers that every avenue he travels seeking meaning and purpose, leads him back down the same alley; a dead-end alley at that. Thirty-seven times in his journal, our exasperated seeker makes the same lament about life: "meaningless, meaningless, all is meaningless." Not exactly a ringing chorus for a modern praise tune, or title for the next Christian best-seller! This is the wrenching cry of an empty heart, the foul fruit of a fruitless quest. Koheleth, looking for

---

1 This is from the Hebrew word that appears 7 times in Ecclesiastes, and is translated "Preacher" (ESV, KJV) or "Teacher" (NIV).

some abiding meaning to life "under the sun," found none.[1] He kept a record of this quest to find a purpose, a "point" if you will, and concluded that at the end of the day, there was none. No purpose. No meaning. No point. Instead of a glorious destination just over the rise of each new road, he found himself redundantly circling back to where he started, alone with himself and his questions. And we've already seen that being wrapped up in ourselves is a small package indeed. However, though his conclusions were empty, his questions were full. They were not only valid, they were—and continue to be—profound, as we shall see in the chapters ahead.

Koheleth, the Preacher, lived nearly a thousand years before Christ—thirty centuries ago. Surely, we've made some progress in the quest for meaning since then? With over 1,000,000,000,000 web pages cataloged by Google in 2008, surely out there somewhere are the answers Koheleth sought? Unfortunately, the evidence is growing to suggest that although our modern search for meaning has the aid of search "engines," we've not developed any lasting answers despite the increase in horsepower for the search. Higher download speeds apparently don't correlate with reduced search times and increased "hits" when it comes to meaning, purpose, and truth. Teenagers cannot get a satisfying answer to a simple question about whether they are "ugly" or "pretty,"[2] even if 600,000 people weigh-in on the question, much less to something with a little more substance like, "what should I do with my life?"

Lost And Still Looking

But, the search goes on. Books sales have skyrocketed in recent years on topics related to finding some reason to be alive. And this is true across a continuum as wide as Oprah's Book Club to Christianbook.com. With nearly 50,000 titles and products on Amazon related to purpose and meaning, the evidence suggests that it remains more of a market for seekers than finders. Predictably, the Christian world is no different. Millions of people have read a multitude of books by Christian authors from a variety of backgrounds, all promising an uncluttered path to personal meaning. Obviously, many religious-minded people are as unsure, unhappy, or uninformed about the question of "What's the point?" as their unbelieving neighbors. And yet, despite all the ink that has been spilled to assist us in our quest, there is scant evidence that the millions who've read just these two books have found what they were seeking any more than Koheleth. At this juncture, I need to make a strong disclaimer. After making a bold assertion that the quest for meaning has been largely unmet for the past 3,000

---

1 The phrase, "under the sun," is a interpretive key to Ecclesiastes. It appears 28x, and in all but 3 of the book's 12 chapters. It points to a quest in the material world; one that excludes the intervention of a covenant-keeping God. Of the 40 occurrences of "God" in the book, *none* are Yahweh, the covenant name of God. All are Elohim, the "normal sense" of the use of the word, rather than the personal and intimate association Yahweh had with His people.

2 http://abcnews.go.com/US/teens-post-insecurities-youtube-pretty-ugly-videos/story?id=15777830#.
T5HNU44jW9Y

years, it would be audacious for me to suggest what has evaded everyone's grasp since the days of Solomon, will unfold on the pages that follow. Although that might be the promise of a late-night televangelist to anyone who mails in their wallet, I am *not* claiming a panacea for the question of purpose. What I *am* suggesting instead, is that I believe many people are wandering in a wasteland of purpose because of inadequate *questions,* more than insufficient answers. And, more often than not, as we saw earlier,[1] the nature and depth of our questions are more a product of our values than of our worldview.

Forty years ago, Gordon Dahl, writing critically of a shift in values in his day, captured in "50 words or less" what is at the heart of our waning sense of meaning:

> Most middle class Americans tend to worship their work, work at their play, and play at their worship. As a result, their meanings and values are distorted. Their relationships disintegrate faster than they can keep them in repair. Their lifestyles resemble a cast of characters in search of a plot.[2]

Dahl's description of our values inversion exposes an illusory understanding of life itself *and* our place in it. When it comes to life's most important questions then, apparently we need to get the *questions* right, long before we set out in search of answers. Because disillusion is the child of illusion, and fulfillment comes from following design instead of desire, getting this issue of design right, or as close to right as possible, is vital. "Design," when it is applied to things, is merely the composite of form and function. But, when we are talking about people, our understanding of "design" is really a function of our anthropology—our convictions about what it means to be "human" in general. And when the spotlight turns to ourselves in particular, we are in the world of meaning and purpose (or the lack of it). Those outside the faith community, almost without exception, subscribe to one version or another of the 150-year old notion that we are products of time, chance, and the impersonal. Richard Dawkins, one of the most popular contemporary spokespersons for this viewpoint, believes we need to put on our big boy pants and deal with the fact that there *is* no design to our universe. We are cosmic orphans:

> The universe we observe has precisely the properties we should expect if there is, at bottom, no design, no purpose, no evil, and no good, nothing but blind, pitiless indifference.[3]

> Natural selection, the blind, unconscious, automatic process which Darwin discovered, and which we now know is the explanation for the existence and apparently purposeful form of all life, has no purpose in mind. It has no mind and no mind's eye. It does not plan for the future. It has no vision, no foresight, no sight at all. If it can be said to play the role of watchmaker in nature, it is the blind watchmaker....Evolution has no long-term goal. There is no long-distance target, no final perfection to serve as

---

1 cf., statistics of the American Council on Education data on the questions of lifestyle versus meaning in Chapter 1.

2 Gordon Dahl, *Work, Play, and Worship in a Leisure-Oriented Society.* (Minneapolis: Augsburg, 1972), 12.

3 Richard Dawkins, *River Out of Eden: A Darwinian View of Life.* (New York: Basic Books, 1995), 133.

a criterion for selection, although human vanity cherishes the absurd notion that our species is the final goal of evolution.[1]

This controversy has probably generated more heat than light between Christians and secularists, and it is not my intention to revisit that scorched earth. I used to revel in similar arguments with Christians, dwelling in the hallowed halls of academia as a vertebrate zoology major and premed student. In fact, at the apex of my agnosticism, I railed,

> "If man was made in the image and likeness of God, I sadly say that I think less of him than I do his worthless creations. I can only hope that somewhere in the abyss we call space, there is a creature worthy of the label, 'God's creation,' and they shall someday soon dominate and squash us plastic artifacts."[2]

Not exactly what megachurch advocates would call a "seeker," do you think? Fortunately for me, I didn't stay mired in this intellectual and spiritual swamp. In 1969, a quarter century before Michael Behe's highly controversial and contested book on Intelligent Design, *Darwin's Black Box: The Biochemical Challenge to Evolution,* I had an existential wreck of my own. And, in an ironic way, I had my college professors to thank. In the arena of higher education—maybe in the whole realm of education for that matter—teachers rarely, if ever, engage in intramural scholarship. "What happens in zoology stays in zoology," or something akin to it seems to be the mantra of academia. This compartmentalization conveniently eliminates the possibility for a collision of ideas, and creates an illusion of cohesion in the arena of god-less thought. For example, in Comparative Anatomy I was told I was the product of an impersonal, random process, and related to cartilaginous fish. But, in Psychology 101 I was told I was unique and special, and had value. Then, in Philosophy 101 I was told there were no absolutes, but I could create my own. Then onto Sociology 101 where I was told Democracy was evil and Castro was messianic (something I eventually learned you can believe only if you don't live in Cuba or China!). But, after my philosophy prof was fired for having sex with a coed (apparently *somebody* believes there are absolutes), my sociology professor killed herself in her garage (creating personal meaning is not so simple), and another prof advocating Communism lost his commune's shared wealth in a pool game (Dawkins will later call this a "selfish gene"), I slowly came to the end of my ideological party. I concluded that although each of these disciplines' attack on biblical faith made sense in their respective classroom, there was no comprehensive worldview that could contain them. They were, at the end of the day, mutually exclusive in many ways. I had more questions than answers about life's meaning and purpose, and who I was. "What's the point?" was a question I asked, not because I was curious, but because I was desperate. And the halls of agnosticism and

---

1 Richard Dawkins, *The Blind Watchmaker: Why the Evidence of Evolution Reveals a Universe Without Design* (New York: W. W. Norton & Co., 1996), 5 and 50.

2 This is excerpted from a journal entry, "On Ignorance" which I wrote in the fall of 1969. I was a college sophomore at the time and at the peak of my disillusionment with religious *and* secular arguments for meaning. I would come to genuine faith in Jesus Christ about five months after penning these words.

atheism, though fun places to stroll, were no place to dig a foundation and build a home. My life had stalled, and I was stranded. I discovered for the first time that you can be sincerely...wrong.

Life's Four Questions

However, having just stripped naked my secular roots and their inability to supply an answer to the question, "So, what's the point?", I need to issue a caution. For people of faith not to have thought through what *their* anthropology is, and not just what it *isn't*, is to be no better off than an unbeliever when it comes to "design," and the subsequent questions of purpose and meaning. Disbelief is not understanding. Arguments *against* are not answers *to*. Showing something to be false is not synonymous with finding what is true.

Design applied to things may involve only form and function, but the notion of "design" when applied to people is richer, more nuanced, and mysterious. A biblical anthropology—one that is informed by the Judeo-Christian Scriptures—does not allow for a blind watchmaker. Instead, the question of what it means to be human is framed within the circumference of God Himself. Discussion about humanity becomes inseparable from deity. And here, the deity in question is the covenant-keeping God of antiquity known as Yahweh. In historic Christianity' doctrine of the Incarnation—when heaven and earth intersected in the flesh of Jesus—the question of *Jesus'* identity was a vital prerequisite to grasping the movements of Yahweh in first century Palestine. Getting *his* identity right became life's most important question. Jesus teased out of his disciples their understanding of his identity one afternoon while walking through the pagan shrines near Banias north of Galilee:

> Now it happened that as he was praying alone, the disciples were with him. And he asked them, "Who do the crowds say that I am?" And they answered, "John the Baptist. But others say, Elijah, and others, that one of the prophets of old has risen." Then he said to them, "But who do you say that I am?" And Peter answered, "The Christ of God."[1]   –Luke 9:18–20

A few years later, a Roman procurator named Pontius Pilate, would be struggling to tread water, caught in a religious and political whirlpool swirling around the identity of Jesus. He would find himself fighting to survive an ingenious triangular plot that pitted his integrity against fealty to Rome and his own personal safety. The Jewish leaders had already made multiple complaints to Rome about Pilate's ineffectual service to the Emperor. In the heat of the moment, Pilate came to the unfortunate but inescapable conclusion that he had to "do" something with Jesus. The Jewish opposition sealed the deal by pitting Pilate's conscience against his future with the accusation, "If you release this man, you are not Caesar's friend. Everyone who makes himself a king opposes Caesar." Experience informed him he was trapped, and expedience demanded

---

1 The Greek word transliterated "Christ" is the equivalent of the Hebrew word from which we derive our English, "messiah." Both mean "anointed one."

he sacrifice his conscience on the altar of self-preservation. Pilate's rhetorical question, "Then what shall I do with Jesus who is called Christ?" unbeknownst to him, would become the pass-fail essay question of all time. His pained quandary spawned life's most important question; one that every person must face, in this life or the one to come.

But, what we "do" with Jesus the Messiah will be determined by our own answer to the prior question Jesus posed to Peter at Banias, "Who do you say that I am?" Although it is not my intention to provide a thorough answer to that question, I have to say that without a sufficient answer to the question of Jesus' identity, in seeking to lay hold of a purpose of your own, you will find yourself walking down Koheleth's dead end alley. In finding a purpose for our own life, we need to have an answer to another question, life's second most important question: The principle of design applied to people. In its essence, it is Jesus' query to Peter, addressed to myself, in a mirror: "Who do I say that I am?" This is the question of identity-who I believe I am as a person. Not to be confused with self-esteem—what I think about myself, identity is at the core of what I believe about myself. It is a crucial component in constructing a sense of purpose. Even if I have an adequate answer to life's most important question (regarding Jesus), yet lack an answer to this second question, I will find myself disillusioned with life, with Christianity, and ultimately with God Himself. It's that important. Unfortunately, there appears to be a proportional relationship between the significance of something and our tendency to get it wrong.

In the quest for meaning and purpose, both the Church and the larger culture seem to make the journey in reverse. Their unspoken, and uncontested starting point is the notion that who I am is the product of what I do (i.e., mission, vocation). We seem to always refer to our mission or vocation in ontological terms: "I am a teacher," "I am a mother," "I am a lawyer," etc., instead of behavioral terms: "I teach second-graders" or "I practice law." In this popular model, identity comes from vocation or mission. And subsequently, what I do also explains why I'm here. Or put another way, purpose also comes from doing. The end product of this line of thinking is—"I am what I do"; identity based on vocation or mission. Perhaps this is why when the ability to "do" wanes, disappears, or is eclipsed by a competitor, my sense of who I am seems to evaporate. Or, when I reach mid-life and am drowning in self-evaluation, I surface only to realize what I've "done" with my life hasn't yielded the results I anticipated. Suddenly, I find myself in a "crisis," one that can only be solved by dumping my wife, buying a red Porsche and running off with someone twenty years my junior. Seriously, much of the angst psychologists have sought to deliver us from during such "crises," is pure disillusionment, the offspring of an identity promoted by my surroundings, yet rooted in illusion nonetheless.

The reason this illegitimate yet popular model is so persistent and pervasive is that it purports to answer the final three of life's four most important questions: "Who am I?" (identity) "What's my point?" (purpose), and "What's my place?" (mission). There's something deep within us that responds to this model, faulty as it is, because in it we hear faint echoes of a promise for purpose, identity, and mission, the things we innately long for. But, these two models have failed to deliver the goods. Why? Because what is wrong is incurably wrong. The order of presentation is wrong. Beginning with "purpose," or "mission" can never generate the momentum needed to carry someone to the end of the journey, because one can't begin with either of them.

The purpose of anything is determined by its design. Purpose is contingent upon design. This is true of everything from mascara to Google's estimated 2 millions servers. In this book, the principles of design, when applied to people, comprise identity. And because identity determines purpose, and purpose leads to mission, in our quest for an answer to "So, what's my point?", we have to start here. Having a robust and sufficiently true answer to the question, "Who do I say that I am?" is the only starting point that will take us the distance. There's no other way to pursue these three essential ingredients that can beget both a "point" and a "path." Any attempt to do it backwards or from the middle out, will be as successful as pushing a chain; Koheleth's chain at that.

But before we move forward to pursue an answer to the question, "Who do I say that I am?" let's perform an abbreviated rehearsal of where we've been so far.

Looking Back:

- U.S. culture is at a unique crossroad. One whose choices are characterized by generational outlooks, fueled by social networking technology, and polarized by convictions regarding the speed at which change should occur.
- Historically and biblically, the consequences of generational choices outlive those responsible for making them, and tend to include collateral outcomes that could never have been predicted.
- The Sixties' generation tended to prefer peer consensus over that of history, and believed they were wise in doing so.
- Jesus taught that true wisdom, when it came to understanding the present and facing the future, included both a possession of the truth in what was ancient, and in the truth of what is modern.
- The religious and social landscape has undergone monolithic changes that are producing people who are not only areligious or multi-religious, but increasingly selfish, and shallow.
- Anthropology, like the SAT, is experiencing a revolution. People are growing comfortable embracing a view of humanity—consciously or unconsciously—that is more a product of technology than theology, philosophy, or science. We are beginning to resemble our gadgets more than our parents.
- Our conception of space and time is undergoing a revolution also; one of Copernican proportions. Reality, the space where one is most com-

fortable "living," increasingly consists of virtual dimensions instead of human and physical ones. Pixels are replacing people as our preferred social context.

- The Christian community, as a whole, is silent on these trends. Most of the "voices" speaking insight, caution, and counsel are coming from outside the faith community.
- Purpose is the product of design. Design determines purpose. Design, when applied to people, is known as identity.

PART I *Identity*
"Who Do I Say That I Am?"

Snakes and Ladders

It is always interesting to study the slow deterioration of meaning and value ascribed to something as a culture retreats from its roots in the name of progress. An old Indian (dot, not feather) board game called, "Snakes and Ladders" deals with the issue of karma and conduct.[1] It migrated to England where it enjoyed a rich history, and eventually to the U.S. in 1943, where the U.S. edition was neutralized to "Chutes and Ladders." Instead of the connection between deeds and karma (i.e., reincarnation), in the Milton and Bradley version, good and bad deeds determined life outcomes. But that was before the Sixties. Currently, the game has nothing to do with altruism, and is simply a race to finish first. Unfortunately, for many Americans—and the rest of the globe too, thanks to a flat world—life itself has atrophied to a race where gaining speed has replaced reaching a destination. And at the heart of this misdirected effort is a ladder of sorts. A snake too. Or more accurately, a *nachash*, a serpent.

We've just established that our need for a sense of purpose and mission is an unrelenting taskmaster. It seems to goad us forward, yet fails to equip us with any sense of identity, leaving us doomed to die searching, or settling for anything to slake our thirst for a "point." As I read regularly of the growing exodus of twenty-somethings out of church, and fifty-somethings out of marriage, it is becoming more and more apparent that a multitude has discovered that where they invested their purpose and meaning capital, was bankrupt. In all fairness, some of this failure is their own fault. But, a significant portion of it is the fault of the church. Five decades of the *"God loves you and has a wonderful plan for your life"* gospel has yielded a veneer-type faith that lacks depth and substance, though it is rich in image and real estate. David Platt, a young, local prophetic voice that has been granted a national pulpit owed to his best-seller, *Radical*, says it succinctly:

---

1 See: http://www.boardgamegeek.com/image/288406/snakes-and-ladders and also: http://en.wikipedia.org/wiki/Snakes_and_Ladders

"...[speaking broadly] Therefore, when I look for a church, I look for the music that best fits me, and the programs that best cater to me and my family. When I make plans for my life and career, it is about what works best for me and my family. When I consider the house I will live in, the car I will drive, the clothes I will wear, the way I will live, I will choose according to what is best for me. This is the version of Christianity that largely prevails in our culture."[1]

And elsewhere:

We are giving in to the dangerous temptation to take the Jesus of the Bible and twist him into a version of Jesus we are more comfortable with...A Jesus who brings us comfort and prosperity as we live out our Christian spin on the American dream.[2]

In our wandering, whether it's in the world of people or pixels, or whether it's to God or away from Him, we tend to accumulate over time, a collection of attributions that we allow to define us. Some are barnacles that have simply attached themselves through association or relationships. Others we have consciously assumed because they are valued by those we admire. Occasionally, we replace an older "outdated" one with a newer, more vibrant successor, or simply rearrange them in our minds according to an imbibed or imposed hierarchy. In short, we all seem to have a collection of nouns and adjectives that we consciously or unconsciously use to describe ourselves that distinguishes us from others. A sort of resume of descriptors comprising how we "see" ourselves in contrast and comparison to others and the world around us. And because these descriptors are assigned locations in a hierarchy, they can be pictured as a ladder. An "identity ladder," if you will. Words like "married" or "single," "gay" or "straight," "Democrat" or "Independent," "Catholic" or "Presbyterian," "African American" or "Asian," populate the various rungs of our identity ladders. People inside and outside the faith communities live their lives and make their choices based on what's on their ladder, *and* the relative importance they place on each rung. I suppose some would simply call these "values," but they're more dense than values. Values are what we love and the way in which we love them. But, because we chase what we love, and become like what we chase, the rungs of this ladder are more formative than descriptive. They are who we *are* (at least to ourselves), not merely what we value or possess. For example, a person might *value* wealth and possessions, but "rich" or "important" could be among the rungs on his ladder. It's how they "see" themselves in contrast to others, whether or not they employ the word to describe themselves. Each word or rung could be used to complete the sentence: "I *am* (a)...", not simply, "I *have*..."

So, everyone has an identity ladder, believer and unbeliever alike. We all have a spoken or unspoken catalog of nouns and adjectives that we cling to as a sort of rosary, praying that in combination, they will answer the gnawing question, *"Who do I say that I am?"* But, I don't think our lists are working, do you? Is

---

1 David Platt. *Radical: Taking Back Your Faith from the American Dream.* (Colorado Springs, Colo: Multnomah Books, 2010), 70.

2 Ibid., 13.

yours, *really?* What if the items that populate our ladders and the order in which they appear is important? What if, unlike a multiple-choice quiz, what we put on our rungs is pass-fail? What if having a full ladder of wrong items is no better than having none at all? What if one of the greatest pitfalls threatening us is *not* that we'll fail in life, but that we'll succeed in ways that really don't matter? What if life really has a point, and I have a place in it?

I believe the top seven "rungs" of the identity ladder should be the same for anyone who goes by the name of "Christian," *and* be arranged in the same order. From the eighth rung on, the number and order are relatively inconsequential. I realize this is a bold assertion, and one that at first blush sounds very *un*democratic (because it is). But, I have not arrived at this conclusion naively or hastily. It is a composite anthropology forged over four decades of ministry and study, and sixty years of living. You can reject this idea. After all, this is America. We're all free to think whatever we want; until we die that is. Then, the only thing that matters is whether Truth really exists, *and* what it is. I would never claim to *have* the Truth. But, I won't hesitate to say as we start to wade out into the deep end that what follows *is* true. I'd bet on it. In fact, I'd die for it.

As we begin, let me say by way of clarification, the alliteration that follows is less forced than it appears. Based on the volume of ink they receive in Scripture, each of these seven "rungs" is a biblical theme that occupies a significant place in the mind of God. I have been studying this topic for nearly 30 years, and what we will examine in this and the chapters that follow, is the fruit of that study. During that time I have watched these ideas ripen like grapes. What began as two "rungs" in the eighties, has matured into the seven that lay before us. I ask you to refrain from evaluating each of them as you read. Instead, I implore you to look for the broader picture, the image that emerges from all the detail. A portrait of sorts, of how you and I should "see" ourselves as Christians. I anticipate that for some of you, this will be like drinking out of a fire hydrant. There will be a great deal of content, copious Scripture references, and undoubtedly ideas that are either novel, or unusual, or both. I plan to take us outside the box of convention, but keep us inside the circle of revelation, and that's a more delicate dance than it might seem.

Building a Better Ladder

The "rungs" that should occupy the first seven positions of the identity ladder for people of faith are: Adamic, Adopted, Abrahamic, Alien, Apprentice, Ambassador, and Advocate. In that order. The first four comprise the vertical dimension of our identity; a sort of "upward" gaze. They each furnish a partial but an essential answer to, *"Who do I say that I am, in relation to God?"* The final three rungs comprise the "horizontal" dimension and complete the model of biblical identity. These last three each supply a partial answer to, *"Who do I say that I am, in relation to my world?"* Together, the vertical and horizontal dimensions of identity converge to yield an understanding of who I am that is not only consistent with my design, but has the juice to carry me the distance. It is independent of zip code, gender, ethnicity, and age. You can take it with you wherever you go, and I believe, like the Apostle Paul, it holds promise not only for this life, but for the life to come.[1]

Some of you are already groaning. I can imagine it. In an age of image consultants and spin doctors, of sound bites, and Google's strip-mining of "relevant" data,[2] I suspect this already seems like too much work. Let me console you with this assurance: If you take seriously what follows, and internalize it, you will find yourself rich in purpose and hope as you age, instead of impoverished by disappointment and complaint. You will discover a direction that transcends continents and ancestry; one that is robust in the face of life's circumstances. A sense of meaning that is not shattered by divorce, disease, deceit, or desertion. I know this to be true from Scripture. But, I also know it to be true from experience. While the masses move like lemmings toward the unintended destination of becoming a cast of characters in search of a plot, you need not. But, in order for you to walk the road of meaning, you have to first enter the narrow gate of identity. As a fellow traveler who's a bit further down the road, I'd like to help you find the gate.

---

1 cf. 1 Timothy 4:7-8

2 See *The Shallows*, chapter 8 - "The Church of Google," for a fuller discussion of our growing inability to focus, read deeply, and do the kind of mental work necessary to truly understand anything. He likens us to "hunters and gatherers," foragers in a data forest.

Adamic—*Like Parent, Like Child*

Jill and I have been able to do some amazing parent-child exploits with our now grown and married children. Hiking in the Appalachians and multiple mission trips to work in an orphanage in Guatemala with our twin daughters Heather and Havilah, and helping to publish and distribute two books written by our oldest son Ben, to mention a few. But, when it comes to our middle son, Geoff, one adventure always trumps all the rest with him, at least for me. Around his fifteenth birthday, he and I rescued a geriatric, royal blue 1970 VW Beetle that was destined either for the scrap pile or the junkyard. The interior of this 25-year old classic was torn, shredded, and charred, evidence of a fire of unknown origins. It wouldn't start and hadn't been run in a long time; so it had to be towed to our house. The tires were dry rotted, the headliner falling in, and the body proudly boasted of having a rich history of "running into" old friends along the way. For the next 15 months, he and I worked to restore, revive, and recreate a car that was once as much a part of America as Elvis.

We removed all the body trim, the wing vent windows, and every square inch of paint on the exterior. Every scratch and dent was filled, sanded, and primed. I can still hear my brother's behemoth air compressor running in our garage as Geoff spray painted the car's primer coat in installments over many nights. A custom interior was ordered from Colorado and installed. A hole for a moon roof was cut and new floorboards welded in to replace those that earlier had provided a great view of the road...while driving! No one in town would consider redoing the headliner for us because of difficulty. So, true to form, Geoff ordered a "how-to" video (YouTube was a decade in the future), watched it twice, and we did it ourselves. I rebuilt the motor and added a little extra horsepower in the process, to bring it up slightly more than our weed eater. Finally, we found a certified Mercedes repainter who agreed to put an ultra-white base coat on our finished product. After adding custom wheels, window tint, and a keyless entry, the final step was a "stinger" exhaust system that allowed the neighborhood to know when Geoff was within a quarter mile of home. It was a work of art. Geoff drove the car all through college and sold it for $3,200. But, my most permanent memory had to do with the amazing bond that had developed between my son and this menagerie of metal. I'll never forget seeing the tearful look in his eyes, then in his twenties, as the car was loaded on a trailer and hauled away to its new home in Tennessee. The intensity of his involvement in that car was responsible not only for its beauty and uniqueness, but had also created a genuine sense of affection and attachment. It was, in a very real way, a labor of love that had given birth to his own creative intentions.

Design Specs

One of the most majestic and ancient ideas among Jews and Christians is that humanity was the final, most unique, and most important of Yahweh's creative acts. In the Creation narrative of Genesis, Yahweh *spoke* the universe into being. He commanded the night and day to separate, the waters to recede, the seas to populate themselves with fish, and the ground and sky to fill themselves with beasts and birds. And it happened. He spoke, and what is came from what was not. Yahweh's creativity and His sovereignty converged inseparably in Creation. But, when Yahweh reached the climax of His creative work, and prepared to create Adam, He didn't speak. Instead, He stooped. The narrative informs us that the God who created the universe and all that it contains, gathered soil and shaped it. The Hebrew verb here is *yatsar,* the word for the potter at his wheel. God's first connection to humanity was full of attention, focus, and intentionality. Surely, what preceded was not random. But this was different. All Creation, in a sense, has dignity for the same reason a Stradivarius is exalted among violins. The stature of the artist is what gives value to their art, not the canvas, clay, or marble.

The creation of the human race was as much art as power. The heart of the Creator was reflected in this aspect of His creative work in a way that it hadn't been with what had already been made. There was much the first couple had in common with the rest of Creation, especially that part of it that was dependent upon breathing; those creatures Scripture says had "the breath of life."[1] After all, they had to share a common environment. But, Yahweh differentiated between humanity and everything else because of the *tzelem elohim,* the "image of God," and the *demut,* the "likeness of God" that He had given it.[2]

This culmination of Creation included two genders each bearing this "im-

1 The Bible makes a distinction between vegetation and all other life, and a further distinction between animal life and humanity. Vegetation, according to Genesis 1:30, was for the benefit of the rest of Creation.

2 See Genesis 1:26-27; In Genesis 5:1-2, the word "likeness" is used (Hebrew - *demut*), a word that is rendered "model" in 2 Kings 16:10 where King Ahaz requests that a replica of a pagan altar be made for him. Here the word refers to "something made to resemble something else." Together, these two words present a marvelous portrait of humanity that is full of dignity, even majesty.

age of God," or Imago Dei as it is known in theology. Drawing from our field of industrial design, it's as though Yahweh's design specs for humanity consisted of a single design that included two models: a male and a female. It is likely more significant than we know that in the two cases where the "image of God" is mentioned in the Old Testament in the context of Creation, both involve a statement about gender. It's almost as if it took two genders to approximate the likeness of God. That's not to say God is a sexual being, but simply that it is at least feasible that His characteristics are reflected differently in males and females, much like light shining through a prism. And jointly they would reflect a more accurate "image" than independently.

The implication from the fact that we are made *like* God, is that we are also made *for* Him. There is the strong likelihood that humanity's design had a great deal to do with enabling a relationship with Yahweh that was outside the realm of possibility for the animals. Is this not the portrait we see painted for us in the early verses of our Bible? Yahweh is described relating to the first couple in a fashion that points to familiarity, maybe even intimacy. He talks with them, He walks familiar paths in the Garden, and He teaches them. And even when they mount their rebellion and refuse to kneel as creatures before the One Creator, He still clothes their nakedness and gives them hope of a distant redeemer.[1] This is corroborated centuries later by a word from Yahweh to His people as they mounted a rebellion against Him similar to the one in Eden:

> Thus says the LORD: "Let not the wise man boast in his wisdom, let not the mighty man boast in his might, let not the rich man boast in his riches, but let him who boasts boast in this, that he understands and knows me, that I am the LORD who practices steadfast love, justice, and righteousness in the earth. For in these things I delight, declares the LORD. **–Jeremiah 9:23–24**

The word "know" here, *yada,* is the Hebrew word for the sexual union of a man and woman in marriage. In the ancient near east, "knowing" was synonymous with intimacy. Yahweh chides His people for valuing what they knew, what they accomplished, and what they earned (sound familiar?). He challenged them instead to "boast" that they were intimate with Him, their covenant-keeping God. Why? Because He had called them to Himself as a nation, surely. But also because that is what humanity was created for in the first place. You and I are designed—literally hardwired—for a relationship with God. This is one of the things it means to be made in the "likeness" or "image" of God. Ignoring or dismissing this doesn't negate it. This is our design. We were made for God, not ourselves. And because design determines purpose, He *has* to be at the center of it all. When things are used in ways they weren't designed, they typically break and often harm results. The same is true here. You and I were designed for God. Koheleth tried to ignore design in his rabid search for purpose. It shouldn't surprise you that at the end of his journey and the close of his journal, he warned those who might seek a

---

1 cf. Genesis 1:28-29; 2:15-17; 3:8-9, 15, 21

similar quest that at the end of the day, we must face this truth: were made for God.[1]

The Imago Dei has provided a rich and interminable study by people of faith. The really smart people disagree on its full meaning, but most concur that humanity carries within it a dim reflection of Yahweh Himself. We possess a passion for justice because we are made in the likeness of a God that is just. We value fidelity and integrity because He is faithful and unchanging. We value giving and receiving love for the same reason. G.K. Chesterton used the word "centrifugal" to describe the God of Christianity.[2] Mercy, compassion, justice, steadfast love, forgiveness, kindness; these are all centrifugal characteristics. Everything about Yahweh moves *out* from Himself to what He has made. The overused and under-appreciated, *"For God so loved the world that He gave His only son..."*[3] is as clear a statement of Chesterton's claim as any. There is a sense in which God is sovereign yet self-effacing.

This Imago Dei, however, must not be confused with divinity. He remains distinct from all that He has made, and is its sovereign Lord.[4] And though we *are* distinct from the rest of Creation, and not merely part *of* it, we are neither gods nor demigods. But, we are greater than the rest of Creation too. In an anthropology that is rooted in Scripture, the secular designation, "nature" cannot include humanity, The label, Homo sapiens is convenient maybe, for studying biology, but it has no value in understanding who we are as people. We are *not* animals (though at times our behavior seems so). The idea that humanity bears Yahweh's "image" or "likeness," is the basis of human dignity. People have value by virtue of Creation, not belief, birth, or behavior. This facet of humanity, more than social or cultural reasons, was posited in the Mosaic Law as the reason capital punishment was prescribed for homicide.[5]

The dignity of humanity also is revealed in the magisterial role given it by Yahweh at the beginning:

> Then God said, "Let us make man in our image, after our likeness. And let them have dominion over the fish of the sea and over the birds of the heavens and over the livestock and over all the earth and over every creeping thing that creeps on the earth." So God created man in his own image, in the image of God he created him; male and female he created them. And God blessed them. And God said to them, "Be fruitful and multiply and fill the earth and subdue it, and have dominion over the fish of the sea and over the birds of the heavens and over every living thing that moves on the earth.   **–Genesis 1:26–28**

Old Testament scholar, Sandra Richter captures the amazing beauty of the

---

1 cf. Ecclesiastes 12:13

2 G. K. Chesterton, *Orthodoxy.*(Catholic Word, 2008), 33.

3 John 3:16

4 See Psalm 24:1-2; 8:3-5; Acts 17:22-28

5 *Whoever sheds the blood of man, by man shall his blood be shed, for God made man in his own image.* (Genesis 9:6) My intention here has nothing to do with the controversial topic of capital punishment. I merely wish to point out that the seriousness of the offense is inseparable from the *Imago Dei*. It is this facet of human nature that makes killing a human more serious than killing a deer.

purposeful tapestry Yahweh originally wove that included Creation, humanity, and Himself:

> On the sixth day, a steward is enthroned, under the Creator but over the creation: Then God said, "Let us make man (Hebrew - adam) in our image, according to our likeness; and let them rule."[1] Though the outworking of God's ideal design is dependent on the sovereignty of the Creator, it remains the privilege and responsibility of the Creator's stewards to facilitate this ideal plan by living their lives as a reflection of God's image. This was God's perfect plan. The role of the human stewards within the created order is specified in Gen 2:15: Then Yahweh Elohim took the human and put him into the garden of Eden to tend it and guard it. The larger message of these accounts is clear: the garden belongs to Yahweh, but humanity has been given the privilege to rule and the responsibility to care for this garden under the sovereignty of their divine lord. And so God's ideal is set in motion—a world in which adam would succeed in constructing the human civilization by directing and harnessing the abundant resources of the garden under the wise direction of the Creator. Here there would always be enough, progress would not necessitate pollution, expansion would not demand extinction. The privilege of the strong would not require the deprivation of the weak. And humanity would succeed in these goals because of the guiding wisdom of God.[2]

So, these "image-bearers," these centrifugal reflections of the very heart and nature of Yahweh, were given the privilege to rule as co-regents on Yahweh's behalf over the rest of Creation. Everything would be under their care and protection, and they would be under His. This is what it originally meant to be "Adamic." To have the capacity to rule with mercy, to nurture with compassion, and serve in love. That was our *original* design. But that design now has serious flaws; design constants that have little to do with Yahweh and much to do with Adam. Unfortunately for us, the "Adamic" facet of our identity is like a coin. It has another side.

Design Flaws

The third chapter of Genesis is the most important chapter in Scripture. The remaining 1,186 chapters of our Bible deal with God's remedy to catastrophic events that unfold in those 24 verses. It is no exaggeration to say that Christians should have a profound understanding *and* reverence for the set of circumstances recorded there. But we don't. Our ignorance or shallow indifference of Genesis 3 is responsible for much of our disillusionment with church, marriage, work, relationships, and the news feeds to our smartphones. It also accounts for our misplaced hopes, our arrogance, and the glaring self-righteousness that rarely goes unnoticed by the watching world. May God be merciful to those of us who preach and teach, for our neglect of this chapter in our instruction of God's people.

For most of us, the details of what we glibly refer to as "the Fall of Man" in Genesis 3, are typically few and marginally important starting points for talking

---

1 Gen 1:26

2 Sandra Richter, "Environmental Law in Deuteronomy: One Lens on a Biblical Theology of Creation Care," in *Bulletin for Biblical Research* 20.3 (2010), 356-57. [NOTE: I have removed the transliterated Hebrew in places to make this quote more readable. Dr. Richter's meaning has not been altered or obscured.]

about God. Particularly, we Christians tend to move beyond The Fall as quickly as possible in our teaching, to get to Jesus. In our sprint out of the Garden, we grab a handful of biblical stories that become the fodder of Sunday school lessons for children, or videos with talking vegetables. Adam and Eve (marriage), a talking snake (temptation), and Cain and Abel (sibling rivalry) are the most popular. Cute, but elementary both in content and value. Maybe that's why we seem more concerned about how to get around the story of two naked people in our teaching, than revisiting the Garden to understand what really took place there: the good *and* the bad. I want to suggest that the universe tilted that day, so expansive and expensive was the choice made by our ancestral parents. If your theology of The Fall consists of two naked people getting kicked out of the garden and wanting to get past the angel with a drawn sword to get back in, you've bought the talking vegetable version. What actually happened that day, and its long half-life that continues to infect and affect all of life, is of cosmic proportions. The fallout from The Fall is so massive, and so vital, the entire second section of this book will be spent trying to clean a few spots in our theological spectacles so we can get a dim, but better look. Meanwhile, there's one vital idea that impinges upon our understanding of being "Adamic." That has to do with another "likeness" that we now bear.

After the death of Abel and the banishment of Cain, Adam and Eve had a third son named Seth.[1] The narrative announcing his birth is wrapped in the context of the Imago Dei and gender, but also another statement of infinitely more significance:

> When God created man, he made him in the likeness (demut) of God. Male and female he created them, and he blessed them and named them Man when they were created. When Adam had lived 130 years, he fathered a son in his own likeness (demut), after his image (tzelem), and named him Seth.   **–Genesis 5:1-3**

We discover from this tiny statement that Seth was born with *two* "likenesses," not one. Adam and Eve bore the "likeness" of God, but Seth also bore the "likeness" of Adam. It is no exaggeration to say that Adam and Eve alone, among all of humanity, understood what this looked like, although they did not pen these words. They alone *knew* what it was like to live in a world without sin. They alone knew what it was like *not* to possess a sin nature from birth. I am convinced that on that day in the Garden when the first parents rebelled and chose to be like God instead of themselves, a change so profound, so comprehensive, and so palpable occurred, that they let the fruit fall from the mouths uneaten and stared at one another in abject horror. Deep within themselves something new was birthed. And it was something dark, something foreign, something unnatural. It is inconceivable that they did not sense it. It was *this* "likeness" they passed on to Seth, and ultimately, to us. The Scripture goes

---

1 The story of Adam and Eve's rebellion is immediately followed by a rippling effect of sin's power. Their immediate family is decimated with one son murdering another, and the remaining child being banished. The birth of Seth must be understood in the larger light of a set of parents losing both their sons, and knowing full well that in every way possible, they are to blame (cf. Genesis 4).

out of its way to inform of us this facet of Seth's personhood. Humanity now possessed *two* "likenesses." One from Yahweh, and another from Adam. The original Imago Dei was not vanquished, but is *was* vandalized.[1] God's original design would now have persistent design "flaws." Therefore, there now exists an Adamic residue in each of us. And this residue has some persistent features.

The first is a propensity and desire to sin. There is something within us now that is drawn, like a moth to flame, away from God toward autonomy, power, and control. And, truth be told, we enjoy it. At least the Adamic part of us seems to. The sobering thing about this infatuation with disobedience, is that *all* the descendants of Adam possess it, *including Christians.* Paul's near schizophrenic confession in Romans 7 makes a great deal of sense in light of this idea of an Adamic residue that loves sin and shuns God:

> For we know that the law is spiritual, but I am of the flesh, sold under sin. For I do not understand my own actions. For I do not do what I want, but I do the very thing I hate. Now if I do what I do not want, I agree with the law, that it is good. So now it is no longer I who do it, but sin that dwells within me. For I know that nothing good dwells in me, that is, in my flesh. For I have the desire to do what is right, but not the ability to carry it out. For I do not do the good I want, but the evil I do not want is what I keep on doing. Now if I do what I do not want, it is no longer I who do it, but sin that dwells within me. So I find it to be a law that when I want to do right, evil lies close at hand. For I delight in the law of God, in my inner being, but I see in my members another law waging war against the law of my mind and making me captive to the law of sin that dwells in my members.   **—Romans 7:14–23**

Paul, writing as a believer, uses expansive language to describe what we have just labeled an "Adamic residue." His passionate cry for help in Romans 7 concludes with a doxology of sorts, thanking Yahweh for Jesus the Messiah, the only solution to our ancestral bondage in this life and the next. As Christians, we need to continually remind each other that we are simultaneously "in Christ," *and* "in Adam." We do a commendable job helping one another understand our "position in Christ" but a deplorable and anemic job of unpacking what it means to be "in Adam." I believe *this* neglect is at the root of a host of issues in the Church, not least of which is the pandemic divorce rate among Christians.[2] Understanding this facet of our identity provides an adequate answer to why you and I think and say some of the things we do, also why we fail to say and do things we know we should. There's an odd relief that results from embracing this. It's not just you, and it's not just me. It's all of us! Having a desire for sin obviously results in more sinning. That's obvious. But, looking closer at the Genesis narrative, we can quickly see two additional facets of our Adamic residue regarding our behavior when we sin, that also persist in all people.

> We, like our ancient parents, seek to hide our sin. Whether it's a foolish attempt to conceal it from God, as they did running into the underbrush, or from other people

---

1 See Genesis 9:6; James 3:9; In both these cases, the Imago Dei is stated to persist *after* Genesis 3.

2 In an attempt to dam this flood, I developed "Knot or Noose? - Sustainable Marriage in a Facebook Culture," a marriage mini-conference that explores marriage within the context of redemption and transformation rather than sex and finances. (see www.knotornoose.org)

like Cain did by killing his brother in the field instead of in the garage, we are prone to conceal it. And, if we're honest, concealing it is part of the pleasure. Even Job understood the connection between Eden and hiding sin by his play on words in the Hebrew: "...if I have concealed my transgressions as others (Hebrew - adam) do by hiding my iniquity in my heart,"[1]

A third foul fruit that fell from the tree of Adam's folly is our tendency to blame-shift. When the first couple was confronted by Yahweh for their insurrection, God asked for Adam to give an account of what had happened. The first thing he did was blame God (indirectly) by implicating Eve, "The woman whom you gave to be with me, she gave me fruit of the tree, and I ate." You can almost hear between the lines an accusation that Yahweh had given him the wrong woman! Adam's own complicity and guilt are three layers below the surface in his response. Maybe he thought if Yahweh didn't want to take the blame for the gift of Eve, then surely He would hold her guilty for the gift of the fruit, wouldn't He? Adam's actual "eating" is near the end of his excuse, conveniently last in the lineup. "You gave. She gave. I ate." It's a great formula for blame-shifting. I've used it. Haven't you? Eve's rendition of the second verse of the same song draws the serpent into the drama. Surely, the serpent's to blame, she pleads. To her credit, her part in the crime is only two layers deep: "The serpent deceived me. I ate." Running the risk of seeming irreverent, it's always amused me that Yahweh never questioned the serpent. I think it's because the serpent would have done what Satan and every demon in Scripture does when addressing God. He would have told the truth![2]

Having a propensity to sin, and to conceal or convey the guilt are three of our Adamic birthrights. But there is a fourth. It is the one that Yahweh promised to the first couple before they ate. He gave them access to every tree in the Garden, including the Tree of Life, except one tree. This was God's tree. He essentially said, "Look, I love you and have created this garden where harmony and unity are woven into the fabric of life. You can smell, eat, cook, or simply study every fruit in here. But, I've got my own little tree over there. Please leave it alone. It's mine." Then He upped the ante and added, "...in the day that you eat of it you shall surely die." He really meant it. And die they did.

Death: The New Normal

Death is often explained as separation. What the Bible calls the "first death" is the separation of the material self (i.e. body) from the immaterial self (soul, spirit).[3] There is a "second death" in Scripture that has to do with judgment and

---

1 cf. Job 31:33

2 It is amazing to me, that in the Gospels, the only ones who get Jesus' identity right every time are the demons. I believe it's because they knew him as the eternal Son of God prior to his incarnation and prior to their own fall with Satan. They repeatedly cry out, "I know who you are!" or some variation on that confession. Satan and his minions are evil and deceitful, but they're not stupid. Lying to God? I don't think so. That's more of a human vice.

3 See Revelation 20:4-15. The implication here is that there are two deaths. The first is the death of the body (i.e. separation of it from the immaterial self), as those who experience it clearly still exist as persons. The "second death" is eternal separation from God.

final separation from God for eternity. Adam and Eve's first "death" was exclusion from the place where heaven and earth intersected, the Garden. They were cast out from God's garden sanctuary and forfeited the intimacy with Him they previously had enjoyed. But, there was physical death too. In fact, the rest of Genesis is a litany of death. The word appears 60 times in the book, 57 of them after this event. Of the 66 books of the Bible, no other book even comes close to mentioning "death" as much as Genesis. And putting the scientific arguments aside, one thing is clear as you work your way through the Genesis narrative. People live shorter and shorter lives. Eden's curse may be slow, but it's sure. Death is the inevitable end of the race of Adam. This certainty is linked by Paul, in no uncertain terms, to Adam:

> Therefore, just as sin came into the world through one man, and death through sin, and so death spread to all men because all sinned...   –Romans 5:12

Paul is our champion for our *position* "in Christ," using the phrase over 80 times in eleven of his thirteen letters. We owe to him our understanding of the depth of God's irretractable riches to us in Christ Jesus. But, Paul never lost sight of his own connection to Adam, reminding himself and others that there was a residue of Eden coursing through his flesh:

> The saying is trustworthy and deserving of full acceptance, that Christ Jesus came into the world to save sinners, of whom I am the foremost.   –1 Timothy 1:15

> But I discipline my body and keep it under control, lest after preaching to others I myself should be disqualified.   –1 Corinthians 9:27

Paul's recurring theological metaphor of the "old self" as the enemy of spiritual transformation is likely a veiled reference to the Adamic residue. The Greek word he uses for "old," *palaios,* is the root of our word paleontology. It can equally be rendered "ancient." Paul's admonitions to Christians about their spiritual growth pits the Adamic residue (i.e. "ancient self") against the Imago Dei:

> In these you too once walked, when you were living in them. But now you must put them all away: anger, wrath, malice, slander, and obscene talk from your mouth. Do not lie to one another, seeing that you have put off the old self with its practices and have put on the new self, which is being renewed in knowledge after the image of its creator.   –Colossians 3:7–10

> ...to put off your old self, which belongs to your former manner of life and is corrupt through deceitful desires, and to be renewed in the spirit of your minds, and to put on the new self, created after the likeness of God in true righteousness and holiness.   –Ephesians 4:22–24

As we begin this project of constructing an Identity Ladder, our top rung is a two-sided coin called "Adamic." We bear the likeness of the centrifugal God, and so are capable of grand and noble feats. When we exercise generosity, justice, compassion, and love—all forms of giving—something deep within us seems to respond. That's because when we follow design, fulfillment results. But, we also bear the likeness of centripetal Adam. We are prone to think of ourselves before others, and typically find ourselves drunk with power and control—both forms of getting. N.T. Wright masterfully describes the fruit of the two "likenesses" we bear, and God's intention for one to have dominion over the other:

> Whatever you think of the much misunderstood doctrine of original sin, it would be extremely foolish to suppose that humans, left to themselves, have not done amazingly horrible things as well is amazingly wonderful ones. Humans make bombs as well as music. They build torture chambers as well as hospitals and schools. They create deserts as well as gardens. And yet the vocation sketched in Genesis 1 remains: humans are to be God's image–bearers, that is, they are to reflect his sovereign rule into the world.[1]

We humans have dignity by virtue of who made us, and misery by virtue of who begot us. Having a full understanding of this Adamic residue produces genuine humility. The Adamic residue is the one thing you and I have in common with every other person on the planet. Despite how often we are in church, how many mission trips we go on, or how much we "tithe," there's still a part of us that wants on the fast train out of Eden. The observing but unbelieving world *knows* we're like them. G. K. Chesterton said this aspect of our humanity is the one tenant of theology that *can* be proven![2] Yet, we trivialize our unbroken connection to Adam with bumper stickers that say, "Christians Aren't Perfect, Just Forgiven," or deny it completely by assuming "seekers" is a descriptor for unbelievers, instead of Christians. I'm pretty sure Jesus was a "seeker," at least that's what he claimed.[3] In either case, we lose our credibility for speaking into their lives. If you really understand the significance of your Adamic self— both halves of it—you will be more accountable for your impatience with your spouse and neighbors, more tolerant of a rude clerk or server, and you'll be less likely to pass judgment on those around you for some "speck" you've noticed in their behavior. There's likely a "log" in your own, and you now know why.[4] Our attitude should mimic the advice of C. S. Lewis:

> Think of me as a fellow patient in the same hospital who, having been admitted a little earlier could give some advice.[5]

Our ladder has more rungs, and fortunately they're not all this painful. But, this first one was essential. It is the first description Yahweh gives us of ourselves. And until we "see" ourselves in comparison and contrast to Adam, we are only looking out of one eye.

---

1 N.T. Wright, *Simply Jesus: A New Vision of Who He Was, What He Did, And Why It Matters*, (New York: Harper One, 2011), 212.

2 Chesterton, *Orthodoxy*, 19.

3 cf. Luke 19:10

4 cf. Matthew 7:1-5; Some of Jesus's harshest words were spoken to those who had a propensity for pointing out what was wrong with others, while completely oblivious to the weaknesses and sins in their own lives. Many of which, were the same or a variation of those they condemned in others.

5 C. S. Lewis – *A Severe Mercy*, Letter to Sheldon Vanauken (April 22, 1953), 134.

Adopted— New Father, New Family

One of the things our family continues to find both tragic and hysterical, even after twenty years of living in the Deep South, is the volume and variety of refuse that accumulates along our state's roads and highways. Moving to Alabama from Colorado was cross-cultural in many ways, and there were times when we wished we had gone to language school as foreign missionaries. Since then though, we've come to realize every place has its idiosyncrasies *and* its idiots, including what we bring to it ourselves. There is much to love and appreciate about the South, and we do. However, because of my early work as an environmental chemist, and our 15 year tenure as a family in environmentally conscious Colorado, we still can't get over the plethora of road kill and spill that colors Alabama's roadways. It's not unusual on a trip to visit our son in urban Birmingham, to pass a dead opossum alongside the road, inflated by decay, and resembling a beach ball more than a marsupial. An occasional armadillo dots the sideline scenery, punctuated by larger carcasses of deer and dogs. However, it's the chair cushions, mattresses, and occasional washing machines that really get our attention. Our oldest son, driving from the city to the suburbs once swerved to avoid a love seat traveling 50 miles per hour in the lane next to him! It had apparently fallen off the truck where it had clearly been loosely loaded. I'm not kidding!

But, Alabama is not alone in its war against misplaced refuse. Nearly half of the states in the US threaten imprisonment for littering, and may include fines up to $30,000. Minnesota simply charges the guilty party 2-5 times what it costs the state to clean up its mess.[1] One of the ways Alabama and other states have sought to mitigate this blight, is the Adopt-a-Highway Program, in which an organization can assume responsibility for the condition of a one-mile stretch of road. The program began in Texas in the 1980's. Thirty years later, the "Adopt-a-" mantra has been attached to dogs, coral reefs, soldiers, hospital rooms, fire

---

1 See: http://www.ncsl.org/issues-research/env-res/states-with-littering-penalties.aspx

hydrants, land mines, and a multitude of other perceived orphans. "Adoption" in our culture has become a rather loose word, one that conveys a vague continuum of responsibility ranging from distant involvement to total immersion. One may "adopt" a baby rhino *in* Kenya or adopt a child *from* Ethiopia.[1] But, I think there's a difference. The word "adoption" has drifted into that world of vague definition, which is the last stop on the highway to no meaning. And when this ambiguous use of our English word is combined with a robust ignorance of ancient history and theological confusion about being "born again," we have conditions for a perfect storm of misunderstanding regarding one of the most beautiful and variegated aspects of our identity ladder—"adopted."

"Born again," the ubiquitous adjective Christians are quick to employ in differentiating "real" believers from illegitimate claimants to the faith—itself misunderstood—has further muddied the wells of understanding regarding the Scriptural teaching on "adoption." The phrase, "born again," is extracted from the debatable translation of two comments made by Jesus to a confused Hebrew scholar.[2] And they are two of the more popular proof-texts for our understanding of what theologians call "regeneration." In short, regeneration is the *reversal* of what Paul says was our natural condition in Adam: *"dead in our trespasses and sins."*[3] Paul never uses the phrase "born again," but he *does* speak clearly of our regeneration in several places.[4] Theologians have argued for centuries regarding when regeneration occurs and why, but nearly all agree on its result: the ability to relate rightly again with Yahweh. The reason this is important is that regeneration (i.e. being "born again") is *not* adoption! You and I *are* "born from above" by the Spirit, and can rightly respond and relate to the God whose image we bear. But, we were *not* therefore, born into God's family. We were *adopted* into His family. And, there's a huge difference. Most of it is absolutely thrilling. But, some of it, is equally chilling.

Adoption: The Perks

"Adoption" is an idea that is unique to our New Testament. It's also unique to the Apostle Paul. And he mentions it only five times in just three of his thir-

---

1 See: http://www.sheldrickwildlifetrust.org/html/help.html

and http://lifelinechild.org/adoption/international/ethiopia/

2 It is at least worth mentioning that *anothen*, the word translated "again," twice in John 3, can also mean "from above." In fact, in the rest of its fives uses by John in this Gospel, and the other 7 uses in the NT, it is always translated "from above." (cf. Jms 3:17; Jn 19:11). Jesus isn't specifically speaking about a second *birth*, but about a birth *from above*. For a high-ranking Jew who happened to be *the* teacher in Jerusalem, this was startling news. Nicodemus, like the rest of the ranking Jews, believed Abrahamic lineage warranted salvation. Jesus, as he seemed to do in every visit to Jerusalem, turns there theological cart over by insisting that being born a Jew did *not* insure entrance into the Kingdom. Our insistence that one must be "born *again*" rather than "born *from above*," has produced a preoccupation on the conversion event rather than an understanding of the nature of conversion itself as a work of God rather than man.

3 cf. Ephesians 2:1

4 cf. Colossians 2:13; Ephesians 2:1-6

teen letters.[1] None of the other eight New Testament writers address it, and the Greek word Paul uses for "adoption" (*huiosthesia*) is not used anywhere else in the New Testament. This silence is further compounded when one considers that *huiosthesia* also never appears in the Septuagint, the ancient translation of the Hebrew Old Testament scriptures into Greek. To be more specific, the *concept* of "adoption" as propagated by Paul, is a totally foreign idea to the Old Testament. The ancient Hebrew law codes of the Old Testament are totally silent on the subject, and not only is there no equivalent Hebrew word for *huiosthesia*, the concept itself is missing from the language![2] So why does Paul, a Jew, use the term and no one else? Likely there are two reasons, both equally important and less than obvious.

First, Paul was a Roman citizen. The significance of Roman citizenship is evident in the responses of those who discovered too late, that they had imprisoned or beaten him.[3] They were in terror thinking they themselves might suffer for allowing a Roman citizen to be imprisoned and beaten without a trial; one of the many "perks" of citizenship (along with tax loopholes and a no-crucifixion clause). Paul craftily played the "C" card several times to get himself out of a tough spot, and eventually to secure a hearing with the Emperor in Rome,[4] another right reserved for Roman citizens. Citizenship was rarely attained by people without status, wealth, military involvement, or all three. Paul's status as a citizen is a very unobtrusive testimony about his relative significance in the ancient world, even *before* becoming the reluctant, latecomer apostle of Jesus. Paul understood Roman culture, especially Roman Law because he was, among other things, a Roman citizen. "Adoption" is a concept therefore, best left to Paul to unpack. If I were God and wanted my children to understand what it meant to be "in the family," Paul is the person I'd choose to explain it.

The second reason it is reasonable that "adoption" appears in Paul's letters and not those of others, is that the three letters that contain references to adoption were written to regions saturated with Roman influence. So it is fitting he would speak of it when writing to those who understood it best. One letter was written to Rome itself. In it, Paul presents his longest and most lucid discussion of Christian adoption. Unlike life in the twenty-first century, everyone who heard Paul's letters read in Rome, the region of Galatia, and the environs of Ephesus, knew exactly what he was talking about! About 100 years earlier, the most famous Roman adoption in history had occurred; that of the one we know as Augustus by his great uncle, Julius Caesar. Adoption and all it entailed was not an obscure topic in Paul's missionary world. Because of this prior under-

---

1 cf. Romans 8:15,23; 9:4; Galatians 4:5; Ephesians 1:5

2 That is not to say there are not examples of adoption in the Old Testament. Moses was "adopted" into Pharaoh's family via his daughter. However, there are no instructions on how one goes about adopting someone in the OT Law codes, in spite of the fact there are copious laws regarding the treatment of slaves and their children, etc.

3 cf. Acts 16:37-38; 21:39; 22:25-29; 23:27

4 cf. Acts 25:11-12

standing of *Roman* adoption, "adoption" as *sons of God* would be almost over-whelming in its effect on all who heard. And because God's Word to us was first God's Word to someone else, our task here—as everywhere in Scripture—is to labor to become "them" as much as possible in our reading. Understanding Roman adoption, then, is a prerequisite to properly installing the second rung on our identity ladder.

Unlike adopting a baby rhino over the Internet, or an Ethiopian orphan via a local agency in combination with international travel, Roman adoption was conducted before a Roman court, the Comitia Curatia. It was, in many ways, one of the most auspicious and solemn of Roman ceremonies. Roman culture was built on, and often manipulated by a small number of powerful, wealthy, and influential families. There was no "Focus on the Family" in those days, but there was a focus on family. *Familia,* as it was known in Latin, was a core concept and a key value in the fabric of Rome's society. Each Roman family had one head known as the *pater familias* who was responsible to raise good citizens who would marry and yield more faithful Romans. This also ensured the con-tinuation of his own title, property, and wealth. The *pater familias* was endowed with absolute power over his children and the other members of his household and its various extensions. At one time, this power extended to the very life of those under him. This umbrella of power under which all his children (by birth or adoption) lived was known as his *patria potestas* ("power of the father"). It is to this that Paul, without ever mentioning it, alludes in all his teaching about Christian adoption.

In Roman society, a child never had anything approximating adolescence, a bar mitzvah, or any type of "coming of age." Because as long as his father lived, he was under his *patria postestas.* Even as an adult with grown children of his own. Also, a Roman could never be under more than one *patria potestas.* So, for an adoption to take place, either the child had to be an orphan, or his current father had to participate in a legally binding ceremony in which the *patria potes-tas* was transferred to the new *pater familias* (i.e. father). In the case where the boy (or girl) was already in a family, his father had to go through a ritualistic, but very binding, ceremony known as the *Mancipatio,* in which he "sold" and "bought back" his son or daughter twice, and on the third cycle, ceremonially did *not* "buy" them back, thereby indicating that the *patria potestas* was broken.[1]

In the next phase, the *Vindicatio,* the adopting father presented a legal docu-ment called a *Rogatio* which was similar to a piece of legislation needing vali-dation by a vote of the council just like any other piece of civic legislation. The portion of this process known as *the Detestio Sa*corum is probably central in Paul's mind, as he introduces this radically new idea of "adoption" into Chris-tian theology. It was here the adoptee foreswore his own family *and* his family's ancestral gods. He also accepted the ancestral gods of his adoptive family. In

---

1 At times, a high-ranking Roman who was heirless, might seek to adopt the son of another family to secure his own family name and future.

this metaphor, there is the sobering notion of completely severing identification and participation in one storyline to embrace another.

All the debts and obligations of the adoptee to the old family were cancelled, as well as any rights he might have had. But, the adoptee gained all the rights due him as a natural-born child of the new family, including the right to inherit. He had a new *pater familias* because he was under a new *patria potestas*. He was a new person entering a new family. The word "father" would now be addressed to, *and* accepted by, a different man. This legal change was so comprehensive and binding, if an adoptee fell in love with his new father's biological daughter, he would not be allowed to marry her, because legally she was his sister. Such was the case with Nero and Octavia, the daughter of his adoptive father, Claudius. The Roman Senate had to pass special legislation to allow the union. Roman adoption was a serious and significant thing. Paul knew it. Those who listened to his letters read also knew it. And, because all Scripture is God-breathed, it is obvious He wants *us* to know it as well.

God wants us to know that we too have been brought into a new "family." We too have a new Father, and there's something deep within us that makes addressing Him as, "Abba," Father seem natural.

> So then you are no longer strangers and aliens, but you are fellow citizens with the saints and members of the household of God,   –**Ephesians 2:19**

> But when the fullness of time had come, God sent forth his Son, born of woman, born under the law, to redeem those who were under the law, so that we might receive adoption as sons. And because you are sons, God has sent the Spirit of his Son into our hearts, crying, "Abba! Father!" So you are no longer a slave, but a son, and if a son, then an heir through God.   –**Galatians 4:4–7**

Paul's comments in a small portion of his letter to the believers at Rome take on new meaning, now that *we* have been slightly "Romanized" through our study:

> So then, brothers, we are debtors, not to the flesh, to live according to the flesh. For if you live according to the flesh you will die, but if by the Spirit you put to death the deeds of the body [i.e. the Adamic residue], you will live. For all who are led by the Spirit of God are sons of God. For you did not receive the spirit of slavery to fall back into fear, but you have received the Spirit of adoption as sons, by whom we cry, "Abba! Father!" The Spirit himself bears witness with our spirit that we are children of God, and if children, then heirs—heirs of God and fellow heirs with Christ, provided we suffer with him in order that we may also be glorified with him.
> –**Romans 8:12–17** [content in brackets mine]

The amazing transaction that promoted our status from vandalized image-bearers to sons was the life, death, and resurrection of Yahweh's son, Yeshua, on our behalf. Paul links our adoption to something he calls God's "plan for the fullness of time," a purpose, a "mystery" of some kind, in which he says we now play a part:

> Blessed be the God and Father of our Lord Jesus Christ, who has blessed us in Christ with every spiritual blessing in the heavenly places, even as he chose us in him before the foundation of the world, that we should be holy and blameless before him. In love

he predestined us for adoption as sons through Jesus Christ, according to the purpose of his will, to the praise of his glorious grace, with which he has blessed us in the Beloved. In him we have redemption through his blood, the forgiveness of our trespasses, according to the riches of his grace, which he lavished upon us, in all wisdom and insight making known to us the mystery of his will, according to his purpose, which he set forth in Christ as a plan for the fullness of time, to unite all things in him, things in heaven and things on earth.   **–Ephesians 1:3–10**

Our past is gone, our debts are cancelled, our own future is now fully secured and inseparably wed to that of our "elder brother," Yeshua.[1] Whatever His inheritance is, we share in it. This is amazing news. This is great news. There's a Greek word for this great news—*euaggelion*. Our Bibles translate it as "the gospel."

Adoption: The Responsibilities

I told you understanding adoption was thrilling. But, I also said it was chilling. And it is. We need to slow down and remind ourselves that in Roman culture, adoption was really all about the *pater familias*, not the child. And so it is here too. It's a wonderful thing to be part of the family of God Himself because of the finished work of Yeshua on Golgotha and the Garden Tomb. But, unlike the UN's celebrated 1979 declaration of the International Year of the Child, Yahweh doesn't focus on children, or focus on the family, for that matter. Being in His family, like any Roman adoption, means I am expected to embrace the responsibilities that accompany my adoption. And just as in Paul's day, the most crucial is that the life of the child reflects upon the name of the family, especially the father. How I live as His child reflects on what others think of Him, not just me.

This is the true meaning of our overused and misused Christian phrase, "testimony." A testimony is a directional arrow of sorts; it can only point in one direction. My life either points to Abba, or it points back to myself. For over two decades, I sat in chapels at Christian day schools, listening to a variety of speakers and entertainers. Frequently, for no apparent reason, someone would be allowed to speak in chapel that many of us had never heard of. Always young, typically male, and predictably entertaining, they would spend most of their allotted time rehearsing their journey to their present situation. It would contain stories of raucous behavior, foolish choices, and disregard for authority. Near the end would come, with near liturgical precision, a passionate plea for my students *not* to make the same mistakes they did. Those of us who were Bible teachers would have to detour from lesson plans and spend the rest of the day doing damage control over what constitutes a "testimony," and what is simply a story. Testimonies, real testimonies, point only in one direction. John the Baptizer's confession, *"He must increase, I must decrease,"* in itself is perhaps the most selfless statement in the New Testament to fall from the lips of any natural born son of Adam. But, even it was not a testimony. John's "testimony"

---

1 cf. Hebrews 2:11, 17

occurred two chapters earlier when he pointed his own disciples away from himself and to Jesus. How John lived his life was summarized in his confession about "decreasing," but the statement was not his testimony. *His entire life was*. There's a difference between a eulogy and an epitaph in length, but there shouldn't be in substance.

It may seem ludicrous that Yahweh's reputation—what others think about Him—hinges on my lifestyle and yours. But, we didn't set up the rules, God did. And that's just the way it is. As an adopted son of the Most High, you and I either point others to Him or away from Him. That's chilling to me. Paul understood the seriousness of adoption. He told the Christians living in Corinth (a *Roman* city on a Greek isthmus) that we all would stand before Jesus someday and be judged for how we lived in His name.

> According to the grace of God given to me, like a skilled master builder I laid a foundation, and someone else is building upon it. Let each one take care how he builds upon it. For no one can lay a foundation other than that which is laid, which is Jesus Christ. Now if anyone builds on the foundation with gold, silver, precious stones, wood, hay, straw— each one's work will become manifest, for the Day will disclose it, because it will be revealed by fire, and the fire will test what sort of work each one has done. If the work that anyone has built on the foundation survives, he will receive a reward. If anyone's work is burned up, he will suffer loss, though he himself will be saved, but only as through fire.[1] **–1 Corinthians 3:10–15**

Adoption doesn't allay responsibility. It creates it. Addressing the same audience he had just comforted with news of their adoption, Paul expanded the responsibility created by adoption beyond mere behavior to emulation: *"Therefore be imitators of God, as beloved children."*[2] He is even more direct and thorough about the connection between adoption and conduct in a command he gave the Philippians who were *all* Roman citizens:

> Do all things without grumbling or disputing, that you may be blameless and innocent, children of God without blemish in the midst of a crooked and twisted generation, among whom you shine as lights in the world, holding fast to the word of life, so that in the day of Christ I may be proud that I did not run in vain or labor in vain.[3]
> **–Philippians 2:14–16**

But, emulation isn't just for pointing *to* God; it's also for acting on behalf *of* Him. This is more fitting now that we understand the terms of adoption. Throughout our New Testament, from Jesus to John, we are instructed to treat others the way He has treated us because of our relationship to Him:

> You have heard that it was said, 'You shall love your neighbor and hate your enemy.' But I say to you, Love your enemies and pray for those who persecute you, so that you may be sons of your Father who is in heaven. For he makes his sun rise on the evil and on the good, and sends rain on the just and on the unjust. For if you love those who

---

1 see also 2 Corinthians 5:9-10

2 Ephesians 5:1 The verb here is an imperative (a command), and the tense points towards a lifestyle, not merely an occasional choice.

3 The word translated "all" here means "every single one," and the tense of the verb here also points to lifestyle rather than periodic conduct.

love you, what reward do you have? Do not even the tax collectors do the same? And if you greet only your brothers, what more are you doing than others? Do not even the Gentiles do the same? You therefore must be perfect, as your heavenly Father is perfect.   **–Matthew 5:43–48**

Be kind to one another, tenderhearted, forgiving one another, as God in Christ forgave you.   **–Ephesians 4:32**

Beloved, let us love one another, for love is from God, and whoever loves has been born of God and knows God.   **–1 John 4:7**

Adoption, in some ways, is a dramatic reversal of our lost status as children of Adam. We will learn in Part II of God's grand intention to mortify our Adamic residue. But, it appears that even that divine healing is reserved to those who bear His name; who are in His family. If you have taken seriously the implications and ramifications of being Adamic on one hand, and those of being Adopted on the other, a chorus of grateful praise should be working its way to your mouth. Humility is the inevitable consequence of truly understanding adoption. You and I were *not* "born" or even "reborn" into the family of God. We were adopted. Our inclusion was His idea. And although it's a place of privilege, it's never a platform for pride. Arrogance has no legitimate home alongside adoption. They are mutually exclusive. Maybe that's why Yahweh places such a premium on humility.[1] It's the beautiful fruit in the life of one who's adopted and really understands it. But, there's even more to humble us as we consider this vast notion of identity.

One of the things I'll never forget from our trip to Israel was looking down into a hole at an ancient tower near Jericho, while listening as the tour guide informed us the structure was 7,000 years old. Suddenly, I felt very young, and very small. Sometimes, we can be humbled when we realize we're a tiny part of something very, very large, and very, very ancient. To discover our next rung, we'll need to go back much further than Rome.

---

1 cf. 1 Peter 5:5-7

Abrahamic — *"Who's Who" Among the Jews?*

The standard joke is that if you go back far enough in your family tree, you'll find at least one horse thief. Sometimes, you might find something worse. When I was in college, my brother sent me a magazine article that was both intriguing and frightening. Mind you, this is nearly 25 years before Tim Berners Lee would invent the world wide web. Information of substance was rare and definitely hard to come by. I guess that hasn't changed, though, considering data has become a new category of trash.[1] The article talked about a war of sorts among the top five Mafia bosses operating in the U.S. In the midst of this midrash on mayhem, I noticed that the name of one of the key players in the drama looked familiar. Too familiar, in fact. His name was Paul Sciacca![2] My surname, Sciacca, is also the name of a quaint seaport city located on the southwest coast of Sicily, which just happened to be the birthplace of many of the Mafiosi ruling the crime world on the East Coast. This all seemed rather intriguing to me as a naive, 18-year old college freshman. But, when an uncle's name turned up in a pocket ledger of a man killed by a Mafia hit, our family's interest suddenly subsided. Sometimes, if you discover you're barking up the wrong tree, even if it's your own family tree, you need to shoot the dog. But still, ancestry is an amazing thing. We don't think much about the fact that we're each creating it as we live. Choices we make effect our grandchildren and great-grandchildren yet unborn; who they are, where they'll live, even what they'll believe. I know because I traced it in my own family through four generations.

About 4,000 years ago, an idol-worshipping pagan from a city with a mono-syllabic name somewhere in the Fertile Crescent, said "yes" to an outlandish re-

---

1 See: David Shenk. *Data Smog: Surviving the Information Glut.* San Francisco, Calif: Harper Edge, 1997. and *The End of Patience: Cautionary Notes on the Information Revolution.* Bloomington: Indiana University Press, 1999.

2 An excellent article describing what was christened the "Banana War," can be found in the Monday, November 25, 1968 edition of the Miami News.

quest, never knowing you and I would inherit the consequences of that choice. He was the son of a man named Terah. The Bible introduces him as Abram.

When "Jew" Was Something New

It's difficult to think of a time when the word "Jew" had no context or meaning, yet the biblical narrative insists on it. Prior to Genesis 12, "Jew" only existed as a theological construct in the mind of Yahweh, and *not* as an ethnic distinction. The Bible tells us that Terah, Abraham, his wife Sarai, and a nephew named Lot, left their home in Ur to travel to Canaan, but got detoured and detained in Haran, a city near the modern Syria-Turkey border. Somewhere in this story, Yahweh appeared to Abraham and made a startling pronouncement that was also a profound promise:

> Now the LORD said to Abram, "Go from your country and your kindred and your father's house to the land that I will show you. And I will make of you a great nation, and I will bless you and make your name great, so that you will be a blessing. I will bless those who bless you, and him who dishonors you I will curse, and in you all the families of the earth shall be blessed." **–Genesis 12:1–3**

Over the next twenty-five years, Yahweh would fill in the details of this promise, which would include nations, kings, and real estate.[1] And the "great nation" He promised would flow from Abraham's loins would begin with the miraculous birth of a son, Isaac. And as the purposes of Yahweh are slowly disclosed, Abraham is informed that "the families of the earth" that will be blessed in him, will include "all the *nations* of the earth." The Hebrew word for "nations" here, *goy(im)*[2] will eventually become the word Gentile in our Bibles. Yahweh's recruitment of Abraham was to be for the "blessing" of all the *goyim* as well as Jews. In fact, Yahweh informs Abraham that he has been "chosen" from among all men for this task. It is, in a sense, his purpose, and one that he bears a great deal of responsibility to keep alive:

> The LORD said, "Shall I hide from Abraham what I am about to do, seeing that Abraham shall surely become a great and mighty nation, and all the nations of the earth shall be blessed in him? For I have chosen him, that he may command his children and his household after him to keep the way of the LORD by doing righteousness and justice, so that the LORD may bring to Abraham what he has promised him."
> **–Genesis 18:17–19**

It might seem odd to you, that I would spend so much time in a book purporting to be about *your* identity, purpose, and mission, talking about a Jew who lived four millennia ago. And if it that is true, which I suspect it is, it reinforces to me the need. You see, this "Abrahamic" facet of identity is the most crucial determinant of your view of Scripture, your relationship *to* it, and your place *in* it. The pained look on the face of a dear friend who was leading a Bible study, when she recounted to me a statement made at their last meeting by one of the women, is forever etched in my memory. Apparently, the woman emoted, "*I*

---

1 cf. Genesis 15:5-6; 17:4-8, 15-16; 18:17-19; 22:15-18

2 cf. http://www.jewfaq.org/gentiles.htm

just hate the Old Testament! Laws, names, kings, sacrifices. I'm so glad as a Christian it's about Jesus." Her exasperation revealed a deeply rooted, yet transparent conviction that many Christians have about the Bible that is, at the end of the day, mythical.

One unrecognized modern Christian myth is that the English Bible's divisions of Old and New "Testaments," is valid and helpful. After all, isn't it good to know that 1 Chronicles is in the "Old Testament," and 1 Corinthians is in the "New Testament"? It is, but only in the manner in which it's good to know which side of your car the fuel door is when pulling into a gas station. However, the actual *existence* of this division creates the illusion of ending one thing and beginning of something different. And, in our era of light speed data transfer, a descriptive prefix like "Old" automatically blares uselessness and inferiority. This is especially true for the rising generation for whom "old" means outdated. In Israel, Jericho is *old*. In the US, an iPhone 3GS is *old*. Even the word "Testament" is infected with misleadings. It is the Latin equivalent of the Hebrew *berith*, and the Greek *dith k*, which we translate into the English word, "covenant." In an age when many think of a John Grisham novel, a thrash metal band, or a legal postmortem document, the word "testament" hardly conveys anything to do with a boat-side promise to Noah, or a late night pronouncement to Abraham. So, we're off to a bad start before we leave the front door, when it comes to even understanding the *arrangement* of our Bibles, much less the content.

A second myth, the bastard child of the first, is that the "Old Testament" is a Jewish book built around the principle of law, and the "New Testament" is a Christian book built around the principle of grace. We all seem to instinctively know that Law deals with what is "legal," and from there it's a slippery slope to "legalism." Therefore, Law being the declared enemy of Grace, it's best just to keep that "Old" Testament at arms length. Maybe use it for some great lessons taught to us by talking vegetables, or Bible action figures.[1] But, it is surely not the staple of mature, forgiven, believers. After all, didn't John tell us clearly that, *"For from his fullness we have all received, grace upon grace. For the law was given through Moses; grace and truth came through Jesus Christ."*[2] There you have it. Law goes with Moses, and grace goes with Jesus. What could be simpler? Unfortunately, simplistic is very different from simple. John's statement is certainly true. However, it's *not* like sunset and sunrise; the end of one and the beginning of another. Rather, it is more like sunrise and high noon. Tragically, in our unconscious yet very fertile mythologizing, we've created a three-headed monster. Or more accurately, a "three-story" Bible.

---

1 Nearly all the biblical action figures manufactured are of Old Testament characters that fit the modern action figure metaphor of brawn and violence (e.g., Samson, Goliath, Lahmi, David, Joshua). There are no New Testament action figures, although I have to admit my Jesus action figure with the loaves and bread miracle option is quite impressive!

2 John 1:16–17

Our "Three-Story" Bible

The first "story," the *basement* (or crawlspace if you live in the South), is our "Old Testament." A basement is always the first thing built. It serves as the foundation that holds up whatever is built after it, the rest of the structure's "stories." But typically, the basement lies buried and hidden from sight. Have you ever gone to someone's house, only to be greeted with, "Hi, I'm so glad you're here. Let me show you our basement"? It is functionally necessary, but we don't live there, and surely don't draw attention to it. Unfortunately, I think Christians often view the "Old Testament" that way; necessary but not really relevant to life. They see this basement "story" as the story of the people of Israel, the Jews. Oh there's Creation, the Fall, the Flood, and the Tower of Babel, all colorful talking points in the narrative that involve people *other* than the yet existent Jews. But, beginning in Genesis 12 and for the next 917 chapters, we're pretty much immersed in the life of Abraham, the "great nation" he fathered, and its foibles and fickle faith. And, because we are Christians and *not* Jews, although it is important and sometimes interesting, this "Old" Testament is surely *not* an essential item to pack for our own journey of faith. So, we relegate it to children's Sunday school curricula and synagogues, with an occasional season of devotional reading in the Psalms, or Proverbs if you're working with junior high boys. But regularly sustained reading and study? I don't think so. It's the *basement* for crying out loud. Even Christian publishing exposes our bias against the value of the "Old" Testament for believers. A recent online search at the largest Christian book provider on the Internet parsed the results showing only 12% of its titles dealing with the Bible directly were for the "Old" Testament, and the "New" Testament occupied the remaining 88%.

The second "story," or ground floor, is the story about Jesus, provided by our four canonical Gospels. And like any normal dwelling, this is the standard point of entry. Here's where you *really* start, if you're a Christian. The life, death, and resurrection of Jesus are the basis of our faith. Well, if we're really going to be honest here, it's mostly just his death and resurrection. The *"God loves you and has a wonderful plan for your life"* gospel needs these two, but can dispatch with the "life" of Jesus quite easily. For many, maybe most of us, the "life" of Jesus was the composite of exemplary living on his way to finish the job he came to do—to die for you and me. That means that when it comes to the Gospels, the final chapters are the preferred ones. Much like a kitchen on the ground floor of our three "story" Bible. Maybe this is why preachers seem to prefer to preach *about* God and others, or *from* Paul, but tend to avoid spending time *in* the Gospels. If you listen between the lines with some teachers and preachers, you get the distinct notion that the main purpose of Jesus' mission, other than our salvation was to provide Paul with something to write about. Over thirty years ago, one of my seminary professors said that the American church lived primarily in a tiny corner of the shadow of the Apostle Paul's theology—justification by faith. I didn't realize how true that was then—and if it's possible to be "more true"—is now.

The top floor of our "three-story" Bible is the rest of the "New" Testament. It begins with the Book of Acts and ends with Revelation, the final book of our English Bible. This "story" is the story of the early Christians we know as the Church. It's perceived to be full of instruction on how to live as a Christian. Topics like marriage, giving, church government, godly living, sins to avoid, and a gospel to proclaim fill its pages. This is surely the proper place for a believer to live, with occasional visits to the basement and ground floor, or course. Even those who claim they want to be "New Testament Christians" go back no further in their Bibles than the Book of Acts. Indeed, some root nearly all their theology there. This "three story" approach to the Scriptures is not only unfortunate, it's a travesty. The main reason is that Yahweh has only *one* "Story," not three.[1] But, another reason is that it exposes both a lack of understanding *and* a lack of respect regarding the book we glibly dismiss as the Word of God.

Regarding our ignorance, even our supposed distinction between Jewish and Christian portions of our Scriptures simply doesn't hold true. Of the 286 times the word "Jew" appears in the Bible, 200 of them are in the "New" Testament! The word, "Christian," by contrast, appears only three times in our "New" Testament of 188,654 words. Or consider that all but two of the books of the Bible were written by Jews. It's also worth pointing out that our "Jesus" was *never* called that by his own mother. She was an observant Jew, and her son's name was *not* "Jesus," it was Yeshua. No self-respecting Jew in first century Palestine would dream of giving her firstborn son a Greek name. The Bible, from cover to cover is a *Jewish* document. It records the unfolding of a dim promise made in a garden to two individuals who were *neither* Jew nor Christian. It moves over many millennia to the first century when a group of *Jews* obeyed the call of Yahweh to continue the mission of Abraham, a Jew, by taking the very good news of salvation to the *goyim* as well as Jews. Now, we have all found ourselves in a very, very, Jewish story indeed. In the words of Edith Schaeffer, **Christianity is Jewish.**[2] I agree. My only addendum would be that Christianity is *Abrahamic*, which, if I'm not mistaken, transforms our "New" Testament into an "Old" Testament.

This failure to comprehend the ancient and Jewish nature of our faith also bleaches the color out of our understanding of Jesus himself. We are left with a modern, monochrome Jesus whom we tend to misunderstand and misrepresent, and often package more for marketing than for missions. How else do you explain the Jesus action figure resting on my bookshelf? N. T. Wright addresses this anemia in his book, *Simply Jesus,* and warns against a failure to do the hard work to reconstruct the ancient milieu in which Jesus taught and touched:

---

1 This idea is so enormous and vital, that Parts II and III will be devoted to it. I resisted inserting the idea of the "One Story" here, knowing I couldn't unpack it, but concluded it was the best way to present an alternative to the idea of a "three-story" Bible.

2 See: Edith Schaeffer, *Christianity Is Jewish*, Wheaton, IL: Tyndale House Publishers. 1975.

If we don't make the effort to do this reconstruction, we will, without a shadow of a doubt, assume that what Jesus did and said makes the sense it might have made in some other context—perhaps our own. That has happened again and again. I believe that this kind of easy-going anachronism is almost as corrosive to genuine Christian faith as skepticism itself.[1]

Our erroneous 3-story approach to Scripture assures us that the basement of our Bible, the "Old" Testament, isn't actually *for* us because it's really not *about* us. It also assures us that the ground floor of our Bible, the Gospels, is "for" us because it's about Jesus, who's *for* us. And finally, the 3-story Bible model assures us the place to spend your time, if you're a Christian, is the top floor. Especially the Epistles. It's here where we learn how to *live* as Christians. And after all, isn't that what Jesus wants us to do until he comes to take us home? The short answer to that question is quite simple: No! Let's look at the longer answer.

Covenant Confusion

I think one of the culprits in the evolution of a 3-story Bible is the confusion surrounding the "Old" Testament, and exactly what in it was done away with through Jesus. Paul repeatedly had to deal with various factions within and outside the infant church that were making a mess of the transition from Sinai to Golgotha. His and other "New" Testament writers' letters are rife with instruction about the insufficiency of what he called the "old covenant" and that fact that its time to retire had come. In its place, they spoke of a "new covenant" of grace instead of law.[2] The author of Hebrews makes the incapability of the old and new covenants clear when he says:

> But as it is, Christ has obtained a ministry that is as much more excellent than the old as the covenant he mediates is better, since it is enacted on better promises. For if that first covenant had been faultless, there would have been no occasion to look for a second.   **—Hebrews 8:6-7**

Our confusion is not whether the old covenant has been done away with, but *which* old covenant. Paul and every other Jewish writer of our "New" Testament agree on the fact that the Mosaic covenant had become obsolete, *not* the Abrahamic covenant. God's intentions and purposes for Abraham have not changed. Paul argues that even the *introduction* of the Mosaic covenant (i.e. the Law) did not affect the vitality of Yahweh's original covenant with Abraham.[3] Paul's life was in constant danger among the Jews *not* because he was preaching Jesus, but because he was preaching and teaching on the temporary nature of the Mosaic Law (i.e. covenant). But, Paul never claimed or meant that the Abrahamic covenant had also been overturned. On the contrary, the radical center of Paul's preaching was that those exercising faith in Yeshua were the *true* "Jews," the legitimate "offspring of Abraham," and spiritual kin to his son, Isaac. Even the

---

1 N. T. Wright, *Simply Jesus: Who He Was, What He Did, Why It Matters.* (New York: HarperOne, 2011), 21.

2 cf. 2 Corinthians 3:5-13; Hebrews 8:6-13; 9:15;

3 "This is what I mean: the law, which came 430 years afterward, does not annul a covenant previously ratified by God, so as to make the promise void." (Galatians 3:17)

goyim! Let the combined reality of these amazing words wash over you, for it explains who you are as a person of faith:

> Know then that it is those of faith who are the sons of Abraham. And the Scripture, foreseeing that God would justify the Gentiles by faith, preached the gospel beforehand to Abraham, saying, "In you shall all the nations be blessed." So then, those who are of faith are blessed along with Abraham, the man of faith.
> **–Galatians 3:7–9**

> There is neither Jew nor Greek, there is neither slave nor free, there is no male and female, for you are all one in Christ Jesus. And if you are Christ's, then you are Abraham's offspring, heirs according to promise.   **–Galatians 3:28–29**

> Now you, brothers, like Isaac, are children of promise.   **–Galatians 4:28**

> ...and not all are children of Abraham because they are his offspring, but "Through Isaac shall your offspring be named." This means that it is not the children of the flesh who are the children of God, but the children of the promise are counted as offspring.   **–Romans 9:7–8**

> This mystery is that the Gentiles are fellow heirs, members of the same body, and partakers of the promise in Christ Jesus through the gospel.   **–Ephesians 3:6**

For Paul, to be a Christian was to be the offspring of Abraham, even if you were a Gentile. He understood that the Mosaic covenant with its Law and demands had served its purpose. Like the booster rockets on a Space Shuttle, it needed to be released. It shouldn't surprise us that most among the Jews in the first century were infuriated with this teaching. Paul was branded as a heretic and targeted for rapid extinction. One official who was well-acquainted with Judaism, accused Paul of having gone mad after he had insisted that Moses pointed to Yeshua, *and* that the message of redemption was for both Jews *and* Gentiles.[1] Paul taught first century Christians that this was the whole point from the very beginning! And so does modern scholar, Paul Wagner:

> The Abrahamic covenant is the overarching plan that unites God's dealings with his people and bridges the Old and New Testaments. This was God's unconditional plan for his people that he would see through to the end.[2]

In one of the most sweeping and comprehensive statements on this beautiful truth in the Bible, Peter weaves the entire "Old" Testament identity of Israel into a single garment and then wraps his believing "New" Testament Gentile audience in it:

> But you are a chosen race, a royal priesthood, a holy nation, a people for his own possession, that you may proclaim the excellencies of him who called you out of darkness into his marvelous light. Once you were not a people, but now you are God's people; once you had not received mercy, but now you have received mercy.
> **–1 Peter 2:9–10**

In this majestic statement, Peter distills ten descriptors, previously reserved for Jews from nine passages over 1,500 years of Scripture, and pours them lav-

---

1 cf. Acts 26:21-26

2 Paul D. Wegner, *The Journey from Texts to Translations: The Origin and Development of the Bible.* (Grand Rapids, Mich: Baker Books, 1999), 32.

ishly upon his audience which is incontestably Gentile.[1] He gracefully and ef-
fortlessly destroys our mythical 3-story Bible with these words. In its place, he
lays before his first century brethren and the people of God thereafter, a "Two
Testament-One Promise-One People-One Purpose" Story. This is what I mean
when I say *you we* are authentically "Abrahamic." Sadly, the Jews of Peter and
Paul's day got it wrong. But, even more tragically, most of us who call ourselves
Christians today don't get it at all.

The Jews' past and present exclusivity of an "Abrahamic" identity to *themselves*, is the fruit of mistakingly equating ethnicity with election. The scripture
declares from the time of Moses through the ministry of Ezra that the Jews
are Yahweh's "chosen people."[2] Thus, if you were born a Jew, you were part of
this elect group. Interestingly, numerous "New" Testament writers also refer to
Christians as being "chosen" (or "elect").[3] Unfortunately, those of us who boast
that the "New" Testament is our book, in ignoring the "Abrahamic" aspect of
our identity, mistakenly equate election with *adoption*. Sadly, whether I am a Jew
who equates election with ethnicity, or a Christian who equates election with
adoption, the results are equally wrong.

One, it strips us of any compelling sense of mission or purpose, individually
and corporately. Theologians have and continue to argue hopelessly about the
"who" and "how" of election, and seem to have left the "why" off the table of debate. When I begin to understand that what I'm a part of is older than the earthly
life of Jesus, and bigger than Paul, my dash lights should start to come on. Many
of us as Christians, like the rest of middle-class Americans, have become part
of a cast of characters in search of a plot. This neglect to embrace and drink
deeply from the cup from Abraham's vineyard is as much to blame as anything
else. Instead of recapturing the ancient nature of our faith, and submitting to
this aspect of who we are, we've become inebriated with gimmicks, gadgets,
and techniques to make church more modern and sexy. Nearly 25 years ago I
cautioned that the rising generation would become tired of the smoke and mirrors version of Christianity that was beginning to characterize our churches. The
frenzy to attract "seekers" didn't have the desired effect. The seekers, if they exist,
are probably still sitting in the bars and coffee shops of our cities, *not* our sanc-
tuaries. Today, those unaffiliated with any religious faith are among the fastest
growing demographic in America. They've been labeled the "Nones," because
they checked "no religious identity" on the American Religious Identification
Survey.[4] This tendency to buy the lie that those *outside* the community of faith
should be allowed to dictate the forms of worship and spirituality *inside* the faith

---

1 For the sources of Peter's description of these believers, see: Deuteronomy 7:6; Exodus 19:5-6; Isaiah
43:21; 42:16; Hosea 1:6, 9, 10; 2:23; For support that this is a Gentile (or at least mixed) audience, see: 1
Peter 1:14, 18; 2:12; 4:3-5

2 cf. Deuteronomy 7:6; Psalm 33:12; Isaiah 41:8-9; 1 Chronicles 16:13

3 Colossians 3:12; 1 Peter 2:4;

4 The Birmingham News, 1/14/12, "Losing Our Religion," by Cathy Lynn-Grossman, Religious News
Service.

community is nothing new. Jesus' harshest and most howling reproach fell upon the Sadducees, a religious group within Judaism committed to being culturally hip in his day. But, even six centuries before that, as I mentioned earlier, Yahweh warned the Jews of Jeremiah's day to "ask for the ancient paths, where the good way is, and walk in it...". I wonder what He's trying to say to His people today? The similarities between twenty-first century American Christianity and sixth century BC Judaism are chilling. The Scripture admonishes us to "be still and know that I am God." I wonder, if we're not still, can we really know He's God? I suspect we'll have to take the white wires out of our ears, and turn down the worship, to find out. Seeing myself as "Abrahamic" isn't old school. It's *ancient* school, and there's a difference; an enormous difference.

But, the most tragic and devastating consequence of either confusing or neglecting what it means to be "Abrahamic," has to do with the point of Yahweh's "call" to him in Ur in the first place. Yahweh had a plan to bless his offspring *and* the goyim. In fact, He had no other plan. Unfortunately, looking down through time from Canaan to Chicago, it is clear that those who are "chosen" seem to inevitably adopt an attitude of isolation at best, disdain at worst, for those *outside* their "chosen" group. The reason this is so very wrong is that the people who populate the crowds we have distanced ourselves from, or maybe look down upon, comprise what our Bible calls "the nations." These are the ones for whom the "chosen" exist. What's wrong with this picture?

Alien — Just Visiting This Planet

Our family lived in Colorado Springs through the 1980's and early 1990's. We left shortly before it became a suburb of Southern California, or as one friend put it, the Protestant answer to the Vatican. Back then, there was still a residue of the old mining spirit. A high premium was placed on autonomy and independence. Most of our friends were renegades just like us, hailing from a variety of states. Spending holidays with the immediate family was a pretty rare thing, and we tended to gather with friends and their kids instead. In retrospect, it was an unfortunate and regrettable thing. Our four children barely grew up knowing their grandparents, and the rich Swedish, Italian, and Native American history of which they were a composite. I suppose that's partly owed to the diminutive value placed on the past while Jill and I were coming of age in the Sixties. History was the Antichrist back then. Colorado in the 1980's was a pretty eclectic and yet tolerant place. The only visible indicators that we weren't all transplants were the occasional bumper stickers that had the word, "Native" printed above a silhouette of the Rockies. But, even these were no more divisive than a license plate that says "Retired Marine" on it. It was more a statement of pride than prejudice. People were either "Natives" or they weren't. But at the end of the day, we all were Coloradans.

Maybe that's why we cried ourselves to sleep for six months after moving to Alabama. We were reminded at regular intervals that we were "from" somewhere else. Typically it took the form of casual interrogation as to our state of birth. But occasionally, it became obvious that "Yankees" were a people group viewed with suspicion and distant affection. Considering that both our grandparents emigrated to the U.S. *after* the Civil War, and my maternal ancestors were here before the Mayflower, it was puzzling to us who the Yankees really were and how we had landed in that people group. Eventually, we came to realize that the designation "Yankee" had less to do with where you were *from*, than it did where you were *not* from. Hence, you would be considered a Yankee if you were from Brooklyn or Boulder, because in both cases, you *weren't* from Birmingham. The conclusion we all drew from this was that although Southern hospitality is very real, very warm, and very inclusive (we *love it*), we would remain eternal outsiders in the South. In short, we just weren't "from around here," and never would be. Fortunately for us, this realization also served to illustrate and galvanize in each of us, the next vital rung on our identity ladder; that of an "Alien." Running the risk that you conclude I think "all roads lead to Ur," I need to insist that for this next rung, we will need to revisit our ancient ancestor in the faith—Abraham. But, the road leading to the "Alien" rung is a little circuitous. Be patient, I promise we *will* arrive there.

At this stage of our journey together, it shouldn't surprise you that "Old" Testament characters *should* occupy a prominent place in our "New" Testament. And so it is. Names like Abraham, Moses, David, Job, and Elijah get a lot of ink. But, under a little closer scrutiny, some significant and salient distinctions drop out of the mix. For example, a mere 5% of the 1,100 references to David in the Bible are in the New Testament. Or Job, whose name appears only once in our New Testament, is mentioned 55 times in the Old Testament. Obviously, for some characters, what happens in the Old Testament stays in the Old Testament.

However, when you talk about Moses and Abraham, things become very different from David and Job in some startling ways. Take for instance the fact that even in the Old Testament where the name of Moses appears over three times as much as Abraham's, he fades from the biblical narrative after the books he authored.[1] But, the real riches are found in our New Testament's inclusion of these two men. Their names appear nearly the same number of times, but the distribution is striking.[2] In both cases, in nearly half of the times they appear, it is at the end of the pens held by two people: Luke and the author of Hebrews.[3] The writer of Hebrews' main intention is to show the necessary but transient nature of Judaism, something we've just examined. But Luke is different. He is *the* major contributor to our New Testament (more than Paul!), but he is also one of the *goyim*; Luke is a Gentile. It is significant to me that Yahweh, in His sovereignty, when inspiring and shaping the documents that became our Bible, chose a Gentile to talk the most about Abraham. Coincidence? Could be, but I don't think so.

Abraham, in both our Old and New Testaments, is held up as the "gold standard" for the essence of faith—what it *means* to "believe" Yahweh. Particularly the Apostle Paul who devotes the major part of a chapter to him in both Galatians and Romans, his two most theological letters. Of course the audiences of these two letters are very different, and so is his use of Abraham. But, the thing

---

1 Moses' name appears 772x in our OT, but only 122 (16%) of those are *after* Deuteronomy. Abraham, on the other hand, although his name(s) appear only 174 times in the OT, 43 (25%) of those occurrences are *outside* Genesis.

2 Moses appears 78x and Abraham 70x.

3 Luke accounts for 22 (31%) of the uses of Abraham, and 29 (36%) of Moses in Luke-Acts. Hebrews accounts for 11 (15%) of the occurrences of Abraham and 11 (14%) of those of Moses.

they have in common, is that Paul holds him up as the exemplar of what genuine biblical faith is *made of*:

> In hope he believed against hope, that he should become the father of many nations, as he had been told, "So shall your offspring be."...No unbelief made him waver concerning the promise of God, but he grew strong in his faith as he gave glory to God, fully convinced that God was able to do what he had promised. That is why his faith was "counted to him as righteousness." But the words "it was counted to him" were not written for his sake alone, but for ours also. It will be counted to us who believe in him who raised from the dead Jesus our Lord,   **–Romans 4:18, 20–24**

Here, faith has less to do with assent to content as it does submission to a promise. Abraham illustrates that faith means saying "yes" to God's plan to bless the *goyim,* and accepting his place in it. Unbelief is also defined in this passage, though implicitly, as *refusing* to play the role Yahweh had for him in His larger purposes, something Abraham chose not to exhibit. However, later in the narrative his grandson Esau would show forever what constitutes unbelief by "despising" his role in this promised plan. Hence, he would forever be remembered in infamy as "godless" in our New Testament,[1] an example of the unbelief that is the opposite of the faith of his grandfather, Abraham. So, Abraham's enduring half-life from Genesis on into our New Testament assists us in understanding what true faith is made of; what is its *essence.* But, he is also used to point us in the direction of what it looks like; what is its *evidence.*

As much as we in the West have been conditioned to bask in Jesus' gentle call to "come," we tend to forget or ignore that his call to "come" was always accompanied by a command to "go." Faith always believes, but it never basks. That has always been the MO of God. It's Yahweh or the highway, in an ironic sort of way. And here too, Abraham is held up as the gold standard of how genuine biblical expresses itself, for those wondering in the first century. And for us, forty centuries later, it is the same:

> By faith Abraham obeyed when he was called to go out to a place that he was to receive as an inheritance. And he went out, not knowing where he was going.
> **–Hebrews 11:8**

Abraham's faith, we are told, is evidenced by what he *did*, not what he believed, although the two are inseparable if they are real. The marriage of these two aspects of faith—essence and evidence—shows up numerous times in our New Testament.[2] For example, most of Paul's arguments in Romans 4 about the nature of Abraham's faith are understood by his audience in the context of this incident with Isaac, even if we moderns don't immediately make that association.[3] He is *not* contrasting faith and obedience, but faith and circumcision

---

1 Genesis 15:1-6 records Abraham's encounter with Yahweh in which "righteousness" was ascribed to him, and Genesis 25:29-34 records Esau's barter in which he gave up his legitimate place in the drama as firstborn. Hebrews 12:16 refers to Esau as "unholy" (ESV) "godless" (NIV), "profane" (KJV). The word here, *bebēlos*, comes from a word for "threshold," an implies a demeaning or disregard of God as God.

2 cf. John 8:39; Hebrews 11:9, 17; James 2:20-22

3 cf. Romans 4:9, 12, 13

(i.e. the "works" of the Law). Faith, as evidenced and embraced by Abraham and expounded by Paul, was always in motion. It never sat idle, it never rested, and it surely never basked. In this respect, it mirrored grace itself. And there was a reason for that, which has to do with the fourth rung of our ladder. It had to do with Abraham's view of himself—his identity. And just like us, it had two major elements: what he believed about Yahweh, and what he believed about his relationship to the world in which he found himself. Fortunately for us, Paul forever lays to rest what Abraham believed about Yahweh.[1] That's been the substance of this chapter so far. But, to ferret out what Abraham believed about his relationship to the "world," we'll need to first spill some ink on what in the world is the "world"?

What In The World?

Our New Testament employs two different, but closely related phrases in the context of addressing the believer's relationship to the surrounding society and culture. The first and more prominent is the Greek word, *kosmos*, which appears 186 times, and is translated "world" in all but three. Although there are nuances to its meaning, the vast majority of the time it is not referring to a *place* (i.e. the earth), but a *perspective*, an outlook, a conviction, a worldview if you like. This perspective is characterized by two fundamental and equally insidious features that like some predators, seem to hunt in pairs. The first is the endorsement and exaltation of the Adamic residue. The other is the marginalization of God. The best synopsis of this perspective is found implicitly buried in a brief command by the Apostle John. The *kosmos* is a very important idea to him, evidenced by the fact that he is responsible for nearly 60% of its use in our New Testament.[2] You can see both of the two features lurking beneath the surface of his admonition to the believers in Asia Minor:

> Do not love the world or the things in the world. If anyone loves the world, the love of the Father is not in him. For all that is in the world—the desires of the flesh and the desires of the eyes and pride of life—is not from the Father but is from the world.
> –1 John 2:15–16

In short, the "world" is human society's exertion to exalt itself and exclude God. It is merely the persistent presence of the Adamic residue, spilling so far east of Eden that it has covered the planet. But, it dresses differently from age to age, which brings us to our second Greek word. The word *aiōn*—sometimes translated "world," but most often, "this present age"—has a variety of meanings; most of them innocuous. But, it can also be the incestuous cousin of *kosmos*. For a thorough understanding of this word and its contribution to clarifying our "Alien" status, we need to visit an old friend, Paul. His most extensive use of *aiōn* is in his correspondence to the one city that would undoubtedly be chosen if there had been something comparable to "American Idol" in his

---

1 cf. Romans 4:20-24

2 Gospel of John - 78; 1 John - 23; 2 John - 1; Revelation - 3. (Total: 105 out of 186)

day—Corinth. It was a Greek city destroyed and rebuilt by Rome, and therefore very much a Roman city surrounded by Greek neighbors. The Corinthians, both before *and* after conversion, were apparently mesmerized by status and power. The Romans called it *dignitas,* but Paul called it foolishness and sin. They were suing each other, creating celebrity cults built around their favorite preachers, and trying to stay current with whatever the hot topic of the day was. Paul spent much of his first letter to the Corinthians dealing with their love affair with the *aiōn.* So what is it?

I want to suggest that *aiōn* is simply the "window" through which the *kosmos* expresses itself at any given point in time. It has a spiritual director known as the "god of this world *(aiōn),*" has an agenda to choke out the Word of God in our lives, and is characterized by what could honestly be called "the wisdom of friends."[1] But, perhaps the most startling statement in Scripture is that this window through which the *kosmos* leaks, has the suction to draw us through it, and reshape us to resemble itself. Paul's oft-quoted exhortation to the believers in Rome is a timeless warning to any who are Abraham's true offspring:

> Do not be conformed to this world *(aiōn),* but be transformed by the renewal of your mind, that by testing you may discern what is the will of God, what is good and acceptable and perfect.   **–Romans 12:2**

The verbs "conformed" and "transformed" are likely both passive in the Greek, which implies that we don't get to choose whether, only *which* of the two will shape us. Elsewhere in Paul's letters we find two additional references to *aiōn,* one which is encouraging, the other, chilling. Both are very real to him because they involve two men he dearly loved and mentored. The first reference is in a letter he wrote to a man he had led to faith as a child. As an older, yet still young man, he was now the pastor of a church of his own on the Mediterranean island of Crete. His name was Titus. In his short letter to this young man, he made a passing comment about the *aiōn* that is very hopeful. He assured Titus that the grace of God in the life of a believer was more powerful than the *kosmos* or its servant, *aiōn:*

> For the grace of God has appeared, bringing salvation for all people, training us to renounce ungodliness and worldly passions, and to live self-controlled, upright, and godly lives in the present age *(aiōn)*...   **–Titus 2:11–12**

Before Paul was beheaded by the Emperor Nero, he penned one last letter to a young pastor serving in Ephesus, a city near the west coast of what is now Turkey. His name was Timothy, and he was Paul's favorite and most beloved disciple. In this deathbed correspondence, he informed Timothy that one of his inner circle disciples he called his "fellow-workers," had abandoned him in the face of death. That man's name was Demas. He had seen Paul imprisoned before, and had traveled and ministered side-by-side with him. What could cause a man so intimately acquainted with the power of God, so clearly manifested in

1 cf. 2 Corinthians 4:4 ("world" is *ai n*); Matthew 13:22; 1 Corinthians 1:20; 2:6

the ministry of Paul, to turn his back on him and maybe even his own faith, and walk away? Listen to Paul, and be attentive to what he says happened to Demas' affections: *"For Demas, in love with this present world (aiōn), has deserted me and gone to Thessalonica"*[1]

John warned his audience about the danger of loving the world *(kosmos)*, and Paul had alerted his Roman brethren of the inevitability of being conformed to it *(aiōn)*. He even went so far as to say that for a genuine believer, the "native" option was not merely a closed door, it was a burned bridge. We can't go back and enjoy the *kosmos* anymore.[2] A final instructive insight about our relationship to the *kosmos* both for us and for our understanding of what happened to Demas, comes from John:

> Anyone who does not love does not know God, because God is love. In this the love of God was made manifest among us, that God sent his only Son into the world *(kosmos)*, so that we might live through him. In this is love, not that we have loved God but that he loved us and sent his Son to be the propitiation for our sins.
> —1 John 4:8–10

The "world," as we've seen is not a place, but a perspective. And those outside the family of God (and even some *within* it) consciously or subconsciously have absorbed the outlook of the *kosmos,* or a variation of it. It has become a familiar way to think and live for them. They are comfortable there. In some sense, it feels like "home," making them "native" to the *kosmos*. The repeated message of Jesus and those who followed him, was that we were to love the "natives," but hate the *kosmos*. This is very easy to get reversed. In conversations with unbelievers over the years, their biggest criticism of Christians is that they live like everyone else, *and* dislike and distance themselves from unbelievers. They love the *kosmos*, and hate the "natives." That's getting it backwards! And Demas is our poster child for this error. His legacy is showing for all time that in getting too close to lean over into the *kosmos,* you can fall in! Unless of course, you see yourself as an "Alien." Then you have a better appreciation for the suction the *kosmos* exerts.

Stangers In A Strange Land

We have finally arrived at the "Alien" rung as promised, which also means we're back to Abraham. As we begin our investigation, there's some biblical bushes we'll need to push aside to get a clear look. Our entry point to this rich reservoir of truth is found in the one book in our New Testament that speaks the most about him and those like him—the Letter to the Hebrews:

> By faith he *lived as an alien* in the land of promise, as in a foreign land, dwelling in tents with Isaac and Jacob, fellow heirs of the same promise....All these died in faith, without receiving the promises, but having seen them and having welcomed them from a distance, and having confessed that they were *strangers* and *exiles* on the earth.

---

1 2 Timothy 4:10

2 cf. Galatians 6:14 — *"But far be it from me to boast except in the cross of our Lord Jesus Christ, by which the world has been crucified to me, and I to the world.*

For those who say such things make it clear that they are seeking a country of their own. And indeed if they had been thinking of that country from which they went out, they would have had opportunity to return. But as it is, they desire a better country, that is, a heavenly one. Therefore God is not ashamed to be called their God; for He has prepared a city for them.   —**Hebrews 11:13-16**, (NASB)

This composite passage will allow us to triangulate a description of an "Alien," using the words in italics as our three reference points. Each of them in our English Bible derives from a single Greek word rich in nuance and beauty.[1] Together they will give us a multi-dimensional understanding of what it means to be an "Alien," in the *kosmos*, and why Demas gave his affections to the wrong place. Our first phrase, "lived as an alien," is a single word, *paroikeō*. This was the word for an outsider, a non-native. The implication here is that this person was *not* a member, in an indigenous sense, of the community where they dwelt. They were a sort of "resident alien." Although they *lived* there, everyone knew they weren't *"from"* there. Sort of like our family moving to the South. This word was used for the Jews while they were in captivity in Egypt and in Babylon, and for non-Jews living in Israel.[2] It's the word for a sojourner, someone local folks would call a "foreigner."

Our second word, "strangers" is from *xenos*. This is the root of our English word, xenophobia, the irrational fear of other nationalities. In the first century too, no one would extend a warm welcome to this word. It meant an "outsider," similar to *paroikeō*, but carried an added dark and negative connotation. *Xenoi* were always regarded with suspicion and mistrust. Life was typically hard for them because of the constant scrutiny under which they lived. They were the "John Does" of the ancient world, people passing like shadows among the cities in which they dwelled. Judas' betrayal money that he threw back to the Jewish authorities was used to buy the "Potter's Field," and it became a burial place for *xenoi*.[3] They were unknown, unloved, and unimportant. And at the end of the day, they were unwanted as well. They were "outsiders" and would never find themselves as "insiders."

The final word, "strangers," is from *parepidēmos*, a word very similar in meaning to our first word, except the nuance here shifts from the foreign aspect of one's nature, to the temporariness of it. The force of this word points to the fact that where they now *are* is temporary, not that where they're *from* is foreign. Although this person might be thought of as some type of "pilgrim," they were always understood to be eventually returning "home." Our word "transient" might capture some of the wide range of meaning for this word.

Taken together, these three words paint an amazing composite of how we, like our father Abraham, should think of ourselves during our own sojourn in the *kosmos*. The anonymous author of Hebrews, however, is not the only person in our New Testament who taught that the "Alien" rung belonged on the iden-

---

1 The richness of these words is evident by a brief comparative study on how they are translated in the various popular English versions of our NT. For example: "lived as an alien" (NAS), "lived" (ESV), "so-journed" (KJV, RSV), "made his home...like a stranger" (NIV),

2 cf. LXX: Genesis 47:4; Isaiah 52:4; Ezekiel 14:7

3 cf. Matthew 27:7

tity ladder of anyone who claimed to be a Kingdom subject. Jesus, Peter, and Paul also spoke directly to this idea:

> They are not of the world, just as I am not of the world. Sanctify them in the truth; your word is truth. As you sent me into the world, so I have sent them into the world.
> –John 17:16–18

> Beloved, I urge you as sojourners and exiles to abstain from the passions of the flesh, which wage war against your soul.   –1 Peter 2:11

> But our citizenship is in heaven, and from it we await a Savior, the Lord Jesus Christ,
> –Philippians 3:20

The person in our Bibles, however, who provides us with the most thorough and compelling presentation of being an "Alien," is Jesus himself. Two entire chapters of John's record of what we call his "upper room teaching," contain repeated references to the *kosmos,* and what it means to be "in" it but not "of" it. In our haste to turn this concept into a bumper sticker doctrine, we've lost sight of the fact that this has very little to do with behavior. Jesus and the rest are speaking clearly about how we see ourselves in relationship to the *kosmos.* And that's an issue of identity, not conduct. Jesus' desire was *never* that his disciples would abandon the "natives"—the *goyim* for whom we exist—by seeking to escape the influence of the *kosmos.* Listen to Jesus as he pleads to the Father for you and I shortly before his murder:

> But now I am coming to you, and these things I speak in the world, that they may have my joy fulfilled in themselves. I have given them your word, and the world has hated them because they are not of the world, just as I am not of the world. *I do not ask that you take them out of the world, but that you keep them from the evil one.* They are not of the world, just as I am not of the world. Sanctify them in the truth; your word is truth. As you sent me into the world, so I have sent them into the world. And for their sake I consecrate myself, that they also may be sanctified in truth.   –John 17:13–19

Don't lose sight of the fact that this is a prayer! It's not an epistle, or a sermon, or a parable. We are granted in this chapter the rarest and most intimate details of Jesus' prayer life. And Jesus is consumed with how his disciples and those that follow will fare when it comes to battling this thing called the "world." He lays out before us forever, his deepest longings for his people regarding the *kosmos*: full immersion with distinction, not isolation through separation. He's actually sending them *into* the *kosmos!* He equates our mission with his. I call this the "Alien mission." Consider what he did. He entered the *kosmos* in the incarnation. He came *to* the "natives," instead of building a 20,000 seat sanctuary and hiring "David and the Giants" to lead worship. He brought the message of the Kingdom *to* them, took them *out* of the *kosmos* to train them, and sent them back in to start the process all over. And we can't do that if we don't understand the difference between the *kosmos* and the "natives." He wants us to be different *in* the *kosmos,* not untouched by it because we're never around it. I'll never forget having dinner one night with a local pastor prior to the smoke-free restaurant movement. An attractive young woman greeted us, and politely asked, "Smoking or non-smoking?" Before I could say anything, my friend responded,

"Non-smoking. Non-drinking, if you have it." Based on the look on her face, he might just as well have said, "Believer-Only, if you have it." The "natives" are not our enemy, the *kosmos* is, and the Satan who directs the operation. I think the world will start taking the gospel more seriously when we begin to take the "natives" more seriously. But to do that, we've got to get it right regarding what in the world is the "world," and understand that if I'm a Christian, my bridges to it are all gone. I'm a stranger now, an outsider whose living temporarily in a land that is not home. I'll never "fit in," and trying denies who I say I am in the first place. That's the meaning and the cost of being an "Alien." Loving the "natives" and hating the *kosmos* can only happen if I see myself this way. Abraham did. Demas didn't. That's also why Abraham is listed in Hebrews 11 and Demas isn't.[1] Though I suspect you're exhausted from this chapter, we're not quite finished. Before we leave this rung, we need to revisit Demas. I'm afraid he's alive and well in the American church, and I want you to recognize him when you see him around...or in the mirror.

Enjoy Your Stay!

One of Colorado' primary industries when we were there, aside from the military, was tourism. Scenic locations like Garden of the Gods, Cave of the Winds, and the Air Force Academy drew thousands of visitors especially during the summer months. Wintertime beckoned hordes of people to make their way to the slopes of Breckenridge, Vail, Aspen, and Beaver Creek. But, Coloradans pretty much had a love-hate relationship with all the tourists. Their money was an essential facet for the economy, but often they were rude, demanding, and wantonly wasteful. Instead of the "Alien" rung, one of the unfortunate, yet highly popular counterfeit rungs replacing it on many identity ladders in the American church, is what I can only call a "Tourist." A Tourist Christian is really an Alien who's either forgotten or minimized both where their true citizenship lays, *and* the temporary nature of their visit. For them, the Christian life, like a vacation, is intended to produce great happiness with little discomfort or pain. They are charter members of the *"God loves you and has a wonderful plan for your life"* gospel. Maybe that's why books like, *"Your Best Life Now,"* and the plethora of titles promising control of the destiny of your body, your money, your marriage, and your retirement have flourished in the church as much as in the larger culture. Tourist Christians are really orphans in time, and have no real allegiance either to the place they are visiting (the *kosmos*) or where they're real citizenship lies. They tend to dislike the "natives," yet love the "blessings" of the *kosmos*, all the while professing that they're not "of" it. They've developed a theology that substantiates their core belief: God's will for them is to enjoy the visit. So they do. And, as with most tourists, they are typically very distasteful to the "natives" during their stay.

---

1 Hebrews 11 is an excellent list of Old Testament characters illustrating New Testament faith. They lived as "aliens" by aligning their wills with the plan of God rather than the *kosmos*

One final, but very important truth: In the world of biblical identity, *geography* is an important factor, because either my identity affects my surroundings, or my surroundings shape my identity. Who I believe I am in relationship to the *kosmos* will either be a product of my zip code or Scripture. I have no doubt this is what Paul meant about either being "conformed" or "transformed" when it came to "this present age," and why he posited the "renewal of our minds" as the antidote.[1]

Demas had permitted *where* he was to determine *who* he was. His heart had departed long before his body. He lost track of *who* he was by spending his time thinking about *where* he was. But, if my identity is rooted in a deep and thorough acquaintance with what God says about me as Abraham's offspring, then I will bring who I am with me wherever I go. Demas went to Thessalonica because he was *"in love with this present age."* Abraham *"went out not knowing where he was going,"* because he was in love with Yahweh. We chase what we love. And we become like what we chase. Aliens aren't chasing *their* dreams; they're chasing His.[2]

---

1 cf. Romans 12:1-2

2 The "dream" of Yahweh is the subject of Part III.

Apprentice— *Spending Time With a Master*

Our eldest son is a carbon copy of his maternal grandfather. "Pops" knew how to work hard and rest right. A child of the Depression, he, like my own father, never finished high school. The family's needs outstripped the luxury of securing an education. Until they started handing out paychecks for attending class, our dads would be on the job, not the campus. Pops was a Master plasterer. He had worked his way up the union ladder from Apprentice to Journeyman to Master. And these were the times when blue collar labor was sweat-drenched art. Stone masons, carpenters, and plasterers were creative geniuses, using hand tools like a normal framing square to mark and cut hip and valley rafters and stair stringers, and mortising hinges without electric routers. Pops worked with plaster mixed with hog's hair to create greater cohesion, and laid it over wooden lathe. He did crown moldings with a sliding mold. When drywall took over new residential and commercial construction, artistry was replaced by expediency. I stood by as a Master was reduced to a technician, spraying fire-proofing on pipes in Canadian refineries to feed his family, instead of creating and maintaining work that instilled awe and provided satisfaction. This probably isn't as compelling a contrast today in an age when a photo of Michelangelo's sculpture of David on an iPhone is thought to be comparable to standing spellbound in front of it in Florence. Apprenticeship, that first rung of learning on the path to having your own business—the privilege reserved for a Master in a trade—has waned and is gasping to survive. So far is it removed from our lives and education, that most children couldn't tell you a trade where it still exists (e.g., plumbing). And even more distressing, is the realization that the last great apprenticeship—marriage—where a young male was to learn what it meant to be a man, a husband, and a father, and a young female was to learn what it meant to be a woman, a wife, and a mother, seems headed for extinction as well. Killed *not* by the proliferation of gay marriage, but the starvation and neglect by heterosexuals, many who are professing Christians. The rising generation, often the product of broken homes, or surrounded by friends who are, turns to Google for advice on how to raise their children, or improve their marriages, not the church or their parents. I suppose our society may eventually decide to retire apprenticeship altogether. But God won't, of that I'm confident. He has no plan B.

The sixth rung on our ladder, "Apprentice," is doubly important. First, it provides the foundation for everything related to our own spiritual formation, because it deals with the personal disciplines that shape us spiritually. But, it is also the watershed from which God the Spirit draws the resources He needs to mold our thinking into that of an Alien. In a very real sense, becoming an Alien is *His* job, but *being* an Apprentice is *ours*. As usual, Peter again does a masterful job in capturing the synergistic relationship between our own disciplines regarding our spiritual transformation, and our usefulness to God:

> His divine power has granted to us all things that pertain to life and godliness, through the knowledge of him who called us to his own glory and excellence, by which he has granted to us his precious and very great promises, so that through them you may become partakers of the divine nature, having escaped from the corruption that is in the world because of sinful desire. For this very reason, make every effort to supplement your faith with virtue, and virtue with knowledge, and knowledge with self-control, and self-control with steadfastness, and steadfastness with godliness, and godliness with brotherly affection, and brotherly affection with love. For if these qualities are yours and are increasing, they keep you from being ineffective or unfruitful in the knowledge of our Lord Jesus Christ. For whoever lacks these qualities is so nearsighted that he is blind, having forgotten that he was cleansed from his former sins.
> –2 Peter 1:3–9

The actual word, "apprentice" does not appear in our Bibles. But, the Greek equivalent of it, *mathētēs*, is a familiar word in our New Testament, showing up nearly 270 times! It is our word, "disciple." And there are many things about this word that have a great deal to do with our Apprentice rung. One is that *mathētēs*, although it doesn't appear frequently with its sister word, *didaskalos*, it has no meaning apart from it. *Didaskalos* is the word for "teacher." The words "disciple" and "teacher" were like Mormon missionaries in the first century world; they always traveled as a pair. One had no real usefulness apart from the other. In fact, a disciple's identity was *inseparable* from that of his or her teacher. That's why the identity of the disciples of John the Baptist was linked to him, not just what he taught.[1] This also explains why, on one occasion, *Jesus* is held responsible for the conduct of his apostles,[2] and why the night of his arrest and interrogation, we are told, *"The high priest then questioned Jesus about his disciples and his teaching."*[3] And in our New Testament, not only is the word "disciple" dependent upon the word "teacher" for its context, it actually has no meaning apart from Jesus himself. The word does not even appear outside the Gospels and Acts.

Emulation Not Accumulation

Apprenticeship in our day has the same desired outcome: financial inde-

1 cf. John 1:35-36; 3:25

2 And some of the Pharisees in the crowd said to him, "Teacher, rebuke your disciples." (Luke 19:39)

3 John 18:19

pendence assured by the accumulation of skills and knowledge. Eventually, the modern apprentice will "leave home." At least, that's the plan. But, the expected *result* of apprenticeship (i.e., discipleship) in Jesus' day was radically different. And that's what makes our study more significant and more important. The goal of discipleship in the Ancient Near East was *not* independence, but emulation. The *mathētēs* spent time with the Master to become *like* the Master. Of course one goal was to know as much as possible what the Master *knew,* but that was always secondary to who the Master was. After all, it was the Master's *identity* that gave their life meaning, not necessarily his doctrine. Jesus made this idea of emulation unmistakably clear:

> A disciple is not above his teacher, but everyone when he is fully trained will be like his teacher. **—Luke 6:40**

But, emulation can cut both ways. It's not always a good thing. One could emulate the *wrong* teacher. Jesus understood our natural tendency to imitate those in authority over us, and so carefully cautioned first century followers about whom they were emulating:

> Then Jesus said to the crowds and to his disciples, "The scribes and the Pharisees sit on Moses' seat, so do and observe whatever they tell you, but not the works they do. For they preach, but do not practice." **—Matthew 23:1–3**

> Woe to you, scribes and Pharisees, hypocrites! For you travel across sea and land to make a single proselyte, and when he becomes a proselyte, you make him twice as much a child of hell as yourselves. **—Matthew 23:15**

Discipleship was around long before Jesus, and it wasn't just a Hebrew oddity. Because its origins were in Ancient Greece, its influence had permeated the entire Greek-speaking world. It was a concept birthed in the Sophist movement, which emphasized oratory, technique, and wit. It was flourishing in Corinth in Paul's day.[1] So, both as a follower of Jesus and as a Greek-speaking Jew, it was natural for Paul to incorporate discipleship into his own ministry methods, *and* address its excesses in his teaching. And if there is such a thing as malignant emulation, it would have been that which resulted from the itinerant Stoic teachers circulating in the Mediterranean west of Jerusalem, the focus of Paul's missionary efforts. These "Sophists" were virtuoso orators, whose lives had many similarities:

- They possessed a large following (*and* wanted one!)
- They participated in the secular public assembly (*ekklēsia*) of a city[2]
- They were official spokesmen for embassies sent to the governor or emperor.
- They declaimed (argued passionately) on many topics publicly...for a fee
- They owned and operated expensive schools to train the children of the social elite how to argue in criminal and civil courts, and in public.

---

1 Our modern word "sophisticated" is derived from the sophists.

2 *ekklēsia* is the Greek word translated "church" in our New Testament. It was the ancient gathering of people for a specific purpose.

- Their students were called "disciples" (*mathētēs*), and their goal was "imitatio," the emulation of their teacher in dress, demeanor, and skill.

Paul attacked this godless cult of sophist celebrity that had infiltrated the Christian "disciples" in Corinth:

> I appeal to you, brothers, by the name of our Lord Jesus Christ, that all of you agree, and that there be no divisions among you, but that you be united in the same mind and the same judgment. For it has been reported to me by Chloe's people that there is quarreling among you, my brothers. What I mean is that each one of you says, "I follow Paul," or "I follow Apollos," or "I follow Cephas," or "I follow Christ." Is Christ divided? Was Paul crucified for you? Or were you baptized in the name of Paul?...For while there is jealousy and strife among you, are you not of the flesh and behaving only in a human way? For when one says, "I follow Paul," and another, "I follow Apollos," are you not being merely human? [i.e., "Corinthian"] What then is Apollos? What is Paul? Servants through whom you believed, as the Lord assigned to each. I planted, Apollos watered, but God gave the growth.
> —1Corinthians 1:10–13; 3:3–6 [brackets mine]

Under close reading of his letters to them, you will discover that it all had to do with a case of "mistaken identity." They had become "Corinthian Christians," instead of Christians who happened to live in Corinth. Here, we see the incredible power geography can have on identity. The Corinthians had allowed *where* they were, and which teacher they chose to emulate to dictate and determine *who* they were. Have we escaped this yet? I think not. I am made painfully aware as I travel and teach, that many modern believers are not apprentices of Jesus, but followers of some remote teacher who they have come to follow via podcasts or a Twitter feed.

Paul went out of his way to point *his* "disciples" past himself to Christ when he implored them, *"Be imitators of me, as I am of Christ."*[1] He even began his first letter to them with alarming, anti-sophist language to describe himself and his ministry, to ensure that they got the point about apprenticeship to Jesus before he began to respond to the flurry of questions that had prompted this letter:

> And I, when I came to you, brothers, did not come proclaiming to you the testimony of God with lofty speech or wisdom. For I decided to know nothing among you except Jesus Christ and him crucified. And I was with you in weakness and in fear and much trembling, and my speech and my message were not in plausible words of wisdom, but in demonstration of the Spirit and of power, that your faith might not rest in the wisdom of men but in the power of God.   —1 Corinthians 2:1-5

Apprenticeship then, is the path to emulation. And emulation of Jesus is the personal goal God has for all who are Abraham's offspring, according to promise. He wants all His adopted children to resemble *His* Son, Jesus, not *their* father, Adam:

> For those whom he foreknew he also predestined to be conformed to the image of his Son, in order that he might be the firstborn among many brothers.   —Romans 8:29

This was the driving passion of Paul, as teacher and apostle, for all those he "discipled." It permeated his writings and consumed his days:

---

1 1 Corinthians 11:1

And we all, with unveiled face, beholding the glory of the Lord, are being transformed into the same image from one degree of glory to another. For this comes from the Lord who is the Spirit.   −2 Corinthians 3:18

Him we proclaim, warning everyone and teaching everyone with all wisdom, that we may present everyone mature in Christ. For this I toil, struggling with all his energy that he powerfully works within me.   −Colossians 1:28–29

...my little children, for whom I am again in the anguish of childbirth until Christ is formed in you!   −Galatians 4:19

Time With The Master

The life of an apprentice of Jesus is characterized by many things, if it resembles him more and more. Many are public and visible; such as compassion, mercy, sharing the good news of the Kingdom that has come, etc. But, the behaviors that others see must be the *fruit*, not the foundation, of apprenticeship. The foundation of genuine apprenticeship to Jesus is rooted in the nature of apprenticeship itself; time alone with the Master with the goal of becoming like him. I surely endorse and enjoy time spent walking in the woods, or near a stream, thinking and praying. But, that is not the same thing. Indeed, sometimes, time spent in nature is time spent with ourselves more than God. A portrait of discipleship that best captures the heart of apprenticeship is Mary, the younger sister of a brash, but generous Jewish woman named Martha. While Martha was busy "serving" Jesus—providing things she deemed necessary, but he hadn't requested—Mary sat at Jesus' feet, listening to him teach.[1] A woman, publicly sitting at a rabbi's feet in a room full of men in a first century Jewish village, is no less difficult than being alone in a room with an actual Bible, in our modern Facebook culture. Mary said "no" to the distraction of serving that had captured her older sister, so that she could be an Apprentice. Saying "no" to convention, convenience, and the ubiquitous "wisdom of friends," may be an equivalent prerequisite to spending time with the Master in our own day.

I'm referring to intentional, sustained exposure to the the Scriptures, our only source of what our Master valued, how he treated people, what made him angry, and how he related to his Father. Especially the four Gospels. Let me say this clearly and without ambiguity. I'm *not* referring to an electronic devotional distilled from a distant teacher (or an office assistant writing in his or her name) that arrives daily in the Inbox on your laptop or phone. I'm also not referring to the many devotional books in print built around the motto, "A verse a day keeps the devil away," consisting of a solitary Bible verse near the top, followed by several paragraphs an author has provided. We fed our kids strained peas when they were little. But, they're not fans of them anymore. Apprentices hunt and fish for themselves when it comes to the teachings of their Master. If you need help, look for a devotional guide that is open-ended, yet provides enough

1 cf. Luke 10:38-42

structure and direction that you are free for God to speak.[1]

Laying the content of this book aside for a moment, let me make a passionate plea to all of you, especially those of you in the generation coming of age, about your Bible. There's something Denzel Washington has in common with Eudora Johnson, although one is a living African American male and the other a deceased female Stockbridge-Munsee Indian. In the movie, *The Book of Eli*, Washington plays the part of Eli, the guardian of a sacred book that allegedly has the power to save mankind from the Mordor-like darkness and evil that have swept over the land after an apocalyptic event of some kind. The book Eli is carrying turns out to be the Bible. Although the film is saturated with graphic violence, it is an amazing parable of what can happen when the lights go out for good, in a high-tech culture that has wedded knowledge to electricity. They rediscover that there is more power in print than in pixels.

Eudora Johnson was born in the mid-1800's, nearly 100 years before Washington, on a reservation in Wisconsin. She attended Moody Bible College in downtown Chicago, and was eventually ordained a Methodist minister. As a traveling preacher, in the era before typewriters were ubiquitous or affordable, Eudora would write her sermons in blue ink with a fountain pen on scrap paper. Like the Book of Eli, those sermons were on real paper. She didn't have to depend on the power company or scroll a screen to read them. Nor did she have anxiety about a hard drive contracting a virus, erasing her messages entirely. Instead, her sermons could be held, studied, and absorbed. You could ponder what she was thinking or where she was when she wrote them. I know, because I have done all those things. Eudora was my great-grandmother. I have her Bible right in front of me, and four of the sermons she preached, including one on Esther. Why share this with *you*? Because a well-worn, copiously and personally marked Bible is one of the richest and rarest gifts you can leave to your children. My two sons each have a Bible that I carried (and also carried me), for two, twenty-year portions of my life. With some effort and interest, they can reconstruct a partial and perforated version of my spiritual pilgrimage as an adopted, Abrahamic, alien-apprentice of Jesus. The marginal dates, names, notes, and prayers on the worn and sometimes tear-streaked pages will provide the substance. Their imaginations will have to fill in the rest. They can trace with their fingers the path of my feet, through misery and despair, hope and exaltation. On those pages, they can discover the war within my soul during a dark and long journey through depression. They can also discern what the God of Abraham and I talked about when I was deeply in love with a mysteriously deep, young beauty named Jill Anderson; the woman who would someday be my wife and their mother. A Bible is surely the record of God's dealings with the remnant of Adam. But, *your* Bible can also be a memoir of your own journey on the wide path of God's grace. It will tell your ancestors things about

---

1 Some excellent devotional guides that meet these critieria can be found at: http://www.handsofhur.org/HOH/Print.html

Him that *aren't* in their Bible, because it will tell them things about you, His adopted child. I implore you as an aging and passing man; do not neglect this book. And certainly do not replace it with an app running on your smartphone. Your grandchildren will have to scour the heaps of technological paleontology to even know what an iPhone was. But a book, that's a different story, and one that can be retold because it can be held. Even when the lights go out.

This would be a wonderful place to conclude this chapter, on an emotional anecdote wrapped in transparency and dripping with relevancy. However, in fairness to my own purposes in general, and you in particular, we've got to embark on the arduous task of exposing a case of Identity Theft of our Apprentice rung. Unlike the Tourist identity that has corroded our understanding of Alien, the Apprentice aspect has been completely usurped by another identity altogether, that of a "Partner." This is more serious than sarcasm-inviting bumper stickers like, "God is My Co-Pilot," or "Jesus is My Designated Driver." I'm referring to a wholesale replacement of a true identity facet with one that is false. In the world of digital security, it's known as identity theft. In the world of biblical integrity, it's called idolatry. At bottom, it's a spiritual downsizing in which Yahweh gets reassigned from CEO to a management position. He has a voice, but no vote, when it comes to how I live my life as a believer, or how we live our lives corporately as His people. And to make matters slightly more complicated, this bastard identity is the offspring of four illicit unions within American Christianity, each formed by what I can only label as a "common law marriage." It's the only metaphor I can muster that best captures *how* these outlaws became in-laws in the family of God. Common law marriages are unions that are considered legitimate *not* because they have been solemnized, but because the parties have been living together by mutual consent, and present themselves to the world as "married." It just seems as though they "belong together." No one questions; no one wonders. They just accept that it's life as it should be. In our case, Christianity has been in bed with four things that have everything to do with America but *nothing* to do with the gospel. And each of them has given birth to the same bastard, *Partner.* You surely won't find their wedding pictures online or in the Registry at Crate and Barrel, because they're living in plain sight. These four proliferators of the Partner counterfeit are "coming to a church near you," if they're not already there.

Christianity And Wall Street

The first "common law marriage" joined Christianity with Capitalism. I fear that our understanding of the gospel, the Christian faith, and the mission of God are more a product of Wall Street than the Scriptures. You discover this painfully but fully when you visit places like Haiti, Manila, Guatemala, or Romania. You can't offer the "Financial Peace University" courses of Dave Ramsey or distribute books like, *What Would Jesus Eat?* or *The Prayer of Jabez.* Dieting, exercise and weight loss are not components of the gospel we can take to the nations. Faced with an entire society devoid of hope and the means to regain it, these resources that seem so normal in America suddenly seem hollow, and sometimes even embarrassing.[1] A dear friend and apologist, the late Ron Carlson once said, *"If you can't preach the gospel you're proclaiming the same way anywhere in the world, it's not the gospel."* I believe this is true.

It is capitalism, not Christianity that holds forth the notion that hard work in a free market yields results to those who take advantage of it. And, the American Dream always goes upward, in a straight line. When this is married to the gospel, success becomes the inevitable outcome of knowing Jesus. Maybe that's why our banquet speakers are those who've won beauty pageants, Super Bowls, or Dove Awards. We don't feel attracted to Super Bowl losers, or those who've bankrupted their businesses, or lost their beauty, to address us. Especially our youth. Why not? Because the best always rise to the top. That's the beauty of the free market.

There's also an unspoken (sometimes loudly proclaimed) assumption that life will increase in quality and perhaps even in longevity, if one is a dedicated Christian. This too, has more in common with the American Dream than it does God's revealed Word. It also belies a very shallow understanding of what *really* happened that day in the Garden, and that afternoon on Golgotha. In America, you get to live a relatively long life (and demand it, if you're a Baby Boomer!), perforated with occasional, but not intense personal pain, and you spend your sunset years traveling to see grandkids, golfing, and picking up that hobby you neglected all those years because you had to work hard to get where you are. You can tell how sweetly your theology has been sleeping with our economy by how you view suffering and pain. Do you view them as "invaders," or normal and necessary ingredients in the plan of Yahweh to make His children less like Adam and more like Jesus?

> ...and if children, then heirs—heirs of God and fellow heirs with Christ, provided we suffer with him in order that we may also be glorified with him. For I consider that the sufferings of this present time are not worth comparing with the glory that is to be revealed to us.   **–Romans 8:17–18**

> Count it all joy, my brothers, when you meet trials of various kinds, for you know that the testing of your faith produces steadfastness. And let steadfastness have its full effect, that you may be perfect and complete, lacking in nothing.   **–James 1:2–4**

I am grateful to live in a nation with a free economy. And I'm also grateful for the opportunity granted to me and millions of others to raise their standard of living through effort and perseverance. And surely, Christianity and the Bible have much to say *to* Capitalism and my participation in it. But, Capitalism has nothing to do with the gospel. Getting those reversed is devastating. And we've done it. God has been perceived as our "Partner" as we pursue the American Dream, instead of the source of our dreams in the first place.

---

1 This is not an attack on any of these books or their authors. It's simply time for us to admit that these have less to do with the Mission of God than they do with the American way of life.

Christianity And Washington

A second prolific progenitor of Partners is the common law marriage between Christianity and Democracy. I realize this may be the wrong moment in history to appear unpatriotic, but I'm not sure a better moment will appear before I leave the planet. I am deeply grateful to be an American. Don't misread what follows. America is a great place to live. And, the Bible has much to say to democracy, just as it did to capitalism. But, also like capitalism, democracy, while it facilitates much religious liberty, has nothing to do with the gospel. If there's such a thing as the wrong time in history to get something backwards, I would say this is it for Christianity and democracy. Letting these two cohabit has exacerbated the problems inherent in them simply coexisting. Democracy by definition and design, is about individual rights and freedoms and the common good. Given our Adamic residue, this eventually is skewed toward the inevitable focus on the individual in the present, rather than the common good over time. In summary, left to our Adamic selves, life becomes a story about me. Which means that Facebook and social media in a democratic country can easily become narcissism on steroids. Looking back, we see it manifested in the explosion of the "rights" movements since the collapse of the counterculture at the end of the 1960's. But, the nineteenth century French historian, Alexis de Toqueville, saw this trajectory within democracy 100 years prior to that:

> Not only does democracy make every man forget his ancestors, but it hides his descendants and separates his contemporaries from him; it throws him back forever upon himself alone and threatens in the end to confine him to the solitude of his own heart.[1]

The reason this marriage within American Christianity is more dangerous than that with free-market capitalism, is that it accentuates a handicap that is as old as American history itself. We don't "do" monarchies. We're Americans for crying out loud. We are citizens of a country that *overthrew* the throne of England. There's never *been* a "King of America."[2] And there never will be. That's the difference between a republic and a monarchy. And in a democratic republic, we live as voting citizens, free to pursue the things specified in the second paragraph of the document that birthed our nation:

> We hold these truths to be self-evident, that all men are created equal, that they are endowed by their Creator with certain unalienable Rights, that among these are Life, Liberty and the pursuit of Happiness.[3]

When the Church got in bed with democracy, its theology began to *reflect* America instead of reform it. Over the years, we have forged a faith that is rife with individuality and vacuous in places when it comes to solidarity with the global Church. It has also tethered our practical understanding of Christianity's boundaries to the West, except occasional mission trips, mostly to predictably

1 Alexis de Toqueville, *Democracy in America*. (Cambridge: Sever & Francis, 1863), 121.

2 British pop singer and writer, Elvis Costello, titled his 1986 album, "The King of America." The title is obviously a parody on Democracy from the standpoint of someone living in a monarchy.

3 *The Declaration of Independence*, paragraph 2, July 4, 1776.

safe places, and an unusual affinity for Israel. Other than that, we're pretty happy to pursue life, liberty, and happiness here at home. This would be less disconcerting if there were references to private spirituality in the Bible, or democracy for that matter. But, when we open our Bibles, we are met with the very thing we don't "do" well, because we don't "do" it at all—monarchy. If we *really* had given thought to this, we'd all be a mess trying to figure out what to do with it. The Bible speaks of a Kingdom that has come and *is* to come. It speaks of a King who *is presently reigning,* and *will* reign. There are no references to "citizens," in a democratic sense. And we are immediately in interpretive trouble if we lay democratic citizenship over Paul's use of the word in Philippians 3:20.[1] The truth of the matter is, if we are Christians, if we are Abraham's offspring, the adopted sons and daughters of Yahweh, then we are *subjects* (not citizens) of a *kingdom* (not a republic). That changes everything! Instead of an emphasis on individual rights and freedoms, the spotlight shifts to fealty and submission. Instead of the common good, the call shifts to the will of the King. Instead of the American Dream—building my own kingdom—the focus shifts to seeking first *His* kingdom and the righteousness that characterizes it. The honor of my King trumps my own reputation and status. Getting this right renders putting a full color portrait of *myself* on a book purportedly about God, seem preposterous!

I love fireworks as much as anyone. And the Fourth of July is *big* deal down here in Dixie. Patriotism is respected. However, after one of the largest churches in our city hung an American flag the size of a mall parking lot from its roof after the 9/11 attacks, I realized we've really got this wrong. If you and I embrace a spirituality that is monarchial instead of democratic, we will realize that we have more in common with a North Korean, Iraqi, or Palestinian Christian than we do our next door neighbor who's an American but not a believer. It also means that you have more in common with a Republican believer (if you're a Democrat) than you do with an unbeliever of your own party. And finally, it means that as a white man, I have more in common with the African American, Asian, and Hispanic believers here and around the world, than I do with many folks on my own block. And this is also true of you, as you sit and turn these pages. We would all do well to heed the words of a second century apprentice, to his fellow Christians engaged in our same struggle regarding their relationship, as Aliens, to the country in which they found themselves:

> Christians reside in their respective countries, but only as aliens. They take part in everything as citizens and put up with everything as foreigners. Every foreign land is their home and every home a foreign land. They find themselves in the flesh, but do not live according to the flesh.   —*The Epistle of Mathetes to Diognetus*, c. AD 130

Democracy eventually divides people through its emphasis on individual rights. The gospel unites people because of its insistence on a universal King. Christians in the US can, and *should* put "American," on their identity ladders, just not on any of the top seven rungs.

---

1 *"But our citizenship is in heaven, and from it we await a Savior, the Lord Jesus Christ"* (Philippians 3:20)

Christianity And Moralistic Narcissism

The third common law marriage in the Church, is the union of Christianity and Psychology. These two had been dating quite seriously for a few decades, but likely "tied the knot" sometime in the 1980's. This one is particularly difficult to address, because on one hand, two of its main foci—the past and the self—have a different perspective, biblically. Scripture implores us to ignore or mortify the past and the self, as Christians.[1] On the other hand, God's gifts to the church include pastors, teachers, and prophets, men and women unusually gifted in discernment and counsel. But *not* for the purpose of self-help. The real problem is rooted in the reality that not only was Christianity and psychology an illicit marriage, it also became a very lopsided one. In the 1980's particularly, psychology clothed itself in church dress and supplanted theology as the first choice for truth when it came to meeting the emotional needs of people. The number of pastors in that decade that returned to a seminary to acquire a counseling degree skyrocketed. Professional journals for pastors became popular that tended to neglect direct interaction with Scripture in favor of a more clinical analysis of issues within the church. As "soul care" became the domain of trained professionals, the foundational baggage of modern psychology also seemed to slip in the back door. The Church was either not paying attention, or looking in the mirror.

The fruit of all this was the emergence of what can only be called a form of Christian narcissism. Church programs and buildings were constructed to satisfy the felt needs of believers and their families. Running tracks, rock climbing walls, fitness centers, coffee shops, and even restaurants became part of ecclesiastical architecture. Slowly, the idea took root that the primary purpose of the church was the nurture of Christians. A shift occurred, taking us away from the glory of God and the mission of Abraham, to the well-being of His sheep. Industries arose that produced goods and services back to ourselves, leaving less money for ministries to others, especially the poor. In an attempt to become "purpose driven" some churches took on expansive capital campaigns, and found themselves mortgage driven instead. I'll never forget the testimony of a local junior high boy in our city's paper a decade ago. He said, *"My church has everything I need. I don't need to go anywhere else."* The senior pastor of this megachurch saw this as a good thing, the evidence of a successful youth ministry. But, with the focus turned inward on spiritual maintenance, actual church growth became more difficult. In the beginning, there was *apparent* growth from sheep shifting, and the movement of consumer-oriented believers from one church to another. But, not true numerical growth from conversions to Christ. A new form of evangelism emerged and has exploded, to fill this void: "marketing" the church. "Going" into all the world was replaced by "getting to" all the world.[2]

---

1 cf. Philippians 3:12-15; Hosea 6:3; Isaiah 43:18-19 and Mark 8:35; Philippians 2:4

2 George Barna, a leader in cultural analysis among Christians, and founder of the Barna (Research) Group, released a controversial book on this subject in 1988, *Marketing The Church: What They Never Taught You About Church Growth.*

Christianity and Marketing

Our last common law marriage is the union of Christianity and marketing. And, with the advent of social networking, this has rapidly moved from the childhood of direct mail to the adolescence of Facebook and Twitter. And this has affected everything from the way a church constructs its worship, to how it prays. When the megachurch movement took on a life of its own a few decades ago, the unchallenged belief-become-dogma was that those best suited to evaluate what a church should "look and feel" like, were those *outside* it. A tribal conviction evolved that there were large numbers of "seekers" lurking in the neighborhoods and regions outside the community of faith. And, they could be drawn in, with the right sort of ambiance and appeal. Therefore, things that might offend a "seeker" were removed from churches, like crosses, pulpits, Bibles and hymnals. Church architecture shifted to make churches look less, well, churchy. "Campuses" were designed that looked more like the Googleplex or a Civic Center from the curb, than traditional places of worship. Massive parking lots, PowerPoint worship, state-of-the-art audio and video, and praise teams who performed on raised platforms with professional precision and skill. In some churches, one or two videographers, dressed in all-black, would crawl around on the stage, filming the musicians and vocalists whose enlarged images would be projected as a backdrop for the praise and worship lyrics. Because the rest of the world tends to follow the West, I saw this identical genre, complete with the crawling paparazzi, at a church in Manila that met, of all places, in a mall.

I don't want to paint with too large of strokes. Not every church that decided to go outside the box got it wrong. Jill attended a church in Minneapolis that was a converted warehouse. No "churchy" exterior to be sure. But once inside, the lighting was intentionally designed to diminish in intensity as your gaze moved from the rear of the building forward. And when your eyes finally arrived at the front of the warehouse, they were greeted by a large, dimly lit white cross. They had a "praise team," but in true John the Baptizer fashion, they desired to be diminished that Yeshua might be exalted.[1] So, the entire group was located in an orchestral pit below the surface of the stage. Dressed in black, their music stands illuminated by dim but sufficient light, they truly led you into worship because *He* was the only one "one stage" that morning. Jill said it was a worshipful experience. And they did it all without a single video clip of a guitarist fingering his Fender Strat behind the words to "Shine Jesus Shine."

I suspect some of you are offended by the lilt of sarcasm meandering through the last few pages. Be forbearing with me, please. You see, after twenty-five years of Jesus action figures, Testa-Mints, Noah's Ark Beanie Babies, knock-off T-shirt logos, statues of Jesus carrying a football, Jabez prayer shawls, Pastorprenour websites, downloadable sermon and PowerPoint packages, Christian cruises, "Son-Bucks coffee logos," and Six Flags Over Jesus church complexes,

---

1 John the Baptizer's classic confession, *"He must increase, but I must decrease"* (John 3:30) stands for all time as the proper attitude of an Apprentice of Jesus.

I'm a little offended too. And, so are the "natives." I've talked to many of them. Maybe it's time we stood at the crossroads and "asked for the ancient paths" when it comes to marketing our churches:

> Thus says the LORD of hosts: In those days ten men from the nations of every tongue shall take hold of the robe of a Jew, saying, "Let us go with you, for we have heard that God is with you." **–Zechariah 8:23**

> By this all people will know that you are my disciples, if you have love for one another. **–John 13:35**

> I do not ask for these only, but also for those who will believe in me through their word, that they may all be one, just as you, Father, are in me, and I in you, that they also may be in us, so that the world may believe that you have sent me. **–John 17:20–21**

(I think a little of my Adamic residue leaked out in the last few pages. I *would* feel bad about that, but my therapist said it was healthy for me to share my feelings.)

Esau's Back In Town!

Here we are, at the end of our excursion through the world of Apprenticeship and its illicit impostor, the Partner. In the previous chapter, we saw that failing to see ourselves as Aliens would allow our geography to turn us into Tourists. There's a similar pitfall here also. Failing to engage in the spiritual disciplines of an Apprentice will not only slowly morph me into a Partner, it will also lead me down the path of Esau, the road that ends at the shack called "godlessness." The word comes from a root meaning "threshold." It depicts *walking* on God, treating Him with contempt. Godlessness is excluding God from places where He belongs. Mind you, godlessness is not *ungodliness*. Ungodliness is behavioral, visible, and obvious. You can see it. Paul and others give us multiple lists of *ungodly* behavior in their letters.[1] Make no mistake, it's bad stuff. But, godlessness is worse because it's an *inner* attitude, and doesn't attract attention. And among believers whose spirituality has been shaped by Wall Street and Washington, it isn't even visible because it's wrapped in patriotism and common sense. Unfortunately, godlessness is the most common sin among respectable Christians. You can be valedictorian at a Christian high school and be godless. You can be a minivan-driving, carpool mom and be godless. You can be a pastor intent on a new sanctuary and be godless. You can be a cheerleader or team captain, and if you or your parents haven't sought the face of Yahweh about college choices, you're acting in a godless way. Excise the mental image of a pimp or drug dealer, or a Judas or Jezebel from your associations with this word. Esau sold his birthright for a can of soup for goodness sake! But, the key to Esau's sin is hidden in the bushes of that verse. It says he "despised" his birthright. That's why he could sell it so cheaply. The Hebrew word behind it is the same one used to

---

1 cf. Galatians 5:17-21; Colossians 3:5-8; 1 Timothy 1:9-10Titus 3:3; James 3:14-16; 1 Peter 4:2-4Revelation 21:8

describe Goliath's attitude toward the teenage shepherd with a sling in front of him that day on the battlefield. The Scripture says Goliath looked at David, and "despised" him because he was so small, armor-less, and young.[1] Goliath saw David as tiny inconvenience of no consequence, a minor "speed bump" to dispatch and move on. Over the years, many students I taught told me they hadn't even prayed about *where* they were going to college. In Alabama, because of football rivalries, some children have only one choice. Contrast this with a young girl I taught in Colorado who spent a day fasting and praying about the same decision. She knew that she'd likely meet her life partner in college, the trajectory for her life would be set there, and most of her lifetime friendships would be formed. This is the way of the Apprentice. The Partner makes the same decision based on sports, Greek organizations, and proximity to home. As "harmless" as that sounds, it's godless. It leaves God out of the decision, even though He belongs in the center of the process.

The opposite of godlessness is letting God be God. He will be anyway, at the end of the day. We both know that. But *choosing* to submit because He is your King, and spending time with Him because He is also your Teacher, opens the rivers of your soul, allowing His Truth to help you unlearn the untruths that have made themselves at home. And you can't do this alone. Find a fellow Alien to walk and talk with, as you travel this road together. Talking *about* God, especially about *His* thoughts regarding *your* plans, is an antidote against godlessness. Paul says there's a direct cause and effect relationship between leaving God out of my speech, and eventually leaving Him out of my conduct:

> Avoid godless chatter, because those who indulge in it will become more and more ungodly.   −2 **Timothy 2:16**

A genuine Christian, a disciple of Jesus, *is* an Apprentice. And this is true because a response to the Rabbi's invitation to "come," is also an agreement on our part to follow. It's an open invitation. You can come anytime. Even if you've spent the last decade building and climbing the wrong "ladder." And the great news for us is that class is still in session, and there's no enrollment cap, according to philosophy professor and author, Dallas Willard:

> The really good news for humanity is that Jesus is now taking students in the master class of life. The eternal life that begins with a confidence in Jesus is a life in his present kingdom, now on earth and available to all. So the message of and about him is specifically a gospel for our life now, not just for dying. It is about living now as his apprentice in kingdom living, not just as a consumer of his merits.[2]

In Jesus' day, another command seemed to follow the Rabbi's call to "come." It held true for everyone from demoniacs to Pharisees. And that was, to all those who heeded his invitation, after they sat at the feet of Yeshua for a season, he issued a second call to "go."

---

1 cf. 1 Samuel 17:19-49, esp. vv. 41-44.

2 Dallas Willard, *The Divine Conspiracy* (New York: Harper Collins, 1997), xvii.

Ambassador — The Word Of The King

About three thousand years ago, as Israel was entering its age of kings, a king from Ammon named Nahash made life very miserable for some Israelites living on the "other side of the river." He was a distant relative of Lot.[1] The Israelites sent a cry for help to Saul, their recently anointed king. His response was swift, harsh, and complete. Saul made a name for himself and galvanized his divided people by nuking the Ammonites and saving the residents of Jabesh Gilead who had cried out to him for deliverance. Years later, Nahash died. Somewhere between this collision with Saul and the rise of one of his descendants to the throne of Ammon, Nahash had been kind to David. In an amazingly conciliatory and diplomatic move, David sent an envoy to Hanun, the new king, to console him concerning the death of his "father," the king.[2] David's motives were misjudged. The envoys were suspected of being spies, sent in at a time of national weakness. In retaliation for this alleged and false act of war, David's men were publicly humiliated by shaving off half their beards, and their clothing cut off from the hips down.[3] David's reprisal was immediate and decisive. The commander of his army, his nephew Joab, so thoroughly defeated the Ammonite and Syrian coalition of over 40,000 men, that the Scripture tells us, *"...the Syrians were afraid to save the Ammonites anymore."*[4]

In our own era, where messing with people's hair and tearing off half their clothing would make for a great prime time reality show, David's response seems a bit heavy-handed. However, in the Ancient Near East, messing with people's hair or exposing their nakedness in public was a humiliation of in-

1 cf. Genesis 11:27; 19:30-38. Lot was the nephew of the Jewish patriarch, Abraham; the son of Abraham's brother Haran.

2 In the Ancient Near East, the word, "father" was frequently a synonym for "ancestor." It could, but often did not, refer to the person's actual biological father. It could just as easily be a reference to his grandfather, as it obviously was in this case.

3 cf. 2 Samuel 10:1-5

4 2 Samuel 10:19b

tense magnitude. The shaving of women's heads, the shearing of men's beards, and physical exposure were the customary treatments of slaves. The reason David wasn't "overreacting," is that the "servants" that endured this shame comprised an envoy from *him*. They were, in a sense, the representation of David himself, and were therefore expected to be treated with dignity and respect. What the Ammonites did to David's servants, they did to the King of Israel. And in the Ancient Near East, unlike the modern U.S., that's like deciding to have lunch inside the core of a nuclear reactor. Things will get real hot real fast, and your grandkids will glow in the dark. That's pretty much what happened when David heard of their disgrace. The lights went out in Ammon and Syria shortly thereafter.

This is an ancient story, but not an archaic one. Not much has changed. Envoys sent from a ruler to a distant land, to represent him and his interests, had the same function, and the same name then as they do today. They were known as "Ambassadors." This brings us to the sixth rung on our Identity Ladder.

Aliens With A Mission

This aspect of our identity—how we "see" ourselves in relation to God and the *kosmos*—has three *very* close ties to our Alien rung. The first has to do with the Ambassador's citizenship. He was always a *foreigner*, never a native, of the land to which he was sent. Everyone knew that, especially him. In fact, one of the Hebrew words translated "envoy" in our Bibles (*litz*), has the inherent meaning of stammering and having difficulty speaking, the inevitable struggle an envoy would have in a foreign country.[1] The second connection between Ambassador and Alien had to do with his message. An ambassador *always* had a message to deliver, and he always spoke on behalf of the land he represented, *never* on behalf of the land where he was serving. And because he was an outsider on a mission, no one would have expected him to do otherwise. They would have viewed him with suspicion if he had. Ambassadors simply never tried to "fit in." It was antithetical to who they were. The third tie to our Alien identity is the king's name. Earlier, I made a big deal about the importance of an ambassador being a sort of present manifestation of a distant king, when it came to how *he* was treated. But, that sword cuts both ways. *He* and *his* conduct while on assignment were a direct reflection on his king. The honor of his king rested on his own diplomacy and comportment. As an ambassador, he had the power to exalt his king's name, or demean it. And trust me, in the Ancient Near East, the king didn't need a Twitter feed to find out which it was!

It shouldn't surprise us to discover the existence *and* role of Ambassador are illustrated and taught in our New Testament. Jesus apparently considered him-

---

1 cf. 2 Chronicles 32:29; This post-exilic account of Hezekiah's *pre-exilic* encounter with an envoy sent from Babylon may be a play on words as well. Everywhere else in the OT where the word *litz* appears, it is translated "mocked." Because the Chronicler wrote *after* the exile, and with an interpretive insight not available in the the *pre-exilic* accounts in 2 Kings 2:12ff and Isaiah 39:1ff, he may have been editorializing about the Babylonian visit's integrity in the first place.

self an envoy of sorts, looking at the many self-qualifying statements he made:[1]

> The one who hears you hears me, and the one who rejects you rejects me, and the one who rejects me rejects him who sent me.   **–Luke 10:16**

> So Jesus said to them, "When you have lifted up the Son of Man, then you will know that I am he, and that I do nothing on my own authority, but speak just as the Father taught me."   **–John 8:28**

> The Father judges no one, but has given all judgment to the Son, that all may honor the Son, just as they honor the Father. Whoever does not honor the Son does not honor the Father who sent him.   **–John 5:22–23**

> And Jesus cried out and said, "Whoever believes in me, believes not in me but in him who sent me. And whoever sees me sees him who sent me."   **–John 12:44–46**

> So Jesus said to them, "Truly, truly, I say to you, the Son can do nothing of his own accord, but only what he sees the Father doing. For whatever the Father does, that the Son does likewise."   **–John 5:19**

Reeducating A Rabid Rabbi

There is also a very clear implication of this principle of Ambassadorship in Jesus' penetrating question to Saul during his spiritual train wreck on the way to Damascus. The Lord's question, *"Saul, Saul, why are you persecuting me?"* is predicated on the notion that what he was doing to people like Stephen, he was doing to Jesus himself.[2] Much like shaving beards and revealing buttocks, Saul was insulting the King of Heaven by mistreating His envoys, His representative presence here on earth; His "Body," if you will.[3] Perhaps that's why Paul is the only New Testament writer to speak specifically and unambiguously of the identity of believers as "Ambassadors":

> ...To that end keep alert with all perseverance, making supplication for all the saints, and also for me, that words may be given to me in opening my mouth boldly to proclaim the mystery of the gospel, for which I am an ambassador in chains, that I may declare it boldly, as I ought to speak.   **–Ephesians 6:18–20**

> All this is from God, who through Christ reconciled us to himself and gave us the ministry of reconciliation; that is, in Christ God was reconciling the world to himself, not counting their trespasses against them, and entrusting to us the message of reconciliation. Therefore, we are ambassadors for Christ, God making his appeal through us. We implore you on behalf of Christ, be reconciled to God.
>   **–2 Corinthians 5:18-20**

In these, our only two occurrences of *presbeutō* ("ambassador") in the New Testament, Paul adopts this identity for himself, and by implication (i.e., "we"), us as well. And from the above snippet from his letter to the Ephesians, we

---

1 I am *not* suggesting that Jesus was merely "God's representative," in contrast to his full deity. But, I am saying that his representative role can not and should not be minimized. For, as is evident in these verses collectively, he clearly links *our* rearthly ole as *his* ambassadors to his earthly role as Yahweh's.

2 Acts 9:1 (see also Acts 22:7 and 26:14; it is obvious this question of Jesus penetrated Paul with such force that it became an integral part of his own story, something he would carry with him throughout life, for we hear him retelling it, word-for-word, twenty-fives years after it happened.)

3 cf. Ephesians 1:22-23; 5:23,30; Colossians 1:24

can see that Paul never separated his role as an ambassador from something he called the "mystery" of the gospel. This is something we'll touch on briefly, but unpack in detail in Part II. However, regarding our current journey into the biblical world of ambassadors, we can extract a thin, but strong and clear profile of *our* identity as Ambassadors. Our source code is located in three words Paul uses, two from the passages above, and the third from an earlier letter to the believers in Corinth.

In our previous discussion on royal ambassadors, we discovered that ambassadorship involved speaking. The ambassador always had either a message *from* the king for his foreign audience, or one to retrieve *for* the king. The one sent to David was without words, but nonetheless loud. Paul is no different. His ambassadorship is based on and driven by a message. Five times in 67 words, Paul employs the Greek word family, *katalassō*, "to reconcile," as the context for his role as an ambassador. This is a wonderful word, and one that has three shades of meaning, all involving the same feature—two parties estranged from one another. One way to view *katalassō* is to see it referring to the offending party being reconciled *by* the one bearing the offense. A second perspective reverses this by insisting it is the one *offending* who does the reconciling. The third view sees it more of a mutual effort in which the two parties are equally engaged, and a single result is achieved. Depending which of these three you subscribe to, and how adamantly you hold to it, will determine to some extent what you tell people the actual message is you're carrying. Leaving the intramural dogmatics aside for a moment, I would like to suggest that reconciliation is the outcome that Yahweh desires, despite whom it seems has done the most "work" (bad word choice, I know).

It is clear from Paul's passionate entreaty to the Corinthians, that the *message* was more important than either the messenger *or* the intended recipients. The "good news," the ambassadorial message, was that the estrangement created by their ancient Garden grandparents had been remedied! They and Yahweh could be reunited. A way had been made, if you wish, back into the Garden. In the Graeco-Roman culture of Paul's day, reconciliation was the removal of enmity between warring factions, typically secured by both parties sending envoys (ambassadors) to secure the peace. In many ways, reconciliation in the New Testament, is the announcement that Yahweh wants to adopt the race that rebelled; and, that He has done the work necessary for it to happen. Arguing about whether the message is, *"God's not mad at you any more,"* or *"Go tell God you want to be back in the family,"* seems trivial in comparison with the fact that although the gate is narrow that leads back to Him, there now *is* a gate, and Paul says Yahweh wants people to know where it is. And, *that's* the "message of reconciliation" that Paul preached. It is our message too. "Be reconciled to Yahweh" is the official message of His Embassy here.[1]

---

1 cf. 2 Corinthians 5:20; Paul's entire argument about reconciliation is the centerpiece here. "Ambassador" likely was merely a suitable metaphor for those carrying that message.

The second word, one of Paul's favorites, is "mystery" (*mustērion*). In his comments above from Ephesians, he links this "mystery" to his role of Ambassador *and* the proclamation of Yahweh's "good news." We know this simply as the "gospel." This "mystery" of Paul's is a multi-faceted and glorious thing. It is older and larger than our Adamic minds can contain. But, it lies *behind* the reconciliation we offer as Ambassadors, because it's Abrahamic in its essence. Listen to Paul's closing comments from his most scholarly and doctrinal letter. Put your ear close to these words, and you will hear a heart so overwhelmed with wonder, that it yields a seamless transition from theology to doxology:

> Now to him who is able to strengthen you according to my gospel and the preaching of Jesus Christ, according to the revelation of the mystery that was kept secret for long ages but has now been disclosed and through the prophetic writings has been made known to all nations, according to the command of the eternal God, to bring about the obedience of faith— to the only wise God be glory forevermore through Jesus Christ! Amen.   **–Romans 16:22–27**

Paul's final word that helps us clarify our Ambassador identity, also serves to fuse mystery to the message of reconciliation and those who carry it. It is the word, *oikonomos*, the one assigned to distribute the master's resources at the right time and place, to the right people. Our Bible calls this person a "steward."

> This is how one should regard us, as servants of Christ and stewards of the mysteries of God. Moreover, it is required of stewards that they be found faithful.
> **–1 Corinthians 4:1–2**

And again, Paul makes it very clear that the message is what has value, not the messenger. He calls himself a servant and steward of these "mysteries" that belong to Yahweh. The Ambassador identity is also just beneath the surface of his own self-description in the Greek. Paul does *not* use his preferred word for "servant," *doulos* (bond servant), here. Instead, he uses a word that is much closer to an ambassador in function than to a servant, as it is commonly understood. He chooses to use *hupēretēs*, the word for the "assistant," or "officer." John uses this word seven times to refer to those who acted on behalf of the Pharisees when it came to matters of authority.[1] In once case, John actually *differentiates* between *doulos* and *hupēretēs* when describing those around the fire at Jesus' trial.[2]

Five verses later, Paul pens some of the most poetic yet potent words in all of his writings, about the difficult path the adopted, alien-apprentice walks, carrying the good news of reconciliation for all nations, as a "steward" of the "mysteries" of Yahweh:

> But we have this treasure in jars of clay, to show that the surpassing power belongs to God and not to us. We are afflicted in every way, but not crushed; perplexed, but not driven to despair; persecuted, but not forsaken; struck down, but not destroyed; always carrying in the body the death of Jesus, so that the life of Jesus may also be manifested in our bodies.   **–2 Corinthians 4:7–10**

---

1 E.g., John 7;32 and 19:6

2 cf. John18:18

But, Paul joyfully embraced this life of difficulty. Something odd had happened to him that day on the way to The Persecution. His passion was not abated, only redirected. His scholarship was neither diminished nor enlarged. But it was informed. Paul's purposes for himself were inseparable from God's purposes for him. His conversion was a reformation, not merely a redemption. Listen to these words spoken on a beach to a group of leaders, into whose lives he had poured three years of his life. He spoke them around the same time he communicated to the brethren in Corinth. In them, you again hear the recurring themes of Alien, Apprentice, and Ambassador:

> But I do not account my life of any value nor as precious to myself, if only I may finish my course and the ministry that I received from the Lord Jesus, to testify to the gospel of the grace of God.   —Acts 20:24

Looking back one last time, I trust you can see that the previous six rungs of our ladder, while clear and distinct, have begun to run together like colors on an artist's palette. They form a brilliant composite, more beautiful than any could alone. The alien and Apprentice are mutually dependent. And Alien and Ambassador are the form and function of Adopted, Adamic strangers on a mission with a message. But, it is the Ambassador facet of our identity where we begin to crest the hill of our journey and can see in the distance the world of Purpose—the product of Identity. Although "Ambassador" *is* an Identity issue, it begins to tease out of us a host of questions that all begin with the word "Why?"

The previous five rungs were, in a sense, confessional. Individually and collectively they point to *inner* convictions. Things we have come to *believe* about ourselves in relation to Yahweh and the *kosmos*. But this rung, Ambassador, is more *professional*, it is something we *speak* about ourselves by virtue of The Story we proclaim; the one we've found ourselves in. As we've come to see more clearly each chapter, this message, this "good news," is for those who are near (me), but it's mostly for those who are far off—the *goyim*, the nations.[1] Paul's train wreck with Yahweh is a paradigm of this truth. The message Yahweh gave Ananias, the one responsible for bringing Paul to faith and baptizing him, involved a mystery, a message, the nations, and his own election. In short, Yahweh offered him a calling to fulfill, not a club to join:

> And the Lord said to him, "Rise and go to the street called Straight, and at the house of Judas look for a man of Tarsus named Saul, for behold, he is praying, and he has seen in a vision a man named Ananias come in and lay his hands on him so that he might regain his sight." But Ananias answered, "Lord, I have heard from many about this man, how much evil he has done to your saints at Jerusalem. And here he has authority from the chief priests to bind all who call on your name." But the Lord said to him, "Go, for he is a chosen instrument of mine to carry my name before the Gentiles and kings and the children of Israel. For I will show him how much he must suffer for the sake of my name."   —Acts 9:11–16

We are nearly completed the construction of our Identity Ladder. A final rung remains. And it's been lost so far back on the great American Evangelical

---

1 Acts 2:39; Ephesians 2:17; Isaiah 33:13; Zechariah 9:10

Highway, that you might not recognize it; or worse, believe it doesn't belong on *our* ladder. In some folks, it evokes fear and anger In others, dancing and delight. Getting this one back on the ladder, and making it secure, is vital for our own sense of Identity. It's at the heart of the "mystery" we proclaim and protect. And, it's also our only safeguard from becoming like the people of Sodom.[1]

---

1 Sodom is one of a pair of cities destroyed by God during the days of Abraham. Unfortunately, the cause of that judgment has more in common with the modern American Church than we would like to admit. I will explain this unusual comparison in detail in the next chapter.

Advocate—A Voice For The Mute

Our eldest son and his family have lived in the "hood" for the past twelve years. Ben, Sara and our four grandkids are the only white folks on their block. Ben has been associated with Restoration Academy, one of Birmingham's best-kept secrets since he graduated from college in 2000. He's served as a History and Bible teacher and Principal. Most recently he has transitioned to Chaplain. In a city whose public school has a 40% graduation rate, RA boasts of not only a 100% graduation rate, but a 100% college attendance rate! It's breaking the generational cycles of hopelessness, fatherlessness, and joblessness that plague much of urban and rural Alabama. But, Ben wasn't always an urban dweller. To hear him tell the story himself, he was satisfied being a white suburbanite, privileged to have a Christian education his entire life. But, like Saul, Yahweh had planned a train wreck down the track.

Ben attended Wheaton College outside Chicago. An expensive, elite, and selective school that boasted some of the students who didn't get accepted would go to Stanford as a second choice. It was a miracle he was part of the Class of 1996. Sometime early in his second year, we discovered that he seemed to be majoring in intramural sports instead of History. Evenings and weekends were spent playing rather than studying. And this is one of those schools where some students chain themselves to their desks and have food slid under the door. Well, not really, but it was *full* of National Merit Finalists and other brainiacs. My point is, the difficulty of enrollment, combined with the high costs and difficult classes seemed to extrude most students in the direction of the library. For some reason, Ben seemed to end up in the gym. Somewhere shortly before the end of the first semester of his sophomore year, Jill and I had a "let's take a walk to the woodshed" talk with him (that's "Southern" for you're about to get a verbal butt whipping) about his lack of effort and our commensurate lack of money. Watching Jill was like an out of the body experience for me. She was on him like ugly on an ape. I'd like to somehow "share" this with you so that it exudes spirituality and an eye to discipleship. But, bottom line? We were ticked! And, as we would find out later, Yahweh who can use a worm or a talking donkey,[1] used *us* that day. Ben returned to Wheaton suddenly motivated to respond to the incessant plead-ings of a friend to become part of a weekly Saturday ministry at the Cook County Juvenile Detention Center in Chicago. This is no "juvy joint" with game centers and couches. The facility services 30,000 kids annually, aged 10-16 who are waiting to be processed by the court system for crimes rang-ing from shoplifting to homicide. It's the childhood equivalent of the Cook County Department of Corrections facility, which does the same thing for adults. About 100,000 a year. Every Saturday for the remainder of college, Ben and his cronies would take a Wheaton van into the bowels of Chicago's urban core, go through enough security to make you catatonic, and coach basketball teams for what they christened, "Cook County Hoops." Each Saturday session would conclude with a devotional of some type. On one occasion, a young man stopped Ben and said, "Can I ask you something?" Ben said, "Sure," thinking it would be about the devotional. The kid looked Ben straight in the eyes and said, "Where were you before I ended up here?" That question would eventually have the force of the one Saul heard on the road to Damascus. Ben's life goals, his dreams, and his sense of what it meant to serve God were about to be under major reconstruction. Two and a half years later, married and fresh out of college, he turned down an offer to teach at a prestigious Christian high school in Birmingham and chose instead to accept a position at Restoration Academy. All because of a question a young boy in jail asked him. The thing is, he had to be in jail himself to hear it.

Why is it, when we're faced with need, I mean *real* need, the kind that none of the Christian self-help books seem to admit exist, we get all weird inside? Why was it, that this question from a poor kid from the Chicago projects couldn't elicit a suitable answer from someone nearly his age, attending the best college Protestantism has to offer? Why did it create more questions in the one ques-tioned, instead? I believe it's because there's something deep within us—call it an "Edenic memory" if you want—that just knows things aren't the "way they're supposed to be." And there's also something in each of us, at least from time to time that longs to make it right. We love movies when the bad guy gets it in the end. And, in our more unguarded moments, we'd love to be the one bring-ing the heat! Why? Because the "Imago Dei" is leaking out through some of the pores in our Adamic residue.[2] These are centrifugal longings in our centripetal flesh. The memories of Eden *before* we were cast east of it. Justice is important

1 cf. Jonah 4:5-11 and Numbers 22:20-33.
2 It might be helpful to revisit Chapter 4, where both the Imago Dei and the Adamic residue are intro-duced.

to all of us, and Yahweh has so much to say about it that it's a wonder we haven't gone deaf from the roar. Sadly, it turns out we *are* deaf, not from listening too much, but too little.

"Advocate" is our final rung. I didn't save it for last because it's peripheral or extraneous. Hardly. It's essential. I put it last because it's a volatile topic. The heat comes more from the dry wood fuel of the "the wisdom of friends," than the Wisdom of God. This rung seems to bring out what I call the "yah-buts" more than generating conversation about the poor. It seems that when confronted with the needs of the poor around us, or around the world, our knee-jerk response is a disclaimer instead of a comment or question. "*Yah, but* most of them don't want to work," we say, or "*Yah, but* 'poor' means a whole lot more than the absence of money." Or, "*Yah, but* Jesus said, 'the poor you will always have with you.' Poverty is just a fact of life." Or, "*Yah, but* this is America for goodness sake! Anyone who really *wants* to work, can." Obviously, these statements are true, or at least sometimes true. Yet how is it, that issues so convoluted and complex are treated with such simplistic dismissal? Or maybe it occupies a line item on our church budgets but never makes it into a Mission Statement? I think it has more to do with our ignorance *of* Scripture than our convictions *from* it. I closed the last chapter with an irritating statement about us becoming Sodomites. I owe you an explanation.

The Five Sins Of Sodom

During the dark days of the waning southern kingdom of Judah, Yahweh brought out three of His biggest guns to lay the hard stuff on the table for His wayward people: Isaiah, Ezekiel, and Jeremiah. These guys could bring the heat, and they did. We love to read Isaiah beginning with Chapter 40, because it's so comforting. I know, I lived in those chapters during my own dark days. There is warmth and light to be found there. But, there are too many pages to be ignored in these three boys' monographs where the warmth gives way to blistering heat. One of them is in the sixteenth chapter of Ezekiel. It is Yahweh's graphic portrayal of His bride acting as a whore because of her flagrant and repeated infidelity to Him. His bride was Judah. And two-thirds of the way into Yahweh's blistering reproach, He compares Judah to Sodom, and pushes up the ante when He says she's actually *worse*. Before you jump to scenes of New Orleans in February or September,[1] let me introduce you to a little-known truth about Sodomites. They're in our churches! 80% of the Sodomite sins Yahweh throws at the feet of His wayward people, are present, even *celebrated* in many American congregations. Maybe even yours. Maybe even by you.

You might want to sit down, if you're not already. Ok, let's go through this slowly. First, we need to deconstruct our unfortunate but deeply rooted misinfor-

---

1 Southern Decadence, the largest gay and lesbian gathering in America, is held around Labor Day each year. Gay Mardi Gras, the second largest festival, is held in February.

mation about Sodom and Gomorrah. If, when you saw the word "Sodomite," you immediately thought of homosexuals, you would have been following the Majority Report on that passage. However, though homosexuality *was* a Sodomite characteristic, it wasn't the reason we are given in Scripture that God "came down" in the first place. In fact, Ezekiel's midrash on Genesis 18 informs us that there were actually *five* sins of Sodom, not one. And, the first four are presented *ahead* of any sexual deviance, which was fifth on the list. The first four "sins of Sodom," Yahweh informs us via Ezekiel, are nearly *everywhere* in America, including our own homes and churches. They are: pride (too much attention to self), gluttony (too much food), leisure (too much free time), and neglect of the poor (too little compassion). Listen to Yahweh's anguish between these lines of reproach:

> Behold, this was the guilt of your sister Sodom: she and her daughters had pride, excess of food, and prosperous ease, but did not aid the poor and needy. They were haughty and did an abomination before me. *So I removed them, when I saw it.*
> –**Ezekiel** 16:49–50

Understanding this also helps us make sense out of what in the world Yahweh was talking about to Abraham when He said that an "outcry" *from* Sodom and Gomorrah had reached His ears. The Hebrew word used in Ezekiel for "outcry" is also used for Mordecai's anguished "outcry" when he heard the Jews were going to be butchered throughout the Persian Empire. It's the word used by the Jews when they were trapped between the Red Sea and Pharaoh's armed forces. It's also the word used to describe the desperate and typically unheeded cry of the poor that are perishing. And, although it's not the identity word, it's in the same word family as the word used in Deuteronomy to refer to a young woman "crying out" in the countryside while she's being raped.[1] These are descriptions of dire and deadly circumstances. Not a gay parade in the streets of Sodom. I'm *not* minimizing the presence of militant homosexuals in those cities. What I *am* trying to do is throw open the curtains that hide the wide and spacious places in our churches and our lives where the other four faces of Sodomy, properly understood, are welcomed tenants.

Before we swim out into the deep end of this oceanic topic, we need to briefly revisit Sodom. In the dialogue between Yahweh and Abraham in Genesis 18, where Abraham tries to barter a reprieve of mercy for the city because his nephew's condo is there, we find an absolutely radiant composite of nearly everything we've talked about up to now. Yahweh couches His statements about Sodom's pending judgment within the circumference of adoption, election, the *goyim*, the Abrahamic covenant, and social justice. The fact that they are part of the same tapestry is inescapable:

> The LORD said, "Shall I hide from Abraham what I am about to do, seeing that Abraham shall surely become a great and mighty nation, and all the nations of the earth shall be blessed in him? For I have chosen him, that he may command his children

---

1 cf. cf. Genesis 18:20-21; Esther 4:1; Nehemiah 9:9; Proverbs 21:13Deuteronomy 22:25-27

and his household after him to keep the way of the LORD by doing righteousness and justice, so that the LORD may bring to Abraham what he has promised him." Then the LORD said, "Because the outcry against Sodom and Gomorrah is great and their sin is very grave..."   **–Genesis 18:17–20**

Obviously, "righteousness and justice," the proper response to the "outcry" of the poor and voiceless, are important to Yahweh. They seem to show up everywhere in the Bible, sort of theological twins in The Story.[1] One inescapable truth from this passage is that Yahweh chose Abraham for the purpose of "doing righteousness and justice," and that doing so is synonymous with "keeping the way of the LORD." Abraham was to be committed to instill this sense of purpose into the fabric of his children's worldview. It is an integral part of the original Abrahamic covenant, and therefore the Abrahamic mission. And for those of us who celebrate our place in that covenant and enjoy its blessings, we need to now realize that, in the words of one scholar, "if we inherit Abraham's blessing, we inherit his mission also."[2] The preeminence of "doing righteousness and justice," (social justice) over sound theology, fellowship, and worship, is captured in what are likely the most beautiful lines of Hebrew poetry in Scripture:

> With what shall I come before the LORD, and bow myself before God on high? Shall I come before him with burnt offerings, with calves a year old? Will the LORD be pleased with thousands of rams, with ten thousands of rivers of oil? Shall I give my firstborn for my transgression, the fruit of my body for the sin of my soul?" He has told you, O man, what is good; and *what does the LORD require of you but to do justice, and to love kindness, and to walk humbly with your God?*   –Micah 6:6–8

Unfortunately, judging by the incumbent worldview of many of my former students and parents, and the content of the curricula in our Sunday schools, home schools, and Christian day schools, the Abrahamic mission appears to have been hijacked by the American Dream. This, I suspect, is evidence of the place the respectable sin of godlessness—the inevitable fruit of seeing ourselves as Tourists and Partners, instead of Aliens and Apprentices—has in our lives. Hence "the poor," are seen as a social problem to be solved, instead of a distinct people group to be reached, part of the *goyim*. A battered and bruised part to be sure, but a part nonetheless.

The discarded Advocate rung must be retrieved from its ancient past and reinstalled in the Identity Ladder of our lives and the working agenda of the modern church. It's vital to the purposes of God, and our own sense of identity. And, I believe the best contribution I can make is to expose the unbroken connection between Eden and the Cook County Detention Center, *and* just how much real estate the widow, the orphan, the sojourner, and the poor occupy in the heart of Yahweh. The former will be the theme of Part II, the latter will conclude our journey on the path to understanding biblical Identity.

---

1 These two words appear in the same verse 89 times after this reference to Abraham. Over half of those occurrences are from the pens of the prophets, during the dark days of the Jews.

2 Christopher J. H. Wright, *The Mission of God's People: A Biblical Theology of the Church's Mission.* (Grand Rapids, Mich: Zondervan, 2010), 82-83. It is impossible for me to overstate the appreciation I have for Dr. Wright's work. My only regret is that this book was not available a decade ago.

Yahweh The Advocate

In over half of the books in our Bibles, those groups from whom an "outcry" is most likely to be heard, are mentioned over 260 times. "The" widow, the fatherless, the afflicted, the oppressed, the sojourner, the weak, and the poor are distinct people groups in the eyes and heart of Yahweh. Maybe that's why the two books that have the greatest number of references to these people groups are Deuteronomy and Psalms.[1] Deuteronomy contains the great Law Codes regarding treatment of others, the animals, and the rest of Creation. The horizontal dimension of one's life. The Book of Psalms, however, is the ancient hymnal of the Jews and frames one's sense of worship centered around Yahweh and His dealings with His people. It is the vertical dimension of a believer's life. And it's from these two books that we are confronted with the unavoidable truth that advocacy has always been something Yahweh expected His people to embrace. But, it wasn't so they could be "good" Jews (or Christians), but because they were to be like Him, and these things were a part of His very nature:

Father of the fatherless and protector of widows is God in his holy habitation.
    –Psalm 68:5

Because of this, "doing righteousness and justice"—the inevitable fruit of a heart of compassion—was something Yahweh went to great lengths to instill into the spiritual genome of His covenant people. Their Law, the comprehensive tapestry of regulations for social, civic, and spiritual life, had multiple layers of advocacy built right into it:

- they were to sell food at "cost," to the poor.[2]
- they were to lend money at no interest, to the poor.[3]
- they were to leave the "corners" of their fields every year, for the poor.[4]
- they were to provide community meals, open to the poor, through their "Sacrifice of Praise."[5]
- they were to cancel debts every seven years, release bond servants, and restore real estate every 50 years.[6]
- the land was to lie fallow every seven years, and all could enjoy its fruit.[7]

---

1 Of the 264 references to these groups in our English Bibles, there are 39 references in Deuteronomy and 38 in the Psalms. Proverbs, a book primarily about how to live among people, contains 27 references. The prophets, who were Yahweh's "voice" calling His people back into covenant faithfulness, refer to these groups 55 times, collectively. It is worth noting too, that these same words used merely as a noun (i.e., *without* the definite article "the" in front of them), occur 257x, roughly the same frequency.

2 Leviticus 25:37; Deuteronomy 23:19

3 Exodus 22:25

4 Leviticus 19:1-11 (this would have been March - April)

5 Leviticus 19:23-24; Psalm 22:25-26; cf. Leviticus 3, 7

6 cf. Leviticus 25; Deuteronomy 15

7 Leviticus 25:1-7 cf. Nehemiah 7:31 This "sabbath rest" for the land, along with other clear rules in the Law code is strong evidence of Yahweh's deep concern for *all* His Creation, not just humans. Its importance is further illustrated by His statement to the captives of the Babylonian exile that because they refused to grant the land its sabbaths, He would "evict" them for seventy years in order for the *land* to rest! (cf. Leviticus 26:27-35 and Jeremiah 25:11-12).

- God also required a special "tithe" every three years to be given to the Levite, the widow, the stranger, and the orphan.[1]

This exquisitely nuanced and layered system of laws must not be understood as part of what was set aside just for Israelites living under the Mosaic covenant. For although the need for high priests, sacrifices, and a Temple was done away with because of Jesus, the poor were not. This deep and compassionate care of Yahweh extended beyond the children of Adam to all Creation, including soil and cattle. We love to sing that the earth is the Lord's, but somehow fail to remind ourselves that really means we are tenants, not owners. And, one of the requirements of our "lease," is that we exercise justice, righteousness, and kindness in the earth. Why? Because we should be like Him, and that's what He's like.[2] In fact, Yahweh makes compassionate engagement with the weak and powerless a clear barometer of intimacy with Him! Josiah, a good king, had a son Shallum who wasn't so good.[3] And in the ancient past of our faith, a king's primary responsibility was to lead the people in covenant faithfulness, not just in war. The prophets were Yahweh's corrective voice when the kings wandered or walked from that path. Consequently, prophets were more important than kings; but never more popular. Shallum was called out one day by Jeremiah for his flagrant disregard for the covenant, and the Law code of Deuteronomy. How did Yahweh know Shallum had shirked his duties as king? He had neglected the poor, which meant he had despised the Law. Listen to Jeremiah's word from Yahweh to Shallum, and pay special attention to the relationship between truly knowing God, and "doing justice and righteousness," the Abrahamic mission:

> Thus says the LORD: "Go down to the house of the king of Judah and speak there this word, and say, 'Hear the word of the LORD, O king of Judah, who sits on the throne of David, you, and your servants, and your people who enter these gates. Thus says the LORD: Do justice and righteousness, and deliver from the hand of the oppressor him who has been robbed. And do no wrong or violence to the resident alien, the fatherless, and the widow, nor shed innocent blood in this place. For if you will indeed obey this word, then there shall enter the gates of this house kings who sit on the throne of David, riding in chariots and on horses, they and their servants and their people. But if you will not obey these words, I swear by myself, declares the LORD, that this house shall become a desolation.   —Jeremiah 22:1–5

Shallum, however, told Yahweh to hit the highway. Jeremiah's closing comments to him reveal the evidence indicting him for his sin, while validating his father's deep love for God. This was determined by how they treated the poor:

> Does it make you a king to have more and more cedar? Did not your father [Josiah] have food and drink? He did what was right and just, so all went well with him. He

---

1 Deuteronomy 26:12; 14:28. Our modern notion of the "tithe," as convenient as it is, and as indigenous as it has become, is more a product of the metric system than the Bible. Sliding the decimal on our paycheck one place to the left might be expedient, but it's surely not what God had in mind. A study of the Bible's teaching on "tithing" will quickly reveal it was *never* 10%. Perhaps that's why the New Testament teaches regular, proportional, generous, and joyful giving rather than a decimal slide. What we do with what we keep for ourselves is more an indicator of whether we're an Alien or a Tourist than how much we give.

2 cf. Jeremiah 29:11-13; Micah 6:6-8

3 He is also known as Jehoahaz in the Bible.

defended the cause of the poor and needy, and so all went well. *Is that not what it means to know me?"* declares the LORD.   —Jeremiah 22:15–16, NIV [brackets mine]

This idea that one's attitude towards the "poor" is the litmus test for loving God is not limited to a comment by a wild prophet in the court of a wayward king. Solomon posits it as a universal characteristic of a righteous man in general, a righteous political leader in particular, and a godly wife and mother:

A righteous man knows the rights of the poor; a wicked man does not understand such knowledge.   —Proverbs 29:7

If a king faithfully judges the poor, his throne will be established forever.
    —Proverbs 29:14

An excellent wife who can find? She is far more precious than jewels....She opens her hand to the poor and reaches out her hands to the needy.   —Proverbs 31:10, 20

God even goes so far as to lump mistreatment of these people in with the sins of adultery and witchcraft![1] But, one of the most amazing and thorough illustrations of, and evidences for, the value Yahweh places on "doing righteousness and justice," is in the life of one of our favorite biblical characters. Unfortunately, his reputation for perseverance in the face of pain has eclipsed what, at the end of the day, may very well be the main reason his life is in the Bible. His care for the poor. His name is Job.

Finding The Perfect Job

I have always been intrigued, and maybe a little jealous, of the things Yahweh said about Job. He said he was "blameless and upright," and that he "feared God," and walked away from evil. These are amazing attributions to come from the mouth of God about anyone. But, the one that always sent me pondering in the woods of my mind, was the statement that God also said He "had no one else like him." And, He says it in the face of "the Satan" who has just returned from a little recon mission that took him "to and fro, walking up and down" on the planet. Yahweh essentially says, "Yeah, well in all your travels and observations, this guy is one of a kind!" Now, before your mind heads down the basement steps to the dark cellar of pain that Job is best known for, I want to keep you on the ground floor of that statement.

Would you like to hear Yahweh say that about *you*? I mean, if you could be hanging out in the Throne Room of God, wouldn't you like to overhear Yahweh talking with Gabriel about *you,* and say this? Who wouldn't? I began to wonder, what prompted such exclusive and exquisite praise of this man? It couldn't be anything that had to do with suffering, because Yahweh made this proclamation of honor *before* Job's pain began. In fact, He says it *twice* before then![2] And keep in mind that this is an ancient tale told to an audience in an oral culture. That means that they too knew of Job's innocence even before the story began. That

---

1 Malachi 3:5

2 Job 1:8; 2:3

means the account about Job is much, much, more than an epic saga about undaunted courage or undying love.

I started to long for the impossible, or so I thought. I began to ask, "What would it be like if I could peer into a few pages out of Job's pre-pain journal?" I just wanted to see a "Day in the Life" of Job before hell became home. Guess what? I found it! Buried in the layers of dialogues that define this book, is a monologue by Job in which he reminisces about his life before he received an autographed copy of, *Your Worst Life Now.* In chapter 29 we hear the "no one like him" guy reflecting on what he did that caused not only Yahweh but his fellow townspeople to honor him. He was living as an Advocate, carrying out that facet of the Abrahamic mission:

> When the ear heard, it called me blessed, and when the eye saw, it approved, because I delivered the poor who cried for help, and the fatherless who had none to help him. The blessing of him who was about to perish came upon me, and I caused the widow's heart to sing for joy. I put on *righteousness*, and it clothed me; my *justice* was like a robe and a turban. I was eyes to the blind and feet to the lame. I was a father to the needy, and I searched out the cause of him whom I did not know. I broke the fangs of the unrighteous and made him drop his prey from his teeth.   —Job 29:11–17

In the opening verses of this book, Yahweh is honoring Job for his passion for *ministry,* not his perseverance in the face of *misery.* We know this because, as we said, He praised him *before* He tested him. Don't get me wrong, Job *is* a great example of bearing up under the crushing weight of underserved and unexplained pain. But, he's an even better model of what God values more than sacrifice—mercy.[1]

Once we begin to understand the central role advocacy plays in the plan of God, the Advocate facet of identity not only "fits," it becomes vital for both my own transformation and the blessing of the nations, which we will see in Part III. We also begin to finally see what was there in the Scriptures all along; the divinely rich relationship between my care of the poor and my knowledge of God. And, it's not merely "there," it is everywhere. Advocacy is the first cousin of other aspects of our faith that we didn't even know were related, like fasting. This was made clear to me during a recent online search for Christian books that dealt with fasting. It returned over 200 results. Yet, not a single one drew from the longest, richest, and most detailed description in Scripture of God's fast of choice. And, the vast majority of them were peddling "power" to the reader, weight loss, detoxification, more "intimacy" with God, and the clout of being like Daniel. There were audio books, eBooks, paperback books, and even fasting journals. Yet, because of the focus of these books, even someone buying a fasting journal would not fill its pages with what Job filled his "journal" with. With the most lucid words possible, God declares that His "fast of choice" is that made by an Advocate whom, most likely, *had* eaten that day:

> Is not this the fast that I choose: to loose the bonds of wickedness, to undo the straps of the yoke, to let the oppressed go free, and to break every yoke? Is it not to share your

1 cf. Hosea 6:6; Matthew 9:13

bread with the hungry and bring the homeless poor into your house; when you see the naked, to cover him, and not to hide yourself from your own flesh?   —Isaiah 58:6–7

Yahweh defines fasting as giving up to *give away*, not to gain. He even goes on to add that living the Advocate identity is one remedy for one's *own* depression and discouragement.[1] The principle of "saving" your life by "losing" it didn't originate with Jesus.[2] It began with Yahweh. We find a similar thread running through the official hymnal of the Temple, the Psalms. Within its 150 psalms, there are 40 references to the widow, the fatherless, the sojourner, and the poor. Most are references to Yahweh's biased love, and His desire that their needs are met.

The Advocate identity, as we would expect, is alive and flourishing when we get to the first century church, recorded in the New Testament. James, the half-brother of Yeshua, says that genuine faith cannot exist where "blessed deeds"[3] are not flourishing:

> What good is it, my brothers, if someone says he has faith but does not have works? Can that faith save him? If a brother or sister is poorly clothed and lacking in daily food, and one of you says to them, "Go in peace, be warmed and filled," without giving them the things needed for the body, what good is that? So also faith by itself, if it does not have works, is dead....Do you want to be shown, you foolish person, that faith apart from works is useless? Was not Abraham our father justified by works when he offered up his son Isaac on the altar? You see that faith was active along with his works, and faith was completed by his works;   —James 2:14–17, 20–22

Caring for the poor was one of the most powerful and visible characteristics of the first century church in Palestine and around the known world:

> Now in these days prophets came down from Jerusalem to Antioch. And one of them named Agabus stood up and foretold by the Spirit that there would be a great famine over all the world (this took place in the days of Claudius). So the disciples determined, every one according to his ability, to send relief to the brothers living in Judea. And they did so, sending it to the elders by the hand of Barnabas and Saul.
> —Acts 11:27–30

> For Macedonia and Achaia have been pleased to make some contribution for the poor among the saints at Jerusalem.   —Romans 15:26

Even Paul made a point of saying that caring for the poor was one of his main ministry foci.[4] Advocacy was part of his instruction and training of pastors and churches.[5] He went so far as to challenge what we would have known as capitalism in the Corinthian church. Paul insisted that because Yahweh was the giver *and* owner of all things, one believer's excess was divinely intended to

---

1 cf. Isaiah 58:10-12

2 cf. Mark 8:35

3 The Greek phrase, *kala erga,* which we render "good works" can also be translated "blessed deeds." It's interesting, the difference in reaction, when Christians hear these two phrases. We have, unfortunately, become conditioned to believe that "good works" are the enemy of grace and faith, and unfortunate and untrue carry-over from our understanding of the Reformation Fathers.

4 Galatians 2:9-10

5 1 Timothy 6:17-19; 2 Corinthians 8-9

meet the deficit of another believer:

> For I do not mean that others should be eased and you burdened, but that as a matter of fairness your abundance at the present time should supply their need, so that their abundance may supply your need, that there may be fairness.
> −2 **Corinthians** 8:13–14

I suspect this was in Jesus' mind too. He told a parable in Luke 12, about a man who had such a "good year" that his *excess* was excessive; even for him. So, the man rented some space at the local U-Store-It to stockpile all God's "blessings" from that year. But, the parable doesn't have a Disney ending. The man died that night. And the pity *wasn't* that he didn't get to enjoy his investments. It was that he wasn't "rich towards God."[1] In the only place in the entire Bible where these words fall from the lips of God, Yahweh calls this man a "fool." And at this stage of our journey in the world of Identity, there's no dodging what that means and why He said it.

The life and words of Jesus provide our final Advocate stop on the road to biblical Identity. Although surely not surprising, it *should* be amazing, that Jesus opens and closes his earthly ministry with references to advocacy. Both his and ours. He uses it as proof that the Kingdom has come, and it's in his hand, and at the end as the litmus test to determine who's actually in that Kingdom and who isn't.

As Jesus, the son of a general contractor in Galilee, stepped out of the mists of obscurity, and onto the stage as the long-awaited Messiah, he does so with such clarity that it's a wonder how everyone missed it. But, *they* didn't know what we know. And let's not forget that we know *what* we know because *they* eventually figured it out, and then wrote it down. Jesus' first public sermon of record was fewer than 200 words in length; nearly a third of which he borrowed from Isaiah. But, Luke tells us that the text he chose for his first message was one that he intentionally searched for in the scroll that was handed to him. Imagine Jesus unrolling a scroll of papyrus covered with Hebrew words that lacked page numbers, chapter numbers, and verse numbers. A scroll of one, long, unbroken paragraph. He unrolls it, his finger tracing the ancient language until his eyes find the very passage Yahweh had led him to read. He stands in true fashion as a rabbi, reads. This is what his family, friends, and neighbors heard that day:

> The Spirit of the Lord is upon me,
> because he has anointed me
> To proclaim good news to the poor.
> He has sent me to proclaim liberty to the captives
> And recovering of sight to the blind,
> to set at liberty those who are oppressed,
> to proclaim the year of the Lord's favor.
>
> – **Luke** 4:16-19[2]

---

1 Luke 12: 15-21

2 cf. Isaiah 61:1-4

Then, to everyone's amazement, including his family, Jesus says this passage is referring to *him!* But, don't miss the content on a quick jump to what happened next. Jesus establishes that the arrival of the Messiah is "good news" *for the poor.* The Jews who were present who thought contextually, not specifically like us, would have immediately done a mental sweep. They would have known *all* that Isaiah said before and after those verses. And they would have found themselves face to face with language that had to do with the end of oppression and sorrow for those least able to help themselves. This event in a small synagogue in Nazareth marked the debut of the One who *will* "walk in the ways of the LORD," and who *will* "do righteousness and justice on the earth." This was Yahweh in a body! Not a carpenter's son in a synagogue! The intersection of heaven and earth that was once the Tabernacle, and then the Temple, was now standing in their midst. And as Yahweh in a body stepped onto the stage that had been 2,000 years in the making, His first pronouncement as the King who has come, was that God had "anointed" (the root word for Messiah) him to bring 'good news' *to the poor.* Don't miss this. You must not miss this. They did.

Near the end of his earthly ministry, in the midst of a flurry of questions from his disciples about his return (some things never change), Jesus lays out a picture of the final judgment. The "litmus test" Yahweh uses to determine (or verify) intimacy with Him—who knew Him and who did not—should sound familiar, but more personal that you have heard it in the past:

> Before him will be gathered all the nations, and he will separate people one from another as a shepherd separates the sheep from the goats. And he will place the sheep on his right, but the goats on the left. Then the King will say to those on his right, 'Come, you who are blessed by my Father, inherit the kingdom prepared for you from the foundation of the world. For I was hungry and you gave me food, I was thirsty and you gave me drink, I was a stranger and you welcomed me, I was naked and you clothed me, I was sick and you visited me, I was in prison and you came to me.' Then the righteous will answer him, saying, 'Lord, when did we see you hungry and feed you, or thirsty and give you drink? And when did we see you a stranger and welcome you, or naked and clothe you? And when did we see you sick or in prison and visit you?' And the King will answer them, 'Truly, I say to you, as you did it to one of the least of these my brothers, you did it to me.'   —Matthew 25:32–40

In a sense, Jesus' criteria for this entrance interview, is whether an individual had lived out the Advocate facet of Identity. Or put another way, whether they had lived like Job. The beauty of this passage to me, is that these people didn't even *imagine* they were ministering directly to Jesus. Advocacy had become such a part of their lives, there was no choice involved. We also see that the "least of these" were Ambassadors, and what was done to them, was actually done to their King. Advocacy is important to God. It is a vital component of our Identity because it is a necessary part of the Abrahamic mission. But, advocacy is not exactly our strong suit. Especially because of our lack of understanding where it fits in the overall picture of redemption. Consider my own state of Alabama. We not only do *not* sell food to the poor at "cost," we tax them fully for it![1] And this is a state dominated by lawmakers who are unashamedly Christian.

This "theological blind-spot" is even reflected in our hymnody. Of the 750 hymns in a major American hymnal currently in use, only 13 mention the widow, the poor, the fatherless, or the stranger. And half of *those* do so only because they're based on a Psalm that speaks of them. It is one thing to sing what God has already sung. It's quite another to write songs of our own about these people groups. There are close to 140 references to "mercy," that we lift our voices about, but they are *all* are about God's mercy to *us*. This is despite the fact that in the writings of Paul and the teaching of Jesus we are frequently commanded to demonstrate mercy. In a democratic society, the mercy of God is perceived to be an individual benefit, a "blessing." But in a monarchy in which the King extols mercy and has been lavishly merciful Himself, the subjects would never dream of being anything less.

Advocacy, as we have seen, is an expression of *who Yahweh is*. It is not merely something that He *does*. We are commanded to *imitate* this unchanging God of advocacy, whose heart is especially directed to those whose lives sin has rendered powerless and defenseless. And we've also seen that as Apprentices, our goal should be the emulation of him who said: *For even the Son of Man did not come to be served, but to serve, and to give his life as a ransom for many."* Advocacy and Apprenticeship are inseparable. They should also be indistinguishable.

The Identity Ladder

Looking back over the past seven chapters, I think it would help to distill a brief synopsis of each of the seven rungs and try to see them standing together:

I am *"Adamic."* Understanding this creates an unbreakable connection to and empathy for those still stuck in the *"kosmos."* We are related by birth. We have the same ancestry. It also is the basis for realistic expectations in my relationships with others. I have an Adamic residue just as they do.

I am *"Adopted."* Seeing this aspect of my identity properly should create a deep sense of gratitude *and* humility. I was not "reborn" into the family of God. I was adopted. And, Yahweh freely *chose* to include me in His family. My past has no control over me, although it still exists. I can now call the God who created me, "Abba, Father." I also have a new family, one that is ancient, global, and diverse. I have more in common with them, regardless of their ethnicity or geography than I do with those *outside* this family.

I am *"Abrahamic."* This aspect of my Identity creates a sense of participation in a Story that is infinitely larger than me, older than Jesus, and more comprehensive than the doctrine of election.

I am an *"Alien."* I am "just visiting this planet." I am a stranger and sojourner. My mission is to the "natives," I'm not on furlough for myself! The lifestyle and values I reflect should resemble a foreigner, not a tourist on vacation.

---

1 Currently, 31 states have no sales tax on food, 7 have a reduced tax rate for food, and 12 states tax food at the same rate as everything else. (see: www.taxadmin.org/fta/rate/sales.pdf)

I am an "Apprentice." Jesus has called me to "come," which involves sitting at his feet, listening to his voice, and watching his life. Becoming more like Jesus is the intended and inevitable result of spending time alone with Him.

I am an "Ambassador." Jesus has commanded me to "go." I carry a message from my homeland and represent my King. His reputation and character are inseparably linked to my own.

I am an "Advocate." As an adopted child of Yahweh, I have a responsibility to emulate "Abba," *and* as an Apprentice, I should resemble my Master. Both Yahweh and Jesus have made it clear by their words and how they expressed themselves, that they had a biased burden for those who cannot speak or care for themselves. This is the essence of Grace. As an Ambassador, I carry not only a message of Grace, but the power of it as well.

The Identity Assassin

As we draw these last eight chapters on Identity to a close, I'd like to try to draw a wide circle around a great deal of material, and pull it tightly enough together that it begins to take on a shape of its own; an identity, if you like. During our trip to the Holy Land, Jill and I spent much of our time on our tour bus, going from site to site at a dizzying pace. We covered more ground, and heard more stories about more places and times than I could process. My brain screamed, "Stop!" at one point. Reluctantly, I decided to stay back at the room when everyone else went to the Dead Sea. It was suffering from a cerebral hernia of sorts. However, there were two things I learned *on* that bus that I'll never forget. And they both illustrate the power and the need for a biblical Identity to provide the answer to our initial question: *"Who do I say that I am?"* Our driver was a Palestinian Arab who was also a Christian. Our tour guide was a Russian-born Jew who had become an Israeli citizen. He was also a Jew who had embraced Jesus as Messiah. Our host was a seminary professor who was an Episcopalian. We were surrounded by Baptists, Methodists, and non-denominationalists. Jill and I were members of a Presbyterian church. One day, after an exhausting series of study stops, a mental meandering was birthed during a distressing trip to Bethlehem the birthplace of Jesus, the "Prince of Peace."[1] As we approached the town, a concrete wall greeted us, interrupted by a guard tower, and topped with concertina razor wire. That emotional jolt was followed by a physical one, when the bus stopped just outside the gate, and our Israeli tour guide got out and waved us on. We were told that because he was an Israeli and a Jew, he was not welcome inside Bethlehem, now a Palestinian Territory. Another guide stepped on the bus and introduced himself. He, like our driver, was a Palestinian Arab and a Christian. This was all nearly too much to process. My juvenile understanding of Palestinians and Jews seemed to have gotten off the bus along with our guide. That day was monumental in God's slow education in my life about how much of my own faith is a product

1 cf. Isaiah 9:6

of American culture, free-market capitalism, and democracy. On the trip back, I found myself looking around and wondering what in the world our menagerie of misfits had in common? All the descriptors I listed for our busload of pilgrims above circled aimlessly in my head and were quickly dismissed. Not one of them could be applied to all of us. And, to simply say, "we're all Christians" (though tempting), was too simplistic. I realized that day, if each of us was to embrace, internalize, and seek to emulate the seven aspects we've labored through in these chapters, it wouldn't matter whether we were from Bethlehem or Birmingham. But, that's the problem. We don't.

The greatest enemy to Identity, is *not* self-esteem, fabricating a hierarchy of descriptors that fuel my Adamic residue. The real enemy of identity is something that can only be called, "tribalism." At its core, tribalism is the belief that something other than Adamic belongs at the top of my Identity Ladder. And this impostor always seems to hail from one of only a few clans: theology, ethnicity, geography, and tradition. There is no greater source of heat lacking light, than the fierce doctrinal distinctions that divide believers. Divergent views on baptism, spiritual gifts, church polity, wealth, and even the poor, have demolished relationships and erected buildings. Calvinist, Pentecostal, Baptist, Word of Faith, conservative, and liberal are just a sampling of the flags among believers that are run up the pole in the war for unity. But, so are African-American, Asian-American, Latino-American, and the rest of the variety of ancestral labels we pin on our church clothes. Where someone lives or was born can also be the cause of separation more than celebration. Yankee and Southerner, American and Eastern European, urban and suburban, "good" neighborhood and "bad" neighborhood, just to mention a few. When you consider that each of these can be combined in nearly countless arrays, you begin to get the picture. The Apostle Paul, who lived during one of the most class-structured times in history, understood this and was bullish about dismantling it in the early church.

The beauty of his teaching is that he clearly acknowledges the divisive categories of his day: ethnicity, status, religious conviction on gray issues, gender, urban and rural. However, apparently believers, while free to embrace some of these distinctives, were to check them at the door upon becoming part of the community of faith. Paul even goes so far as to say something that in his day would have had the force of insisting that Yahweh was a woman. He says that one of the other things God killed on Golgotha besides our sin was a 1,500 year old enmity between Jews and Gentiles; a divisive hostility based on ethnicity. The division ran so deep that a wall surrounding the main Temple area had been built to keep Gentiles from getting too close. A promise of death was carved in stone, to those who disregarded it. It is to that very "wall" that Paul is pointing in this passage. Like the Berlin Wall coming down in 1989, Paul insisted that the Cross had destroyed the basis of the hostility the only way possible. Jesus created "one new man [race] out of the two":

But now in Christ Jesus you who once were far off [Gentiles] have been brought near by the blood of Christ. For he himself is our peace, who *has made us both one and has broken down in his flesh the dividing wall of hostility* by abolishing the law of commandments expressed in ordinances, that *he might create in himself one new man in place of the two,* so making peace, and might reconcile us both to God in one body through the cross, thereby killing the hostility.   **–Ephesians** 2:13–16

And what Paul said happened to ethnicity on Golgotha, he said happened to all these non-biblical impostors on the Identity ladder too.

There is neither Jew nor Greek, there is neither slave nor free, there is no male and female, for you are all one in Christ Jesus.   **–Galatians** 3:28

Here there is not Greek and Jew, circumcised and uncircumcised, barbarian, Scythian, slave, free; but Christ is all, and in all.   **–Colossians** 3:11

Paul doesn't deny believers the freedom to use these words to *describe* them. He just doesn't want them to *define* them. Getting this distinction right isn't easy. But it's necessary. And the other descriptors, Messianic, Arab, Episcopalian, American, Palestinian, etc., can all have a seat on the bus. Just somewhere *after* the seventh row.

Knowing *who* you are on a bus is one thing. But, knowing who you are in life is an altogether different matter. It contains within it an undeniable obligation to *do* something with the fact that I now know who I am. It pushes me in the direction of getting an answer to a question that's more significant than the first one, yet dependent on it. And that brings us to the doorstep of the question of purpose. Or, put another way, "What's my point?"

PART II *Purpose*
"What's My Point?"

"Plot Hunger"— *Our Need to Connect the Dots*

Surprising my wife is about as easy as nailing Jell-O to a tree. Jill's highly developed intuition and background as a journalist and sociology major means her little gray cells rarely rest. She even "processes" when she sleeps! And definitely faster and more efficiently too, considering that she's not distracted by the world of real people. So, the challenge of choreographing an unforgettable 60th birthday under her nose, unnoticed, would be like parting the Red Sea. And, as much as she enjoys people, she is clearly introverted, so being in a group takes more out of her than it imparts. I have vivid memories of a friend of mine who wanted to give *his* highly introverted wife the fortieth birthday of the century. He invited half the city, a stand-up comedian, and a circus of activities that *he* would have loved. But, that was the problem! She spent the end of the night in the ER from over-extending herself. She'll *never* forget her fortieth birthday! But for all the wrong reasons. I would *not* be "that guy."

I was scheduled to speak at two large conferences in the Upper Midwest, very near where Jill grew up, right around the time of her birthday. We decided to combine the conferences with a few weeks of R&R "back home," and quietly celebrate her birthday there, alone. She was thrilled. Friends who are doing missionary work in Asia, had offered us their home for the duration, which seemed to seal the deal. Jill anticipated we would share this momentous birthday "quietly." But, that's when Operation Oktoberfest was birthed. I realized that our oldest son, Ben, would be at a large urban ministry conference in Indianapolis the week before her birthday. Indianapolis is a mere 3 hours from Chicago where our middle son lives. That only left our twin daughters, one who lived in Mississippi, and the other in Birmingham. I started the ball rolling with a query to the kids. The deal was: all or nothing. It couldn't be two or three kids, it had to be all four, or no go. I told the children I would pay for everything. I had saved some money and had a round-trip credit with an airline. The rest would come from...well, it would come from somewhere. The girls were both able to adjust their schedules at the hospitals where they are nurses. Geoff didn't teach on Fridays at the college, so he could launch that day. And Ben? Well he was "three hours south of Geoff." I knew I also had to draw Jill's cousin in on the plans because she had to arrange *her* work schedule around our stay in Minnesota. And I didn't want her to take off work when Jill would be in the middle of Operation Oktoberfest. In the world of statistics, that's five variables that had to line up flawlessly for this thing to happen. I was asking God for "perfect storm" conditions, hoping to blow a little joy into my wife's sails. About fifty emails and online purchases later, here's what I had in a file folder labeled, "Operation Oktoberfest":

Ben would find a ride from the CCDA conference in Indianapolis to the Megabus station. From there he'd ride a Megabus from Indianapolis to downtown Chicago. Geoff would grab the Metra in Elmhurst and ride it to Chicago to meet Ben. Together they would hop the Orange Line to Midway Airport where they'd both catch the same flight on Southwest to Hubert Humphrey Airport in Minneapolis. Havilah would drive from Mississippi to Birmingham, pick up Heather and they'd drive to Park'n'Fly outside Hartsfield International in Atlanta. Leaving their car, they' snag a shuttle to the airport and take an AirTran flight to Hubert Humphrey. Once there, they'd join their brothers, whose flight arrived 30 minutes earlier, and the four of them would go to Budget to pick up the rental car I had rented. From there, they would drive to Minneapolis' Uptown area to "surprise" Jill and me at Bar Abilene, a popular sports bar and restaurant in that area. One glitch, one delayed flight, or traffic jam, and the whole thing falls like a house of cards. Supportive spouses were left behind; two with our grandchildren.

And, there *were* no glitches. None. Picture this: Jill and I are sitting in Bar Abilene, getting re-acquainted with one of my oldest and dearest friends who owns the restaurant (eating there was his idea, and it turns out, his gift!). Everybody knows what's going on, everyone of course, except Jill. As she's pouring over the book-sized menu, I lean over and whisper, "Happy Birthday" just as the four children are filing in one at a time. My wife's an expressive person, but this was once-in-a-lifetime stuff. First shock, then confusion, then amazement, then a joy that only a mother can know when she's alone with the four children she bore and the husband she loves. In the credit card business, they would label this..."*Priceless.*"

This is a beautiful memory, and always elicits a host of "oh's" and "ah's" when Jill rehearses it for others. But, the real beauty of this story, is that there was a *plot* that was unfolding right beneath her nose, and she had no idea. The tale I just elaborately retold *really does* have a connection to this book. The really important thing for Jill was that once she understood the big picture, a plethora of pithy details from the past few months all fell into place. She could reconstruct the plot *backward* that I had created to unfold *forward*. Unusual phone calls from the children at odd times. My wandering off outside to talk to them.

My computer being active more than she appreciated, and a host of other recollections that began to fit into a larger grid. They had a place, and they had meaning because of the big picture that gave it to them. Alone, details can never design a plot, no matter how exotic, entertaining, or enticing they are. It's plot that gives meaning to details. This was true of Jill and her party, but, it's also true of life itself. Especially for someone who now knows she's an Adamic, adopted, Abrahamic, alien-apprentice-ambassodor-advocate.

Our original premise was that Identity leads to Purpose, and Purpose leads to Mission. Or, *who* I am points to *why* I am, which points to *what* I'm to do, now that I have answers to the first two questions. Hopefully, we've answered the first question adequately, even if not throughly. This brings us to the doorstep of the second, the question of purpose. Or more succinctly, *"What's my point?"* Even before we begin, we know that any answer we arrive at, to be authentic, has to make sense within the context of Identity. That's a non-negotiable, because of our premise. It's got to be an "Identity Driven Purpose," to put it another way.

In Chapter 2, I cited Gordon Dahl's description of middle-class Americans. We're going to repeatedly revisit this quote throughout the book. And each time we do, it will loom larger and richer:

> Most middle-class Americans tend to worship their work, work at their play, and play at their worship. As a result, their meanings and values are distorted. Their relationships disintegrate faster than they can keep them in repair. Their lifestyles resemble a cast of characters in search of a plot.

We humans seem to have an inherent craving for plot. To find one or create one. Sometimes, we resort to mimicking, fabricating, or hijacking one. But, at the end of the day, we want one, and we're going to have one! In this piece of creative prose, Dahl makes a very clear and accurate connection between plot and purpose. No plot, no purpose. Four words. All true. He paints a portrait of a culture in search of a purpose in all the wrong places. And his assessment is as relevant today as it was in the 1970's when he first said it.

Purpose depends on plot because purpose is dependent upon non-randomness, the deep assurance that life is unfolding, not merely happening. No one has ever, in the midst of an auto accident, suddenly stopped and said, "Wait! We need to ponder the significance of all this!" We have places for people who act that way. Everyone knows deep down that there's no purpose to randomness. That's why car wrecks are called "accidents," *not* "encounters." Accidents "happen," but life unfolds. And from our discoveries in Chapter 4, we have at least a partial answer to why humans have a penchant for purpose. It's because of the Imago Dei, the good side of the Adamic coin. We were created in the likeness of a purposeful God. Even the Creation account belies an amazing purpose. There is order, sequence, beauty, hierarchy, and interdependence. Even a cursory reading of the first two chapters of Genesis provides a sense of movement, the specific details all playing a part in which each fades as just as the next appears. The creation of the human race is the obvious apex of the Creation narrative. But even that is not the end. The creation of humanity is the prequel to the Fall of mankind, which becomes the centerpiece of the rest of the Bible for a long time.

Evidence that this need for purpose is part of our DNA, and not a "modern" idea (or one that has emerged from the ashes of boredom of life in the afflu- ent suburbs), is that it is present even in primitive civilizations. The animistic Aboriginal culture of Australia is one of the most intriguing examples of our longing for plot. The late narrative-driven philosopher and author, Bruce Cha- twin, in his book, *The Songlines,* weaves the creation myths of a primitive culture into a novel. Part fact and part fiction, his book introduces the reader to "The Songlines," or "Dreaming Tracks" as Europeans call them, of the Aborigines. These stories, sung meticulously and in proper order, recount the creation of all things and their names, linked to specific geographical spots across the land and sky. The indigenous nomads can navigate their way across the vast expanse of earth, using these songs as a type of melodic GPS. They are part story, part geography, and part theology. In short, a plot from the days of the ancestors that provides direction for today. A metaphysical map of sorts, dressed in mythology and sung by pre-moderns. But, beneath it all is a story, an ancient story that gives the Songlines purpose, even today for those who know them.

The Real Hunger Games

Our own plot hunger drives much of the scriptwriting in Hollywood. And in an ironic way, serves to move our money into their bulging bank accounts. It is no coincidence that the Internet Movie Database website owned by Amazon. com, has a "Plot Summary" and "Storyline" entry for each of its over a million and a half titles. But, the movie industry itself is our greatest witness to both the plot hunger and how to tease it or slake it.

The 1998 release of *The Truman Show,* is an example. The lead character, Truman Burbank (Jim Carey), lives a scripted life, unbeknownst to him, in front of the world via television. The viewers, and us by extension, get to watch a real man, living a "real" life (to him) the plot of which is totally controlled by others. Everyone knows this, including us. Everyone that is, except Truman. I still recall finding myself rappelling up and down an emotional rock face from laughter to sorrow, vacillating between the fact that this was just a movie, yet it was so tragic. Someone else was scripting Truman's life. There was a plot that was, by design, created to genuinely gratify the hunger of the *viewers,* and yet only arti- ficially do so for the main character. It was funny but sick.

The Wachowskis' ground-breaking film, *The Matrix,* was released the same year. The notion of "plot" was the centerpiece of this film as well. Not just the plot conceived by the Wachowski brothers, but the artificial, virtual *sense* of plot that was fed digitally into each of the humans living in the electronic chrysalises created by an evolved computer collectively known as "The Matrix." As viewers, we were drawn into the insidious nature of a *virtual* plot that has no substance in the world of people. One scene in the movie was prophetic, given the rise of reality TV, which exploded as a genre the same year. Cypher, one of the characters rescued out of the virtual delusion, decides that he wants back into the zombie digital existence. All because a virtual steak dinner in a virtual restaurant, while his body is intubated with circuitry cables, is "easier" to live with. Author Chris Hedges believes Cypher is now the new normal, in his book, *Empire of Illusion: The End of Literacy and the Triumph of Spectacle.*[1] If *The Truman Show* sickened us because of the duplicity, *The Matrix* frightened us because of the near plausibility. Although we all could say, "it's just a movie," when the credits rolled, deep down, a gnawing question kept bubbling to the surface like a decomposing lake bottom: "I wonder if this could ever happen?" Hedges believes it has. We're just not intubated, we're infatuated. And that's because we're plot hungry, and maybe a little *too* hungry.

But, maybe the two best Hollywood films to bait and then eviscerate our need for plot, were directed ten years apart by the same person, Christopher Nolan. The first was *Memento*, released in 2000. The genius of this film lay in the presence of *two* versions of the same plot, one played forward in black and white, the other in color and in reverse. The main character, Leonard Shelby, suffers from a malady where he can no longer build new memories. Throughout the film, Shelby tries to find his wife's murderer, his last memory. But, because everything he discovers one day will be forgotten the next, he compiles a plethora of notes, clippings, even tattooing data on himself, in his race to unravel this memory within a memory. Nolan is so successful directing this film that those watching it are as confused as Shelby! The movie's *confusion* of plot prompted one cinema sleuth to create an actual diagram of the film's progression with each of the two plots running in opposite directions, in an attempt to make sense of the movie![2]

Apparently not satisfied that he had scrambled the minds of enough people, Nolan directed a second film a decade later that will, most likely, go down in history as the most convoluted film of all time. It was as though he dropped our plot hunger and the movie script into a Vitamixer and poured out the film, *Inception.* If *Memento* was a memory within a memory, *Inception* was a dream within a dream within a dream within a dream. In a world where the extraction of people's ideas had become commonplace, Dom Cobb, the protagonist, is challenged to do the opposite, *plant* an idea. It requires a level of penetration into the subconscious four levels deep, and the plot slowly becomes a house of mirrors for the viewer. It even ends with no real resolution regarding what's real and what's fabricated. We walk in and out of these films, knowing we'll be confused no matter how often we see them. But, at the very root of both our attraction, amazement, and mental nausea, is our love of, and need for plot.

We *love* plot. And not just in films. We often find ourselves drawn, almost

---

1 Chris Hedges, *Empire of Illusion: The End of Literacy and the Triumph of Spectacle.* New York: Nation Books, 2009.

2 See: http://en.wikipedia.org/wiki/File:Visual_Map_of_the_Film_Memento.png

irretrievably, into novels and feature stories crafted by skilled wordsmiths who also know how to exploit this longing. Modern best-selling authors like J. K Rowling *(Harry Potter)* and Susan Collins *(Hunger Games)* have gotten wealthy mining the riches of the deep reservoir of our need for plot. Partly because they know how to tease out our interest, but what they don't know, is we are *divinely* hardwired to connect the dots, to make sense of things. This is just as true of little things like why a car won't start, as it is of big things like what is justice, what is truth, and what's my purpose. We *need* to know, deep down that the profusion of dots on the radar we call "life," are connected, not random. We need the assurance that there's a beginning and an end to things, whether it's cancer or adolescence, we are made to think this way. Cause and effect. Choices and consequences. And that there's *continuity* from one to the other. In short, we need to know that's there's a plot, or put another way that there's a *point* to this thing we call life.

I'm not talking about "trying to find ourselves" here, any more than I was referring to self-esteem in the previous chapters on Identity. Many among the rising generation who've boarded the "find yourself" treadmill, have not done so in search of purpose, but as an escape from boredom, the inevitable off-spring of a tiny world. When your world is small, and you occupy a large part in it; you become bored. Or arrogant. But, plot hunger is different, and more vital. I'm referring to something, which once understood, is as comprehensive, compelling, and inescapable as Identity, and just as variegated. More like a tapestry than a quilt.

Tapestries are made up of weft and warp threads. The warp threads run from top to bottom, and the weft threads run from side to side. Unlike cotton, where both types of threads are visible, a tapestry's beauty is derived from the variety of colors in the weft threads, which are visible, and it's strength comes from the warp threads which are not. In the world of story, which is a type of literary or oral tapestry, it's much the same. A plot serves as the warp threads. It supplies structure and direction, even "purpose" to the story, all the while remaining unseen to everyone, except to the one who created it. The multitude of names, cities, events, emotions, and personalities sequentially paraded before us—the narrative—serves as the weft threads. The provision of narrative is variety and beauty. Both are necessary, but narrative is where we really live because it's all we can see. It not only surrounds us, in a very real way, it defines us, according to philosopher and author Larry Tauton. *"Whether it is a family history or the history of a nation, the narrative of one's past is critical to identity,"*[1] according to Tauton. Applying this metaphor of a tapestry to life itself, there are really only three possibilities regarding the weaving together of plot and narrative. And they can't all be valid, because they're mutually exclusive.

---

1 Larry Tauton, *The Grace Effect: How the Power of One Life Can Reverse the Corruption of Unbelief* (Nashville: Thomas Nelson, 2011), 157.

Three Plot Possibilities

The first possibility we've already visited. It's the dismal reality that there really *is* no plot. What we *think* is a metanarrative or "Story," is merely the accumulative chronicles of what was happening at any given point in time. We give it a variety of labels, like "history," "sociology," or "anthropology." But, when all's said and done, it's just information, data to be collated, stored on Google's servers, and mined for its usefulness, and sorted by the algorithm of relevance. Life, as Richard Dawkins preaches, has no design—only structure, order, and movement. Therefore, it is not linear, and can have no inherent script. But, if design determines purpose, a world lacking a plot, becomes a world lacking a purpose. And if life has no purpose, and you're alive, you have no purpose either. As we discovered earlier, this option has already been thoroughly tested and distilled into three words: *"Meaningless, meaningless, meaningless."*

A second possibility, and surely as popular as Angry Birds, is that there is a metanarrative, a grand Story that gives meaning and purpose to life. But, it's the one *you* decide to live, based on what's important to *you*. Picture life as a sort of "Chart Your Own Adventure," (CYOA) in which *you* get to write the script *and* be the star. Imagine being able to ad-lib a storyline in which your greatest strengths and achievements, or the things you have the most control over, are the most valuable commodities on earth. You'd have purpose, meaning, and you'd be happy. Or, if you are more of a "dark drama" fan, then your pain, sorrow, and your feelings of victimization and neglect (the "unfairness" of life), can become the central themes of *your* story.

In this idea of metanarrative, what would really matter in life at the end of the day, would be what *you* think about, what *you* talk about, what *you* live for. This is *your* adventure, and that's what gives it value! It becomes the justification of all that you want or don't want, and your source of identity. Why? Because if your *story* is important, you must be too. In the world of American publishing, the Choose Your Own Adventure genre of fiction has sold 250 million copies of its over 200 titles. Directing the outcome of others' lives is apparently a popular pastime. However, choosing to decide how to end the Abominable Snowman out of 28 possible choices is one thing. Determining whether you have any value in the universe is quite another matter.

This way of thinking is like *The Truman Show* 2.0, where you're not only Truman, but the script writer as well. And instead of the world watching you on TV, they can find you on Facebook and follow you on Twitter. In an era of limitless bandwidth, electronic toys beyond imagination, and the social networking power to amass a global audience from your bedroom overnight, this paradigm on the question of narrative has a horde of investors. And why shouldn't it? It's like taking your centripetal Adamic residue to the spa. I love Jean Twenge's assessment of this "Choose Your Own Illusion" approach to one's personal narrative:

American culture's focus on self-admiration has caused a flight from reality to the land of grandiose fantasy. We have phony rich people (with interest only mortgages and piles of debt), phony beauty (with plastic surgery and cosmetic procedures), phony athletes (with performance-enhancing drugs), phony celebrities (via reality TV and YouTube), phony genius students (with grade inflation), a phony national economy (with $11 trillion of government debt), phony feelings of being special among children (with parenting and education focused on self-esteem), and phony friends (with the social networking explosion).[1]

The "Chart Your Own Adventure" story generator, upon closer scrutiny turns out to be the twenty-first century version of Bobby McFerrin's 1988 mindless chart-topping hit, *Don't Worry, Be Happy*. Someone should have told Koheleth about this option thirty centuries ago. If they had, Ecclesiastes would likely have begun with, "Happy, Happy, Everyone can be happy." For some reason, I'm having trouble thinking how to spin this for the refugees in Darfur or the people living in Buffalo County, South Dakota where the per capita income is slightly over $5,000. Or, how to tell it to the mom & pop businesses that never recovered from lost revenue from the BP oil spill on the Alabama coast? As for me, looking into the eyes of a 5-year old Guatemala orphan rescued from the nightmare of sexual abuse, or those of a 30-year old former student who's wife dropped over dead in a doctor's office, I can't picture myself telling them it was time to write a new chapter in *their* adventure. For those of us who've lived a while, we realize life isn't something you accessorize to suit your circumstances like your iPhone. Sure, life *may* be adventurous at times. But, at other times it can be tortuous. And during those trying times, you don't get to choose much, especially how you want it all to unfold.

Fortunately, there's a third possibility regarding this idea of narrative. It's the suggestion that there really *is* a metanarrative, a single, grand Story that makes sense of all of life as we know it. A Story worth knowing. A Story worth retelling. This was the hope for Samwise Gamgee in *The Two Towers*, when all other hopes were gone that because there *were* such stories, he and Frodo might be *in* one:

> I know. It's all wrong. By rights we shouldn't even be here. But we are. It's like in the great stories, Mr. Frodo. The ones that really mattered. Full of darkness and danger, they were. And sometimes you didn't want to know the end. Because how could the end be happy? How could the world go back to the way it was when so much bad had happened? But in the end, it's only a passing thing, this shadow. Even darkness must pass. A new day will come. And when the sun shines it will shine out the clearer. Those were the stories that stayed with you. That meant something, even if you were too small to understand why. But I think, Mr. Frodo, I do understand. I know now. Folk in those stories had lots of chances of turning back, only they didn't. They kept going. Because they were holding on to something.

What if there really *is* A single Story that has meaning, because it has a plot and because it has an Author? And what if, because a story's only as old as the

1 Jean M.Twenge and W. Keith Campbell. *The Narcissism Epidemic: Living in the Age of Entitlement*. (New York: Free Press, 2009), 4.

one who creates it, that this one is Eternal? What if this story is *so* grand that it is completely inclusive? A story that reaches so far back behind the curtain of the past, that it fades into the mists of what can be known, but also passes through the present into a future that extends beyond death. What if it's so expansive, it has "room" for everything and everyone? A place for good and evil, for tsunamis and dew, a place for Alzheimer's and adolescence, childbirth and stillbirth, celebrities and outcasts. And what if this story were completely adequate yet still not exhaustive? What if it provided enough answers to keep me sane, but not enough to make me proud? And what if you discovered that you were *made* for a Story like this? That your own purpose was inseparably intertwined with the plot of this Story, because your design fit the fabric of the tale. Wouldn't you want to *know* this Story? And better yet, what if you could *join* a Story like this? Wouldn't you sign-up?

Typically, this would be the point where a writer would pivot into a rich section to satisfy all the anticipation I created in that last paragraph. But I can't. At least not yet. You need to know something at this juncture of our journey that is as almost as important as the Story itself. It's this: the whole *notion* of narrative is receding into the mists of history as I write. By the time most of you reading this are my age, textbooks will be a term associated with the *archives* of American history. But not used to study it. Cursive will have become a lost alphabet left to researchers and paleographers.[1] Books like the one you're holding will be, to your children, what phonograph records were to mine. Most tragic will be the near loss of narrative itself. We are at the precipice of creating a world made up of the very random dots we currently are desperately seeking to connect. Nicholas Carr's assessment of this inevitability is clear. Listen to his appraisal of Google's goal to digitize the world's books, taken from "The Church of Google," a chapter in *The Shallows*:

> But Google, as a supplier of the Web's principal navigational tools, also shapes our relationship with the content that it serves up so efficiently and in such profusion. The intellectual technologies it has pioneered promote the speedy, superficial skimming of information and discourage any deep, prolonged engagement with a single argument, idea, or narrative. "Our goal," says Irene Au, "is to get users in and out really quickly. All our design decisions are based on that strategy."[2]

Carr, in speaking of an unintended consequence of Google's obsession to make all knowledge searchable, also indirectly predicts the death of narrative:

> To make a book discoverable and searchable online is also to dismember it. The cohesion of its text, the linearity of its argument or narrative as it flows through scores of pages, is sacrificed.[3]

His assessment of Google should be extremely disconcerting to us Chris-

---

1 As of this writing, 46 states have adopted the Common Core Standards, a set of educational guidelines. Teaching cursive is *not* among them. (http://articles.cnn.com/2011-08-10/living/handwriting.horror_1_cursive-teaching-handwriting-love-letter?_s=PM:LIVING)

2 Carr, 156.

3 Ibid., 165.

tians who maintain that life is both purposeful and linear. We believe that there was a beginning, and there will be an end to life as we know it. That there is, in the biblical vernacular, a "present life," and a "life to come." And, even more important, that there is unbroken continuity between the two. And this is the very fabric of narrative. But Larry Page, co-founder of Google will never think about narrative, because he believes the human brain, instead of a masterpiece of Yahweh, is a hard drive made of meat. At least that's what it sounds like in this excerpt from a 2007 keynote speech to the American Association for the Advancement of Science:

> My theory is that, if you look at your programming, your DNA, it's about 600 mega-bytes compressed, so it's smaller than any modern operating system, smaller than Linus or Windows... and that includes booting up your brain, by definition. So your program algorithms probably aren't that complicated; [intelligence] is probably more about overall computation.[1]

Even the intrusion of digital readers like Kindle, Nook, and the iPad threaten to push the narrative into obscurity. At least author Stephen Johnson thinks so:

> I fear that one of the great joys of book reading—the total immersion in another world, or in the world of the author's ideas—will be compromised. We all may read books the way we increasingly read magazines and newspapers: a little bit here, a little bit there.[2]

Carr calls this approach to reading, which Google provides in broad band-width at high speed, the "strip mining of 'relevant content' [which] replaces the slow excavation of meaning."[3] Without realizing it, Carr is addressing the enormous principle that meaning depends on narrative. And what he is asserting about books, I believe is true about life.

So, here we are, face to face with the very real challenge of competing and defeating options regarding the issue of life having a narrative, and a purpose. It's not automatic. It's a choice. But, it also has a "default" setting, like Microsoft products. Each of us *has* to have a story, and, it's either going to be my own, or someone else's. And, *who* that "someone else" is, really matters. If I don't pursue the One Story, I'm left with *my* own CYOA, or someone else's. It's that simple. And that serious.

To complicate matters, we are also living when the *idea* of narrative, much less its value, is quietly being kidnapped. And, by the looks of it, there will be no ransom demands any time soon. These scenarios are cause for alarm; at the very least, attentiveness and alertness. But, what is even more distressing to me is that all the alarms about narrative's death by neglect are sounding from the secular culture. We Christians seem to be too preoccupied updating our Face-book profiles, downloading books to our Kindle, or putting wireless networks and flat panel TV's in our churches, to notice. And if that weren't nasty enough,

1 Cited in Carr, 172.

2 Cited in Carr, 103.

3 Ibid., 166.

we don't even *think* in terms of narrative when it comes to our faith. Why? Because of our mistaken understanding of the Bible that *contains* the One Story in the first place.

The Hole Truth Is Not The Whole Truth

One of my former students is now around thirty. A seminary grad, he is presently a husband, father, and pastor of a small church in Northeast Alabama. We are also close friends. I respect him for *where* he is, and who he has become. His tiny congregation is nestled near the convergence of the Alabama-Georgia-Tennessee junction, near the tail of the Appalachians. Very few people would recognize the name of the town that is home to his tiny flock. But, millions of Americans know of the region, thanks to our obsession with Reality TV. The area is called Sand Mountain. It has become legendary for two reasons, both the work of the media. Unfortunately, because of this exposure, "infamous" would likely be the adjective du jour attached to the region. At least to most outsiders, although for some who live there or visit, the infamy is a drawing card.

That's because the area close to the church has also been christened "Meth Mountain." It was the focus of a 2008 special episode of "Intervention." The show, an A&E's reality-show-posing-as-documentary, features addicts and their families wrestling with the traumas associated with drug abuse and intervention. It's there, and it's a serious issue. My young pastor and friend has had to face it himself, dealing with people he has grown to know and love in the area who for one reason or another have found themselves or those they love in a fatal attraction with either dealing or doing this drug. While it's an obvious attraction for some folks, it's unlikely "Meth Mountain" will show up on a TripAdvisor.com search.

The second reason Meth Mountain, and the surrounding areas have been in the nation's spotlight, is owed to Dennis Covington's 1996 book, *Salvation on Sand Mountain*. In this piece of investigative journalism, Covington writes about an extended stay in the Sand Mountain area, and his introduction to the Church of God With Signs Following. The unusual name for the church belies an abbreviated embodiment of a disputed text[1] in Mark's Gospel, which had become the signature feature of its worship, and a criminal case involving the pastor and his murdered wife:

> And he said to them, "Go into all the world and proclaim the gospel to the whole creation. Whoever believes and is baptized will be saved, but whoever does not believe will be condemned. And these signs will accompany those who believe: in my name they will cast out demons; they will speak in new tongues; they will pick up serpents with their hands; and if they drink any deadly poison, it will not hurt them; they will lay their hands on the sick, and they will recover." —**Mark 16:15–18**

Because of Covington's book, "snake-handling" is synonymous with Sand Mountain. The book, still in print, was nominated for a national award and put Sand Mountain on the National Registry of Places to Talk About But Never Visit. That's probably because some might recommend *not* going anywhere with such a close connection between cooking crystal meth and messing with rattlesnakes. You wouldn't have to twist *my* arm too far to get me to join that reticent retinue. Avoiding the obvious, I want to briefly return to this church's founding theology, and the actual text that theology is built upon. Because, in this rural setting where rattlesnake poison and crystal meth get along like second cousins, this church's theology reveals an error just as prevalent in churches that have Purell dispensers in their lobbies instead of rattlers on their altar.

The Church of God With Signs Following could be the poster child for "Adventures in Missing the Point," when it comes to the Bible. But, they also serve as representatives of a larger tendency that characterizes much of Christianity in the U.S. Now, don't jump immediately to the snake handling part, because that's merely a result, not the cause. Lots of churches have their own version of "snake handling." Misuse, neglect of scholarship, and intentional proof-texting by religious leaders, have been used to justify things that are just as serious, although they're not quite as spectacular. It might lead to a rock-climbing wall in the 24/7 Youth Complex, a refusal to use instruments in worship, or spending more money on flowers than missions. The most glaring error on Sand Mountain had less to do with the snakes in the cages than it did with the preacher in the pulpit.

The text in Mark speaks of snake handling, poison, and healings. That's obvious. But, the opening statement, which is the context for all that follows, was absent from the preacher's teaching, because at the end of the day, his was a "Chart Your Own Adventure-Christian Edition." He either didn't know the Bible, or he knew how to *use* the Bible to substantiate what *he* wanted all along. And, for any personal, self-generated version of The Story, the Bible is a vital ingredient. Even if you're abusing it more than using it. Let's face it, the Bible has been used to justify everything from castrating slaves to bombing Iraq, not to mention constructing larger buildings with elaborate furnishings. Of course,

---

1 Many biblical scholars consider Mark 16:9-20 an unauthentic later addition to the Gospel of Mark. The two main reasons are: (1) it does not appear in some of the oldest existing witnesses, and (2) it is reported to be absent from many of the Church Fathers' writings.

it has also been the impetus to launch sacrificial efforts of mercy and redemption. I've not lost sight of that. But, being able to tag a Bible verse onto a vision or movement doesn't automatically authenticate it, any more than affixing a postage stamp to an armadillo will get it from Little Rock to Newark.

Even in Mark's account (assuming for the sake of argument that it *is* authentic), Jesus' command is clear, and unequivocal: "Go into all the *world* [the nations], preach the gospel, and make disciples." The rest of what follows is a *description* of what those who "go" might experience, not a *prescription* for what they should do if they decide *not* to go. It's significant that at the Last Supper, when Jesus told his apostles to do what he had just done (wash each others' feet), he was holding a towel, not a viper. Encountering snakes while "going," is very different from staying home and collecting them. Jesus is talking about snakes on the path of obedience to the Abrahamic mission, *not* those stored in boxes in the basement of the church. If you follow the narrative in Acts, all these things happened to the Apostle Paul, except drinking poison. And, using Paul's experience as an illustration, Jesus is clearly referring to his apostles being protected from those seeking to extinguish the light of the message of reconciliation, not serving up an arsenic latte during worship. What we do *with* the Bible is always a product of what we think *of* it. Sometimes it results in snakes on the altar, other times it results in treadmills in the Family Life Center. The one thing these misrepresentations all seem to have in common, though, is that the gaze of onlookers is directed to people and things, instead of Yahweh. A church full of people fondling snakes is just a twisted version of American Idol, not a modern expression of the Apostle John on the island of Patmos. Whenever people are drawn to us, our architecture, our pulpit, or even our worship, something's wrong with our theology in practice. And you can always tell where our attention is fixed. Just listen to what we talk about. As we swim deeper into the waters of narrative and purpose, we need to attempt to get the story straight on the Story. And that has to do with what we really *think* about this marvelous book in our hands, the Bible.

As Christians, we are quick to assert the Scriptures to be the Truth of God. A claim that's getting tougher to defend and more difficult to discuss, in our postmodern world where the category of truth itself is under siege. Some of that conflict is the inevitable consequence of living in the modern, globalized *kosmos,* which by nature is opposed to God. But, another reason the Christian understanding of truth has lost its place at the table in the public square, may also be traced to our understanding of truth generally, and how we relate it to the Bible specifically.

Three Takes On Truth

Truth is an ancient and complex subject, garnering its own discipline in the larger field of Philosophy, known as epistemology. And although I am an admirer from a distance, and have a friend who's so astute in it, that talking to him is like chasing a jet, I make no claim to be a philosopher. Therefore, I suspect what follows will surely disappoint some of you, although I would indulge your patience, and ask that you try to see this section in the larger context of the narrow context of this book.

I want to suggest that truth is tripartite, not a solitary thing. What I mean is that it has three different facets or "faces" by which it presents itself to us and the world. The first, for those of us who still believe it's a valid category, truth is *propositional*. It consists of words that have meaning. It depends on the rules of grammar and logic to make sense, and to be made sense of. Usually, it is either true or false. I am counting on this being true as I write, anticipating that you will know what I actually mean by the words I am putting into print. The propositional nature of truth is vital for meaningful communication, whether it's at a Middle East Peace gathering, or a Boy Scout Eagle ceremony. For believers, it means that there's a valid place for evangelism and apologetics, the presentation of the message of reconciliation, and the defense of truth in the face of error. Truth as proposition is certainly vital for us Christians. Even those who can't spell epistemology, are dependent on this aspect of truth. And those who *deny* truth's relevance depend on this property of language to tell us so, as J. I. Packer so cleverly points out:

> It is the nature of truth to be public; that is to say, what is true for anyone is true for everyone. Granted, some today dispute this. Popular post-modernism has recently caused a stir by seeming to affirm that there is no such thing as public truth, only personal, private truth that differs for each individual. But, if this affirmation itself is offered as public truth, it can only be true by being false, and thus refutes itself. If it is offered as the personal truth of the offerer, there is no reason why anyone who already has a different idea of truth should take any notice of it.[1]

The propositional nature of truth has been a mainstay in education and learning from the days of Adam to the present. Even the serpent questioned the very meaning of the command God had given our ancient parents, with the words, "Did God actually say...?". There is a strong connection made in the Fall narrative between obeying and disobeying the *words* of God. They were held accountable for their sin because they *knew* what God had said, *and* what He meant by it. The Abrahamic blessing and the mission it entailed was dependent upon instruction, which was dependent upon this aspect of truth.[2] In short, we need words, and we need their meaning to remain constant between people. More important, and more relevant to the intention of this book, is the fact that truth is vital to the notion of *narrative* when God is the author. In a sense, reality is simply life as God "sees" it. And truth can be understood as His *description* of what He "sees," past, present, and future. And, it's His choice regarding how lucid or fuzzy that description is. That means that truth, in its most basic sense, is itself a narrative—*the* Narrative. What is at stake in the arena of apologetics,

---

1 J. I. Packer, in *Grace And Truth in a Secular Age*. Timothy Bradshaw, Ed., (Grand Rpaids: Wm. B. Eermands, 1998), 245-46.

2 cf. Genesis 18:19

the defense of our faith, is really the question of competing narratives vying for the prize of "truth." Postmodernism's approach to truth is akin to Agatha Christie's approach to homicide in *Murder on the Orient Express,* in which all the suspects in a murder are guilty. In our modern case, truth is no longer allowed to be exclusive, so your "truth" is as good as my "truth." Under the disguise of being tolerant, this is really being so open-minded that your brain falls out. Truth is propositional. It's either true or it's not true.

But, truth is also *incarnational*; something that, unfortunately, we have tended not to emphasize since the turn of the twentieth century. This means truth not only includes words that can be validated by logic and history (i.e., propositional), truth can also be *seen* and authenticated by observation. In fact, in cases where propositional truth (words) and incarnational truth (lifestyle) communicate conflicting messages, it is always the propositional side of truth that loses. Jesus understood the fragile marriage of these two forms of truth. In his amazing prayer after the Last Supper, he implied that the *kosmos* would be justified in denying his own identity, purpose, and mission, if the lives of his followers (*including us*), were characterized by disunity:

> I do not ask for these only, but also for those who will believe in me through their word, that they may all be one, just as you, Father, are in me, and I in you, that they also may be in us, so that the world may believe that you have sent me.   —John 17:20–21

This visible, verifiable aspect of truth is a quiet, but clear facet of the Incarnation itself. John's Gospel begins in a radial fashion, unlike the other three. No genealogies, no birth narratives, no angels and shepherds, no manger. It's a veritable wasteland of fodder for children's Christmas pageants, but a treasure trove for understanding the nature of truth in the plan of God. His Gospel opens introducing us to the preexistent Son, whom he describes as the eternal "word," the *logos*. This "word" was in an intimate relationship with Yahweh, the Father. But, he left that "face-to-face" relationship to enter another one of a very alarming nature. He took on flesh and "moved into the neighborhood" of the children of Adam, in the words of Eugene Peterson.[1] Or, reaching back to the other book in our Bibles that opens with, "In the beginning..." we see the "Potter" of Genesis 2 who created the human race, in a very sobering sense, has become a "pot" in John 1. A scandal to the first century Jewish mind, and a conundrum to all who have lived since,[2] including me!

But, the writer of Hebrews draws us back to a second quality of truth, something we seem to have forgotten in our infatuation with its propositional nature. He tells us that Yahweh was *speaking* in the Incarnation, not just reconciling and redeeming. The Incarnation was more, much more, than the necessary first step for our sins to be forgiven. It was the final, most majestic, and most

---

1 cf. John 1:14, The Message

2 The dual nature of Jesus Christ, his humanity and deity occupied the minds of the best scholars in the 5th century at the Council of Chalcedon. It was decided the best way to understand this enigmatic reality was to posit that Jesus had two complete, but distinct natures existing in one person. It was known as the "hypostatic union."

thorough message from God we will get this side of the new heavens and earth.

> Long ago, at many times and in many ways, God spoke to our fathers by the prophets, but in these last days he *has spoken to us by his Son*, whom he appointed the heir of all things, through whom also he created the world.   —**Hebrews 1:1–2**

Yahweh was speaking *in* Jesus, not speaking *through* Jesus This was categorically different from what He had done earlier with the prophets. Jesus wasn't a prophet on steroids, he was *God in a body*. And, He was speaking on behalf of the Father, *about* the Father![1] All the descendants of Abraham (through Isaac) were also eagerly waiting for this information, even those only half-related.[2] The Samaritan woman at the well, during her life-changing encounter with Jesus, told him that when the Messiah arrived he would "tell us all things." Jesus said that day had arrived with him.[3] The "all things" they were waiting to hear, it would turn out, had to do with the one grand narrative, and the God who owned it. It had arrived. The Kingdom had come. That's why Jesus could say to Andrew that anyone who had seen him, had seen Yahweh![4] God in a body, truth in skin. No wonder they didn't get it! But, we're not the sharpest knives in the drawer either, when it comes to this living and variegated aspect of truth.

The incarnational nature of truth has strong implications for us today as well. Particularly when we realize that in a very real and mysterious sense, we have become *part of the message*, part of incarnational truth. A recurring idea that flows freely from the pen of Paul, is that we are all now part *of* the Story not mere responders to its offer of grace. This is true, because according to him, *we are the presence of Christ on earth*. He is still here, living his life through us.[5] We are his "body," through which Yahweh now completes what He began in the Incarnation. In the words of one author, "the incarnation is not over."[6] This involves our participation in the expansive idea known as redemption, which we will spend all of Part III unpacking. But is also involves our reinforcement or demolition of the "truth that is in Jesus," by the way we live.[7] Because the truth of the gospel is *both* propositional *and* incarnational in nature, and because propositional truth always is dismissed when it's not validated incarnationally, *we* become vital components of the gospel itself. The *spoken* message of recon-

---

1 John 1:18 *"No one has ever seen God; the only God, who is at the Father's side, he has made him known."* The phrase, "made him known," is the Greek word from which we get our English, exegesis, the "unpacking" or explanation of something, like a text of Scripture. John says here that Jesus was "exegeting" Yahweh. It doesn't get a whole lot richer than this, in this life.

2 The Samaritans in the Gospels were the descendants of an era of intermarriage between Jews and a gaggle of Gentiles imported into the region between Jerusalem and the Sea of Galilee by the Assyrians in the 8th century B.C.. The children from these unions were not only biracial, they were bi-spiritual, embracing paganism and Judaism (cf. 2 Kings 17:41). As a result of this and a long history of deceit and warfare, enmity between the Samaritans and orthodox Jews persisted to the first century and beyond.

3 cf. John 4:25-26

4 cf. John 14:9

5 cf. Galatians 2:20

6 Sweet, *Carpe Manana*, 26.

7 cf . Romans 2:24;

ciliation is rejected where the *living* message contradicts it. Paul hinted at this reality in a comment buried within an argument about his own credibility as an apostle, something challenged by a faction within the Corinthian believers:

> You yourselves are our letter of recommendation, written on our hearts, to be known and read by all. And you show that *you are a letter from Christ* delivered by us, written not with ink but with the Spirit of the living God, not on tablets of stone but on tablets of human hearts.   –2 **Corinthians 3:1–3**

In the esoteric world of Christian jargon, this is glibly known as a "testimony." And in the manner in which it typically is presented, it is a narrative of sorts, purportedly part of a grander narrative. Unfortunately, if my "testimony" is mostly about me, and in the end, *my* life or journey is the abiding memory of others; it's more of a CYOA with Jesus adding "juice" to my story. And, often it's a domesticated Jesus more suited for the manger than the Throne. If we don't take Jesus seriously, our "contribution" to the narrative discredits the gospel and what the *kosmos* believes about Jesus from watching us, as N. T. Wright so astutely points out:

> We want a "religious" leader, not a king! We want someone to save our souls, not rule our world! Or, if we want a king, someone to take charge of our world, what we want is someone to implement the policies we already embrace, just as Jesus' contemporaries did. But, if Christians don't get Jesus right, what chance is there that other people will bother much with him?[1]

Historically, especially since the rise of Fundamentalism in the early 1900's, we have been relatively weak on "doing" in our war to protect "believing."[2] I believe, however, the time has arrived for the propositional message of the gospel and its incarnational brother to be identified as fraternal *twins*, products of the same birth who appear different yet say the same thing. Unfortunately, this will not be easy for two reasons. The first is that propositional truth, is considered by most to be an only child, or at least an *elder* brother, and the third facet of truth is an unknown, distant cousin to most of us.

This third and nearly anonymous aspect of truth, one that we've addressed already, is that at its very core, truth is narrative. Not "narrative," as in fiction or nonfiction, where the genre determines whether a story it is actually true. That was the approach in the 1920's when the church essentially divided over this idea. This is really in the domain of propositions, whether they are true or false. And, that is the realm of apologetics. What I'm positing here, is that the very *nature* of truth, what it is in itself, is narrative. The implications of this are

---

1 Wright, *Simply Jesus*, 5.

2 Although it is beyond my intentions in this book, it is worth noting that, at its core, the Liberal-Fundamental controversy of the early 1900's raged around the reliability of Scripture. There was an informal parting of ways in which the "Liberals" walked away with "doing" and the "Conservatives" walked away with "believing." That divorce has yielded a plethora of problems for the modern evangelical church when it comes to finding a place for "deeds" in its theology. Combine this with the explosive growth of the popular view of the "any moment" Rapture, a Calvinist view of election, and a business model for the church, and you have the perfect storm for minimizing the involvement of Christians in the world, beyond a "four points and a prayer" genre of evangelism.

vast and varied, deserving a book of their own. But for my purposes, the one that intrigues me most, is that narrative has a unique type of *authority* that neither propositions nor incarnation can claim, though the authority of narrative depends on both of its twin cousins for its bite.

The authority of narrative demands an adherence to a storyline that appears to be linear. Ad libbing and deviations from the storyline can be hilarious, evidenced by the popularity of the often comical "out takes" at the end of movies. But, what we're talking about here is a little more serious than *Toy Story* 3. The obvious corollary from this, is that if there really is a metanarrative that comprises truth itself, there is no place for the CYOA approach to life. It is ludicrous to think of. Imagine you are watching a gripping semi-historic film like *War Horse,* and right in the middle of the movie, where the horse is imprisoned in barbed wire, a scene from *Terminator* 5 appears, and then just as quickly, the film returns to *War Horse.* You'd look around the theater like, "What was *that?*" Although both films portray combat, violence, good and evil, and have a plot, it just isn't right. You *know* it doesn't "fit." It's not "the way it's supposed to go." At that moment, you'd be experiencing the incredible authority of narrative, and its power to judge the "rightness" of things by the standard of whether they belong in the storyline. This is narrative's contribution to truth, but it's a stranger to most of us who live in the shadow of propositions and a vague recollection of incarnation.

These three components, propositions, incarnation, and narrative, all have a voice and should be allowed to speak into our understanding of the nature of truth itself. And because what we believe is *the* truth (i.e., *God's* Truth) is contained in the only record we have of it, the Scriptures, our "take" on truth will also color our view of the Bible itself.

The Bible As Truth

If my understanding of truth weighs-in heavily in the "truth as propositions" camp, the Bible will take on many of the qualities of a textbook. And because its authorship is divine, it is the source of *all* relevant truth. That is, it contains truth statements that can be used to judge other truth claims. Although I may profess that the Bible is the "Word of *God,*" my primary focus will be on the "Word" portion of that profession. An emphasis will be placed on exegeting, understanding, studying, preserving, and defending "Truth" as an epistemological category. Postmodernism, at its worst, is an enemy of this facet of truth, denying that it has any objective existence. The Bible becomes a sort of citadel of Truth that must be held, adhered to, and protected at all costs from the enemies of Truth who assail it and disregard its precepts or teaching. Christians frequently evaluate the culture using this model, and are incensed at the "unbiblical" way it lives and thinks. Scripture references are often cited to reveal improper thinking, conduct, and choices of those outside the faith. Using this approach to the Bible, believers are often held accountable to the *words* of the

Bible regarding marriage, parenting, drinking, giving, the age of the earth, etc. The emphasis here is on using the Bible's *content* as the standard regarding how to *think*. Developing a "Christian mind," one able to discern which ideas, world views, and behaviors are true or false, right or wrong, good or bad, is the goal of Christian education. Scholarship and systematic theology in particular, are viewed as paramount. A believer's responsibility to the Bible is to know it, study it, and *defend* it.

Stressing "truth as incarnation" renders the Bible a sort of Christian Handbook, or "Disciplopedia," telling believers how to *live*. This perspective on the Bible views the content of Scripture in a sort of "wisdom" mentality, with a focus on the *ideas* and "big picture" of the Bible instead of the words. A sort of forest versus trees mentality. But, the motivation laying behind this view is the critical importance of *doing* what the Bible teaches, not merely defending or accurately explaining what it says. This is much of the focus of what attracted the label of "Emergent Christianity" a few years ago. The just criticism they leveled against Evangelicalism is that it had ignored the clear teaching of Jesus and the Scriptures as a whole, to *live-out* the Incarnation, not just dissect it as a doctrine. This would involve loving and ministering to people, serving them, and being "present" in their pain. Seeking to "incarnate" Christ became the centerpiece. The credibility vacuum that had been created after decades of an imbalanced propositional emphasis made this reaction understandable. The propositions of the Bible lost their credibility because the *content* of the message-bearers often did not match the *life* of those carrying it. Brennan Manning, though not among the emergent cloister, has always stressed the *evidence* of intimacy with Christ over mere conversation about it:

> Sheer scholarship alone cannot reveal to us the gospel of grace. We must never allow the authority of books, institutions, or leaders to replace the authority of knowing Jesus Christ personally and directly. When the religious views of others interpose between us and the primary experience of Jesus as the Christ, we become unconvicting and unpersuasive travel agents handing out brochures to places we have never visited.[1]

One of the unfortunate things about many conservative responses to those within the emergent camp, is that they failed to *listen* to the critical voices because of the weak emphasis (even denial) of the importance of propositional truth. Scholar D. A. Carson, a critic of what deserved critical attention in the emergent movement, in his fair-handed critique of the "Emergent" Church, also recognized the danger of leaving out the incarnational nature of truth. *"In the realm of morality, often obedience is as foundational to understanding as is exegesis."*[2] When the incarnational aspect of truth is the primary focus, the emphasis shifts from *knowing* to *being*, evidenced by doing. This has become a very popular clarion call among the rising generation, weary of the "work-less,"

---

1 Brennan Manning, *The Ragamuffin Gospel*. (Sisters, OR; Multnomah Press, 2000), 45.

2 D. A. Carson, *Becoming Conversant with the Emerging Church: Understanding a Movement and Its Implications.*(Grand Rapids, Mich: Zondervan, 2005), 118.

nearly exclusive emphasis on believing. Books like Shane Claiborne's *Irresistible Revolution,* Tom Davis' *Red Letters,* Gabe Lyons' *The Next Christians,* and David Platt's *Radical,*[1] all exhort the Church to do the same thing; namely, to take seriously the *words* of Jesus. But, they mean we should *obey* them, not study or defend them. I find this ironic, considering that words have been the private property of the propositional camp for decades. In the truth-as-incarnation camp, the believers' responsibility is to know the Scriptures by studying them with an eye to obedience. But, more often than not, this too seems to lack the internal momentum to carry even the most dedicated disciples the distance. Veteran saint and sage Eugene Peterson so aptly points out why, and it has to do with the third facet of truth:

> We have grown up in a culture that urges us to take charge of our own lives. We are introduced to thousands of books that we are trained to use—look up information, acquire skills, master knowledge, divert ourselves... whatever. But use? Well-meaning people tell us that the Christian gospel will put us in charge of life, will bring us happiness and bounty. So we go out and buy a Bible. We adapt, edit, sift, summarize. We then use whatever seems useful and apply it in our circumstances; however we see fit. We take charge of the Christian gospel, using it as a toolbox to repair our lives, or as a guidebook for getting what we want, or as an inspirational handbook to enliven a dull day. But, we aren't smart enough to do that; nor can we be trusted to do that. The Holy Spirit is writing us into the revelation, the story of salvation. We find ourselves in the story as followers of Jesus. Jesus calls us to follow him, and we obey—or we do not. This is an immense world of God's salvation that we are entering; we don't know enough to use or apply anything. Our task is to obey—believingly, trustingly obey. Simply obey in a "long obedience."[2]

The third perspective on truth, seeing it as narrative, understandably views the Bible as a Story Book, *the* Story Book (although *not* a storybook). And, I suppose one can't be too critical, considering that nearly half of our Bible consists of narratives of one type or another. It might surprise you to learn that almost 60% of our *New Testament* is narrative. But, unlike a literary anthology, these stories are all related to, and dependent upon the same meta-Story for their ultimate meaning. For instance, the amazing love story found in the Book of Ruth centers around three characters, Naomi, her daughter-in-law, "Ruth the Moabitess," and an older man, Boaz. The story is full of intrigue, valor, suffering, and redemption. But, the author of Ruth, with a little help from his Publisher opens and closes his book with two invaluable pieces of historical information that catapult his story into a broad narrative sea. The story of Ruth opens in a manner worthy of a Tolkien epic, revealing its historical setting: *"In the time when the judges ruled..."* This was a time of darkness in the history of the Jews. It closes with a ten name genealogy that reaches back through Boaz to Judah, the progenitor of the Messianic line, and forward to King David, yet unborn. Matthew, a thousand years later will reach back into this story and weave it into a longer genealogy pointing to Yeshua, the real reason for all the names leading up to his.

1 See Bibliography.

2 Peterson, *The Pastor,* 248–49.

Instead of viewing the Bible as a long collection of propositions to be understood, preserved, and defended, or as a collection of instructions on how to live and treat others, this view sees the Bible as one, long, Story that has a beginning, an end, and most importantly, a storyline; a plot. Ruth was part of something much older and longer than she could ever know. And, that Story isn't over...yet. That also means the Books of Judges and Ruth have *everything* to do with *our* lives too, not just theirs. If the weight of that is beginning to settle on you, I have been successful...so far.

When someone we know or love has a "break from reality," and is living in a fantasy or delusional world of their own making, we are deeply troubled because we know that they are not living the way "they're supposed to." Sometimes we have to do more than feel bad. From time to time, out of options, money or strength, we are forced to institutionalize people like this. We medicate them. We monitor them. We deprive them of certain liberties. Some aren't ever allowed to be around children (pornographers, child molesters, etc.)

This all makes sense to us because of the "power" of narrative. If there really is a way that things are "supposed to be," then living or trying to live in contradiction to that is wrong. Not for propositional or incarnational reasons. But, because the presence of a storyline creates the shores within which everyone must float their craft.

As we close this chapter, if I say that not all truth is black and white, that statement should have a different shade of meaning to you now. True truth is polychromatic, a beautiful, yet unrelenting thing. I believe our apprehension and portrayal of truth must draw a wide enough circumference for its propositional, incarnational, and narrative nature to merge into the tapestry it is to the God whose existence frames it. It should come as no surprise then that our understanding of truth will shape our view of the Scriptures. If we favor one aspect of truth over another, or deny any, it will be reflected in our convictions about what the Bible *is,* and from there, what we *do* with it. We might launch out to change the world in Jesus' name, or sadly, just go buy some snakes.

"Let's Work Our Way Backwards"

James Baldwin's classic statement, *"Children have never been very good at listening to their elders, but they have never failed to imitate them,"* is as true now as it was when he wrote it. I was eleven then, and had never heard of him. As a matter of fact, the only black man I ever saw before college was Hank Aaron at a Milwaukee Braves game with my Boy Scout troop! As a man who's at "retirement age" (whatever that means), I've surely had opportunity to test this aphorism. My four children are a partial reflection of me (as I'm sure I wear my own father's imprint). I see it in many ways, now as adults in the early stages of creating a family system of their own. Our home was always characterized by laughter, creativity, hard work, and spontaneity. That last item, though, was the mosquito pond of irritation when there were six of us under the same roof. Changed minds, altered plans, forgotten chores, to mention a few of the existential gnats regularly buzzing around my Adamic residue. I'm not the last word on order myself. My closet resembles a place where clothes come to die or at least get lost. But, when it comes to going somewhere, whether it's a family vacation or a trip to Tortuga's, (the best pizza place on the planet), I have to man up. My family, especially the ones with the most estrogen, seem oblivious to the cumulative effect on the clock or the odometer, that the incremental additions or alterations have on our itinerary. Combine this with the fact that four out of six of us have *serious* issues with low blood sugar. Around 4:00 every afternoon, they may either become serial killers or manic depressives. This, combined with the " let's just..." additions to our schedule, family outings to eat can degenerate into a scene from *The Hunger Games!* Well, not really, but it can get pretty tense. At some point, in my efforts to keep peace, and protect my feelings, I came up with a rubric that has allowed us to realistically decide whether there was enough time, gas, or whatever, to *do* everything that was under consideration. It had to do with "working our way backwards" from our final destination to our first, using the time of day when we wanted or needed to actually *be* at the end of our journey. It simply meant approximating the time necessary to get from one thing to another, and keeping a running tally. Keep in mind, I don't do time management workshops when I'm not writing books, but I suspect my years as Chief Chemist forged an appreciation for the principle of contingency, that things depend on what preceded them, and shape what follows. So, "Let's work our way backward" is now both a family algorithm *and* a source of "smack" talk around the dinner table at holidays. My kids and their spouses have enjoyed much hilarity wielding this phrase, while rehearsing greatly "spiced" revisionist versions of their childhood. And I have to admit, it gets pretty, fall-off-the-chair, wet-your-pants sort of funny. And, because the rubric really works, it's become a staple in the war against chaos-theory when it comes to planning in our family. But, I believe it also has application in our study of our grand narrative, the Truth of God known as the Bible. So, let's work our way backwards, and begin at the end of the Story.

Discard your eager hopes of finally getting an answer to whether the beasts in Revelation 9 are weaponized horses, mutant insects, or purely figurative. I don't know, and neither do the guys who tell you they *do*. Sorry. Meanwhile, if you need a little hermeneutical relief, consider that the word "like" is used by John 9 times in four verses *trying* to describe their features. That means even John himself who *had the vision,* didn't have categories to make sense out of it all! So, if you get frustrated reading this book, be thankful you weren't him! It sounds like a bad acid trip to me. He most likely could never forget what he saw and didn't understand, yet was commanded to record. You and I only have to *read* about it.

As we begin at the end, I want to lay this before you to consider as we go there. The Revelation of John, as difficult as it for us twenty centuries later to make sense of, makes *no sense,* unless the Bible is one grand Story. Its content is one of the most powerful arguments we have that the Bible is a narrative. *Not* a textbook or a handbook. Imagine, as we move into this, that this is the only book of the Bible you have.

The first thing you encounter is the name of someone called "Jesus" who also has the attribution "Lord" attached to his name. Your dash lights should come on or at least flicker right here. In the first century, in a Romanized world, it was *illegal* to attribute the title "Lord" to anyone except the Emperor. Already we're on dangerous political footing. And, this "Jesus," you just don't know (unless you can draw in the four narratives where his name appears over 600 times). So, the last six words of book have no meaning at all, left alone. Moving five verses "ahead" (remember, that's backward), you run into someone with the nickname, "the root" that is a descendant of another person named "David." Again, no clue who David or this "root" are (unless you go to the books of Ruth and Isaiah). But, as I said, you don't have them. Moving "ahead" a little further you hit a triad of weird, paired descriptors: "Alpha and Omega," "first and last," and "beginning and end" which are obviously related, and point to someone.

But, again, you're out of luck (unless you go to Isaiah). Then comes a "Lamb," whom you will discover landed a lead role in this book, with 29 appearances. This one stumps you too (unless you go to John's Gospel and Peter's letters, to find out it's Jesus). Next, you run into a pair of phrases that sound alike, and are as equally confusing: the "book of life," and the "tree of life." Too bad you don't have Genesis and Exodus to provide some help. Moving "forward," you come to a veritable swamp of names, metaphors, and descriptions of a city. I'll list them, but remember, you have absolutely no idea who and what they are, or which, if any of them are significant, from this book.

There's this "holy city," which a couple verses "ahead" you'll discover has a name. It's called Jerusalem. Without knowing for sure, it *seems* like "12" is an important number, because it pops up nine times in the two chapters you are swimming in. For instance, there's 12 gates in this "holy city" as well as 12 foundation stones. That's not cause in itself to become anxious, except there are 12 people with names, called "apostles"(whatever that is), associated with each of the foundation stones, and a tribe with a name associated with each of the gates. And, to make matters more difficult, the tribes are all descended from a man whose name is given, as if that helps. It's "Israel." Now, I know this is cheating, but let's pretend there's somewhere to go for help (you know like your lifeline phone call in "Who Wants to Be a Millionaire?"). You would discover that "Jerusalem's" a popular place, showing up in over 800 times in 35 *other* books. And, you'd discover that it makes its first appearance under an alias known as Salem, in (you guessed it), Genesis. Its grown up name is "Jerusalem," which a book called Joshua provides. You would be led to the Gospel of Mark to learn what an "apostle" is, and as a bonus, get their names. Back to Genesis for the names of the twelves tribes, *and* the identity of Israel; he used to be "Jacob," a twin, and a person from whom you definitely would *not* want to buy a used chariot! A little confusion (curiosity?) is stirred in by the fact that 1,500 years separates the names on the stones and gates.

Whew, that was a workout! Moving a few chapters "ahead," you run into someone who apparently is pretty tight with the "Lamb." His name is Moses. It's the only time his name appears in the book, so you think you're done with him. At least until you discover it shows up a little fewer than 900 times in 30 other books, *and* the first time he hits the radar is 64 *books "later"* in the early part of Exodus. This is about 1,500 years *before* John! Seeking to make sense of something even more confusing, you learn that the "end" of our Story, has a chorus singing the "Song of Moses," *and* the "Song of the Lamb"!

I realize that this excursion was a little juvenile. Some of you more sophisticated types might have felt a little underwhelmed. But, I did this, tongue-in-cheek, to show that as believers, the book that provides us with so much hope in this life, has absolutely no comprehendible meaning apart from the rest of Scripture, *especially* the beginning of our Bible. It's no coincidence that the author of our last book of the Bible began the Gospel he wrote—the same time as Revelation—with the phrase that began the Jewish Scriptures, "In the beginning..." John got it. He understood that there was an unbroken plot line between what he and Moses had written. But do you know what he *didn't* do? He didn't write a 16-book fictional series about the *events* of this book, centered on an event that's not even *in* it! Instead, he did what all of us will do when we begin to understand the majesty of this Story, whose mere *ending* I just rehearsed for us:

> I, John, am the one who heard and saw these things. And when I heard and saw them,
> I fell down to worship at the feet of the angel who showed them to me.
> **–Revelation 22:8**

He worshipped. And, as we'll see in the chapters ahead, so did Paul every time he pondered on paper what this thing we call the Story really entailed. It's what you and I are going to do at the end of the story too. We, and everything in heaven, on earth, and under the earth.[1] Awe, and on-your-face-before-the-throne worship. That's what has *really* been "left behind" when it comes to understanding the place of prophecy in the overall Story of God. But more on that later.

Stuck In The Present

We post-Edenic children of Adam seem to resist looking back too far, though our hearts point us to eternity, according to our friend, Koheleth.[2] The very idea of a Story that points *back* to the beginning of time, and forward into an unknown eternity is somewhat frightening. And, with the advent of Twitter and Instagram, our lives are mired in the ever slippery present, which seems increasingly difficult to manage as it slides into the past even before we can process or enjoy it. We can't seem to remember yesterday or even *think* about tomorrow. How can we possibly make time to ponder an ancient past or the eternal future? But, this antipathy isn't a byproduct of technology. It seems to be a universal quality of all of us who trace our family tree to the same Garden. Eviator Zerubavel, in his study of how different cultures "map" time, found that only 9 in 191 countries formally mark on their national calendars any events over the eight centuries between 680-1492.[3] We Christians aren't much better, although we claim to own the oldest Story on earth. *Our* "church calendar" goes back 4,000 years to Ur of the Chaldeans, or even further if we penetrate the Garden and go back to Adam. But unfortunately, it is rare for any non-liturgical church to *follow* a church calendar instead of merely *publish* a current one. And most references to Protestant church history in our churches only point back as far as the Reformation in the sixteenth century. As if that's when genuine Christians first appeared. There's much in *our* Jewish heritage worth keeping (like the Mosaic celebration that we've reduced to wafers and grape

---

1 cf. Philippians 2:8-11

2 *"He has made everything beautiful in its time. Also, he has put eternity into man's heart, yet so that he cannot find out what God has done from the beginning to the end."* (Ecclesiastes 3:11)

3 Cited in Jackson, *Distracted*, 224-25.

juice). There's nothing in the Jewish festival of Passover that is hostile or con-
tradictory to any of our theology as Christians. Why we didn't adopt the whole
celebration instead of the Pauline redaction of it in 1 Corinthians to bread and
wine, has always puzzled me. But, speed and efficiency are the yin and yang of
the modern world. So, I won't be surprised, if a communion drive-thru finds its
way onto the architectural drawings for a suburban church.[1] We have drifted far
from any connection to this vital part of His Story, which is *our* history. The creation of Israel out of a horde of Egyptianized Jews is a miracle that even Yahweh
seems proud of.[2] The Exodus event, which Yahweh built into their religious and
agricultural calendar, as well as their hymnal,[3] was just the *beginning* of the very
tangible and visible fulfillment of a promise He made to a wandering Chaldean
named Abram. But, because of what it represented, it is also one of the most
dramatic and definitive events in our *own* spiritual heritage. According to mis-
siologist Christopher Wright,

> The exodus was not a movement from slavery to freedom, but from slavery to cov-
> enant. Redemption was for relationship with the redeemer, to serve his interests and
> his purposes in the world.[4]

Passover was Yahweh's means to guarantee that His covenant people would
never forget their *corporate* history, of which their own *personal* history and
meaning were dependent. Even the Feast of Booths, which is also celebrated
by practicing Jews, is linked to the Exodus. The feasts of Purim and Hanukkah
have historical roots in the 5th and 2nd centuries before Jesus. As believers, we
have abandoned, or at least neglected, this essential view of the continuity of
redemptive history. The story of Israel is an indispensable prelude of the story
we find ourselves in. Their history is our history. It doesn't matter whether they
embrace that. The reason this notion of The Story should be vital for us, is that
it will become increasingly difficult to preserve *or* present a true and intact gospel in a culture that devalues genuine narrative. The Story will never Tweet. Of
that I'm sure.

It is worth pointing out another thing that is unmistakable at the *end* of The
Story that somehow has fallen out of our biblical suitcase since the first century.
John makes it indisputably clear where The Story ends. It is *not* in "heaven."
Instead, the drama of amazing grace ends where it started, in a garden *on earth*.
The reason I need to camp here will be abundantly clear by the end of the book.
For now let me say our misunderstanding of this tiny piece of biblical truth is
responsible for a multitude of erroneous thinking, conscious and unconscious.
It affects the way we share the gospel, and how we talk about eternity. Usually,

---

1 As outlandish as this sounds, I am at the place where I believe nearly anything is possible in the world of
ecclesiastical creativity. Perhaps the final straw for me was the introduction of ATM's (Automatic Tithing
Machines) into some churches! See: www.securegive.com/

2 *cf.* Deuteronomy 4:34

3 cf. Psalm 78

4 Wright, *Mission of God's People,* 101.

we get it wrong. Talking about "spending eternity in heaven" is not right. That's *not* where The Story ends. There's a ton to be said about what happens *after* death but *before* the resurrection. Our Story ends *after* the resurrection, and we're on a "new earth" in resurrected bodies! Jeremiah will be there, Luther, Adam (I really want to whine to him about the weeds and fire ants in my yard!), Saint Francis, and the "cloud of witnesses" listed in Hebrews 11. Getting this right is *huge!* It transforms how we share the gospel. But more important, it shapes how we live in the present. Paul made it perfectly clear that there is an unbroken cause and effect relationship between this life and the next:

> Have nothing to do with irreverent, silly myths. Rather train yourself for godliness; for while bodily training is of some value, godliness is of value in every way, as it holds promise for the present life and also for the life to come. The saying is trustworthy and deserving of full acceptance. For to this end we toil and strive, because we have our hope set on the living God, who is the Savior of all people, especially of those who believe.
> –1 Tim. 4:7–10

It's of special interest to me, that "godliness" was a topic that Paul addressed only to Timothy and Titus, two pastors who were teaching those in their churches.[1] The pursuit of godliness was to be the passion of all believers. They needed to be taught that, and how to cultivate it. The modern idea that the experience of all Christians in eternity will be identical, has no grounding in the Bible. In fact, the opposite is taught. Jesus' teaching on "storing up treasure in heaven" was contrasted to hoarding it here.[2] But, it is meaningless unless it's true. And if it is a fact, then some folks have treasures and some folks don't. Jesus' parables about the talents end with different "rewards" for varying efforts.[3] Don't immediately jump to "works" or "legalism" here. I'm not talking about the entrance exam. I'm simply saying though it would be pleasant to think that the eternal state for believers is an equal-opportunity-provision, it isn't. Am I saying it makes a difference how I live now, even as a Christian? Let me make this completely clear: Yup!

Paul's teaching of the Corinthians makes it very clear that our lives as believers will be "tested by fire," based on whether we've spent our energy for The Story or for ourselves. Some folks will still be "in," but they'll smell like ashtrays.[4] Well, that's not quite what he says, but you get the idea. I think we've assumed or been taught that after judgment, we all sort of mosey on into "heaven," find our mansion, then go play golf, or whatever we loved doing on earth. Some imagine that eternity will be a socialistic sort of deal, with everyone getting an equal share. Sorry, that's not the case! Though I don't fully understand it, it doesn't work that way. I thought something like this for a long time myself. But, after reading and studying my Bible more carefully, I discovered that

---

1 cf. 1 Timothy 2:2; 3:16; 4:7–8; 6:3, 5–6, 11; 2 Timothy 3:5; Titus 1:1

2 cf. Matthew 6:19-20

3 cf. Matthew 25:14-30

4 cf 1 Corinthians 3:10-15

it was a dangerously popular error. The seriousness and pervasiveness of this line of thinking, was illustrated by the guests and their comments on the 2005 ABC Barbara Walters Special on "Heaven." She interviewed Ted Haggard, the President of the National Association of Evangelicals, Rev. Dr. Calvin Butts, the pastor of New York's Abyssinian Baptist Church, Imam Feisal Abdul Rauf, the founder of the American Society For Muslim Advancement, and Rabbi Neil Gillman, a professor of philosophy at New York's Jewish Theological Seminary. Her last guest was the Dali Lama, considered by some to be the reincarnation of Buddha.[1] An all-star lineup for an interview on any network, or TEDS talk for that matter.

They were each given the opportunity to talk about "heaven" from the perspective of their religious faith. Jill and I watched the entire show. I thought she would have to call 911 to care for her husband before it was over. The Christian voice was so far from the Scriptures, we were incredulous. Butts said that heaven was a fourth dimension. The Bible does teach that God is in "heaven" until the last judgment. But still, "heaven" *isn't* the location of the end of The Story, no matter which way you slice it. And *neither* of the Christians pointed that out. One of them even said heaven was our ultimate "home." It was where we were going to spend eternity. In the interview with Walters, I do not recall a single reference to Jesus in his comments. And, he was given the most airtime. The Jewish voice at least mentioned the resurrection of the body and the final judgment. But, the Muslim scholar won the prize for the most statements that agreed with Scripture: a cause and effect continuity between this life and the next, a *physical* existence that included things we do in this life, no sin, and a final judgement. Obviously, he veered "off track," basing one's destiny on their behavior instead of grace. And the really big issue, as Timothy George so aptly puts it in the title of his book, *The Father of Jesus is Not the God of Mohammad,* he got the very identity of God wrong. I'm guessing *that* makes a difference when it comes to eternity. The Dali Lama was the most likable and "real" of those interviewed. Both Jill and I agreed that if we'd tuned-in to these interviews with no spiritual background, but some spiritual hunger, right now we'd both be Buddhists, not Christians.

But for our purposes, it's a travesty that the Evangelical emissary for The Story tells millions of viewers—most of them unbelievers—that living to "spend eternity in heaven" is the goal of every Christian. Even when the Bible says just the opposite! Not just that "heaven" *isn't* our destiny, but even more important, that's *not* what we're supposed to be living for. That is the Tourist identity on display, and on that night, it went viral. The new *earth* is where we'll we be when we're done doing what we're *living* for. Having a mistaken idea of "heaven" then, can make a huge difference back here on earth. It not only affects how we *live*, but also how we talk, when it comes to this Story. And, if we don't have

1 A synopsis of the show is here: http://abcnews.go.com/International/Beliefs/story?id=1374010&page=2#. T7RrQb8jW9Y

the *end* of the Story straight, most likely we've got the rest of it screwed up too, which we do. Because our Identity Ladder is Yahweh's way of fitting us *for* the Story, having The Story wrong will lead to us revising our identity to match *our* version of it. Which we do. Aren't you glad *you're* not God?

Here And Now — Here And Then

I want to wade into one final idea to wrap up our brief trip to the *end* of our Story before we close this chapter. It's a biblical theme that has the momentum to move us all the way back to Genesis via every book between. It's found in a passage in our "ending" book:

> And when the seven thunders had sounded, I was about to write, but I heard a voice from heaven saying, "Seal up what the seven thunders have said, and do not write it down." And the angel whom I saw standing on the sea and on the land raised his right hand to heaven and swore by him who lives forever and ever, who created heaven and what is in it, the earth and what is in it, and the sea and what is in it, that there would be no more delay, but that in the days of the trumpet call to be sounded by the seventh angel, the mystery [*mustērion*] of God would be fulfilled, just as he announced [*euaggelizō*] to his servants the prophets.
> —Revelation 10:4–7 [italics and brackets mine]

The book that closes our ancient, eternal Story uses two words that are essential for us to understand in the context of John's final words. They point us back to the beginning of the Story and give meaning to everything between. They are the words "mystery" and "announced," *mustērion* and *euaggelizō* in Greek. *Euaggelizō* is a member of a word family from which we derive our English word, "evangelism," the proclamation or announcement of the "good news." In our New Testaments, *euaggelizō* is synonymous with "preaching," particularly the preaching of the "good news." John tells us that Yahweh had "preached" a "mystery" to the prophets, and obviously He had done so *prior* to the days of Jesus. The combination of these two words at the *end* of the Story is very, very significant. Especially when we realize that "mystery" turns out to be Yahweh's favorite genre of literature, and that of his most prolific theologian, Paul of Tarsus. Preachers often tell us that in the Bible a "mystery" is something that was hidden, but has now been revealed. That's helpful, but only marginally, because it reveals to us what the Greek word *means*, but fails to inform us of what this "mystery" actually *is*. And it turns out that knowing that is the prerequisite to truly understanding this Story of which Revelation is the dramatic conclusion. To do that, we need to examine the reeducation of a rabid rabbi. A brilliant Benjamite Jew from Tarsus named Saul; the greatest "mystery" writer in the Bible.

New Eyes, Not Restored Sight

In the summer of 2007, I led a small team of eighteen on a short, but intense trip to an orphanage for girls in Monjas, Guatemala called Shadow of His Wings.[1] Shortly before our departure to return home, we had been dubbed, "The Extreme Team"! Because of prior involvement with the ministry there, and a deep love and respect for its Director, I pulled together a heterogeneous group of compassionate believing friends from four states for the task. Our mission: to do whatever the orphanage desperately needed done and had neither the manpower nor skill to do. Our team consisted of nurses, industrial designers, a contractor, two IT specialists, a dance teacher, a preschool teacher, a campus ministry leader, a recent seminary graduate, a medical software salesman, and a young man involved in a Catholic housing ministry in rural Appalachia. Three of the team were my twin daughters and Jill, and five were former students. The team custom-designed and built an entire office complete with free-hanging bookshelves, and semicircular desktops. They painted, preached, pulled electrical wire and CAT5 cable, taught dance, did basic medical hygiene workshops for house parents, and played with the orphans nightly. I taught the staff, house parents, and a few local pastors during the day. It was a once-in-a-lifetime trip where every person on the team met a need in the field, some which didn't arise until *after* we were there.

My attachment to this place was the fruit of my heart for its mission: the vision and dream of its Executive Director who had become a dear friend. I had met Joanne six years earlier when both of us were doing something different. I was in Peronia, Guatemala on my first trip out of the country. She was the liaison between the native host church and our team. During that trip, I had an epiphany while watching one. I was working with the construction crew, mixing concrete by hand on the ground, and carrying it up makeshift ladders in buckets to the second floor where we were pouring a new roof. I had tied steel

---

1 See; http://www.shadowofhiswingsorphanage.org

on that roof the previous two days. During one of our breaks, I decided to poke my head in on some of my other team members. They had setup a rudimentary eye clinic, which was essentially a dispensary of used eyeglasses from the States. Each pair of glasses had been cleaned and packaged with a label that had the prescription of the lenses on it. It was an impressive operation orchestrated by some folks who obviously knew what they were doing. On the wall, were two identical eye charts similar to the ones used in American offices, except instead of a series of letters of decreasing size, ours had a series of objects. For instance, instead of the enormous "E" that tops all U.S. charts, ours had a coffee cup, then a row with a smaller flower, bird, and so on. It was an ingenious system, relying only on a small handful of Spanish words to function, but able to provide a ballpark diagnosis on the patient's relative vision.

It just so happened that while I was there, an elderly woman was going through the final stages of her "exam," and was being fitted with a pair of glasses. The style was so dated that it was easy to understand why they were discarded. When they slipped the gaudy spectacles on her wizened face; she began to weep. She kept saying the same thing over and over, in Spanish. We had no idea what she was saying, but there was no doubting what she was feeling. She could *see*! For the first time in who knows how long, this dear woman could see. Someone's donated, outdated glasses, teacups on the wall, folding chairs for exam couches, and suddenly she could focus on what had been there all along. And from that day on, so could I.

I think that was the birth in my own heart of a burden for the compassion that must accompany the gospel. I saw, maybe for the first time that there was more to the "gospel" than four points and a prayer. There was more wreckage to be moved out of the road from that one fruit fiasco in the Garden than simply getting folks back in there. In the words of one scholar:

> The redemptive work of God through the cross of Christ is good news for every area of life on earth that has been touched by sin—which means every area of life. Bluntly, we need a holistic gospel because the world is in a holistic mess.[1]

So, I had a major adjustment in my own prescription that afternoon in a town that used to be a garbage dump. Like the man that was healed in John 9, I could say, "I was blind, but now I see." Jesus understood the dismal truth that some people with 20/20 vision can't see when it comes to certain parts of the Story,[2] and he continually found himself on the wrong side of the Law whenever he exposed it. Some don't see the Story clearly, others don't see it at all. That afternoon I was in the first group for sure. But twenty centuries ago, Saul of Tarsus was stuck in the second.

1 Wright, *Mission of God's People*, 110.

2 Jesus's encounter with a nameless man born blind occupies the entire 9th chapter of John's Gospel. It is really the story of a blind man and a blind mob. There are over 30 references or allusions to "seeing" in this story. And although there are 10 references to the blind man, there are nearly twice that many to the "blind" Pharisees. The elderly woman in Peronia was in group one, I was in group 2.

Paul Never Became A Christian

The story leading up to Saul's conversion was a big deal to Yahweh. Maybe more important than the conversion itself. At least, there's that possibility considering how much time we spend studying Paul and yet not "seeing" the relationship between the details of his conversion and the ministry it spawned. God seems to have gone out of His way to make sure that we understood not *that* it happened, but *how*. Paul's story is the only narrative in the Book of Acts that appears more than once. The beheading of James, the stoning of Stephen, even the events of Pentecost each get one detailed spot.[1] Paul's encounter with Yeshua on the road to Damascus is told *three times*. Once by Luke, the author, and twice more by Paul himself. Why put the same story in one book three times? As a veteran teacher of nearly 25 years, I know why *I* repeated certain things to my students, and I think you do too. Here's Luke's original account, which of course, he received from Paul because he wasn't there when it happened:

> But Saul, still breathing threats and murder against the disciples of the Lord, went to the high priest and asked him for letters to the synagogues at Damascus, so that if he found any belonging to the Way, men or women, he might bring them bound to Jerusalem. Now as he went on his way, he approached Damascus, and suddenly a light from heaven shone around him. And falling to the ground he heard a voice saying to him, "Saul, Saul, why are you persecuting me?" And he said, "Who are you, Lord?" And he said, "I am Yeshua [Jesus],[2] whom you are persecuting. But rise and enter the city, and you will be told what you are to do....Now there was a disciple at Damascus named Ananias. The Lord said to him in a vision, "Ananias." And he said, "Here I am, Lord." And the Lord said to him, "Rise and go to the street called Straight, and at the house of Judas look for a man of Tarsus named Saul,...So Ananias departed and entered the house. And laying his hands on him he said, "Brother Saul, the Lord Jesus who appeared to you on the road by which you came has sent me so that you may regain your sight and be filled with the Holy Spirit." And immediately *something like scales fell from his eyes*, and he regained his sight.   —**Acts 9:1-6, 10-11, 17–18**

A funny thing happened to Saul on the way to the persecution. Paul had a train wreck with Yahweh, the God he was zealously defending against the heresy that was spreading in Jerusalem. Little did he know, he would become its most potent diplomat. I think it's really important for us to walk through this encounter carefully, and with a little conjecture and some Scripturally-informed imagination, try to fill in the gaps. But, before we even leave the front steps, it's essential that you remove from your mind and vocabulary the notion that Saul "became a Christian" on this trip. Nobody "became a Christian" in the Book of Acts, in the sense that we mean it today. Saul was a Jew when he left Jerusalem, and he was still a Jew when he was hauled, blind, and deeply shaken into Damascus. And the man

---

1 cf. Acts Stephen's stoning *is* mentioned a second time, but not so much as a recollection of the event, as much as a testimony to Paul's zeal as a Jew. He shares is as part of his testimony before the Jews in Jerusalem, hoping to add credibility to his conversion.

2 (cf. Acts 26:12-180 In the words of Paul, when rehearsing the story of his conversion before King Herod Agrippa II, he informs us, *"I heard a voice saying to me in the Hebrew language..."* When Paul inquired who was speaking to him, Jesus would have responded in Hebrew, which would have been "Yeshua." In Greek, this is "Jesus."

who "led him to Christ," was also a Jew, as were all the people he fellowshiped with over the days that followed. Yet, if we read the complete account attentive to details, we have to say that in a sense, Saul *was* a Jew, and he *wasn't* a Jew. He was the same person, radically changed. And the change had less to do with his religious preference as it did his view of the Hebrew Scriptures. The important thing for us at the start, is that we do not overlay a twentieth century vocabulary and context over a first century narrative. We need to lock that hermeneutical misfit in his room, and keep him away from all our interpretations of the Bible. He's already wrecked enough havoc in our heads. For example, if every time you read the word "gospel" in your Bible, you think of a Four Spiritual Laws tract, or the Roman Road, you've fallen into this interpretive reversal. What is called the "gospel" in our Bible, as we will discover, is inseparable from the Story. And the Story, as we've seen from looking at just its *ending*, is a narrative that defies a PowerPoint reduction to four points and a prayer.

When I began to understand the centrality of the Story motif in Scripture, and look for its presence in the life and teachings of Paul, it was like making progress in an eye exam. You know what I mean, the rapid-fire litany of *"Which is better,* 1 *or* 2*?"* questions, while the optometrist rotates that gaudy sequence of rotating lenses on the road that eventually leads to your eyeglass prescription. Almost immediately, I began to grasp the nature of the radical transformation of Saul into Paul, the understandable fury he felt towards those who messed with "his gospel," and why he was so passionate about the temporary nature of Judaism. Although we have no record to substantiate it, I believe that shortly after this account in Acts, Paul never offered another sacrifice in the Temple, though he continued to frequent it.[1]

Combining Luke's narrative account, with his record of Paul's two recounts of his encounter with Yeshua that day on the road, a fuller (though incomplete)[2] version can be garnered, including a command to share this experience. But, in the opening account, which is actually more about Ananias, we are told that Saul was struck blind, and that he "regained his sight" when Ananias laid hands on him. What follows next is likely more complex than our quaint image of Ananias looking across the table at skin-contained malice and quaintly saying, *"Saul, Yahweh loves you and has a wonderful plan for your life! You need to invite Yeshua into your heart so you can spend eternity with him in heaven."* Instead, he repeated Yahweh's words to him, words that included kings, and Gentiles, and Jews, and pain. Saul's story is unique to the Bible,

---

1 There is a single reference to Paul making "an offering" in connection with a ceremonial purification ritual in Acts 21:26. However, the word employed there, *prosphora*, is not the word used for a blood sacrifice throughout the Book of Hebrews, *thusia*, which appears 15x.

2 It is clear from Luke 9:26-27, that when the early church refused to entertain the possibility that Saul had come to faith, Barnabas must have sought him out, and listened to his story. He not only risked his life in doing so, but also undoubtedly forged the bond of trust that would characterize their relationship for many years. In Luke's description of *Barnabas'* account of Saul's conversion, the events on the road as well as in Damascus are presented. He could have only gotten those from Saul. This incident provides a strong suggestion that there were many times when he would share this "testimony."

both in its explanation, and I believe, its intended result. This is the only account of literal blindness in Acts, compared to nearly 50 references to it in the Gospels, and 11 events of its healing. However, there is a *second* reference to blindness being healed in Acts, and it also involves Paul. This second reference provides added insight into the obviously intentional *manner* in which Saul's healing occurred. We are told that "something like scales fell from his eyes" as he was restored to sight. We don't know whether Ananias is the one who saw them or if Saul *felt* them leave his eyes, or both. We don't know whether they persisted or dissolved like manna. None of that information is there for us, as much as we'd love to know it. But, "scales" did fall, of that we are sure. Why "scales"? No one in the Gospels experienced this kind of healing. And an even more important prior question is, why *blindness?* Blindness and scales. Why not a vision and its illustration, like Peter on the roof in Joppa? Or, how about an angelic appearance during prayer like Cornelius, the one Peter was called to teach in Joppa in the story that immediately follows Saul's conversion?[1] I believe that answer comes from the lips of Paul himself 17 chapters later, while as a prisoner in Caesarea, he recounted the Damascus Road incident to King Herod Agrippa II. Here, Paul's description of his dialogue with Yeshua on the road is a much-expanded version of the story; twice the size of the previous two combined:

> And when we had all fallen to the ground, I heard a voice saying to me in the Hebrew language, 'Saul, Saul, why are you persecuting me? It is hard for you to kick against the goads.' And I said, 'Who are you, Lord?' And the Lord said, 'I am Yeshua whom you are persecuting. But rise and stand upon your feet, *for I have appeared to you for this purpose*, to appoint you as a servant and witness to the things in which you have seen me and to those in which I will appear to you, delivering you from *your people and from the Gentiles—to whom I am sending you to open their eyes*, so that they may turn from darkness to light and from the power of Satan to God, that they may receive forgiveness of sins and a place among those who are sanctified by faith in me.'
> –Acts 26:14–18

Apparently Yeshua said more to him that afternoon than, "Get up, dust yourself off and head into town." The reference to "opening the eyes" of the Jews and Gentiles would have caused Saul's mental eyes to pop open, even while his physical eyes were glued shut. Yeshua's is drawing directly from a messianic promise in Isaiah 42 that links the ministry of the Messiah with opening blind eyes, *and* refers to the servant of Yahweh as being blind himself. Saul, a dedicated Pharisee, would have done a first century version of a mental Google search, hearing these words from Yeshua. Without having the *whole* picture yet, Saul's tiny world of Judaism suddenly had no room for its own Yahweh and His Story, which they assumed was exclusively their own. Oddly enough, what happened to Saul on the Damascene highway is best summarized by Jaron Lanier, an unbeliever, speaking about adjustment to rapid technological change in his book, *You Are Not a Gadget*:

---

1 cf. Acts 9:Acts 9:36-10:23

> Someone who has been immersed in orthodoxy needs to experience a figure-ground reversal to gain perspective. This can't come from encountering just a few heterodox thoughts, but only from a new encompassing architecture of interconnected thoughts that can engulf a person with a different world view.[1]

Saul *definitely* had a "figure ground reversal" that day, and was most likely overwhelmed by the new mental "architecture" required to house the volume of unlearning and relearning he was headed into. Mike Mason, writing on marriage (another unlikely well into which to drop my bucket), paints an equally graphic description of what it must have been like to be Saul of Tarsus that weekend. Mason says that a person set in his ways is like a densely populated city. To build anything new in its heart, something else must come down.[2] Lanier and Mason, talking out of the other side of their mouths when it comes to Saul, hit bullseyes regarding the Noahic-size shift required in Saul's thinking. And this would be true from that roadside wreck, all the way up to when he lost his head, literally, to Nero. But, to accommodate this new *mind*, he also needed something else. And, I believe that's why we have a record of the "scales" in this story. Yahweh hadn't merely restored Saul's sight. He'd given him new *eyes*!

New Paul—Old Story

Saul had to come to grips with some incredibly uncomfortable—and as he would quickly discover—unpopular revisions. The first blew the covers off both ends of what amounted to his own "short story" version of redemption. He was faced with the necessity to abandon his understanding of the *purpose* of Judaism, and place it in something larger than itself. What he thought was the *whole* story, turned out to be a mere "chapter" in a Story much older than Abraham, much wider than the Jews, and much deeper than election and Law-keeping. That day on the road, Saul's personal, theological, and spiritual universe was beginning to be reordered, a shift on the order of magnitude of admitting and embracing the idea that the earth was *not* the center of our solar system.

> It is the story that stretches from Genesis to Revelation, not merely as a good yarn or even a classic of epic literature, but fundamentally as *a rendering of reality*—an account of the universe we inhabit and of the new creation we are destined for. We live in a storied universe. And once again, such a rendering of reality carries its intrinsic authority. For if this is truly the way things are, how they have become so and where they are going, then there are all kinds of implications for how we should respond individually and collectively.[3]

And although Luke's record of Paul in Acts includes very few details of this tectonic shift in outlook, the record of his three missionary journeys, his arrest and imprisonment in Jerusalem and Caesarea, and his transport to Rome and imprisonment are there. They provide us with snapshots of his theology, his constant warfare with orthodox Judaism, and the growing Gentile compo-

---

1 Jaron Lanier, *You Are Not a Gadget: A Manifesto.* (New York: Alfred A. Knopf, 2010), 23.

2 Mike Mason, *The Mystery of Marriage.* (London: Triangle, 1997), 14.

3 Wright, *The Mission of God*, 55-56.

nent of his audiences. But, Acts also provides us a chronological framework, a timeline in which Paul wrote all but three of his letters.[1] This means that from within his correspondence to the churches in the Mediterranean and mainlands of Asia, Macedonia, and Greece, we can extract even more pieces to the puzzle coming together in that rabbinic mind of his. And this, sends us back to our clue factory for figuring out everything that precedes it. The end of the Story, particularly, the two words we culled from John's vision near the middle of Revelation. The fulfillment of a promise made by Yahweh to His servants the prophets, is back on the table, or more specifically, the desk, of Paul:

...there would be no more delay, but that in the days of the trumpet call to be sounded by the seventh angel, the *mystery* [*mustērion*] *of God* would be fulfilled, just as he *announced* [*euaggelizō*] to his servants the prophets.   —**Revelation 10:7** [fragment]

"Mystery" and "preach," are peppered throughout Paul's writings and those of his personal physician and traveling companion, Luke. Of the 54 times the specific word "preach" appears in our NT, all but eight are from the pens of these two men. The same for "mystery," only Luke isn't in the game on this one. Paul is responsible for 20 of the 27 occurrences of the word in our New Testament. Apparently, this idea of "mystery" is a big deal to Paul. Just as it was to Yahweh. And *why* it's a big deal is no mystery either for those whose scales have been removed, or their "veil," if you prefer Paul's own word for it.[2] "Mystery," for Paul became the hatrack for everything he came to know and believe about his new, infinitely expanded Story. It was the source code or genome of redemption. Everything came back to it *and* was derived from it.

Tracing the use of it in his writings is exceedingly instructive, although frequently frustrating, taking us above our interpretive pay-grade in terms of comprehension. The first thing we discover, is who *didn't* "get it" when it came to full disclosure from on high. Paul tells us that this mystery had been "hidden for *generations* and *ages*," words that point to very long and yet distinct time periods[3] and the people associated with them. Specifically, it's startling to discover that those most likely *to* understand were precisely the ones who *didn't*—the authors! Peter, writing a few decades after Paul, informs us that even the prophets who were writing about what we now know as the "mystery," had no idea what they were actually being moved to write.[4] He goes further and says that even the

---

1 There is disagreement regarding *where* Paul actually was when he wrote his four "Prison Letters"—Colossians, Philemon, Ephesians, and Philippians. Some believe they were written from Caesarea. Paul's three "Pastoral Letters," to Timothy and Titus, according to some, were penned *after* a release from Rome, and inbetween a second arrest and subsequent death. However, conservative scholars agree that Galatians, the Corinthian and Thessalonian correspondence, Romans, and the "Prison Epistles" were written during Acts.

2 cf. 2 Corinthians 3:12-16

3 cf. Colossians 1:24-28.

4 That these compositions were in fact a synergistic effort in which Yahweh used their backgrounds and vocabularies, empowered and inspired by the Holy Spirit, is also clear in Peter's second letter (cf. 2 Peter 1:16-20). These were divine oracles committed to writing. The sheer reality of knowing the *source* of your prophecy yet not the meaning, must have been both majestic *and* frustrating.

angels have not been given backstage passes into this truth, but instead have to sit in the audience along with the rest of humanity and learn:

> Concerning this salvation, the prophets who prophesied about the grace that was to be yours searched and inquired carefully, inquiring what person or time the Spirit of Christ in them was indicating when he predicted the sufferings of Christ and the subsequent glories. It was revealed to them that they were serving not themselves but you, in the things that have now been announced to you through those who preached the good news to you by the Holy Spirit sent from heaven, things into which angels long to look.
> **–1 Peter 1:10–12**

Paul validates *and* terminates this heavenly censure, informing us that Yahweh's current intention is that the church is to be the stage from which the hosts of heaven, hell, and humanity, will obtain a progressive understanding of this mystery that has been hidden from sages for ages:

> To me, though I am the very least of all the saints, this grace was given, to preach to the Gentiles the unsearchable riches of Christ, and to bring to light for everyone what is the plan of the *mystery* hidden for ages in God who created all things, *so that through the church the manifold wisdom of God might now be made known to the rulers and authorities in the heavenly places.* This was according to the eternal purpose that he has realized in Christ Jesus our Lord,   **–Ephesians 3:8–11**

In a beautiful moment of personal disclosure, clothed in third person language, we gain an insight into the cause and connection between Paul's unending gratitude for his apostleship on one hand, and his ambassadorship with the King's message that the veil of the mystery has been lifted. We also gain an answer to the gnawing question of whether Saul's theological insight was immediate or gradual. If Emily Dickinson is right, that "the truth must dazzle gradually or every man go blind,"[1] the fact that Paul went blind at his *initiation* into truth is quite telling! In his Corinthian correspondence, Paul shares a snippet of how he came to further understand what had been hidden for centuries from prophets and kings, and for aeons from angels and archangels:

> I must go on boasting. Though there is nothing to be gained by it, I will go on to visions and revelations of the Lord. I know a man in Christ who fourteen years ago was caught up to the third heaven—whether in the body or out of the body I do not know, God knows. And I know that this man was caught up into paradise—whether in the body or out of the body I do not know, God knows—and he heard things that cannot be told, which man may not utter. On behalf of this man I will boast, but on my own behalf I will not boast, except of my weaknesses—though if I should wish to boast, I would not be a fool, for I would be speaking the truth; but I refrain from it, so that no one may think more of me than he sees in me or hears from me.
> **–2 Corinthians 12:1–6**

The life-altering nature of that experience, paired with what he saw and learned, especially that he was first the child of Adam to do so, apparently launched him on a trajectory that was destined to land him in trouble. Not just with his fellow Jews, but with Yahweh Himself. The verses that immediately follow his vision *must* be understood in the context of it. In short, what he

---

1 Cited in, *The Pastor: A Memoir,* Eugene Peterson, (New York: Harper One, 2011), 128.

experienced was so totally removed from the experience of any living person, including the twelve apostles up to now, Yahweh had to quarantine the inevitable ascent of arrogance. He did to him what He did to Jacob, 18 centuries earlier—He crippled him. Only Saul didn't come away from the experience with a limp. Yahweh gave him a thorn instead; a physical limitation whose very nature would remind him to be humble. We don't know what it was. But it was severe, permanent, and in the "can't touch this" zone regarding prayer.[1]

> So to keep me from becoming conceited because of the surpassing greatness of the revelations,a thorn was given me in the flesh, a messenger of Satan to harass me, to keep me from becoming conceited. Three times I pleaded with the Lord about this, that it should leave me. But he said to me, "My grace is sufficient for you, for my power is made perfect in weakness."   **–2 Corinthians 12:7–9**

So Saul, like Noah, Abraham, Moses, and Jonah before him, joined the long line of chosen vessels who discovered that submitting is preferable to running. He accepted *both* the privilege of becoming "Paul," and the thorn that accompanied it. In exchange, he was given insight into "the *mystery* of Christ, which was not made known to the sons of men in other generations."[2] For Paul, this *mystery* included Christ himself, Christ and the church, the will, wisdom, and grace of God, and the gospel itself, so broad and yet cohesive.[3] And Paul was shown that the mystery began before time and reached back as far as Adam, *not just* Abraham. It included "all things, and all nations," not just Israel and the Jews.[4] And according to Paul, the "plan for the fulness of time" had finally arrived:

> ...making known to us the mystery of his will, according to his purpose, which he set forth in Christ as *a plan for the fullness of time, to unite all things in him, things in heaven and things on earth*   **–Ephesians 1:9–10**

> But when *the fullness of time had come*, God sent forth his Son, born of woman, born under the law, to redeem those who were under the law, so that we might receive adoption as sons.   **–Galatians 4:4–5**

Yahweh's Highways

For Paul, there must have been at least an echo of familiarity to the thoughts ricocheting in his head. A "storied" universe, characterized by a layered revelation available to some and hidden from others, was not a novel notion. It was part of the fabric of the Jews' holy book, and therefore their own history. What Paul labels a "mystery" in his own writings had been Yahweh's MO since the beginning. Repeatedly in the Jewish scriptures, God separated His "ways" from

---

1 God's refusal to listen to Paul's plea for the removal of this "thorn," is a sober truth about the nature of prayer itself. We need to continually remind ourselves that God does not "work" for us, and respond to our beckon call like a butler. Also, as any good parent knows, "no" is a valid answer to any request a child makes. Too often, we speak about God "not answering our prayers," rather than simply saying, "I asked the Father, and He said, 'no,' at least for now." And finally, we learn from Paul's self-disclosure that sometimes what we want *out* of our lives, God wants in.

2 cf. Ephesians 3:4-5

3 cf. Ephesians 1:9; 3:3,4,9; 5:32; 6:19

4 cf. Ephesians 1:4; Revelation 13:8; 1 Corinthians 15:22,45; Colossians 1:19-20

his "acts," *and* who was and was not privy to each. And, upon closer examination, it's obvious His "ways" are a reference to His plans in a much grander reality He is controlling. There is a clear indication of intention, progress, and purpose to these "ways," a narrative of sorts. This being the case, the pleading of Moses to the Lord, *"Now therefore, if I found favor in your sight, please show me now your ways, that I may know you in order to find favor in your sight,"* must be understood as a desire on his part to understand just what in the world God was doing, and why.[1] We see this same sense of a "storied reality" even in the Hebrew hymnal, the Psalms, *"He made known his ways to Moses, his acts to the people of Israel."*[2] The psalmist separates God's "ways" from his "acts," the former apparently hidden and classified. And apparently, Moses has been granted "clearance" from Yahweh and is the recipient of the deeper understanding of what God was doing, and had access to these "ways." Considering that the Scripture elsewhere speaks of Yahweh's relationship with Moses as one of a friend,[3] we see here evidence that Yahweh is giving Moses an "insider" understanding of what is unfolding before him, *and* enfolding him also. Moses is granted a brief and privileged glance at a fragment of a bigger picture; namely, the Story. He comes to realize that his own destiny is now inseparable from its plot.

It's the prophet Isaiah, however, that alerts us to the divine nature of the Story, *and* why Paul was "caught up into the third heaven" to comprehend it.

> For my thoughts are not your thoughts, neither are your ways my ways," declares the LORD. "For as the heavens are higher than the earth, so are my ways higher than your ways and my thoughts than your thoughts. For as the rain and the snow come down from heaven and do not return there but water the earth, making it bring forth and sprout, giving seed to the sower and bread to the eater, so shall my word be that goes out from my mouth; it shall not return to me empty, but it shall accomplish that which I purpose, and shall succeed in the thing for which I sent it."
> –Isaiah 55:8–11

Yahweh's "ways" and "thoughts" are categorically different from ours. We reason and conclude differently, but also in an infinitely inferior way. They are also "higher" than ours and beyond our power to comprehend. Again, there is this notion of the "ways" of God being far removed not only from our knowledge, but our ability to recognize. This is infinitely more than an issue of degree. The classic theological case for our need of "divine revelation," doesn't help here, as if we merely needed *God* to help us understand some deep idea. It is, rather, the boundless truth that there is something at work here, a grand drama that is sovereignly unfolding above our senses, and beyond our sensibilities. And, for the present, Moses, Isaiah, and a long line of faithful people all the way up to John the Baptizer, are given an appetizer and told that the main course will not be served in their lifetime. His "ways" are the truth, the whole truth, and nothing but the truth. Unfortunately, no one could handle the truth...*then.*

---

1 cf. Exodus 33:13

2 Psalm 103:7

3 cf. Exodus 33:11

Jesus even seems to make an allusion to the reality of narrative at the Last Supper, when he announces a change of status for his apostles, and what that entails: *"No longer do I call you servants, for the servant does not know what his master is doing; but I have called you friends, for all that I have heard from my Father I have made known to you."*[1] At the time, it was limited to private explanations of parables, teaching around campfires and homes during his three years of ministry, and exclusive experiences at the Transfiguration, and later that night in Gethsemane. But, unbeknownst to them, friendship with Jesus would soon include "insider information" regarding Yahweh's plan for the fulness of time, a plan that would engulf them and redefine their own purpose and mission. A storyline so powerful, which once understood, it would set the trajectory for the rest of their lives. It would also determine the cause of their deaths.

Even Paul, whose transformation launched us on this majestic study of story, never became fully comfortable in his understanding of the breadth and length, and height and depth of this mystery. It is perhaps no more apparent than in the concluding comments of his elaborate, yet incomplete discussion on the difference between national and spiritual Israel, near the end of Romans, his most theologically astute treatise. This notion of God's "ways," a reality far removed from our grasp, is evident in Paul's near doxological conclusion after attempting to outline Yahweh's purposes for His "chosen people" throughout time in the preceding three chapters:

> O the depths of the riches, and the wisdom, and the knowledge of God! How unsearchable are his judgments, how inscrutable his ways!   **–Romans 11:33**

It is tragic indeed that for many moderns, these chapters have become only a theological meth lab to cook the doctrine of election, instead of seeing them as a spell-binding synopsis of the role of some key players in this mystery, this Story. Paul got the point, even though he didn't have the whole picture. He, more than any, *knew* that Yahweh's thoughts were higher than his. He had gotten a taste of the former and had a lifelong diet of the latter. He was grateful to have a few crumbs of understanding that had been brushed his direction from the table of God's ways. That's why he ends his discussion of the purpose of God's elective plans for Israel on his knees, instead of in an armchair in his library. But, Paul didn't stay on his knees. The new eyes he'd been given, and the thorn that accompanied them, seemed to work in tandem in his life, preserving his humility while stoking his intensity. This man who had tried to extinguish the light that had arisen among his people, discovered he had caught fire, and its flame now consumed him. And like the bush that attracted a young Moses, Paul would become a light to the Gentiles—the very thing the children of Abraham were supposed to have done all along.

---

1 John 15:15

15

Epitaphs—A Final Bumper Sticker

"All men are cremated equal." Although this is the title of a current book on midlife dating,[1] I first encountered the phrase in Apple evangelist Guy Kawasaki's first book, *The Macintosh Way*.[2] That was over twenty years ago when I was running System 4 on my 8 MHz Mac Plus. The quote immediately found its way to a prominent location in my covert educational curriculum, a collection of strategically placed, thought-provoking quotes peppered across the walls and ceiling of my classroom. They each lurked silently, waiting to ensnare and inspire any whose mind's had somehow lost their way during my teaching. Another favorite was, "There are no atheists in hell." I'll never forget the day a varsity cheerleader stayed after class, and with a furled brow, deep in thought, walked over to the quote about deceased disbelievers, and said, "Mr. Sciacca, then where *are* they?" It's days like that when you walk to your car wondering if you should consider being a greeter at Wal-Mart.

But, because I had fourteen students or former students die in a decade and a half, death was no stranger to me. Especially the "premature" death of teenagers. The quotes on my walls were intentional. From tragic, but typical car and motorcycle deaths, to drowning on a honeymoon and everything in between, I had travelled the road littered with the fruit of Adam's folly with my students and their friends and families too frequently to be shocked. The death of peers in high school often seems to leave a larger crater than elsewhere. I suspect it's the fusion of naive thoughts of immortality and the constant exposure to each other that only high school affords. I pondered the mystery that I'd never lost any students on mission trips. It seemed to always be around town, or traveling to and from college. Our youngest daughter, Havilah, lived with the Kuna In-

---

1 Elizabeth Fournier, *All Men Are Cremated Equal: My 77 Blind Dates*, (Bloomington, IN: iUniverse, 2009).

2 Guy Kawasaki, *he Macintosh Way*, (Glenview, IL: Scott, Foresman and Co., 1990), 3.

dians in Panama's Darien Jungle one summer when she was 15, and returned safely. Yet, a classmate of hers was permanently disabled driving home from school that same year. Every year, life in the fast lane of high school is stalled by a tragedy of some sort, typically involving a car. But, the brevity of life never really seemed to sink in. Students didn't entertain the possibility that the person they waved a goodbye to on Friday would be dead by Monday. Or more soberly, it might be them.

I'm not sure if I made a difference regarding my students' choices regarding recreation or vocation, but I initiated a project in my senior Bible elective, *Twenty-First Century Faith* that involved writing their own eulogy and designing an epitaph for their tombstone. For the assignment, they died on their 75th birthday, and had become the person they dreamt of becoming. God allowed each of them to sit invisibly in the back of the church at their funeral, while they were eulogized. What would they want to hear? It was an excellent way to catapult a group of graduating seniors, beginning a new life, to focus on the very end, and make them ponder what and whom they had become. Not the normal fodder for graduate conversations. I kept their projects, and mailed them to each student a year after they graduated.

One assignment is tattooed to my cerebral cortex. Kendrick was a gregarious, and charming guy, loved by his family and wrestling teammates alike. But, his choice of friends and what he did on weekends never left my radar. He always seemed to be drawn or squeezed toward darkness as a moth is attracted to light. That's why news of his death, six-months after graduation, arrived with the force a hurricane. He had been playing Russian Roulette at a party. When the day arrived to mail out the projects, I couldn't find the strength to send Kendrick's to his grieving mother. Jill, who's made of stronger steel than I in the face of tragedy, hand-delivered it. His eulogy was full of reflections. He had lived sacrificially, given over to fatherless kids. He also had spent many hours coaching youth. He had been a godly husband and father. All those hopes had been snuffed out prematurely. And tragically, at least part of the reason for how and when he died, had to do with how he was living. His dreams for himself were distant ideas. He couldn't know the choices we make in the present often are the ingredients that either create dreams, or twist them into nightmares. Knowing what you want said about you at your funeral, or engraved on your tombstone for that matter, is a summation of purpose. It is not morbid to think about such things while still living. Such was the case with Paul.

Likely in solitary confinement (possibly even in Rome's infamous Mamertine Prison), no longer the minimum security of "house arrest," Paul is awaiting his execution. The inevitable day when the separation of his head from his body will end the separation of himself from his Lord. In his final letter, Paul writes what could easily be his epitaph: *"I have fought the good fight, I have finished the race, I have kept the faith."* All three of the verbs in his joyful profession as he faced death, carry within them the force of finality, of arriving.[1] But most important, and consistent with what we've discovered about this single-minded saint, is his choice of words for "kept." Remove forever from your minds any mental notions of clinging to or holding onto something. The opposite of "losing" one's faith. Paul chooses a word here that has a wide circumference of meaning, all circling around the central idea of vigilance and protection from harm. Paul is boasting that as his own chapter in the grand Story is about to close, he has neither lost nor mishandled the mystery which he was entrusted. "Keeping" the faith was a holy passion for Paul, one that eclipsed most others:

> But I do not account my life of any value nor as precious to myself, if only I may finish my course and the ministry that I received from the Lord Jesus, to testify to the gospel of the grace of God.   —Acts 20:24

A decade earlier, Paul had said this to a group of elders from Ephesus. He did not know that finishing the race and keeping the faith would also entail the loss of this life he counted of so little value in comparison with his place in the Story. I believe when Paul finally saw clearly the connection between *who* he was (which he so richly explains in his letters) and this "mystery" of which he was given privileged access, his own purpose was defined and driven by it. The enormity of it had defied both the limitations of the wineskins of conventional Judaism and the theological myopia of first century Judaism's greatest crusader. The torn veil of Jerusalem's Temple on Good Friday was not merely symbolic. It marked the beginning of the end of mystery.[2] Paul and the early church had a name for this death and resurrection of understanding, this "mystery." They called it the "gospel." But again, it *wasn't* four points and a prayer. It was the One Story of the One God. A plan for the fulness of time to unite all things in heaven and on earth in Christ. And this, according to Paul, didn't begin in a manger outside the holy city. It began in a tent somewhere on a journey from Ur to Canaan. It was something that Yahweh "pre-preached" to *Abraham*.

> And the Scripture, foreseeing that God would justify the Gentiles by faith, preached the gospel beforehand to Abraham, saying, "In you shall all the nations be blessed."
> —Galatians 3:8

We have here the conflation of all the key elements of everything we've been gathering in our journey to this point: sin, justification, faith, the gospel, and the nations. This is what captured our rabid rabbi on the road that day, and held him a glad prisoner from that day forward. It is impossible to read Paul without concluding that he was a man *consumed* by the message he carried. In his own writings and Luke's Acts narratives, it is nearly impossible to distinguish

---

1 cf. 2 Timothy 4:7; Paul uses the perfect tense here, which in Greek is a beautiful way of speaking of an action occurring indefinitely in the past, but stopping at some point, yet the results of the action enduring on into the future. A condition or state has been arrived at, in a sense.

2 cf. Matthew 27:51; The veil in the Jewish Temple represented the barrier and distance that existed between Yahweh and His people. The Gospel writers are eager to report that that separation was dismantled as a result of the death of Jesus on the cross. Access to Yahweh was made possible through Jesus. This was the plan that had been hidden. This was the "mystery hidden for ages."

between the man Paul and the mystery he proclaimed. For him, his past credentials as a Jew were like dung in comparison to knowing Christ. His pedigree, the currency of credibility in a culture saturated with sophistry and posturing, came to mean nothing to him in comparison with his status as an adopted son in the household of Yahweh.[1] But, he harbored more than feelings of a satisfied mind. His own biographer tells us that Paul was energized by threatening and slaughtering Christians.[2] But, he did not find his fury *quenched* after his roadside wreck, merely *redirected*. His "figure ground reversal" seemed to energize him, like a fallen runner still bent on winning a race, redoubling his effort. Paul's passions were not abated. They might have actually been intensified. The truth tends to do that. Paul's intensity of emotion and resolve spilled over into his ministry to the recipients of grace *and* the opponents of it.

We read from his own pen, a humble testimony of tireless and selfless service to the One for whom he was a *doulos,* a bond servant. And, his service was always to *others*, those he sought to draw into the Story of the mystery hidden for ages and then equip to do the same for others.[3]

> Him we proclaim, warning everyone and teaching everyone with all wisdom, that we may present everyone mature in Christ. For this I toil, struggling with all his energy that he powerfully works within me.   —**Colossians 1:28–29**

"Mature in Christ," for Paul had less to do with the acquisition of information than it did transformation. In a similar comment to the believers in the region of Galatia, he lamented how he was in the *"anguish of childbirth until Christ be formed in you!"*[4] For him, spiritual formation, the increasingly visible presence of the risen Christ in the very lives of those whose sins are forgiven, was to be the new norm. What he anguished over regarding *their* lives, he expected for himself too.

> I have been crucified with Christ. It is no longer I who live, but Christ who lives in me. And the life I now live in the flesh I live by faith in the Son of God, who loved me and gave himself for me.   —**Galatians 2:20**

No More Storytellers

Paul taught, both with his mouth and his lifestyle that those who have heard The Story, and responded *to it,* are also now in it! All his teaching regarding believers being the "offspring of Abraham" as children of promise by faith, points to this. As we saw in the last chapter, it's impossible to inherit Abraham's bless-

---

1 cf. Philippians 3 contains his most detailed description of his resume *and* his dismissal of it in contrast to simply being in the Story. It is no coincidence that in the context of this discussion, he uses as one of his key arguments, an element of identity—our alien status as Christians (3:20).

2 Luke's description in Acts 9:1, combined with Paul's own confessional sorrow elsewhere in Acts, creates a very strong case for violence and murder at his hands. (cf. Acts 22:3-4; 26:9-11; Galatians 1:13). This is helpful insight for understanding the deep remorse that never seemed to leave Paul's heart, even as an older man. While he was convinced of Jesus's removal of his guilt, he knew the Lord could never take away his regret, a function of memory not maturity.

3 cf. 1 Corinthians 15:10 and 2 Corinthians 11:23-29

4 Galatians 4:19

ing, and not inherit his mission with it. The good news of this Story, the unfolding of this mystery, this plan for the fulness of time is *not* like a beautiful photograph or even a wonderful film that we want people to notice. It's not even like the story of your own conversion, a past event with present implications and future promise. God's Story *isn't* over. Easter Sunday is the centerpiece of the Story, and everything led up to that grueling weekend. But, Golgotha was the curse of Eden beginning to work its way backward. Everything now flows *from* it. Grace is always in motion. It putrefies when it's hoarded, by individuals, churches, or systematic theologies. The Story isn't something to point people *back* to. It's something to draw people into. We often picture evangelism as casting life preservers from the bank to people drowning in a river. We want to rescue them and drag them to safety. But, I picture it more like throwing a rope to people standing on the *bank*, and yanking them into the raging torrent of grace and truth we've found ourselves in. The *"God loves you and has a wonderful plan for your life"* version of the Story, an erroneous one, is casting life preservers from a cruise ship. The real Story, Yahweh's Story, is *"God is God, and has a plan for the fulness of time to reconcile all things in heaven and earth in Christ. And, He has a place for you in this ancient Abrahamic Story as an adopted, alien-apprentice, ambassador-advocate."* This is no tale for cowards or narcissists. Annie Dillard, in her inimitable style, paints an intriguing and lucid portrait of this Book that *is* The Story:

> This Bible, this ubiquitous, persistent black chunk of a bestseller, is a chink—often the only chink—through which winds howl. It is a singularity, a black hole into which our rich and multiple world strays and vanishes. We crack open its pages at our peril. Many educated, urbane, and flourishing experts in every aspect of business, culture, and science have felt pulled by this anachronistic, semi-barbaric mass of antique laws and fabulous tales from far away; they entered its queer, straight gates and were lost. Eyes open, heads high, in full possession of their critical minds, they obeyed the high, inaudible whistle, and let the gates close behind them.[1]

Yahweh's not interested in "saving" a horde of Story-*tellers*. His plan has always been to create a family of Story-*dwellers*, people who like Paul, cannot separate their own purposes from His—the One Story given to us in this grand narrative, the Bible. The unquenchable fire that was Paul's penchant for persecution had been transfigured into a passion for the sons and daughters of Adam—*"Woe to me if I do not preach the gospel!"*[2] Like Jeremiah before him, Paul and others found themselves without options, held fast as joyful prisoners of the grace that had captured them:

> If I say, "I will not mention him, or speak any more in his name," there is in my heart as it were a burning fire shut up in my bones, and I am weary with holding it in, and I cannot.   **–Jeremiah 20:9**

One Saul of Tarsus had been transformed from a murdering Yeshua-hater

---

1 Annie Dillard, "The Book of Luke," in *The Annie Dillard Reader.* (New York: HarperCollins Publishers, 1994), 266.

2 1 Corinthians 9:16; see also Jeremiah 20:29

into Paul the Apostle, a bond servant of the One he hated. His new confession and conviction? *"For me, to live is Christ and to die is gain."*[1] In a heart surrendered to Yahweh, this is the power of narrative unleashed. Paul had become a Story dweller. However, not all the embers of his past fury had found a place in the hearth of ministry. Paul, like Yahweh and Yeshua, still had wrath to spare when it came to those who restricted, edited, or ignored this Story that had discovered him.

The propensity to mess with the storyline is apparently in our Adamic DNA. Before there even exists a casting pool from which to draw leading characters, Yahweh makes it clear that unauthorized "editing" of *His* Story is punishable, by death!

> But the prophet who presumes to speak a word in my name that I have not commanded him to speak, or who speaks in the name of other gods, that same prophet shall die.' **–Deuteronomy 18:20**

And during the Dark Ages of Judah, the years just prior to the Babylonian destruction of Jerusalem and its Temple, most of the *unauthorized* scriptwriting was coming from those entrusted with speaking on behalf of Yahweh, His prophets and priests:

> I did not send the prophets, yet they ran; I did not speak to them, yet they prophesied. But if they had stood in my council, then they would have proclaimed my words to my people...How long shall there be lies in the heart of the prophets who prophesy lies, and who prophesy the deceit of their own heart...What has straw in common with wheat? declares the LORD. Is not my word like fire, declares the LORD, and like a hammer that breaks the rock in pieces? Therefore, behold, I am against the prophets, declares the LORD, who steal my words from one another.
> **– Excerpted from Jeremiah 23:21–31**

This predisposition to distortion has a long half-life and receives the harshest and most vitriolic words to fall from the lips of Yeshua six centuries later:

> But woe to you, scribes and Pharisees, hypocrites! For you shut the kingdom of heaven in people's faces. For you neither enter yourselves nor allow those who would enter to go in. Woe to you, scribes and Pharisees, hypocrites! For you travel across sea and land to make a single proselyte, and when he becomes a proselyte, you make him twice as much a child of hell as yourselves. **–Matthew 23:13–15**

Paul, following in the footsteps of Moses and Yeshua, upped the ante in his only letter that withholds praise and thanks for the faith of its recipients. Writing to the Galatians, he pronounces a damning curse on those who mess with this Story, the gospel Yeshua entrusted to Paul:

> I am astonished that you are so quickly deserting him who called you in the grace of Christ and are turning to a different gospel— not that there is another one, but there are some who trouble you and want to distort the gospel of Christ. But even if we or an angel from heaven should preach to you a gospel contrary to the one we preached to you, let him be accursed. As we have said before, so now I say again: If anyone is preaching to you a gospel contrary to the one you received, let him be accursed.
> **–Galatians 1:6–9**

....

1 Philippians 1:21

Apparently, in the brief interval between when the "mystery hidden for ages" had first stepped out from behind the curtain of Yahweh's protection, and the early days of Paul's ministry, it had experienced revision. Paul, throughout his life, is constantly having to distance himself from the growing numbers of charlatans, and theological contortionists who are twisting the Story to suit their liking. He described them as carnival "peddlers" of the Story, driven by cunning and greed, using "disgraceful and underhanded ways" to "tamper" with the storyline. Their goal? To amass a following by shaping it to allow the hearers to play leading roles in their new version. Others, according to Peter, *twisted* the story to make it say what they wanted. Since the Story began, hijacking it has always been a profitable business, putting the Adamic residue on center stage, all dressed-up in church clothes.

But, information is only as appealing as our interest in it, or our use for it. And in a culture like ours, characterized by a "narcissism epidemic," as Jean Twenge warns, the *only* information whose stock is up right now, is that which I generate about myself, or you give me that will serve the same purpose. Churches with both feet in the present have found themselves in the scalding water of the electronic age. The only way to keep from being burned—other than getting out—is to keep dancing. May God be merciful to many of us who've hijacked God's plan for the fulness of time, and rewritten it into an opportunity to talk about, promote, and pamper ourselves. Or maybe worse, to propagate a version of The Story that puts us at the center of redemption instead of Yahweh Himself. Best-selling books like *Your Best Life Now* and *It's Your Time* may be appealing promises, but thinking this way leads us back to Eden, not to the New Jerusalem and the Lamb.

I said earlier that Paul's passion was redirected into his ministry to the recipients of grace *and* the opponents of it. His life, which by his own admission, was no longer precious to him, now found its meaning in the Story, the mystery of God's ways, long hidden and now unveiled. He had also come face to face with the reality of who he was in all this. His letters open with the self-attribution, "apostle," or "servant of Jesus Christ," as do Peter's letters and James, the half-brother of the Lord. Their answer to the question of identity, "Who do I say I am?" was galvanized to this Story. They, like Paul, had discovered their purpose, the answer to *"What's my point?"* because they now knew there was a plot, and they had been pulled into it. But, Paul also was convinced that the plan for the fulness of time meant the fulfillment of the Abrahamic covenant and the reversal of Adam's folly. To him, these two were inseparable and interdependent. Discovering why this is true, and what it means for each of us in this life, brings us to our final question, the question of mission, or *"What's my place?"*

PART III *Mission*
"What's My Place?"

"Plot Anemia" — *What We Don't Know Can Hurt Us*

Today's rising generation has very little appreciation for the transparent redundancy in our culture when it comes to entertainment. Streaming video providers like Netflix and Amazon Prime, not to mention bit torrent sites like EZTV, render the notion of "missing" something on TV or film a rather ancient anxiety. Production times for film series have also been reduced so much that often a sequel is released while the memory of the parent film is still quite fresh. I try, unsuccessfully, to evoke empathy from my adult children for the fact that we had to wait three years for *Return of the Jedi,* after we found out that Darth Vader was Luke's father at the end of *The Empire Strikes Back!* But, it was even worse when I was a child.

My family may have had the first flat panel TV in America. I was born when television was just leaving the technological nursery and headed for mainstream America. We were too poor to own a color television. That luxury was the prerogative of the wealthy paper mill executives my parents served through Reliable Cleaners, our family dry cleaning business where we all worked. Our own home, a tiny story and a half, two bedroom, one bath house of maybe 900 square feet was modest, even by our town's standards. But, we had a "rec-room" in the basement, complete with a full bar my dad had fabricated using bowling alley butcher-block laminate for the bar surface. It had a small refrigerator, shelves lined with glasses and all the mixology tools required of any bartender. It was from this basement nightclub that the crooning of Harry Belafonte, Peggy Lee, and Pat Boone rose like a pop fragrance to the ground floor during my early years.

In the middle of the wall next to the bar, my dad had cut a square hole through the mahogany paneling. He picture-framed it, and on a shelf on the backside, placed our black and white TV so it faced out into the room. For all those in the rec-room, the television became a glowing portrait amid the paneling...a flat panel TV, if you like. I spent many hours in that room as a child, watching the weekly antics of dogs like *Lassie* and *Rin Tin Tin,* who seemed to have auditory vocabularies comparable to many of today's high school graduates. It was in that room as an eighth grader I witnessed live the assassination of Lee Harvey Oswald by Jack Ruby. No replays. No slo-mo's. Just low-tech bliss. Technology's debutante ball hadn't happened yet, but it was coming.

Twenty-five years later, while we were living in Colorado Springs, some friends of ours had been watching a very lengthy Masterpiece Theatre series each week. If I recall, it was 20 episodes, maybe more. They were going to be out of town for the final episode and asked for me to record it on our VHS video recorder. I don't know whether it was me or a power outage that knocked out the timer, but I didn't get it. Can you imagine the angst (and likely anger) returning home to watch the final episode of an extended series that sufficiently has captured your interest to secure a twenty-week commitment, only to discover it is not happening? No plot resolution, no character recovery, no answers provided to questions deliberately raised throughout the series. And worst of all, no recourse. No way to "download" that episode, or pull it off your DVR or your neighbor's for that matter. As we saw in chapter 13, the ending of the Story is vital. But, so is the scope and sequence of everything leading up to it. And unfortunately, though we are created with an intense plot *hunger,* we seem to be suffering from an acute case of plot *anemia* when it comes to the Bible. We don't naturally *think* in terms of The Story, because in truth, we don't *know* it. And because we don't know The Story, we find ourselves *living* in light of our own, the default setting for our Adamic residue. Instead of seeking to find our place in His Story, we foolishly try to squeeze Yahweh into ours. I suppose we think it will give "juice" to our story, like getting Denzel Washington or Brad Pitt into it. But, our puny stories cannot contain the God of eternity. They simply collapse, or become illusory as we re-imagine Him as a domesticated deity whose greatest joy is making us happy, not the other way around. This is serious, but thankfully not terminal. One needs to get the story straight to know where to find her place in it. We examined the narrative nature of Truth in chapter 13. Now, we need to unpack the Narrative itself.

The first step in treating our plot anemia is to discard our high fat, low iron view of the Bible as a two-Testament treatise. In its place, we will posit a five act drama comprising a single Story.[1] I believe it is neither coincidental nor inconsequential that a chorus of voices are being raised from among God's people regarding that need for a narrative approach to biblical interpretation and theology. Because God's word to us was first His word to someone else, and because the Bible can never say what it has never said, we are fettered to our Abrahamic past. And in an ancient oral culture where hearing was the medium, narrative was the message. Turning our eyes into ears is no easy task, but it is a prereq-

---

1 This perspective is not unique to me, nor did it originate with me. I am indebted to scholars like Craig Bartholemew, Christopher Wright, N. T. Wright, and Walter Wangerin for assuaging my plot hunger and modeling for me the art of reading Scripture as God intended.

uisite to understanding the storyline of the Story we are now in. This makes it imperative. However, a more ominous threat to the Story lies on the road ahead. As I mentioned earlier, we are very likely on the cusp of watching the actual notion of narrative itself sink beneath the shifting sands of digitized sensibilities. What postmodernism has done to Truth, technology is doing to narrative. At least, that's the message the unbelieving world is throwing over the high fences of ignorance Evangelicalism has erected:

> Some thinkers welcome the eclipse of the book and the literary minded fostered. In a recent address to a group of teachers, Mark Federman, an education researcher at the University of Toronto, argued that literacy, as we've traditionally understood it, "is now nothing but a quaint notion, and aesthetic form that is as irrelevant to the real questions and issues of pedagogy today as is recited poetry—clearly not devoid of value, but equally no longer the structuring force of society." The time has come, he said, for teachers and students alike to abandon the "linear, hierarchical" world of the book and enter the Web's "world of ubiquitous conductivity and pervasive proximity"—a world in which "the greatest skill" involves "discovering emergent meaning among contacts that are continually in flux."[1]

The above assessment, I believe, is prophetic *and* accurate. And this is not the assessment of a lone journalist. Education's leaders are marching like lemmings to the Cupertino Pipers when it comes to what learning should look like, and more important, what it means to "know" something. "Knowing" is degenerating into an instrumental skill of knowing where and how to *find* something, but never to know innately what that something is. In a nation lamenting the loss of jobs to China, it is ironic we are outsourcing our semantic memories, and along with them the ability to think sequentially. But, this has greater significance than merely in the world of education and learning. It should cause all the dash lights of believers to be flashing bright red. Without a commitment to narrative itself, any "gospel" that purports not only to be *a* story, but *the* Story, will have no traction. And Christians who do not understand *this*, will find themselves stuck in a revolving door of meaning, thinking that propositional apologetics is the answer—defending the bits that Google has mined. And I fear that while we are distracted, arguing over words, the Story itself will be sinking beneath the waves of "emergent meaning." If we Christians thought postmodernism's attack on truth was the war to end all wars, we are mistaken. The real battle being fought for the future of the gospel is the transparent coup technology is waging on the value of narrative. Getting the Story straight will only matter in a world where narrative itself is still valued. But, that's another story in itself. One that is beyond the scope of this book. So, what's the story on the Story?

"In The Beginning..."

ACT I — "COMMENCEMENT" (Genesis 1-2)

Our Story commences, like any good narrative, with an introduction of sorts. A stage is set, key characters make initial appearances, and a relational context appears that creates a connection between the "who" and the "where." The majestic account of Creation in Genesis 1 catapults us in rapidly from the macroscopic level of the universe to the microscopic level of a single couple placed in a perfect garden called Eden. They are given a charge to "be fruitful and multiply," and to "fill the earth and subdue it." God had established them as co-regents, ruling on His behalf over all He had made.[1] They were to expand their influence beyond the Garden, as image-bearers of God Himself. They were, in a sense, to "Edenify" the rest of Creation. This was, in the words of one scholar, God's "Creation Project." It was a peaceful arrangement. Everything that breathed was given everything that didn't, for food. He was pleased with the way things were. *Very* pleased, in fact, and He christened them "very good." Genesis 2 serves as a sort of divine soliloquy, expanding our introduction to the one whose name in Hebrew is a reflection of humanity's place at the top of Creation.[2] Things are as they are supposed to be.

The Genesis account, so familiar to us living 35 centuries later, is actually the "backstory," a sort of *prequel* to the story of a distinct "chosen people" that begins with the birth of Moses in the next book, Exodus.Consequently, the first audience of this narrative—the Jews recently freed from Egypt—would have found themselves spellbound as they listened to Moses rehearse it in their hearing. Surely there were earlier, fragmentary, oral accounts of *some* of the people and events in Genesis, which Moses' listeners were familiar. The sheer magnitude of the genealogical records alone testifies to written sources. But, our belief in divine inspiration demands that Moses' account was richer, more nuanced, and

---

1 The name of God that is used throughout this Creation account is *Elohim*.

2 cf. Genesis 1:28, 31

more thorough than anything they had ever heard. And *what* they heard was breathtaking. A Creation filled with beauty, wonder and grace. It was a very unusual Creation story indeed, totally unlike anything they would have heard living in Egypt for four centuries. No blood, no deific sex, no violence. A world in which everything flourished because all Creation was doing exactly what it was designed to do. It was a Creation characterized by purpose and endowed with fulfillment. And yet, most likely, as they listened they must have wondered how such a place of beauty and peace had become the arena of hatred, mistrust, and brutality that characterized their lives as slaves. Where did the world *they* knew come from? They were about to find out as Moses continued to speak. Enter the serpent.

ACT II—CONFLICT (Genesis 3-11)

I've always struggled with the press release in Genesis 3 on the serpent: "more crafty than any other beast of the field the Lord God has made." As the plot unfolds, the serpent doesn't strike me as the sharpest knife in the drawer when it comes to temptation. And maybe that's because we've been conditioned to believe that the "Devil wears Prada" somewhere on our spiritual journey. I've learned by living and by watching that he wears camo, not Prada, and he always attacks from the rear not the front. Here too. The serpent hijacks God's Creation Project, Edenifying the rest of Creation with evil instead of God. His strategy was masterful and successful. If you read the account slowly and carefully, you'll discover that his work with Eve was finished long before she ate the fruit. By carefully getting *her* to introduce the Tree of the Knowledge of Good and Evil into the discussion, it was easy for him to talk about the tree Eve had brought up. Forget all the things you've heard about her "adding" to what God had told them, when she responded to the serpent by saying they were not allowed to *eat* from or "touch" the tree. While that idea makes for some great preaching, it's not in the account. First, we have no idea what all God had instructed them. To assume that what we have in the first two chapters is the extent of their instructions is quite presumptuous. And, from a purely practical standpoint, it doesn't seem likely that God told them, "Hey guys, you can fondle the fruit, smell the fruit, lick the fruit, just don't take a bite." Really? I don't think so.

The serpent effectively turned Eve's focus from what she *had* to what she *didn't* have. They were given freedom to eat from every tree in the garden. Every tree! Except the one that belonged to Him. God had *His* tree in the garden that they were to tend. Caring for it, and not eating from it, was their only assignment with a restriction. The serpent's original question about God's prohibitions was designed to have her turn and point to a single tree. And at that point, as I so unprofessionally tend to say, she was "meat on the grill." It was over. Much like an illusionist who accomplishes his illusion ten minutes before we think he has, the serpent had wrapped up his work before her hand ever reached for the fruit. He really *was* the craftiest thing in the garden. He still is. That little "turn your gaze from what you have to what you don't" ploy sounds pretty familiar doesn't it. Crafty isn't a synonym for creative, but it is synonymous with effective. And when it comes to our Enemy, that's all that matters. In the chapters that follow, we're going to take an extended walk deep into the theological forest of what unfolded in the garden. But for now, discard all your mental images of two naked and embarrassed people getting kicked out of the pool. I believe the universe tilted that day, and they both knew it.

The rebellion that was launched through that piece of fruit spread like the shadow from Mordor out from the garden and wove itself into the fabric of humanity. From family disintegration and domestic violence to global evil stoppable only by near human extinction, aquatic style, the "knowledge of good and evil" spreads. But, it was light on good, and heavy on evil. After a global flood, God gives Noah and his sons a "Take Two" on the Edenic charge to "be fruitful and multiply, fill the earth and subdue it." But, almost as though the seeds of failure are inherent in this second attempt, God adds a caveat to the charge. Capital punishment for capital murder is the new normal. Why? Because humanity bears the Imago Dei,[1] the Image of God. Moses' audience has an answer, abbreviated as it is, to why life in Egypt had been so hard for so long. Things are no longer as they are supposed to be. Then, almost as if the Author had anticipated the despair that nine chapters of dark narrative would produce, He decides to introduce a protagonist. A man with a two-syllable name from a one-syllable city enters the story, Abram of Ur. His name will emerge nearly 300 times in the Story from this point on, making itself at home in slightly fewer than half of the books of our Bible. Only they don't know what you know, so he'll just seem like a wandering pagan to them. At least for a while.

ACTS III—COMPLICATION (Genesis 12 - Malachi)

Before we move forward, I need to drag two valuable insights onto our path. The first is a vital puzzle piece for understanding what follows, and will determine whether we read the Bible as a narrative or merely as an anthology. Our "Old Testament" begins with Genesis and ends with Malachi. They constitute the "bookends" of this portion of the Story. But, because we are trained to view the Table of Contents of our Bible like any other book, we assume that it provides us with the linear unfolding of the Story. It doesn't. The portion of the Story that is in our Old Testament concludes with Nehemiah. The next piece of the Story we have is the entrance of John the Baptizer in Mark's Gospel. That means that the 22 books *after* Nehemiah should be read and understood as *supplemental,* but not sequential material for the Story. For example, twelve of the prophets lived and spoke during the time period recorded in 2 Kings. In my thirty plus years of teaching, I am still amazed at how few Christians know this. So, as we move into Act III, it's crucial that we understand how the *arrangement* of the books of our Bible fits when it comes to the Story itself.

1 cf. Genesis 9:6

The second insight, also an excellent traveling companion on our rehearsal of this Story, has to do with the notion of "Jew." As we turn the page and step into Act III, it is worth noting that "Jew" has no existence in the world of Adam. It is a theological construct in the mind of Yahweh, nothing more. Grasping this is vital because the first audience of Genesis, as we have seen, although they have no *national* identity, they do have a very distinct racial identity. They are a people distinct from the Egyptians. But, that was not always the case. In fact, the remaining 39 chapters of Genesis, the early developments of Act III, will provide the newly emancipated Hebrews with an answer to *who* they are, and *why* they exist. Or, in the language of this book, their *identity* and *purpose*. And, this part of their "backstory" opens with a fuzzy statement of their *mission* as well. It's all there, easily visible to us in hindsight, though surely not to them at the time. It's revealed in what theologians refer to as the "call " of Abram:

> Now the LORD said to Abram, "Go from your country and your kindred and your father's house to the land that I will show you. And I will make of you a great nation, and I will bless you and make your name great, so that you will be a blessing. I will bless those who bless you, and him who dishonors you I will curse, and in you all the families of the earth shall be blessed." **–Genesis 12:1–3**

With these words, Yahweh unveils His plan to rescue the Creation Project, to turn the events of Eden backwards. The "blessing of the *goyim*" through an elect people. What has been in the mind and heart of Yahweh since eternity past, is now incarnate in the person of an itinerant Chaldean. From here, the Story continues to unfold for nearly 40 more chapters, growing in complexity and depth. Names like Isaac, Jacob, and Judah populate its pages, while others like Lot, Ishmael, and Esau appear and then exit offstage. And oddest of all, Joseph occupies more narrative real estate than anyone else in Genesis, yet is reduced to bones that are carried and buried a few books later. But, if you are the recent refugees from Egypt, this man is a vital link in your own lineage, for he is the reason you and yours were in Egypt for ten generations. Moses' audience *needed* to know about Joseph, though *we* know that though obscure in Act III, Judah will be the son of Jacob who carries the Story to completion.

Act III also contains the most significant event in the entire Old Testament. Maybe one of the top three or four in the Story itself—the Exodus. Because we falsely assume the Exodus of the Jews from Egypt was a deliverance from bondage to *freedom*, we miss not only the significance of the event itself, but its role in the life of modern believers. The Exodus was *not* a deliverance from bondage to *freedom*. It was a deliverance from bondage to *covenant*, a different type of servitude. Their liturgical, agricultural, and civic calendars were centered around this event. It still is. But, understanding what was in the mind of Yahweh before and after this event is essential. Getting this wrong not only blurs our perception of what happens from this point on, it also separates us modern Abrahamic believers from our own purpose and place in the Story. Yahweh's election of Israel was *purposeful* and corporate, not just providentially selective. Once He got them out of Egypt, He needed to get Egypt out of them. Hence, a host of laws making them distinct among the nations. But, His purpose for them had to do with their role in The Story, not their ease and retirement in Canaan. Yahweh took the Jews out of Egypt, yes, but He brought them to Mt. Sinai, *not* to Club Med. The Exodus cannot be separated from the "call" of Abram and the "blessing" of the nations:

> Say therefore to the people of Israel, "I am the LORD, and I will bring you out from under the burdens of the Egyptians, and I will deliver you from slavery to them, and I will redeem you with an outstretched arm and with great acts of judgment. I will take you to be my people, and I will be your God, and you shall know that I am the LORD your God, who has brought you out from under the burdens of the Egyptians. I will bring you into the land that I swore to give to Abraham, to Isaac, and to Jacob. I will give it to you for a possession. I am the LORD."   **–Exodus 6:6–8**

They existed for mission, the mission of Abraham, their father. Unfortunately, "election" would become the distorted grounds for *failing* in that mission rather than fulfilling it, as the remainder of Act III will bear out.

From the Exodus event to the close of Act III, we witness the thickening complexity of the Story. A plethora of people groups make appearances of varying lengths in the narrative. Philistines, Hittites, Assyrians, and Babylonians make excursions into the world of the Jews. Most of them unpleasant. Nations rise and fall. We hear a litany of names, some of them familiar, most of them not, playing major and minor roles in this unfolding drama of redemption. Joshua, Ruth, Samuel, David, Ahab and Josiah, to name a few. But as the record shows, the stewards of the Story of "blessing" find themselves becoming more and more a reflection of the cultures that surround them, than the God who chose them *out* of those cultures. Instead of resembling the Story-dwellers Yahweh had intended, they increasingly become Story-*quellers*, as the "nations" are either emulated or envied. As a result, a new role in the Story is needed, that of the *navi*, the "prophet." There had been periodic previous appearances of individuals who spoke on behalf of Yahweh, but as God's chosen people begin to choose their *own* adventure, He raises up nearly twenty men in rapid succession to reign in those whom He had appointed to lead His people in covenant faithfulness. The job description of a Jewish king was fairly straightforward: maintain righteousness and justice in the kingdom. The prophet's job was to provide the king with real-time evaluation of his performance. For this reason, in the Story, prophets play a more major role than kings. Understanding the role of prophets in the Story is crucial. Our own failure or refusal to do so is at the heart of a great deal of theological imbalance *and* best-selling books. Prophets in the Bible are typically divided into groups based on when they lived, whether or not they wrote, who their audience was, and a number of other factors. But, for our purposes we only need to separate their *messages*, not them, and fortunately there are essentially only two types of prophecies in our Story.

The first is what we might call "prescriptive" prophecy, messages that tell people how to live. Some call this "forth-telling." The *majority* of prophecy in our Bibles is of this type, and had to do with *their* present, not *our* future. This comes as a surprise to many modern believers, who've been conditioned to equate the word "prophecy" with the "end times." But once we begin to see them in relation to the kings rather than the people, our understanding changes. I like to think of prophets who deliver these types of messages as confronting the "traitors." Whether it was naive stupidity, like Hezekiah providing classified information to the Assyrians, or blatant idolatry and perversion such as that introduced by Ahab and Jezebel, prophets were primarily dispatched to address the sins of kings.[1] The majority of prophecy in our Bibles is of this type. And, it is also this type of prophecy that speaks loudest into our own day, if we give it a voice:

> ...for my people have committed two evils: they have forsaken me, the fountain of living waters, and hewed out cisterns for themselves, broken cisterns that can hold no water.   –Jeremiah 2:13

The second type of prophetic message, less frequent yet by far the most popular among modern believers, is often called "predictive" prophecy, or "foretelling." Prophetic oracles of this type always have to do with the future. They are frequently enshrouded in imagery and allusion, and regrettably serve as fruitful soil for unscrupulous or impetuous teachers in our own day. Under closer scrutiny, "Bible prophecy" is often merely a euphemism for Christian astrology, a quest for the power that results from insider information. Knowing what others don't, or speaking with certainty about future events creates a sort of gnostic aristocracy, an illusory religious version of Silicon Valley. Undressed, we discover our Adamic residue finding one more avenue of expression in its quest for power and control. Christian publishers and film makers have had a heyday exploiting this illicit marriage of plot hunger and our Adamic remnant. When I was younger, a book was released taunting the notion that the UPC barcode system could be the mark of the Beast.[2] The date of the "rapture" is also a fertile nursery birthing books and celebrity preachers. I still have a copy of, *88 Reasons Why The Rapture Will Be In* 1988 sitting on my bookshelf. I suspected that it might be a collector's item someday, like a Michael Jordan rookie card. So I kept it.

But, if Yahweh *didn't* provide us with predictive prophecy so that we could create charts, write books, produce movies, and split churches, what *is* its purpose? Fortunately for us, the Apostle Peter anticipated that question in the first century:

> But do not overlook this one fact, beloved, that with the Lord one day is as a thousand years, and a thousand years as one day. The Lord is not slow to fulfill his promise as some count slowness, but is patient toward you, not wishing that any should perish, but that all should reach repentance. But the day of the Lord will come like a thief, and then the heavens will pass away with a roar, and the heavenly bodies will be burned up and dissolved, and the earth and the works that are done on it will be exposed. *Since all these things are thus to be dissolved, what sort of people ought you to be in lives of holiness*

---

1 cf. 2 Kings 20:12-21 and 1 Kings 21:20-26

2 cf. Robert Van Kampen, *The Sign.* (Wheaton, IL: Crossway Books, 1992), 243-44.

and godliness, waiting for and hastening the coming of the day of God, because of which the heavens will be set on fire and dissolved, and the heavenly bodies will melt as they burn! But according to his promise we are waiting for new heavens and a new earth in which righteousness dwells. *Therefore, beloved, since you are waiting for these, be diligent to be found by him without spot or blemish, and at peace.* **–2 Peter 3:8–14**

Peter informs his readers (and us 20 centuries later) that predictive prophecy's purpose is to serve as "trailers," for the Story. Yahweh gives His people snapshots from time to time of what is ahead to provide hope *and* incentive to live the life of a Story dweller *in the present*. He gives us glimpses of future scenes and the *end* of the Story so that we may have hope and strength in the *midst* of the Story. Especially for our own role in it. It turns out, that just like its cousin, prescriptive prophecy, the primary application of predictive prophecy is the *present*, not the future. It is significant that each time Jesus is questioned about the "last days," his first response is to warn the one asking about being misled in the present.[1] Even at the Ascension, when the apostles are still anxious about "end times" details, Jesus immediately draws them back to their present place and purpose in the Story. In slightly more gracious words than mine, he tells them it's none of their business.[2] This is similar to what Jesus told Peter when he was wondering what Jesus had in mind for John's future.[3] It was almost as if Jesus had said, *"You're going to be crucified upside down in Rome, and John's going to die of old age on a Mediterranean island with a 5-book contract. Do you have a problem with that, Peter?"* Two different men. Two different roles. One Story. Our Adamic residue will always struggle with role envy. Isn't that what got Adam in trouble in the first place? Understanding this is especially relevant for us today, when tempted to compare our place in the Story to others around us. The Bible has a word for satisfaction with one's role in the Story. It's called "contentment." Paul said it was a secret he had learned.[4] But then again, if there was ever someone who *knew* his place in the Story, it was him.

To interpret prophecy properly, it is essential that we understand its role. Prophecy serves the Story and exists for it. It has no purpose outside it. Biblical prophecy either addresses the "traitors," or it provides the "trailers." But in *both* cases, its intended purpose impinges on the *present*, not the future. To the degree that you and I only think futuristically about biblical prophecy, to that same degree we've got it wrong. Prophecy comprises about one out of every three words of the narrative. It is a major player, and needs to be treated like one. But, if we get its purpose wrong from the start, prophecy will soon find itself wrested from the storyline and exploited to provide "proof" for the latest CYOA-Last Days Version. Okay, back to the Story itself.

Genesis 12 through Malachi, which we've dubbed Act III, turns out to be

---

1 cf. Matthew 24:1-4; Mark 13:3-5

2 cf. Acts 1:6-8

3 cf. John 21:18-23

4 cf. Philippians 4:11-13

a very long Act, spanning some 1,500 years. It began with the introduction of Abram, a solitary and migratory figure. It ends with the return of a tattered fragment of a king-less nation to the ruins of Jerusalem. Yahweh had surely brought forth nations and kings from the loins of Abraham, as He had promised. But, the flames of those hopes had dwindled to smoldering ash. Israel declined from a unified kingdom, to a divided kingdom, to no kingdom. In four centuries. Imperceptible to those whose lives ebbed and flowed between these bookends of glory and disgrace (but not to us), the "mystery" of the Abrahamic promise and mission continued to unfold. Remember, this is *not* Ancient Near Eastern history. It is *our* history as well, because it's the One Story we are a part of.

As the lights are fading to darkness at the conclusion of Act III, we "watch" Nehemiah rebuilding the wall around Jerusalem. We see Ezra rebuilding the people's hopes and identity through covenant renewal. Finally, and rather abruptly, Yahweh closes the curtain to rebuild the stage for Act IV. And, as in all compelling dramas, it was time for an Intermission.

"Intermission"—The Bible's Missing Page

I have always marveled how deftly, and efficiently stage crews can work their magic behind closed curtains between acts. What was an elegant British mansion when the curtains close, can be magically transformed into a quaint peasant cottage, complete with a sleeping sheep dog when the curtains reopen. Stage transformations have been a challenge throughout history. The Roman coliseum was transformed in seven hours into an aquatic battleground for ships, by the mere addition of 4 million gallons of water, redirected from an aqueduct. But, what Yahweh accomplished during the Intermission of His Story was of such a magnitude, that four centuries or so of silence seems too short for all that got put in place.[1] The curtain on Act III *closes* with these words:

> Behold, I will send you Elijah the prophet before the great and awesome day of the LORD comes. And he will turn the hearts of fathers to their children and the hearts of children to their fathers, lest I come and strike the land with a decree of utter destruction.   **–Malachi 4:5–6**

The curtain on Act IV *opens* right where Malachi left off during the days of Nehemiah, seemingly without skipping a beat:

> The beginning of the gospel of Jesus Christ, the Son of God. As it is written in Isaiah the prophet, "Behold, I send my messenger before your face, who will prepare your

---

1 The actual length of this "blank page" era is disputed among scholars, largely because of the difficulty in ascribing exact dates to the events recorded in Ezra and Nehemiah. The return of the Jews from Babylon under the leadership of Zerubbabel and the blessing of the Persian king, Cyrus is well-established at 538-39 B.C. However, the actual dates of the arrival of Ezra and Nehemiah are more difficult to fix. Dates of 458 BC and 445 BC have been suggested. But there is debate surrounding which Persian king actually ruled during the return of Ezra to Jerusalem. However, it is likely safe to assume that our books of Ezra and Nehemiah were in their present form sometime in the 5th century BC, or shortly thereafter. This is where the "400 years" of the Intertestamental Period is derived. We must remind ourselves that we are *not* seeking to create a time *line*, but rather a time *window* in which God was "silent," from the prophetic standpoint.

way, the voice of one crying in the wilderness: 'Prepare the way of the Lord, make his paths straight,'" John appeared, baptizing in the wilderness and proclaiming a baptism of repentance for the forgiveness of sins.[1]   **–Mark 1:1–4**

Yet, at least a four century Intermission separates these two comments, and what happened backstage is not only vital to the continuation of The Story, it is crucial to properly reading and understanding the rest of it, our New Testament. New groups with unusual names like, "Pharisees," "Sadducees," and "Herodians," and "scribes" populate the pages of the Four Gospels. A single family, the Herodians, dominates the first five books of our New Testament. Buildings called "synagogues," replete with a sophisticated system of leadership and liturgy, appear to be everywhere in the then-known world. Yet, none of these groups, families, or buildings are ever mentioned in our Old Testament! They were all carefully and strategically put into place by Yahweh during the Intermission. While the curtains on The Story were closed, He was constructing three extraordinarily significant cultural highways that would converge on a tiny piece of real estate in the Western Mediterranean about the time the curtains on Act IV open. We need to spend some time traveling backward on each of these roads before we return to our seats for Act IV.

In the closing scenes of Act III, we witnessed the rise and fall of the Hebrew monarchy, and listened to the oracles of sixteen prophets whose words make up nearly half of our Old Testament. And in our preoccupation with the storyline of Scripture, we are tempted to assume that its storyline *is* The Story. It's not. Though its contents are sufficient, they are hardly exhaustive.[2] The Story we've been looking at—this "plan for the fullness of time," this "mystery hidden for ages"—is the *composite* of Yahweh's "ways." Even with the amazing help provided by the inspired Word, we must continually remind ourselves that The Story must be comprehensive enough to contain all people of all time. Its inscrutable nature has not changed because He has given us *some* of its details.[3] In truth, the fact that The Story exists in the mind of Yahweh, surely means it *exceeds* the boundaries of the Bible, though when we seek to journey there, we have to do so without any help from Him. Or, put another way, The Story is immensely bigger than the Bible, so all history that is *not* in the Bible, is still in The Story.

1 The appearance of John the Baptizer, in Mark and Luke's Gospel, signals the resumption of the Story. It is especially significant that Mark, whose Gospel is likely the first one recorded, literally begins with John's appearance. Luke provides us with a very detailed narrative of John's parentage, his miraculous conception, and subsequent retreat into obscurity prior to "coming out" as the fulfillment of Malachi's prediction. The Story resumes with John, not Jesus.(cf. Luke 1:1-24, 57-80)

2 The Apostle John's classic statement at the close of his contribution to Act IV, reminds us of the sufficient yet incomplete nature of Scripture when it comes to the Story: " *Now there are also many other things that Jesus did. Were every one of them to be written, I suppose that the world itself could not contain the books that would be written.*" (John 21:25)

3 Paul's doxological statement in Romans 11:33 was made *while* he was giving us the most extensive insights we have on the election of Israel. May God forgive us for thinking we understand His "ways" simply because we have His Word! Whenever we are tempted to feel smug about who God is and what He's doing, it would be advisable to re-read the closing chapters of Job.

This means the nations that make cameo appearances (by comparison) within the story of Israel, are important in their own right to Yahweh. The rise and fall of the Assyrians, Neo-Babylonians, and Persians all play enormous roles in Act III of The Story, although their combined ink would occupy less than a single chapter in our Bible. A Persian king whom Yahweh calls His "anointed one," was responsible for keeping The Story alive by financing 50,000 Jews a return trip to the rubble of Jerusalem.[1] They rejoiced at the thought of being allowed to return to their homeland, not knowing the role they were playing in The Story. We now know they were part of the "stage crew," each doing his or her part, rebuilding the city and its Temple, fulfilling their role, that Yahweh's plan for the fullness of time might continue.

The Greek Chapter

Our record of The Story fades to dusk in the books of Ezra and Nehemiah, with Artaxerxes as the current ruler of the vast Persian Empire.[2] The Bible, remember, *contains* The Story, but itself is not the *complete* Story. World history provides us with what transpired after our record went blank. In the fourth century BC, a usurper to the throne of Persia named Darius III, found himself facing the most brilliant military commanders in history. A youthful protege of his father, Philip of Macedon, Alexander was bent on owning the world. The result was the death of Darius III by his own people, and the end of Persia as a world power. However, Alexander's empire was not long for this world either. But, in the NASA-level trajectory of his rise to power, Alexander would unwittingly play an enormous role in setting the stage for Act IV. As a pupil of Aristotle, Alexander had a passion for learning. He carried copies of the *Illiad* and the *Odyssey* with him on military campaigns (Imagine if he'd had a Kindle!). This young but brilliant war hero also had a private agenda of making Greek culture the new normal in the world. For the first time in history, the "West" was the dominant cultural force in the Ancient Near Eastern world. Alexander built the largest library in the world in Egypt, a city he conveniently named after himself—Alexandria. The Apollos of our New Testament undoubtedly studied in Alexander's library, and Stephen our waiter-apologist, found himself arguing with Jews who were also educated there. Even Paul felt the influence of Alexander, for the two ships which he sailed as prisoner to Rome, were likely built in the harbors of this amazing city.[3]

But, Alexander's two most lasting legacies are his unwitting contributions to Yahweh's Story. The first was his drive to unify the known world under the umbrella of Greek culture and learning. The second, which would be the vehicle of the first, was to spread the knowledge of the Greek language.

---

1 cf. Ezra 1:1-66 and Isaiah 44:28

2 This is most likely Artaxerxes I, the son of Exerxes, the Ahasuerus of our Book of Esther. He likely reigned during the early part of the 5th century BC. (cf. Ezra 7 and Nehemiah 2:1; 5:14).

3 cf. Acts 18:24; 6:9; 27:6; 28:11

He was highly successful in both. Not, so much because of his tenacity, as his unconscious role in Yahweh's Story. The Greek language became the lingua franca in the entire known world. Especially in the Mediterranean Basin, which became the radiating center for The Story's movement to the *goyim*, the nations. The Jewish scriptures were translated from Hebrew to Greek in Alexandria. The Sadducees of Jesus' day were aristocratic Jews who embraced Greek culture and much of its philosophy.[1] But, Alexander's most significant contribution to The Story was the spread of Greek as the language of the known world. Yahweh didn't desire that the whole world *become* Greek. That was the passion of Alexander. But, it's safe to say that Yahweh did want the whole world to *know* Greek. Alexander's ambition was an important facet of The Story. When the rabid renegade rabbi named Saul is converted 350 years later, a universal language is in place that he and others can exploit to spread the news of Jesus and the "mystery of the kingdom" *everywhere*.

Alexander's ambition to *unite* the known world also served as an important ground-breaking idea. It served to till the soil in preparation for the doctrine of adoption. The notion of a single human race comprised of a variety of ethnicities is at the heart of the mystery hidden for ages. Alexander, again unwittingly, laid the foundation for the radical words that would fall from the lips of Paul centuries later:

> But now in Christ Jesus you who once were far off have been brought near by the blood of Christ. For he himself is our peace, who has made us both one and has broken down in his flesh the dividing wall of hostility by abolishing the law of commandments expressed in ordinances, that *he might create in himself one new man in place of the two*, so making peace, and might reconcile us both to God in one body through the cross, thereby killing the hostility.   –**Ephesians 2:12–16**

In a sense, what we know as the Universal Church, or the Body of Christ, emerged in a tribally-oriented world that had been prepared by a brilliant pagan in the fourth century before Jesus. In a very ironic way, what Christians affirm in the confession: *"I believe in...the holy catholic church, the communion of saints,"* in the Apostles' Creed, owes *something* of its acceptance in the first century to Alexander's vision of unity.[2] The Greek contribution to the transformation of the stage during our Intermission is enormous. From it, we are bequeathed our New Testament. We also received a reorientation toward the relational unity that characterized Eden prior to the one-fruit fiasco.

---

1 The belief in the immortality of the soul while denying a physical resurrection, is a Greek idea. (cf. Acts 23:6-8)

2 I am not suggesting anything more than the idea that the existence of a common language, which allowed familiarity with Greek literature and culture, helped prepare the world for the larger notion of a unified human race in Christ. To assume that this transition was fluid and simple is to be ignorant of the hostility that existed between Jews and Gentiles in the first century, *and* the portions of our New Testament that address this tribalism.

The Roman Chapter

The second set of actors laying another highway to Act IV was from Rome,[1] the Republic-turned-Empire that conquered the shattered mosaic that Alexander bequeathed to the world upon his death. In 63 BC, the Roman commander Pompey, conquered Jerusalem and squashed the corrupt Jewish priest-king dynasty that had emerged from the ashes of Alexander's empire scattered there by one of his generals, Seleucus, three centuries earlier. A non-Jew named Antipater, had danced an ancient version of the "Potomac Two Step," artfully switching sides during the tumultuous era of Rome's move from Republic to Empire. In the process, he also endeared himself to the Hasmoneans, the Jewish priestly family ruling in Jerusalem at the time. When the Jewish house of cards collapsed and Rome finally squashed what remained of a Jewish "kingdom," Antipater found himself the benefactor of both of his associations. This is all very important, because one of his sons, and *his* descendants would dominate the biblical landscape for the next three generations. His name was Herod the Great.

It is *this* Herod that is credited with the infamous "massacre of the innocents," the wholesale killing of children two years and younger, in his frantic attempt to destroy the one called "the King of the Jews." But, it is also this Herod who is responsible for the very Temple in which Jesus would eventually teach and cause trouble. It was *this* Herod who built a spell-binding artificial port on the Mediterranean coast named Caesarea. It was at this seaport city that Peter would bring the gospel to a Gentile named Cornelius, and from which Paul would sail under guard for Rome. Herod was still dealing from both sides of the deck, trying to placate the Jews *and* Rome in his world class construction projects. Herod's personal life would have provided enough raw (in every sense of the word) material for ten seasons of daytime television, so sordid, convoluted, and demented was his life. His privileged children were educated in Rome, and Herod himself was on Marc Anthony and Cleopatra's short list for parties. This baby killer was in the elite class, comfortable with the movers and shakers of his day. However, he was only a puppet on Rome's larger stage, and as a non-Jew, a suspicious outsider at best to the descendants of Abraham living in Jerusalem. Rome's real presence in Palestine was in the form of a series of prefects, or governors who were appointed to rule an unruly people. The fifth such prefect is history's best known. His name was Pontius Pilate.

The Roman presence in Jesus' day was as prevalent as the dust it inhabited. Tax collectors, currency, legions, officers, and halls of judgement dotted the land like date palms. One could not travel five miles in any direction without a temptation to think that Rome, not Yahweh, ruled the world, and this little corner of it. Unlike Alexander, an individual with a vision of a Greek world, Rome was

---

1 Alexander, at his death, was heirless, so his empire became the object of an intense and enduring intramural conflict among a number of his generals. One of them, Seleucus and his descendants ruled Palestine until the Jews revolted and regained control during what has been called the Maccabean Revolt. The modern festival of Hanukkah (Feast of Dedication in John 10:22) is an enduring remainder and reminder of this era.

a war machine with a vision of domination. So, instead of providing us with a universal language, Rome's legacy to the first century had to do with military expansion and aristocratic prominence. Militaristic regimes need to facilitate troop movement to protect borders. They also need to stimulate commerce and collect taxes to finance its operation. Rome did this by building paved roads, some 50,000 miles of them throughout the Empire. Little did the Emperors in Rome realize they were constructing Yahweh's highways for the gospel, four centuries later. Paul and the rest of the missionary movement emanating from Jerusalem, relied heavily upon the Roman road system in their efforts to bring the *musterion* to the nations. (Most of their movements were over land, not water.)

Roman law, created to benefit the citizenry, also allowed Paul to move with near impunity through the legal system of the Roman cities in which he often found himself in danger. More than once he used his citizenship as a "get out of jail free" card.[1] But, perhaps the most significant way Yahweh employed His Roman stage crew was the fact that Rome had created a time of relative peace. With the end of the wars surrounding the fall of the Republic, a time of peace was instituted by Augustus, called the "Pax Romana." It is into this relative calm that the "fullness of time" Paul wrote of, was consummated. It takes no imagination to picture Jesus being born in Bethlehem today! Now a Palestinian territory, Joseph and Mary would not even be allowed access to the city! So, Rome provided the stage with safe and efficient travel, a just system of law, and a season of relative international peace. No small contribution to the plan for the fullness of time, even if none of it is in our Bible.

The Jewish Chapter

The third contributor to the stage during Intermission was from Yahweh's own chosen people, the Jews. Unfortunately, when we read our New Testament, we often rush to get through the Gospels. Our journey hastens to Paul and his ministry to the Gentiles. We forget that the early church was a *Jewish* church. Thoroughly Jewish. The original center of the faith was Jerusalem, not Antioch or Rome. The first converts were all Jews, as were the Apostles themselves. All the converts on Pentecost—three thousand of them—were all Jews. But, because election has more to do with purpose than ethnicity, Yahweh also used the Jews as He did with Alexander and the Romans. But, He also used them in unique ways. One was the unique way in which He strategically redistributed them. The relocation policies of the Assyrians in their destruction of the northern ten tribes of Israel in the eighth century BC, and the deportation tactics of the Babylonians in their annihilation of the Temple and the southern two tribes in the sixth century were His vehicles. By the first century, Jews were scattered throughout the known world. We have an illustrative persuasion of this reality in the Pentecost narrative in Acts 2, some six hundred years after the fact:

And at this sound the multitude came together, and they were bewildered, because

1 cf. Acts 22:25-29; 23:27

each one was hearing them speak in his own language. And they were amazed and astonished, saying, "Are not all these who are speaking Galileans? And how is it that we hear, each of us in his own native language? Parthians and Medes and Elamites and residents of Mesopotamia, Judea and Cappadocia, Pontus and Asia, Phrygia and Pamphylia, Egypt and the parts of Libya belonging to Cyrene, and visitors from Rome, both Jews and proselytes, Cretans and Arabians—we hear them telling in our own tongues the mighty works of God."   —Acts 2:6–11

Yahweh's initial insistence to Moses that His people be limited to a single shrine in one city, was a deterrent to the idolatry and polytheism that characterized their neighbors. However, its destruction at the hands of the Babylonians also cut the soul out of a people whose very identity was inseparable from their ritual. Separated from their Temple and the sacrificial system it provided, local venues of worship called "synagogues," were created. These sacred places helped assuage this loss, but were no replacement for the national shrine of Yahweh that had been in Jerusalem. For ardent Jews, synagogues were a poor substitute for the Temple, but they did provide a unique sense of identity in the cities where they dwelt as "strangers and exiles." Only those of us with the benefit of retrospect can see God's larger purposes in the demolition of their Temple. In its destruction, Yahweh didn't merely judge His people for their idolatry as He promised in His covenant with them. Out of its ruins He would extract the raw material to add to the stage He was building during the Intermission, upon which Act IV would play out. This "diaspora" of Jews created a network of starting points for Paul and others like him as the message of the mystery of the Kingdom moved out from Jerusalem to Judea and Samaria, and to the ends of the earth.

Another way Yahweh was able to draw His elect people into the unfolding of this mystery hidden for ages, was their expectation of a Messiah. The early stewards of the gospel did not have to educate the Jews about the nature of Jesus' mission. They were faced with validating the authenticity of it. The Jews were already *expecting* a Messiah, unlike the Greeks and Romans who weren't. It was part of the warp and woof of Jewish theology and life. The early apostles' task lay in explaining how a *crucified* Messiah fit the prophetic model. Paul's arguments with the Greek philosophers in Acts 17 stand in stark contrast with his arguments with orthodox Jews everywhere he went. The latter had a *place* in their thinking for a Messiah, the resurrection, and a God who was in the habit of revealing Himself personally throughout time. The Romans had deified the Emperor, and the Greeks had a pantheon of gods and goddesses whose behavior was at times less moral than the Greeks themselves. In short, the "learning curve" for Jews was very small. Unfortunately, so was their tolerance for the scandal of a message in which the long-awaited Messiah not only *died,* but he did so for Gentiles as much as for Jews!

Like the elements of a perfect storm, the three highways of Greek, Roman, and Jewish cultural influence, all converged to create a single stage awaiting the curtains to open for Act IV of this drama. Or, in the words of the Apostle Paul,

"But when the fullness of time had come, God sent forth his Son, born of woman, born under the law..."[1] It was "time" for the curtains to open, for the drama to continue. And continue it does, with the raspy voice of an eccentric rural preacher, fulfilling the words of an ancient prophecy, *"Prepare the way of the Lord, make his paths straight."*[2] Something was stirring behind the curtain. It is impossible for us living in the twenty-first century, to fathom the tumultuous effect of this voice breaking the silence of ten generations! This was a significant as the thunder the Jews heard when Moses was on top of Mount Sinai. Yahweh was speaking to His people...again.

---

1 Galatians 4:4; Paul's use of *pleroma* ("fullness") here denotes something being completed, similar to a container finally being "full."

2 cf. Mark 1:1-3; John 1:19023; Isaiah 40:3

Looking Back To The Future

John the Apostle tells us that the "world could not contain the books," if one were to record all that Jesus taught and did. Accepting that wise counsel, I surely won't attempt to prove him wrong in this brief chapter! In our Story of Five Acts, Act IV is by far the most important. It is the high point of The Story, and the fulcrum of all history. Everything either leads up to Act IV, or flows from it. Nothing in The Story has any purpose apart from it. As we learned earlier, Yahweh has *"a plan (plot) for the fullness of time, to unite all things in him* [Jesus], *things in heaven and things on earth."*[1] In Act IV, the "him" of that plan walks onto the stage that Yahweh had been building for four centuries! This is holy ground. We should probably take our shoes off when we read the four Gospels. Unfortunately, Christmas compels us to keep them on.

ACT IV—"CLIMAX" (The Four Gospels)

I've gotten myself into trouble more than once by suggesting that the Christmas carol, *Away In a Manger* should be changed to, *Away With The Manger*. I've never been a fan of Nativity Scenes, especially the "living," drive-thru versions in which the mules and sheep have more curb appeal than the Savior. The serenity and sterility they portray, and the domesticated Jesus they present and perpetuate, just doesn't match the facts. There is an irony of eternal magnitude in the fact that when the Herods and Caesars were living in opulence, the God of the universe made His incarnate entrance in a matrix of cattle manure and the obscure. Sometimes I fear the perennial parade of children in bathrobes in Christmas pageants neuters the power of that event much like the ubiquitous presence of Santa with children numbs us to the sea of consumerism we find ourselves floating in, weeks before Thanksgiving. I suppose a baby in swaddling clothes is cute and is compatible with Santa. But, the absence of birth narratives in three of the Gospels, and a careful reading of Luke's long account, should

---

1 Ephesians 1:10

make us think otherwise.[1] Luke's obvious purpose for *including* a detailed birth narrative in his lengthy and highly-detailed Gospel, appears to have more to do with the enormity of the occasion's place in The Story than to give us a family album of Jesus' childhood. The contrast between people's reactions to this birth versus that of John the Baptizer is striking. Everyone that encountered this child found themselves on their knees before him in one fashion or another, not softly smiling or thinking the ambiance was quaint.[2] Out of a woman's womb in Bethlehem, the God of eternity had stepped into time. In the later words of John the Apostle, Yahweh had "pitched His tent" in the midst of the sons and daughters of Adam.[3] A new type of Temple had appeared, one of which Jerusalem's Temple was merely a prototype.[4] Heaven had intersected earth. In an event as universe-tilting as the sin of our First Parents, deity took on flesh. If there is a hierarchy in the list of the "ways" of Yahweh that are not *our* "ways," surely this event and what it implies is near the top. The Creator had become a creature. The Potter became a pot. The manger, it turns out, was far more humiliating than the cross would ever be. That's why "drive-thru" nativity scenes tend to obscure in their effort to endear. But, that's running ahead of ourselves. Act IV finally introduces some "good news" into The Story, after what had become a long downward spiral since Act II. Before we can fully understand what happens in Act IV, we've got to get some things cleared up. Let's begin by blowing away some of the fog that has accumulated around our understanding of this "good news," or "gospel" as it is called in our New Testament.

The English word "gospel" is cut from a different cloth in our Bible than other common words like "baptize" or "king." And I think this sets us off in the wrong direction from the start. For example, "baptize" is merely the English transliteration of the Greek verb, *baptizō,* and "king" has a one-to-one correlation with the same idea in the Greek language. But, the English word "gospel" in our Bibles has its roots in Old English, *not* Greek. It is derived from *goodspel* ("good" + "story"), which over time was reduced to *godspel.* Unfortunately, in the minds of most modern Christians, their understanding of "gospel" is entirely vacant of any idea of "story," much less *The Story.* Instead, "gospel" has become a synonym for an abbreviated evangelistic effort consisting of four bullet points concluding with a prayer. And to make matters worse, we tend to superimpose

---

1 Luke is the only Gospel writer to provide us with any information surrounding the birth of Yeshua (Jesus). But even a careful reading of his text shows that his intention was to expose the variety and depth of reaction by *others* to the realization of the intersection between heaven and earth that was occurring in this birth. He doesn't portray a "cute" Jesus as much as a prostrate humanity. From the annunciation to Mary by Gabriel to the worship of the wise men, the picture that emerges is that of eternity touching time. Manger scenes allow us to smile and nod, forgetting the scene they are portraying where homage and worship are the norm.

2 cf. Matthew 2:1,11; Luke 2:8-20, 25-38

3 The Greek word John chose, *sk na* , is used throughout the Greek version of Exodus to refer to the Tabernacle, the tent-like dwelling place of Yahweh on earth. John's deliberate connection to the Old Testament Story is obvious by his opening words, *"In the beginning..."*

4 cf. John 2:19; Matthew 12:6

this meaning for "gospel" backwards onto every occurrence of it in our Bibles. So, when we read that Paul was not "ashamed of the gospel," we unconsciously envision him sharing some first century version of the Four Spiritual Laws. But, you can't bullet-point The Story. It's too big, too old, and too rich to be reduced to a PowerPoint slide.

In our New Testament, *euaggelizō*, the Greek word translated "gospel," has the features of a coin. It has two sides. One side is a verb, the activity of "proclaiming" or "preaching." The other side is a noun, the *content* of that proclamation. And we are repeatedly told this content is "good news" of some kind. I think it is both interesting and significant that in contrast to the modern four points and a prayer approach, the "gospel" in the four Gospels has less to do with the forgiveness of sins than it does an *announcement* of a major plot-line change in The Story. John the Baptizer and Jesus himself made unbreakable connections between the "good news" (i.e. gospel) and something they both call the "kingdom of God" that has broken into time and space.[1] And, whatever this "kingdom" is, it's obviously something people have been longing for, and thus its arrival is hailed as good news, a "good story," or "goodspel" if you will. And we know it is not just a "good" story, it is *The Story*, a mystery hidden for ages, a "plan for the fullness of time." Mark, in his signature abbreviated style, distills it best, attributing the "good news" to Yahweh, and linking the kingdom, the "fullness of time," and the gospel:

> Now after John was arrested, Jesus came into Galilee, proclaiming the gospel of God, and saying, "The time is fulfilled, and the kingdom of God is at hand; repent and believe in the gospel."   **—Mark 1:1, 14–15**

Don't miss me here. The message of forgiveness of sins *is* a dominant theme throughout the Gospels, running from start to finish.[2] But, the forgiveness of sins is *never* associated with the word, "gospel" *in the Gospels*, as it is in the modern message we proclaim under that banner. In fact, there isn't a single place in our New Testaments where "gospel" and "sin," or "gospel" and "forgiveness" appear in the same verse! The "good news" in the Gospels is directed more to the poor, the sick, "the nations," and the dead, than the guilty.[3] When we equate the "gospel" with news about justification from sin and guilt, our gaze is turned from The Story to ourselves. "Faith" is reduced to a means to justification (*my* justification), instead of a life of submission to a larger Story, as God intended. Paul understood this clearly, and so opens and closes Romans, his most thorough and theological letter on the topic of the "gospel," with a statement about faith that is infinitely larger than mere personal "belief":

> Paul, a servant of Christ Jesus, called to be an apostle, set apart for the gospel of God, which he promised beforehand through his prophets in the holy Scriptures, concern-

---

1 The phrase "the kingdom" appears nearly 100 times in the four Gospels, 79 of which are in Matthew and Luke alone. (cf. Matt 4:23; 9:35; 24:14; Luke 4:43; 8:1; 16:16)

2 cf. Mark 1:4; Luke 1:76-77; 3:1; 24:45-47

3 cf. Matt 4:23; 9:35; 11:5; 24:14; Luke 7:22; 9:6

ing his Son, who was descended from David according to the flesh and was declared to be the Son of God in power according to the Spirit of holiness by his resurrection from the dead, Jesus Christ our Lord, through whom *we have received grace and apostleship to bring about* **the obedience of faith** *for the sake of his name among all the nations,* including you who are called to belong to Jesus Christ...Now to him who is able to strengthen you according to my gospel and the preaching of Jesus Christ, according to the revelation of the mystery that was kept secret for long ages but has now been disclosed and through the prophetic writings *has been made known to all nations, according to the command of the eternal God, to bring about* **the obedience of faith**— to the only wise God be glory forevermore through Jesus Christ! Amen.
    –**Romans 1:1–6; 16:25–27** [emphases mine]

To make faith private and personal, instead of public and behavioral is to heist Act IV from the rest of The Story and plug it into a story of our own. And whenever faith becomes privatized, The Story will inevitably be hijacked by whatever CYOA is close at hand within the Church. Why? Because somewhere along the line we were told that the gospel is: *"God loves you and has a wonderful plan (story) for your life."* The forgiveness of sins is surely one of the *benefits* of the "good news." But, it isn't the good news itself. The gospel is the proclamation of a Kingdom arriving, not sins departing.

The four Gospels (Act IV), in their larger Story context, introduce us to the vital Act in a Story that's *older* than Jesus and more expansive than the Jews, or any people group for that matter. These four men's contributions to the larger Story simultaneously *explain* the fuller meaning of Acts I–III, and create the context for Act V. And, they have to do so in a way that is consistent with the Abrahamic blessing and mission. Is it any wonder then, that Matthew opens his Gospel reaching back from Jesus to Abraham, and closes it with Jesus sending his disciples to "the nations"?[1] What we call the Great Commission—taking the "good news" to the nations—began with Abraham, not Jesus.

> Know then that it is those of faith who are the sons of Abraham. And the Scripture, foreseeing that God would justify the Gentiles by faith, preached the gospel beforehand to Abraham, saying, "In you shall all the nations be blessed." So then, those who are of faith are blessed along with Abraham, the man of faith.   –**Galatians 3:7–9**

Perhaps this is why Matthew interprets Jesus' life and ministry as the fulfillment of prophecy no fewer than 15 times across the span of his narrative. For Matthew, what were "trailers" in the Old Testament—pointers to future hope-inspiring aspects of The Story—were now being fulfilled in the life of this one from Galilee. Our only Gentile author, Luke, also puts Abraham on center stage in his Gospel.[2] He mentions him twice as much as Matthew, a Jew.[3] Even the apostle Paul, whom many perceive as lobbying against the Mosaic Law, appar-

---

1 cf. Matthew 1:1; 28:20

2 Luke was Paul's personal physician and frequent traveling companion. It is reasonable that his own theology was highly impacted by Paul, and perhaps even a product of it. (cf. Colossians 4:14; 2 Timothy 4:11; Philemon 1:24)

3 Abraham played an enormous role in Paul's theology. In fact, Paul mentions him twice as frequently as he does Moses, and does so most in his two most theological letters, Romans and Galatians. Luke mentions Abraham 10 times in his Gospel, compared to Matthew's 7.

ently believes Abraham to be a more central figure to the "gospel" than Moses. He refers to him twice as much in his letters.[1] Jesus' cryptic statement to the Jewish elders in John's account, *"Your father Abraham rejoiced that he would see my day. He saw it and was glad,"* makes sense because of the shared purpose between him and Abraham.[2] In Act IV, the time had come. The mystery hidden for ages would be disclosed. *Everything* had been leading up to this Act. Jesus knew and accepted this. Jesus clarified his own leading role in The Story, *and* exposed our tendency to miss the larger picture. In a private theological lesson near the very end of Act IV.

> And he said to them, "O foolish ones, and slow of heart to believe all that the prophets have spoken! Was it not necessary that the Christ should suffer these things and enter into his glory?" *And beginning with Moses and all the Prophets, he interpreted to them in all the Scriptures the things concerning himself*....Then he said to them, "These are my words that I spoke to you while I was still with you, that *everything written about me in the Law of Moses and the Prophets and the Psalms must be fulfilled."* Then he opened their minds to understand the Scriptures, and said to them, "Thus it is written, that the Christ should suffer and on the third day rise from the dead, and that repentance and forgiveness of sins should be proclaimed in his name to all nations, beginning from Jerusalem." **–Luke 24:25–27, 44-45**

Seeing the Gospels as Act IV of an unbroken Story, instead of the first four books of a "New Testament," is essential to properly read and understand them. I fear that many of us are like the Levite in the parable of the Good Samaritan who ran past the injured man in his hurry to reach Jerusalem. We rush past Good Friday to get to Easter, and I suspect we sprint through the Gospels to get to Golgotha and the empty tomb. Unfortunately, in the process, we run right past the eternal purposes of God. This is because we tend to read and think in terms of our story instead of *The Story.* But, this isn't unique to us. The Jews of Jesus' day seemed prone to the same "fixate on the destination and miss the journey" syndrome. So, as we look at Act IV, we need to begin by stepping back from our aggregated but erroneous notion that the whole point of the four Gospels is to tell us the "good news" that our sins are forgiven. Therefore, we can have a personal savior and a private salvation. Jesus lived nearly 40 years, not 40 hours. Why? Was there a "point" to all that he did prior to Golgotha?

Thy Kingdom Come, Thy Will Be Done

When Jesus first appeared as the Messiah in his home synagogue, he chose a passage in Isaiah from which to read that was dripping with connections between the Messiah, "good news," and the poor and oppressed.[3] These were all

---

1 Paul mentions Abraham 19x compared to 9 for Moses. This is consistent with his insistence that Mosaic Judaism was, by design, a temporary feature in the larger Story which was Abrahamic in nature. Paul's two most theological treatises, Galatians and Romans, rely heavily upon Abrahamic connection to the gospel. It is also likely that his repeated attack on "the works of the Law" is best understood to reflect his belief that the Law has no place in the life of a believer because its purpose has been completed. For Paul, the Law held no real purpose even for a Jew, much less a Gentile convert.

2 John 8:56

3 cf. Isaiah 61:1-3

common Jewish themes, but they were typically associated with the end of all things. They were the hope of first century Jews. But, for most, they were part of a distant future, something to look forward to, or maybe for your children to enjoy. But that Saturday in the synagogue, as Jesus rolled up the Isaiah scroll and handed it back to the attendant, he asserted: *"Today this Scripture has been fulfilled in your hearing."*[1] The energy that statement unleashed is an indicator of just how deeply ingrained these messianic longings were. Some were ecstatic, suddenly realizing the hope of the ages might be birthed in their lifetime. Maybe in their very midst! But, indignation and anticipation collided explosively as hope was birthed in one heart, and hostility in another. This was *not* the way it was supposed to unfold! Certainly not a quiet announcement in an obscure town by an itinerant laborer! At least, that's what some thought. Those who anticipate or dictate *how* Yahweh must act, always seem to be either incensed or distracted when He finally does. That day in Nazareth was no different. They missed the first press release of the mystery because it wasn't what they expected. And, that's because Yahweh wasn't who they thought He was either. One author masterfully connects this reality with another unavoidable truth in the Gospels, namely that Jesus' fan base came from the weak, needy, and uneducated, not the rich and illustrious:

> Jesus, telling stories about a sower sowing seeds, about weeds among the wheat, and about a vineyard where the tenants refuse to give the owner the fruit, is allowing these ancient echoes to take root in the fertile and scripture-soaked minds of his hearers, to try to get through to them the message that what they have longed for is happening at last, but it doesn't look as they thought it would! God is at last doing the great new thing he's always promised for Israel—but the wrong people seem to be getting the message, and many of the right people are missing it entirely![2]

This case of mistaken identity runs throughout the four Gospels. It will eventually be used by Yahweh to send some angry Jews to Pilate to seek his murder, and draw others to Jesus to seek His Kingdom. Because *The Story* wasn't their story, many missed God in skin when He came to town. But, those who *had* no story, the poor and powerless, were spellbound watching Jesus touch and teach. Their plot hunger was aroused as he unveiled what the arrival of this Kingdom would look like. They no doubt hung on every parable that began with, "The Kingdom of God is like..." Their plot hunger was being slaked, at least a little. For them, this definitely *was* "good news." At least, that's how it began. But, as we work our way through the Gospel narratives, we see perplexity growing right alongside hostility. Even Jesus' entrance into Jerusalem on Palm Sunday was a mixed metaphor. He was hailed as a king, yet rode on a donkey's colt, a

---

1 Luke 4:21b; It is significant to me, that Luke's account of this puts Jesus' comment in the perfect tense in Greek. This tense is typically used to refer to an action whose effects continue indefinitely. Jesus is speaking here of a very permanent "fulfillment." In our modern idiom, he was saying, "The game you've been waiting for is on!" Or, as he says elsewhere, "the kingdom of God is at hand."

2 Wright, *Simply Jesus*, 90-91.

symbol of peace not victory.[1] Though Matthew, reflecting years later, informs his readers that this event was a fulfillment of a fifth century BC "trailer."[2] It is reasonable to assume that a common laborer riding a baby donkey was not what they anticipated for the one to shatter Rome's yoke. But, how could they know that Jesus was *not* coming to save the Jews from Rome? He had come to bring a Kingdom that was "not of this world." But, even this is still hidden from sight. It will take Paul (who was still the unconverted Saul), to guide believers to see the unbroken connection between Adam in Eden, Abraham in Ur, and Jesus in Jerusalem. This was new wine indeed. But, not everyone had the new skins to contain it.

The atonement for sin that Golgotha secured enabled humanity and the God whose image it bore, to be reconciled at last. Just as Jesus had promised.[3] But, it also marked a turning point in a war that began in Eden, not Italy. Rome was not the enemy, merely a pawn of the real Enemy. What happened that ancient Friday when hope had fled hand-in-hand with daylight, and the souls of the hopeful were rent in half along with the Temple curtain, was *not* just that humanity's sin debt was paid. It was! And, that is surely good news. *But, it isn't the gospel.* The *real* "good news" always has to do with the *Kingdom*, not its subjects. In speaking of his impending crucifixion, Jesus had said, *"Now is the judgment of this world; now will the ruler of this world be cast out."* That meant the oldest "trailer" on record for Act IV, found near the end of Act II, was in the queue and about to play itself out in The Story for real:[4]

> The LORD God said to the serpent, "Because you have done this, cursed are you above all livestock and above all beasts of the field; on your belly you shall go, and dust you shall eat all the days of your life. I will put enmity between you and the woman, and between your offspring and her offspring; he shall bruise [crush] your head, and you shall bruise his heel." **–Genesis 3:14–15**

Those who *insisted* they knew what The Story should look like, had hardened their hearts and galvanized their plans. But, even those who were truly "looking for the kingdom," including John the Baptizer himself, seemed to grow more and more confused by Jesus' obvious intention *not* to restore the throne of David.[5] Their frustration stemmed from not *knowing* The Story, the former's

---

1 cf. 1 Kings 1:33-35

2 cf. Zechariah 9:9

3 cf. John12:31-33

4 A few years later, Paul will assure the Colossian believers with a similar thought, drawing a tight circle around their justification, Jesus's death, and the spiritual victory of that weekend: *And you, who were dead in your trespasses and the uncircumcision of your flesh, God made alive together with him, having forgiven us all our trespasses, by canceling the record of debt that stood against us with its legal demands. This he set aside, nailing it to the cross. He disarmed the rulers and authorities and put them to open shame, by triumphing[1] over them in him.* (Colossians 2:13–15). Paul's Roman imagery here is unmistakable. He is pointing to the Roman "triumph," the victory parade in which victor and vanquished are paraded before the populace in Rome. This is a public spectacle. One of great honor for the victor and great shame for the vanquished. He uses an even clearer reference to the "triumph" in 2 Corinthians 2:14. In Paul's thinking, what happened on Good Friday was a shift in kingdom supremacy.

5 cf. Luke 17:18-20; Mark 14:3-11; Matthew 20:20-28

hostility from not *wanting* The Story as it was unfolding. One led to murder, the other to abandonment. As Act IV unfolded, the hostility of a minority, as is often the case, trumped the confusion of the majority. By the time Good Friday arrived, less than a week after Palm Sunday's grand procession, Jesus found himself abandoned on a Roman cross, his accusers present, and his disciples absent, save for John and a few women. And from this final cruciform pulpit, he cried out, "It is finished," the public proclamation of what he had said privately in prayer with his disciples the night before, "I have finished the work you gave me to do."[1] With this seemingly anticlimactic announcement, The Story appeared to stall. The expectations of all Israel were hanging dead on a tree atop a desolate hill. For portions of the next two days, we can only imagine the desecration of hope that spread through Jerusalem like a plague. Jesus' last words, "It is finished," would have been repeated countless times, as eyewitnesses rehearsed the events of that afternoon to those who were absent. All hope was past tense. Jesus was right. It really *was* "finished."

The Day Death Died

The one thing that had prevented the arrival of the Kingdom, the very thing that stopped it dead in its tracks just as it was arriving, was Death. The threat looming over the Tree in Eden had ruled supreme and unchallenged since that fateful and infamous choice. And Death had surely been the victor on Golgotha. How could there be a Kingdom? The King had died. It was "finished," but, it was not over. The Story doesn't end here.

No one could have imagined that Death itself could die. And die it did, early on the first day of that week. The death of Death has another name; resurrection. And resurrection marked the beginning of what was next in The Story, now that the work on Good Friday was finished—the coming of the Kingdom in power. Mark tells us at the end of his Gospel that after ascending into heaven, Jesus "sat down at the right hand of God."[2] His reign as King began after his ascension. He is the King of Kings and Lord of Lords *now*, not eventually. No more mangers, no more swaddling clothes, no more nativity scenes. And, from the throne of God we hear a word from his lips that informs us that what happened on Golgotha was bigger than sin and the human race:

> And he who was seated on the throne said, "Behold, I am making all things new."
> Also he said, "Write this down, for these words are trustworthy and true."
> –**Revelation 21:5**

The work Jesus had "finished" made possible the work that was still to be done, the blessing of the nations. Jesus told his disciples that because he was returning to the Father, *they* would be able to continue "works" he had begun:

---

1 John 17:1-5 and 19:30

2 Mark 16:19; Although this statement appears in a disputed section of Mark, its truth is substantiated by numerous other New Testament references by Paul and others (cf. Ephesians 1:20; 1 Peter 3:22; Hebrews 1:3).

Truly, truly, I say to you, whoever believes in me will also do the works that I do; and greater works than these will he do, because I am going to the Father.
–John 14:12

The entire *life* of Jesus has to be perceived as playing as large a role in The Story as his death. Jesus distills his mission here to two facets, of which only one is related to Golgotha and Good Friday: *"For even the Son of Man came not to be served but to serve, and to give his life as a ransom for many."*[1] If we're not careful, we'll be preoccupied with his suffering, dying, and rising. We will miss the inseparable connection he repeatedly made between his role as Messiah, and his ministry of feeding, touching, and healing.[2] When this type of theological myopia combines with our tendency to make the gospel synonymous with sin and justification, the stage is set for the CYOA version of purpose and mission that has hijacked much of American evangelicalism. Our individual justification is inflated to be the primary purpose for the Incarnation. And, as we've seen, justification is *not* the gospel. The gospel is the announcement of the Kingdom; Golgotha, the Empty Tomb, and the Ascension to the throne of Yahweh. The final moments of Act IV marked the beginning of something bigger than my forgiveness. It's true that the gospel *involves* me and my guilt, and justification is surely one of its blessings. But it's not *about* me. It's about the Kingdom coming on earth as it is in heaven. And *that* is a "good Story," one that would surely be a blessing to all who hear it. It's a Story worth taking to the nations, which is exactly what happens in Act V.

---

1 Mark 10:45; cf. Matthew 20:26-28; Luke 22:26-27; Titus 2:14

2 cf. Matthew 4:23; 9:35; 11:2-6; Luke 4:16-21

Looking Ahead To The Past

ACT V — "CONSUMMATION – Scene 1" (Acts thru Jude)

Act V, the final Act in The Story, is book-ended by Jesus' Ascension at the beginning, and his Second Coming at the end. And by "end" here, we really mean the end! It is, somewhere within Act V that we must locate ourselves. Act V is *long*, longer than Act III that took us from Abraham to Artaxerxes. And similar to Act III and its place in the Old Testament, Act V comprises most of our New Testament. Let me lay a word of caution here, however. The volume of ink must never be used to determine relative value. Act IV is still the centerpiece of The Story. And Jesus, not Paul, is the key figure. I am amazed and saddened by the relative unimportance placed on the words of Jesus compared to those of Paul. Between the lines of some preachers and theologians, you get the distinct impression that the primary purpose of Jesus was to give Paul something to write about. Yet, Jesus told Andrew, *"Anyone who has seen me has seen the Father."* The writer of Hebrews tells us that "*He is the radiance of the glory of God and the exact imprint of his nature."*[1] Act IV (the four Gospels) affords us the clearest, most exhaustive, and final portrait we have of Yahweh in a body. Don't ever forget that. Whatever you're reading, whomever you're reading, make sure that Act IV is at the top of that list throughout all of life.

Luke, the largest contributor to the New Testament, serves as liaison between Act IV and Act V[2] by putting the Ascension of Jesus and the events surrounding it at the center of his 2-volume effort, Luke-Acts. The event appears at the place both books nearly touch each other, the *end* of his Gospel and the *beginning* of Acts. This nearly seamless transition yields a beautiful continuity

1 John 14:9 and Hebrews 1:3

2 Luke, a Gentile, made the largest contribution to our New Testament, nearly 28 out of every 100 words. This is more than the apostle Paul, even though Paul provided 13 letters, compared to Luke's 2 books. Luke's volume is greater. I believe it is significant that Yahweh, in compiling our only record of his Story, uses a non-Jew as a major player in the record of final two Acts, in which the blessing of Abraham is actually getting to "the nations" (i.e., the *goyim*).

to The Story, with Jesus' missional mandate to the Apostles to go to the nations, and his ascent to rule at the right hand of the Father as the shared piece. In Luke, it is Jesus' final command. In Acts, it serves as the introduction and outline to the book. What we glibly call the "Great Commission" is *not* a call to evangelize. It is a command to take The Story to the nations. In fact, this is the entire *purpose* of the Church because it is the purpose of God. Not understanding this creates a fast track to believing the Church exists for itself, and getting people to "come to church" is the fulfillment of the Great Commission. This is to get things backwards regarding purpose, which inevitably means getting things wrong about mission.

> It is not so much the case that God has a mission for his church in the world, as that God has a church for his mission in the world. Mission was not made for the church; the church was made for mission—God's mission.[1]

Understanding the equivalence between the mission of Abraham and the mission of the Church is the only deterrent against the encroachment of the self into the gospel. It also curtails a CYOA approach to the "Mission Statement" of any local community of believers. The refusal to see it this way is at the heart of tribalism among Christians. A "market share" approach to ministry prevents churches and individuals from locking arms and pooling resources to bring The Story to the nations. God has never negotiated with His people regarding what *they* felt their mission should be. He never will. There is only one mission because there is only one Story. To the degree that you and I and the groups of believers with whom we gather understand this, to that degree we are truly the Church, the "people of God." And of course, the inverse is also true. Scholar and author Christopher Wright takes it a step further and *disqualifies* any group from *being* the Church, if it refuses to submit itself and its plans to the One Story: *"In this age, the church is missional or it is not the church."*[2]

Scene 1 of Act V presents to us the immense challenge of a predominately Jewish Church to accept the temporary nature of Judaism, and embrace the eternal purpose of Yahweh to bring the blessing of Abraham to all peoples. Luke's Book of Acts also provides the chronological matrix within which most of Paul's letters were written. Between Luke and Paul we can construct a partial but glorious picture of the spread of the good news from Jewish Jerusalem, to biracial Samaria, and onto "the nations," the Gentile peoples living around the Mediterranean Basin. Luke's detailed account provides us with valuable insight regarding the conversion of Saul, the death of Stephen and James, and the early persecution of believers. It also informs us of a significant role reversal in the narrative. Namely, the withdrawal of Jesus and the preeminence of the Holy Spirit who averages two appearances per chapter, more than any other book in the New Testament. We are front row spectators as the good news moves in concentric circles outward from the place Jesus was last seen, to parts of the

1 Wright, *The Mission of God*, 62.
2 Wright, *The Mission of God's People*, 93.

world he had never visited. We learn of radical conversions, churches planted, and ultimately of a new "chosen people" drawn from the very social strata the Jews were careful to exclude:

> For as many of you as were baptized into Christ have put on Christ. There is neither Jew nor Greek, there is neither slave nor free, there is no male and female, for you are all one in Christ Jesus. And if you are Christ's, then you are Abraham's offspring, heirs according to promise.   —**Galatians 3:27–29**

> ...and have put on the new self, which is being renewed in knowledge after the image of its creator. Here there is not Greek and Jew, circumcised and uncircumcised, barbarian, Scythian, slave, free; but Christ is all, and in all.   —**Colossians 3:10–11**

> Do not be deceived: neither the sexually immoral, nor idolaters, nor adulterers, nor men who practice homosexuality, nor thieves, nor the greedy, nor drunkards, nor revilers, nor swindlers will inherit the kingdom of God. And such were some of you. But you were washed, you were sanctified, you were justified in the name of the Lord Jesus Christ and by the Spirit of our God.   —**1 Corinthians 6:9–11**

Scene 1 of Act V has been christened by some as the "Apostolic Age" because the infant Church was led by men and women who were connected in varying degrees of proximity, to the original disciples who were trained by Jesus. Luke gives us a partial record of their movements in Acts, and the remainder of Act V provides us with much of their correspondence to various churches. These remaining letters, which themselves claim divine inspiration, constitute the majority of our New Testament.[1] Our doctrine of the inspiration of Scripture demands that we ascribe to them the same status we give to the Old Testament. However, when it comes to the actual movement of the apostles and other stewards of the mysteries of God, it becomes clear that there was a degree of improvisation occurring,[2] unlike the obvious outlines followed in their letters. In other words, this "gospel to the nations" stuff was virgin territory for all of them. The Jewish Law had worship and obedience down to rocket science. If there was ever such a thing as "cookbook" religious behavior, they had the recipe. Everybody knew their place and their part. No confusion. But, the coming of the Holy Spirit in power at Pentecost changed all that, forever. It was messy, and it pretty much stayed that way throughout the narrative in the Book of Acts. It was surely a stretch for the Jewish Christians to extend the hand of fellowship to the biracial Samaritans. For most first century Jews, the only good Samaritan was a dead one. We find the early Church convening, trying to figure out what to do with Samaritans who claim to be believers. Jesus never gave specifics on

---

1 2 Peter 3:14-16 is an excellent illustration of this point. Peter, in speaking of people twisting Paul's writings, includes *them* in the category of "Scripture."

2 Luke's account of Paul's various *attempts* at ministry in regions of Asia is an excellent example of this. While it is obvious that God knew exactly what he wanted Paul to do, and how and where, as one reads the account, it is obvious Paul doesn't have a clue. He simply keeps trying new avenues, hoping one will open up. (cf. Acts 16:6-9). Also, it is obvious that Paul and Barnabas could not agree on the qualifications for a missionary companion, and actually had a "falling out" over the issue, and it appears that even Barnabas's home church sided against him and in favor with Paul (cf. Acts 15:36-40). All this is simply to say that much of the certainty with which modern ministry moves forward, has no abiding counterpart in Acts, even when it involved first order Apostles.

this one![1] Then, the good news of The Story extends to Gentiles, then to women, then to slaves, prostitutes, homosexuals, and so on. Where is this all going? You can almost feel the frustration, and intuit the "heat," that some of these early deliberations must have produced.

Fortunately, Scene 1 of Act V is directed by Spirit-led, Apostolic leadership. It was new territory for everyone, but at least they had some of Jesus' veteran Apostles to help work their way into the unknown. And we too have inherited a wonderful byproduct from their efforts, failures, and victories—our New Testament. Because we now find ourselves in a different Scene of the same Story, what they've left us is very, very important. But remember, God's word to us was first God's word to someone else. We have to continually remind ourselves of this as we read the inspired letters that endured. They were written by Spirit-led Apostles, speaking into specific contemporary circumstances, seeking to assist the newcomers to this Story idea; what it meant to be a "Story-dweller" in first century culture. These letters are brilliantly insightful, and contain timeless truth that spills well beyond the boundaries of their own time. But, even collectively, they do *not* comprise a specific "handbook" for church planting. Any attempt to hatch a "New Testament church," using them as a *script*, is doomed to failure or exclusivity. What we have in our New Testament; therefore, is an amazing record of Spirit-led improvisation when it came to fulfilling the mandate Jesus gave just prior to his exit. For our part, this should lead to a modicum of humility regarding the way we interpret what it all means for the twenty-first century. The certainty without apology or reservation that characterizes much modern Christian verbiage about life and ministry, is rightly interpreted by the watching world as arrogance. I dare say that God is irritated too.

ACT V—"CONSUMMATION – Scene 2" (The Present)

Scene 2 of Act V is basically a continuation of Scene 1, with one major difference—no first order Apostles are left on the planet. Symbolically, it looks like this:

[Spirit-directed, Apostle-led improvisation] – Apostles = Spirit-led improvisation

Add to the absence of first order Apostles the fact that we have *no* written script. At least those living in Scene 1 could draw on the letters that were circulating. Not so for Scene 2. Surely we must have *something*! We don't. When it comes to the Bible's record of The Story, this is the *only* part of it where the Scriptures are silent. What about the New Testament? Helpful. But, it's a record of Scene 1, remember? And Scene 1 is over. We're in Scene 2 now. I don't know about you, but to me, this is pretty significant, considering that Scene 2 is where I live! Even the churches in the episcopal traditions who claim unbro-

---

1 We do have a beautiful story of an encounter between Jesus and a Samaritan woman in John 4. In the story, Jesus not only speaks to her, and teaches her, but she come to faith in him and becomes an evangelist to her own village! Jesus and the disciples apparently stay in the Samaritan village for several days, teaching. Jesus set an example here, but there was no clear instruction to take the gospel to them as a distinct people group. An "occasional" Samaritan or Gentile convert is one thing. To have entire regions of Samaritans and Gentiles seeking to join the young church is quite another.

ken spiritual lineage back to the Apostles are out of change on this one. This is Spirit-led improvisation on steroids! Whenever I teach on this fact, I can feel some people's blood pressure rising. They just don't want to think of life and ministry in this context. It doesn't seem right. But the truth is; it doesn't seem very "American." We want to be in control, or pretend to be. But, when it comes to Scene 2 of The Story, we don't have a detailed script. My point here is huge, but its importance has more to do with *attitude* than aptitude. How we go about *doing* ministry not how good we are *at* it. And, if you've been around folks in ministry as much as I have over the past 40 plus years, you know that many of us act as though we *really* know what God is doing, and are eager to tell you. But, the inconvenient truth (something anyone who's been engaged in significant ministry for any length of time knows), is this: *we really haven't got a clue what we're doing.* And that's the truth. Let me unpack what I mean.

First, this is an attitudinal issue. It simply means that at the end of the day, because God doesn't have a Twitter feed or a Facebook page, he's *not* in the business of providing updates on how The Story is doing. In addition, self-promotion is outside His skill set, and buried deep within His sovereignty is the liberty He has granted people to make choices, which He seems to honor. There is also at least *some* evidence that Christians make mistakes, can't get along, tend to take their Adamic residue to church with them from time to time, and that more churches have gone broke from too much ego than too little money. All this to say, *we really have no clue on what we're doing for The Story, in The Story, or to The Story.*

This is compounded by an Enlightenment gene I'm convinced has wormed its way into the Christian genome sometime after the eighteenth century. We, more than any other religious tradition, seem to be obsessed with needing to *tell* people what God is "doing" in our lives. We also expect others to give us a report on their own Christian experience. I'll never forget someone asking me what God was "teaching" me through two family divorces, my mother's death, and a personal bout with cancer complete with complications. I felt a wave of embarrassment crawl across my soul when something didn't immediately come to mind. I guess I assumed that for an inquiry as "spiritual" as this *something* should immediately present itself; sort of like an appointment on my smartphone. But, nothing did. Staring blankly at the person, I confessed, "I don't know." He looked at me as though God must have sent a memo, and I missed it. Something deep inside me wanted to respond a little more aggressively, "How could I *possibly* know the answer to that?" Now, before you judge me, let me "update" that report. Of course cancer brought me back to square one. Of course, cancer fueled my prayer life. Of course, cancer caused me to deal with compassion to others who've suffered before me. Of course cancer rocked my world and drove me to God. And, the combination of that with the divorces, death, and about five other things I failed to mention, turned my heart inside out. But, to be asked to report on what *God* was "teaching me," I really couldn't say. *He* hadn't told me. Oh, I surely had *something* to report. And that's what we do, don't we, find *something*? At least that's what I did that day. I lied. I'm a Bible teacher for crying out loud. I'm *supposed* to have an answer to a question like that. But, the bottom line is; I didn't know. And, I still don't. I *do* know I'm not the same person. I *do* know that God's deafening silence at a time of great need caused me to struggle in a new and fresh way with His goodness *and* His God-ness. I *do* know that the pain wore away my thin little Jesus veneer and besieged my previous quick-to-respond reporting of what God was "doing" or "saying" in my life. But to attribute something to *God* with certainty? Well, I think that requires more burning-bush sorts of attributes, instead of a warm feeling of brokenness while having a quiet time or weeping. And if I *don't* have an answer, is it pride or fear that prompts me to respond as if I do? Wouldn't it be richer and more honoring to Him to simply say, "I'm not sure. But here's some things I now know," or something a bit more honest and true to reality?

Even worse, sometimes, we *abuse* other Christians using what God has "told" us as a stick to beat them into submission. How in the world do you respond when a pastor tells his congregation that *God* has "told" him they need to build a bigger building, or move to a new location? It's easier to feel unclean or at least unspiritual, than to question such a proclamation. Who am I to question what God has "told" anyone? I'm pushing this point because of my initial comment: this is about *attitude*, not aptitude. We Christians exude a certainty without humility about things we simply don't know for sure. Part of it is that we don't want to appear immature to other believers, or incompetent around unbelievers. But in the end, no one benefits, including God. And, it repulses many people, especially those who think and feel deeply.

This does *not* mean we should be hopeless or conclude that we are helpless. Or that God doesn't make some things very clear. It *does* mean, however, that we should be humble, both in living and in ministry. It means that we acknowledge our Adamic residue that wants to be first, wants to be right, and wants to be noticed. It demands that we *listen* to others when they speak into our lives or our plans, things that run counter to them. It means our commitment to The Story always has priority over any contribution we want to make in it. It means that we admit to ourselves, and maybe to others from time to time, that we really *don't* know what on earth God is doing. To do otherwise, to pretend to always know, is pride all dressed up and ready for Church. This is serious, though, because God said in His Word He is *opposed* to the proud.[1] He's *against* them, not merely disappointed with them. And to make matters worse, when it comes to spiritual progress or ministry, pride dams up grace. It prevents it from flowing. If there's anything we Christians need, it's grace. And if there's anything we don't need, it's pride. Admitting that we don't always know what God is "doing," "teaching," or "asking" might be a step in the direction of spiritual maturity, not infancy. Veteran pastor, Eugene Peterson, believes that God

1 cf. I Peter 5:5

does His best work when we admit that we are in over our head when it comes to what God is doing:

> Well-meaning people tell us that the Christian gospel will put us in charge of life, will bring us happiness and bounty. So we go out and buy a Bible. We adapt, edit, sift, summarize. We then use whatever seems useful and apply it in our circumstances however we see fit. We take charge of the Christian gospel, using it as a toolbox to repair our lives, or as a guidebook for getting what we want, or as an inspirational handbook to enliven a dull day. But we aren't smart enough to do that; nor can we be trusted to do that. The Holy Spirit is writing us into the revelation, the story of salvation. We find ourselves in the story as followers of Jesus. Jesus calls us to follow him and we obey—or we do not. This is an immense world of God's salvation that we are entering; we don't know enough to use or apply anything. Our task is to obey—believingly, trustingly obey. Simply obey in a "long obedience."[1]

Scene 2 is where we live. It's the "in-between" time since the death of the Apostle John on the Island of Patmos, and the return of the King riding on a white horse. We live in the "here, but not yet" portion of The Story. And, it's a tough place to pitch your tent, because like the early Church, we are improvising. But, *unlike* the early Church, the Apostles have all left the party. Paul, a late comer to The Story, but partner with us in it, offers these words of comfort:

> Not that I have already obtained this or am already perfect, but I press on to make it my own, because Christ Jesus has made me his own. Brothers, I do not consider that I have made it my own. But one thing I do: forgetting what lies behind and straining forward to what lies ahead, I press on toward the goal for the prize of the upward call of God in Christ Jesus. Let those of us who are mature think this way, and if in anything you think otherwise, God will reveal that also to you. Only let us hold true to what we have attained. Brothers, join in imitating me, and keep your eyes on those who walk according to the example you have in us.[2]

Paul's counsel is this: *"Set your heart on the very thing that God set His heart on you for in the first place—His plan for the fullness of time and your place in it. Make that your one holy passion. And, if you get off track, God will let you know. But, meanwhile, seek out some people who've got The Story straight, and study how they do it."* When it comes to The Story, be humble, be diligent, be teachable, and be available. Paul says if you get off script, Yahweh Himself will let you know. That's really good news about the "good news"!

ACT V—"CONSUMMATION – Scene 3" (Revelation)

I realized that I probably should have packed a lunch, when a recent online search on a Christian book site returned 1,625 titles or subtitles that had "The Book of Revelation" in them. But, then I decided I wouldn't be staying for lunch after all. Upon scrolling through phrases like, "Breaking the Code," "Unlocking," "Understanding," "Explaining," and "Unveiling," side-by-side with statements that a particular book was for "Dummies," "Blockheads," or "Idiots," two things became immediately clear. The first was a general ambiance of confu-

---

1 Peterson, *The Pastor*, 248-49.

2 Philippians 3:12–17

sion enveloping the Book of Revelation. The second was an equally pervasive attitude of certainty from author to author, regarding their acute ability to liberate the reader from that confusion. However, given the polarity of opinions offered in the titles, I had to conclude that nearly all the contributors fell into that class of people who are often mistaken, but never in doubt.

Why would God make the last Scene of His epic Story the most difficult to decipher? What's the point of that? How are we supposed to make sense of God's final installment about His plan for the fullness of time, if it has to be unlocked, unveiled, and its "code" broken? Having just impugned the army of authors who have tried to "unveil" Revelation, I would hardly offer my interpretation! What I would like to proffer in its place; however, is a warning. I think we are in danger of losing our moorings when we spend our strength winnowing opinions as we search for interpretive certainty, and neglect viewing Revelation in the larger light of its contribution to The Story. I've labored to almost force you—gently of course—to keep returning to the metaphor of story regarding how you read and think about the Bible. In so doing, I am fully aware of the interpretive crater I've created on the level of particulars. But, I also am comforted knowing that multitudes of scholarly men and women have taken that work upon themselves. Bookshelves and Kindles are full of the fruit of their labor. *So, What's Your Point?* has been about identity, purpose, and mission. Purpose depends on plot, and plot depends on Story. We've worked arduously to birth and nurture a narrative approach to the Bible. Revelation is the end of that narrative. Its contribution has to fulfill that role, even if its complexity evades a final and complete (or comprehensive) understanding. Put simply, how does The Story end, and what effect should that have on your life and mine?

The full answer to those two questions will occupy the remaining chapters. The short answer is that The Story ends with a masterful conclusion that resolves all the problems created in Act II. The Abrahamic mission is completed successfully, evidenced by "the nations" singing together around the throne of Yahweh and the Lamb. Then, the "credits" roll, and time is swallowed up by eternity. If you're among those who stay for the "credits" at movies, secretly hoping for an "out-take" or two, then you've watched a million lines of text, honoring people with roles that defy understanding, like "gaffer," "key grip," and "cutter," just to mention a few. There are also the leading roles, supporting roles, screenwriters, etc. The list seems to be without end. No one appears to be left out. Our Adamic residue, deep down, longs for The Story to end this way. Something hardwired into our fallen selves seems to hope that if we sat long enough, surely our own name would appear on the screen. Even if just for a moment. But it doesn't. If there *are* credits that roll, they will read something like:

WRITTEN AND DIRECTED BY **YAHWEH**

STARRING **YESHUA MOSHIACH**

PRODUCED BY **THE HOLY SPIRIT**

Abraham won't get a nod. Moses won't either. In light of that fact, I don't think you or I should wait to see whether we do either. God alone will be glorified. It was *His* plan for the fullness of time to unite all things in him, things in heaven and things on earth. Start to finish, it was Yahweh working by grace, in us, through us, and for us, to reverse and restore what Adam had ruined:

> Then I saw a new heaven and a new earth, for the first heaven and the first earth had passed away, and the sea was no more. And I saw the holy city, new Jerusalem, coming down out of heaven from God, prepared as a bride adorned for her husband. And I heard a loud voice from the throne saying, "Behold, the dwelling place of God is with man. He will dwell with them, and they will be his people, and God himself will be with them as their God. He will wipe away every tear from their eyes, and death shall be no more, neither shall there be mourning, nor crying, nor pain anymore, for the former things have passed away." And he who was seated on the throne said, "Behold, I am making all things new." Also he said, "Write this down, for these words are trustworthy and true." –**Revelation 21:1–5**

"Behold, I am making all things new" is a summary statement of the consummation of The Story. God here gives us a preview snapshot of the closing Scene, where His grand Story is headed. It is a glorious sight, and a blessed hope. The certainty of this outcome is to be a source of strength for those of us still living in Scene 2. You and I *know* how The Story ends! Of course, we have only snippets in this passage, a biblical version of a travel brochure, I suppose. But, we *are* given the end of The Story, and it's an amazing ending. This is a case where a "spoiler" doesn't really spoil anything. It merely creates greater anticipation.

But, we must never forget that although we are *longing* for Scene 3, we're still *living* in Scene 2. And one of the unfortunate consequences of not thinking about where we are in The Story, is minimizing the harsh realization that we are still in the jaws of what Yahweh calls "the former things." This is the world of tears, death, mourning, crying out, and pain.[1] It is the world of Adam's folly. And, it is our world too. It is *this* world that will finally and thoroughly be undone when He "makes all things new." A question immediately arises for the people of God living during the time of the "former things." What is *our* responsibility? Or put another way, what is our mission? Because the mission of God has always been the mission of God's people, we need to fully understand what are *His* plans for Scene 2, the time of the "former things"? And for that, we'll need to take a slow walk in an ancient garden.

---

1 It is worth noting that the Greek word translated "crying" (*kraugē*) means to "cry out" or "wail." It is the same word used in the Greek Old Testament referring to the "outcry" against Sodom and Gomorrah by the poor and oppressed (cf. Gen. 18:20). The point here is not merely sorrow. "Mourning" and "tears" includes those emotions. This is a reference to hopeless despair caused by oppression, the plight of the poor, the widow, the fatherless, and the sojourner in the Ancient Near East.

Milton Got It, Why Can't We?

In the latter part of the seventeenth century, a twice-widowed, blind, and impoverished man, dictated an epic poem of 10,000 lines of blank verse to his daughters. The publisher paid about $7 for his efforts. It would turn out to be what most literary critics now consider the greatest English-language poem of all time. John Milton's *Paradise Lost* is a masterful retelling of the events that were responsible for the beginning of the long, long half-life of "the former things." In the poem, Milton recasts the fall of Satan, his subsequent takeover of Earth, and his temptation and conquest of Eve and Adam as a serpent. In doing so, he brilliantly captured the onset of Act II of The Story, what theologians call the Fall of Man. Buried deep in the bowels of *Paradise Lost,* somewhere after the first 9,000 lines of poetry, is a conversation between Adam and the archangel Michael that occurs as a vision. For the next 1,000 lines, Milton unpacks in vivid poetic detail The Story of Yahweh, which, on the stage of human choices, was necessitated by their decision to listen to the Serpent instead of obey God.

> But him the gentle Angel by the hand
> Soon rais'd, and his attention thus recall'd.
> ADAM, now ope thine eyes, and first behold
> Th' effects which thy original crime hath wrought.
> In some to spring from thee, who never touch'd
> Th' excepted Tree, nor with the Snake conspir'd,
> Nor sinn'd thy sin, yet from that sin derive
> Corruption to bring forth more violent deeds.[1]

Adam is taken on a tour of human corruption that flows out from the first couple in Eden like a dark shadow. He learns of the future murder of their son Abel by his brother Cain in a grisly and lurid portrayal that is as moving as it is accurate. The Flood, the Tower of Babel, disease, sickness, and death parade

---

1 http://www.ccel.org/ccel/milton/paradiselost.xi.html

themselves before Adam like a lineup of ghastly characters in the drama. Michael walks Adam through the entire Story from the demise in Eden to the return of Christ, or in our language, Act II through Scene 3 of Act V.

> Rarely be found: so shall the World goe on,
> To good malignant, to bad men benigne,
> Under her own waight groaning, till the day
> Appeer of respiration to the just,
> And vengeance to the wicked, at return
> Of him so lately promis'd to thy aid,
> The Woman's seed, obscurely then foretold,
> Now amplier known thy Saviour and thy Lord,
> Last in the Clouds from Heav'n to be reveald
> In glory of the Father, to dissolve
> SATAN with his perverted World, then raise
> From the conflagrant mass, purg'd and refin'd,
> New Heav'ns, new Earth, Ages of endless date
> Founded in righteousness and peace and love,
> To bring forth fruits Joy and eternal Bliss.[1]

On his visionary sojourn, Adam is graphically and repeatedly confronted with the enormity and perpetuity of a solitary choice. In this spectacular poem, it is clear Milton understood something vital that appears to have fallen out of the theological backpack of most of us modern believers. But, we most likely wouldn't wade through 9,000 lines of poetry to retrieve it. In our comfortable world of spiritual simplicity, where redemption is reduced to justification, and the gospel is the proclamation of that reduction, *Paradise Lost* seems like a perfect synopsis. That is, if you and I are resigned to believe that all that happened in Eden that morning was a married couple getting kicked out of Paradise. Unfortunately, this pale theology is precisely what seems to be underlying much of the popular understanding of the nature and effect of sin, especially that *first* sin. And, getting *this* wrong will affect people's perspective of themselves, others, the gospel, and the mission of God. Or to put it differently, identity, purpose, and mission will be all wrong. Our understanding of sin sets the trajectory for our entire lives as Christians. To get this wrong, is to get it all wrong. However, to get it *right*, or close to right, will draw everything we've talked about together so far into a cohesive whole. I know this seems like an overstatement, but it's not. So, let's see whether we can get it right. Two non-negotiables need to be on the table before we begin. The first is that it's an error of enormous magnitude to limit our understanding of sin to guilt. The second is that there is a proportional relationship between the depth of our understanding of sin, and our understanding of redemption, and our place in it. Or, as one writer succinctly put it, "Whatever we say about sin will qualify whatever we say about

---

1 Ibid.

grace."[1] And to thicken the stew, these two ideas are inseparably connected.

How Big Is Your Gospel?

Let's work our way backwards, and examine the second one first. What I mean is that if you or I have a tiny view of sin, it will yield a tiny view of redemption. Tiny in both depth *and* breadth. Conversely, if my understanding of sin is immense, it will generate a view of redemption that is immense in depth and breadth. Perhaps the easiest way to determine the "size" of your sin-view, is by thinking about what comes to mind when you hear the word "saved," in the context of salvation and redemption. Do you, or those you know, refer to a specific time when you were "saved"? Does your church talk about people getting "saved" in numerical terms, especially after certain meetings, or upon returning from mission trips? To use past tense language that is final and complete, when referencing someone coming into the family of God, tends to be a good indication that someone's understanding of sin is limited to the issue of guilt. And that's a "tiny" view of sin because it's one-dimensional. And sin, among other things, is *anything* but one-dimensional, which we'll see in vivid color in a moment. One of the many foul fruits found on this tiny tree, is the inevitable tendency to think of the gospel as the vehicle of getting people "saved." But, an even more debilitating malaise is the gradual but inevitable loss of purpose and mission it engenders. And this can happen to entire churches, not just the individuals in them. If people are encouraged (or coerced) to "invite Jesus into their hearts so they can be forgiven of their sins and go to heaven when they die," they tend to adopt what I call a "2-snap" understanding of salvation. For instance, as a young college student, my own forgiveness was the result of an instantaneous declaration by God. Sort of like snapping His fingers. Snap! I'm forgiven. And the other half of the evangelistic promise—"going to heaven"—I suspect takes the same amount of time. If the return of Jesus occurs in my lifetime, it will be even shorter, a "twinkling of the eye," according to Paul. Another short snap. In this scenario, "salvation" is reduced to two snaps; one at the beginning of my Christian journey and the other at the end. What have I left out? Not much! Just my entire life! What *should* I do then, between the "snaps"? That is the question many believers don't ask, and the churches they attend don't address it either. The implied (or proclaimed) answer to that unasked question, is "Be good, tithe, go to church, and help other folks get 'saved.'" Hence, evangelism (getting folks "saved") often becomes the fuel to keep church folks excited after the glow of their own "salvation" has flickered and diminished. Fortunately for us, redemption is wider, deeper, longer, and higher than getting "saved" and "going to heaven." And that's because sin is so much bigger than guilt.

Maybe it was the inevitable stepchild of the marriage of the "four-points-and-a-prayer," and the "God loves you and has a wonderful plan for your life"

---

1 Cornelius Plantinga. *Not the Way It's Supposed to Be: A Breviary of Sin.* (Grand Rapids, Mich: Eerdmans, 1995), 6.

versions of the gospel. I'm not sure, but deep within the theological assumptions of both is an emphasis on sin and guilt. Illustrations of cancelled debts, open prison doors offering release, and judges dying for condemned criminals, abound in the world of evangelism. We labor tirelessly to convince relatively good people that they are evil and guilty before God.[1] *Are* we guilty before God? Absolutely. No thinking Christian, and many thinking *unbelievers* live with the reality of their own guilt, or that of someone else. We all instinctively seem to remember we've been kicked out of the Garden, and that Paradise has indeed been lost. We cling to the truth that the death of Jesus Christ on our behalf was caused by that guilt. Jesus paid the penalty for the life I've *lived*, but shouldn't have, and He credited me with the life I *should* have lived, but didn't. Paul assures us of this repeatedly in his letters.[2] We call this forensic transaction, "justification." Our doctrine of justification is God's answer to our guilt. But, Paul *also* informs us that sin has a second identity, one that is perennial, powerful, and persistent.

> Since, therefore, we have now been justified by his blood, much more shall we be saved by him from the wrath of God. For if while we were enemies we were reconciled to God by the death of his Son, much more, now that we are reconciled, shall we be saved by his life.   **–Romans 5:9–10**

Sin also produced *corruption*. It's not something anyone, or anything is easily "saved" from. At least not until Scene 3. An expansive view of sin is one that has a full and robust understanding of both guilt *and* corruption. And subsequently, this produces an expansive view of redemption, one characterized by a thorough understanding of what *God* has done, is doing, and desires to do regarding *both* aspects of sin. To forge an expansive view of redemption and our place in it, we need to walk back into the Garden one last time. And as we do, we're going to discover that there was infinitely more than Paradise "lost" that day.

In Act I, the Creation narrative records for us that God does much "saying" and "seeing." Eight times He *speaks*, and the Creation comes to life. And seven times we are told He *looks* at His finished work in stages, and makes a judgment about it. He sees it as "good." In fact, His final assessment, when His Creation project is completed, is that it is *"very* good." God is pleased with things as He

---

1 For some reason, we Christians refuse to admit that "goodness" is a relative category, and as such, has degrees of expression. Osama bin Laden and Mother Teresa were surely unequal in regard to their goodness. And because "goodness" is a relative term, it is not quantifiable. There's no way to measure it, or to know when one is "good enough," in terms of God. Scripture tells us that God's standard is "righteousness," *not* goodness. The standard by which we are judged is the Judge Himself. It too, is not quantifiable, because it is infinite. It can only be "imputed," or ascribed, to someone by God. This levels the playing field by justly pronouncing all people guilty, regardless of how "good" they've been. However, to fail to *distinguish* between goodness and righteousness in our attempts to share the "gospel" with people, communicates a total disregard for whatever they've done that is admirable and good. I think the difference is significant, and our failure to distinguish does more to alienate than enlighten. We would be more effective in our evangelism *and* true to the gospel itself, if we gave-up trying to convince good people that they're evil, and helped them see that they're *not* righteous, instead.

2 cf. 2 Corinthians 5:21; Romans 8:1-4; see also 1 Peter 2:24.

sees them. They are just as they're supposed to be, because of the One responsible *for* them. And then, just once in Act I, He *speaks* about what He sees. And, it's *not* "good":

> Then the LORD God said, "It is not good that the man should be alone; I will make him a helper fit for him."...So the LORD God caused a deep sleep to fall upon the man, and while he slept took one of his ribs and closed up its place with flesh. And the rib that the LORD God had taken from the man he made into a woman and brought her to the man.   **—Genesis 2:18, 21-22**

Apparently, God understood that in order for things to be the way they're supposed to be, for them to truly be "good," there must be the possibility for relationship. As Act I closes, it is implied that with Eve in the script, everything *is* now "very good." As the curtain closes, there is, at the very core of the world, an abiding and pervasive sense of harmony, mutual interdependence, and safety. Everything is "working" as it should. In a word, "peace." The Hebrew language has a beautiful word for this spacious and sublime idea. It is the word, *shalom*.

> The webbing together of God, humans, and all creation in justice, fulfillment, and delight is what the Hebrew prophets called shalom. We call it peace, but it means far more than mere peace of mind or a cease-fire between enemies. In the Bible, shalom means universal flourishing, wholeness, and delight—a rich state of affairs in which natural needs are satisfied and natural gifts fruitfully employed, a state of affairs that inspires joyful wonder as its Creator and Savior opens doors and welcomes the creatures in whom he delights. *Shalom, in other words, is the way things ought to be.*[1]

To understand sin, we need to understand shalom. Shalom is perhaps the only word large enough to provide an expansive understanding of sin, because it is the only word that is capable of containing all that was lost. We didn't just lose Paradise that day. There was the catastrophic loss of *shalom*; the way things were "supposed to be." This means things *aren't* the way they're supposed to be anymore. Nothing is. Everyone is infected. Nothing was unaffected. God can't look at Creation today and say everything is "very good" as He did on the sixth day of the Creation account. Everything, everywhere, from that day on down through the long corridor of time, has felt the tremor of shalom's departure. And the vacuum its absence created has been filled with an unending stream of posers, pimps, and patrons of every type of counterfeit peacemakers imaginable. Hopefully, you are beginning to see how huge, how pervasive, and how serious this thing called sin *really* is. Do you see why our cliché, "getting saved," doesn't seem to reach quite far enough into the abyss to serve as a euphemism for redemption? The spoiling of shalom in Act III marked the beginning of the "former things" that pass away in Scene 3. But for those of us still in Scene 2, they're not "former." They're "now." Very, very "now." Keeping a razor sharp and brutally honest perspective about the reality of sin in Scene 2 is vital to the success of the gospel. Why? Because it preserves grace as it really is—*costly and expansive*:

> To speak of sin without grace is to minimize the resurrection of Jesus Christ, the fruit

---

1 Plantinga, 10.

of the Spirit, and the hope of shalom. But to speak of grace without sin is surely no better. To do this is to trivialize the cross of Jesus Christ, to skate past all the struggling by good people down the ages to forgive, accept, and rehabilitate sinners, including themselves, and therefore to cheapen the grace of God that always comes to us with blood on it. What had we thought the ripping and writhing on Golgotha were all about? To speak of grace without looking squarely at these realities, without painfully honest acknowledgement of our own sin and its effects, is to shrink grace to a mere embellishment of the music of creation, to shrink it down to a mere grace note. In short, for the Christian church (even in its recently popular seeker services) to ignore, euphemize, or otherwise mute the lethal reality of sin is to cut the nerve of the gospel. For the sober truth is that without full disclosure on sin, the gospel of grace becomes impertinent, unnecessary, and finally uninteresting.[1]

But, this also means the gospel, if it truly is "good news" about a Kingdom arriving, a Serpent being crushed, and God's plan to unite all things in heaven and on earth in Christ unveiling, then it *has* to bring "good news" to the spoiling of shalom. It *has* to somehow deal with the restoration of things to "the way they're supposed to be." Just as The Story has to be comprehensive enough to make some sense of all of life over all time, so too the gospel must be large enough to be proclaimed to every corner of the universe from which shalom has been abducted. And if my purpose and yours are now inseparable from God's purposes, then our lives too, are intertwined with all this. As we shall see, a restorer of shalom is what it means to be a Story-dweller. What does the "way things are supposed to be" look like? To appreciate that, we'll need to first take a painful look at the spheres where shalom is now absent, and what has grown up in its place.

The Loss of Shalom Between Humanity and God

The first and most obvious realm where things are not "as they're supposed to be," involves humanity and God. We see in the Creation account a very personal and liberal relationship between God and the two that bear His image. They are to serve as co-regents in God Creation Project, ruling in His place, exercising dominion over the rest of Creation. This was what they were designed to do, and this is the way things were supposed to be between the Creator and His image-bearing creatures. And, this is what shalom looks like between God and humanity, because it was actually happening. But, sin spoiled that. The first couple was asked to exit the Garden, and were excluded from His presence. This, the most central of all relationships, and the definer of what it means to be human, was vandalized. The apostle Paul is even more graphic and revealing, insisting that part of us died that day, and remains so until quickened by God Himself.[2] A separation between God and humanity, the inability to rightly and freely relate to one another, replaced shalom. In an almost instinctive fashion,

---

1 Ibid, 199.

2 Paul's statement in Ephesians 2:1, that we "were dead in our trespasses and sins" has generated a great deal of debate among very qualified scholars. They disagree on just how "dead" we are, or more specifically, what Paul meant by his use of that verb.

humanity frantically sought to fill the void shalom's absence had birthed, with gods of its own making. And, we still do. The ancient idols of money, sex, and power persist, merely changing their costumes from wood and stone, to silicon and metal. We worship what we believe will bring us peace. Yahweh was replaced by Moloch in the Iron Age. Today, He's been reduced to the great iAm, as we begin to look more and more like our gadgets than our parents.

The gospel we proclaim, this unveiled mystery of which we are stewards, is God's appeal to humanity to embrace the remedy He initiated, to repair the loss of shalom between Him and them. To respond to this offer requires that one first *admit* to being a shalom-breaker, a sinner. The Bible calls this repentance. But, this offer can also be rejected. People can refuse to agree that things are not as they're supposed to be between them and God. It would be amusing, if it weren't so tragic that the same people who rail *against* God because things aren't as they should be *around* them, refuse to apply the same argument to themselves. And to *refuse* to be reconciled, it would seem, is sin sneaking in the backdoor instead of the front, because it too is a disturbance of shalom. Maybe of an even darker shade:

> Perhaps we think most often of sin as a spoiler of creation: people adulterate a marriage or befoul a stream or use their excellent minds to devise an ingenious tax fraud. But resistance to redemption counts as sin, too, and often displays a special perversity.[1]

The death of humanity's relationship with its Creator, has produced the largest void of all, one that is irreparable unless God intervenes. Thankfully, He did. The Apostle Paul spins a theological web connecting the finished work of Christ on Golgotha, our justification, God's plan for the fullness of time, and the restoration of shalom in the relationship between God and humanity.

> Therefore, since we have been justified by faith, *we have peace [shalom] with God* through our Lord Jesus Christ. Through him we have also obtained access by faith into this grace in which we stand, and we rejoice in hope of the glory of God....For in him all the fullness of God was pleased to dwell, and through him to reconcile to himself all things, whether on earth or in heaven, *making peace [shalom]*[2] *by the blood of his cross.*
> **–Romans 5:1–2; Colossians 1:19**

So, shalom has been restored between God and humanity. At least substantially. Its full restoration is in Scene 3, when the "former things" are truly gone, and the dwelling of God is on the new earth. But, the fact that the enmity between us and the One whose vandalized image we bear, has been restored to shalom, even if it's in its infancy, is good news. It's gospel.

The Loss of Shalom Within Humanity

The curtain on Act I closes with the announcement that the "man and woman were both naked and were not ashamed." Although it is a reference to a man and his wife, it is a beautiful portrait of shalom within humanity. The absence of

1 Plantinga, 8.

2 The Greek word most often used by Paul and others in the New Testament is *eirēnē*, which though not a one-to-one correspondence, is a near equivalent of the Hebrew *shalom*.

fear, and the presence of freedom between two people, was the way it was supposed to be. But that portrait was quickly desecrated. As Act II unveils itself, we are presented with a stark contrast to the close of Act I as interpersonal relationships deteriorate in the absence of shalom. Fear and shame, the first to arrive on stage, degenerate to murder and mayhem, as Act II unfolds. Fratricide is followed by homicide, and humanity's distrust for itself usurps the place shalom once held. It is telling that centuries before there was such a thing as a divine law code, God saw fit to put in place a policy of capital punishment for capital murder.[1] Apparently, folks weren't getting along too well outside the Garden! James, writing in the first century, indicates nothing had improved by his day:

> What causes quarrels and what causes fights among you? Is it not this, that your passions are at war within you? You desire and do not have, so you murder. You covet and cannot obtain, so you fight and quarrel. You do not have, because you do not ask. You ask and do not receive, because you ask wrongly, to spend it on your passions.
> –James 4:1–3

Tragically, this isn't ancient history. We are still immersed in the offspring of Cain's animosity to his brother. Hourly, headlines arrive via our RSS feeds and remind us of shalom's absence, evidenced in humanity's unending war on itself. Thousands of young girls are taken out of Southeast Asia and funneled into the sex trade industry every year. And this sickening exploitation of the world's most helpless inhabitants is *not* limited to foreign shores. Estimates of trafficking in the U.S. are in the hundreds of thousands, annually. Drive-by shootings occur frequently within miles of my son's home each year in urban Birmingham. Child soldiers carry AK-47s and are trained to kill in the Lord's Resistance Army across the globe in Uganda. Hundreds of thousands of North Koreans languish in rural concentration camps. My own state's prisons can't safely accommodate their bulging inmate populations. Nearly 15 million children in Sub-Sahara Africa, live as orphans because their parents have died of AIDS. Until recently, thousands of U.S. children were packed like cattle in nearly 3,600 tiny apartments stacked sky-high in urban Chicago, living without fathers, and in constant fear. Statistics such as these have become so monolithic they've turned our hearts to stone. It is true that news like this is typical but is it normal? Is this the way it's *supposed* to be? Does all this bother you? It bothers God, because this is what the absence of shalom looks like between people made in His image. Well then, why doesn't He *do* something about it? He did.

Four times in six verses, Paul informs us that the death of Christ did *more* than restore shalom between God and humanity. Jesus' death was intended to restore shalom between *people* too. That was part of His plan all along.

> But now in Christ Jesus you who once were far off have been brought near by the blood of Christ. For *he himself is our peace,* who has made us both one and has broken down in his flesh the dividing wall of hostility by abolishing the law of commandments expressed in ordinances, that he might create in himself one new man in place of

1 cf. Genesis 9:6

the two, *so making peace,* and might reconcile us both to God in one body through the cross, thereby killing the hostility. And he came and preached *peace* to you who were far off and *peace* to those who were near.   **–Ephesians 2:13–18**

But, by far the clearest and most glorious portrait of what humans living in shalom could have looked like in the Garden, is in one of the last "trailers" for The Story. God actually gives us a depiction of what redeemed humanity will look like, united in worship instead of divided by the pride of ethnicity and the xenophobia propagated by sin:

After this I looked, and behold, a great multitude that no one could number, from every nation, from all tribes and peoples and languages, standing before the throne and before the Lamb, clothed in white robes, with palm branches in their hands, and crying out with a loud voice, "Salvation belongs to our God who sits on the throne, and to the Lamb!"   **–Revelation 7:9–10**

Our Loss of Shalom As Individuals

Sin's long tentacles have tainted the very fabric of our individual humanity as well as everything around us. Every aspect of our lives bears its imprint. The spoiling of shalom means that each of us is not as we are supposed to be. Theologians throughout the centuries have spilled much ink about this malady under the rubric of "depravity." Unfortunately, they haven't done an equally thorough job helping those of us who live with its reality day in and day out to understand it holistically and redemptively, so we know what to expect and how to respond. And this is particularly true because at its very core, sin turns us against ourselves before it turns us against others.

... sin qualifies as the worst of our troubles because, among other things, it corrupts what is peculiarly human about us. Sin attaches to intention, memory, thought, speech, intelligent action—to all the special features of personhood—and transforms them into weapons.[1]

And because, as N. T. Wright puts it, *"We are not saved as souls but as wholes,"*[2] the restoration of shalom has to extend to every area of our being from which it was stolen. And the doctrine of depravity informs us that sin emptied the vault of shalom. Left to ourselves, we are bankrupt when it comes to the way we're supposed to be.

Our mind, the ability to reason and trust our conclusions, has been affected by sin. We are, as the Scripture says, "darkened in our understanding" and can't see life clearly because of sin. In fact, there's a part of us that doesn't *want* to see things the way they're supposed to be.[3] Paul admonishes us that part of our spiritual transformation and worship is to allow our *minds* to be "renewed," so we can again begin to think within the circumference of the plan and purposes of God.[4] We have to unlearn the untruths and relearn the truth. And, sin's as-

1 Plantinga, 76.

2 Wright, *Surprised By Hope,* 199.

3 cf. Ephesians 4:18; Romans 7-8; Colossians 1:21-22

4 cf. Romans 12:1-2

sault was not limited to our minds. It affected our conscience, muddling our ability to discern what is right, and our will, crippling our ability to choose what is good.[1] However, there is also something more tangible that is not the way it's supposed to be either.

Although it is beyond proof, I suspect that the human genome, surely fully present in Adam, was itself maligned by Eden's folly. I believe we didn't just inherit a sin *nature* from him, we also inherited a genetic map that is "not the way it's supposed to be" either. That means that sin has a *physiological* long half-life, not just a metaphysical one. One that is so pervasive, only a new body will be able to remedy the damage. Meanwhile, our bodies bear and reflect the loss of shalom in perhaps the most convincing ways, because they are the vehicles in which our immaterial self relates to the rest of Creation. We can witness the longing for shalom on the psych floors of our hospitals. We see it on the faces of loved ones whose brains have been hijacked by Alzheimer's disease. Take a visit to a children's hospital in any city, or a late-stage AIDS patient's room in any hospital. You will walk back to your car thinking; this just isn't right. Hearing loss, diabetes, ED, infertility, the chameleon called cancer, and a litany of other assaults on our bodies remind us daily that something's wrong. And it is! Because something's missing. We're merely beholding what has replaced it.

It should make perfect sense why the "Prince of Shalom," in Isaiah's "trailer,"[2] spent half of his life healing bodies, not just "saving" souls. Restoring health is restoring shalom, because the absence of disease is the way things are *supposed* to be.[3] Even the cases of demon possession in the Bible must be understood in this light. The demoniac who mutilated himself and ran around naked, is "clothed and in his right mind" after Jesus exorcises the demon. But, the account also gives us one very important detail as well. He was *sitting* at Jesus' feet. For the first time, shalom had returned in its fullness, and he sat. And the man crippled from birth, when his mobility was restored, he danced. He *didn't* sit.[4] When shalom is restored, we move in the direction we've been unable to move because of the shackles of sin that had its grip on us. And one day, when Scene 3 arrives, our *bodies* will again be restored to their full image-bearing beauty:

> Beloved, we are God's children now, and what we will be has not yet appeared; but we know that when he appears we shall be like him, because we shall see him as he is.
> **–1 John 3:2**

> But our citizenship is in heaven, and from it we await a Savior, the Lord Jesus Christ,

1 cf. Titus 1:15 and Hebrews 5:15; Romans 7::14-24 and Philippians 2:12-13.

2 cf. Isaiah 9:6

3 HInts of this are visible in Yahweh's promise to the newly formed covenant people of Israel: "*You shall be blessed above all peoples. There shall not be male or female barren among you or among your livestock. And the LORD will take away from you all sickness, and none of the evil diseases of Egypt, which you knew, will he inflict on you, but he will lay them all on those who hate you.*" **–Deuteronomy 7:13–15**

4 Luke 8:35 and Acts 3:1-8.

who will transform our lowly body to be like his glorious body, by the power that enables him even to subject all things to himself.   **–Philippians 3:20–21**

The Loss of Shalom Between the Rest of Creation and Humanity

I hate to introduce bad news, but the idea that sin got Adam and Eve kicked *out* of the Garden, and Jesus invites us back *in*, fails to make room for what I believe is a very important detail: Adam and Eve never *wanted* to go back in. I may lose a few of you more scientific folks here, but I'm merely giving an opinion about something the Bible seems to imply but never says.[1] I wasn't there, but I don't think Adam and Eve ever swallowed whatever fruit it was dangling within arm's reach. I believe that bite fell from their mouths, as they gawked first around them and then at each other, realizing that things *really* were no longer the same. I suspect that the shalomic stillness of the Garden was shattered by the cries of death and pain. Blood, guts, feathers, squealing, and zoological pandemonium engulfed them as the Creation turned on itself. The animals that Adam had named as he calmly interacted with them,[2] were suddenly killing one another, trampling the vegetation, and threatening his own safety. When God finds Adam and Eve, they are hiding and afraid. But, I don't think their fear is all because of guilt. I think it's because they realize they're no longer in charge. And, they're scared spitless!

Predation, I think, was sin's firstborn child in the nonhuman world, when shalom was shattered. From a botanical garden and petting zoo, the Garden morphed into Jurassic Park right before their eyes. That made them the only two human beings in all history who would ever fully understand the power and nature of sin. And because regret is a function of memory, I don't think they ever slept well again. The loss of shalom between the rest of the breathing part of Creation and humanity that began that day, is still a resident of life on earth. And, it is everywhere. From fire ants and mosquitoes, to rabid pit bulls and sharks, we find ourselves vacillating between mild irritation and outright paranoia[3] when it comes to our multiple-legged cohabitants. The BBC series,

---

1 My argument for predation as a product of sin is based on my belief that there was no death before Adam. Christians who espouse pre-Adamic death, in my opinion, limit redemption primarily to justification, thus making sin purely a forensic issue between God and man. Jesus's substitutionary death is the solution to man's guilt, and the case is closed. However, this fails to address the expansive evidence in Scripture to the contrary. The Genesis account is clear that everything that had breath ate vegetation when things were as they were supposed to be (Gen 1:29-30). The emergence of "thorns and thistles" as part of the curse on the earth suggests a change in the genetic make-up of plants (Gen 3:17-18). A parallel change in the animal kingdom is therefore plausible as well. Surely, if we hold to an ontological change in human nature of the magnitude our doctrine of depravity suggests, an equally significant change in the order of Creation must be admissible. But, most importantly, the repeated description of shalom within the animal kingdom found in the Prophets points to a *return* to pre-Fall conditions within all of Creation, not just humanity (Is. 11:6; 65:25). And the statement that a lion will "eat straw like an ox" points to a physiological change which I believe is a *reversal* to shalomic conditions.

2 cf. Genesis 2:18-20.

3 I have a special vendetta against fire ants. Here in Alabama, they are just "thug" insects, looking for a fight rather than a meal. Find me a purpose for them, and I'll rethink my theology! And don't give me the

Planet Earth, sometimes serves as a running documentary on the loss of sha-lom within Creation; every episode depicting some new footage on carnage in the wild. But, as I've watched it, mesmerizing as it is, I also knew that's not the way it's supposed to be; an all-you-can-eat buffet, where all the items were devouring each other! But, if *Planet Earth* isn't shalom in action, what *should* it look like? We may actually have a blurry reference to a moment of restoration of shalom between Creation and humanity in Mark's two-verse abbreviation of Jesus' temptation by Satan in the wilderness. Sandwiched between a refer-ence to Satan and another to a ministering angel, we are told Jesus was "with the wild animals."[1] There are some—and I'd throw my lot in with them—who see this as a foretaste of the return of shalom. I can't really picture Jesus, after successfully facing and defeating in a *wilderness,* the Enemy Adam couldn't handle in a *garden,* cowering behind a rock, fearing the "wild animals." No, I imagine the beasts at ease with their Creator, even if it were temporary. It was still real. And, I suspect that in the words of The Creator, it was "very good." But, there is even clearer evidence in Scripture. I think the "trailers" in Isaiah are more than beautiful Hebrew poetry. They are a picture of what Creation looks like when God "makes all things new," when shalom is restored on the new earth:

> The wolf shall dwell with the lamb, and the leopard shall lie down with the young goat, and the calf and the lion and the fattened calf together; and a little child shall lead them. The cow and the bear shall graze; their young shall lie down together; and the lion shall eat straw like the ox. The nursing child shall play over the hole of the cobra, and the weaned child shall put his hand on the adder's den. They shall not hurt or destroy in all my holy mountain; for the earth shall be full of the knowledge of the LORD as the waters cover the sea.   **–Isaiah 11:6-9**

It will be powerful to experience what Adam once knew; safety and wonder in the presence of God's variegated handiwork. That is Scene 3. And it helps us understand more fully what is *not* said in Act I about Creation before the Fall. The full flourishing of Creation will cause us to worship. But, there is more in Creation than plants and animals that have felt the full force of shalom's departure. Paul tells us that we and the beasts are not the only ones awaiting its return:

> For the creation waits with eager longing for the revealing of the sons of God. For the creation was subjected to futility, not willingly, but because of him who subjected it, in hope that the creation itself will be set free from its bondage to corruption and obtain the freedom of the glory of the children of God.   **–Romans 8:19-21**

---

food chain argument. There's plenty of other tasty ants around, and they don't control any other insect population themselves. An ant that holds on to you with its jaws, and then stings you repeatedly, inject-ing venom, just for fun doesn't strike me as the "way things are supposed to be." I could be wrong. But, I doubt it.

1 cf. Mark 1:12-13. The Greek here is supportive of this idea as well. The preposition translated "with" means "amidst" or "in accompaniment with." And the word for "animal," (*th rion*) is only used of danger-ous animals, predators, and is the word used nearly 40 times in Revelation to describe heinous visionary creatures. Jesus, in other words, was "with" animals that he should have run from.

What the ancients called "earth, wind, and fire," and the unbelieving world knows as "nature," we call Creation. It was another victim of sin. The Creation account reveals an amazing world of order and rhythm, of dividing and joining, of "kinds" and boundaries. We are told that the waves are given limits, beyond which they were not to pass.[1] In the South, we still savor the remnants of God's artistic love, watching the sun drop behind a mountain in North Carolina. The sky ablaze with fading ribbons. Shades of orange and blue and gray. We listen to the surf through a high-rise patio door in Gulf Shores at night, spellbound by the rise and fall of the surf. These sounds and sights are so soothing that entire industries exist to help us enjoy them. Something deep within each of us joins the chorus of humanity that sings, "*This* is the way it's *supposed* to be." But, it's not always like this. These echoes of Creation are frequently and unpredictably interrupted by sin's curse working its dark magic. The melodic waves breaking on the shoreline are transformed into hurricanes and tsunamis, leaving devastation and death in their wake instead of delight. Waterfalls and lazy rivers turn into raging torrents, sweeping away homes and personal histories. Winds that rustle the leaves in the autumn sometimes become dark and ominous funnels of fury, razing entire cities to rubble. Creation can be cruel and heartless. When shalom drains out of the pool of Creation, humanity is left naked and helpless. Doppler radar can report to us what's coming, but it sure as heck can't stop it.

I realize that this last paragraph raises the issue of the Sovereignty of God in all this. Aren't there tons of verses that clearly teach He's in charge? Yes there are, and yes He is. He does *allow* these things to happen. But, why do unbelievers and sometimes believers blame Him: "How could a good God do these things?" By this time, you should have at least a partial answer to that accusation. We do not dethrone God, as if anyone could. We simply look at Creation at rest in Scene 3 *and* Creation at war since Act II, and agree that the tornados that leveled much of my own neighborhood a year ago, and entire neighboring towns the same day, demonstrated that this is *not* the way it's supposed to be. That's all. And, I believe the life of Jesus points to such a view as well.

"All Things" Is All Things

There's a well-known story in Mark's Gospel where Jesus is asleep in a boat full of panicked disciples, rowing to keep afloat and alive on a very agitated Sea of Galilee. Upon being rudely and hastily awakened, Jesus turns to the storm and says, "Peace! Quiet yourself!"[2] The story goes on to reveal two things that happened immediately. The first was that the storm "ceased" and calm returned. The second was that the disciples freaked out, and wondered what kind of person could speak to the wind and waves, and they would obey? Jesus gave

---

1 Job 38:4-11; Genesis 1:1-9.

2 cf. Mark 4:35-41.

a *command*, "be at shalom!" and Creation obeyed. Tumults and disasters at sea, apparently, are not the way things are supposed to be. Jesus gave his disciples a taste of shalom, and they were wonder-struck. I'm not trying to minimize the complexity of disasters within Creation, or disagree with the insurance industry that calls them all "acts of God." I'm simply suggesting that what we call "natural disasters" are actually *un*natural disasters. They're expressions of shalom's absence. An expansive understanding of sin demands this courtesy. If some folks want to view tsunamis and tornados as God playing His own version of Angry Birds, that's their call. I just want us to keep pushing deeper and deeper into the void that shalom's departure has created. Because, as we'll soon find out, our own purpose and mission are inseparable from what happened in Act II. And if we haven't been gripped by just how far humanity fell, and how much of Creation fell with them, we might spend our lives telling folks, *"God loves you and has a wonderful plan for your life...pass it on."*

Obviously, Creation can be fun. But, it's certainly not safe. At least not anymore, and *not yet*. But neither are we, as we've seen. Put these two together, and we'll have to confess that we haven't been too kind to Creation either. I happen to live in a region of the country that has been the poster child for "natural disasters" over the past few years. Multiple hurricanes and tornados have surely secured us copious airtime, presidential visits, and ink. However, it was the largest oil spill in history that put Alabama on the map in the twenty-first century with nearly the drama the Civil Rights Movement did in the 20th. Make no mistake, when over 200 million gallons of crude oil is allowed to flow for nearly three months into a small, semitropical area, it's not the way it's supposed to be. The fishing industry, wildlife, and the general habitats of the area were rocked. Some will never recover. There was loss of life, loss of income, loss of livelihood, and loss of hope for many people. Most of it never made the press. I don't want to minimize that. But, the accident itself, is just one of multiple ways the assessment of an aging Native American woman of the Wintu living in northern California, proves true, *"How can the spirit of the earth like the White Man?...Everywhere the white man has touched it, it is sore."*[1] The dominion bestowed upon us by God as His co-regents, the charge to "tend" and "guard" the Garden, slowly degenerated into domination. Tending turned to tearing, and protecting turned to pimping, as we slowly and steadily filled our waterways with trash and our air with particulates and hydrocarbons. This is what sin in humanity has done to God's good earth, and everything on it. This is our personal contribution to the spoiling of shalom. Listen to the same message from a 2,800 year old prophet:

> Hear the word of the LORD, O children of Israel, for the LORD has a controversy with the inhabitants of the land. There is no faithfulness or steadfast love, and no knowledge of God in the land; there is swearing, lying, murder, stealing, and committing

---

1 *Touch The Earth: A Self-Portrait of Indian Existence.* Compiled by T.C. McLuhan, (New York: Promontory Press, 1971), 15.

adultery; they break all bounds, and bloodshed follows bloodshed. Therefore the land mourns, and all who dwell in it languish, and also the beasts of the field and the birds of the heavens, and even the fish of the sea are taken away. **–Hosea 4:1–3**

Even the modern recycling movement, as altruistic as it seems, and as good as it makes us feel, belies the fact that we still won't face the uncomfortable truth that consumption is the major cause of pollution, not improper disposal of our waste. Our desire for more goes back to the Garden. I am even disappointed at the attitude of the American Church when it comes to Creation and its care. Conversations seem to range from ignorance and indifference, to animosity and arrogance. This is particularly true among believers who have wedded the gospel with capitalism. The "earth" is viewed as something God gave to us to use, instead of something that belongs to Him, and upon which we are custodial tenants. The scriptures are very clear on this subject; however. And, as it turns out, we're tenants on *His* property. We don't own it, despite what the mortgage company tells us. It's His. All of it.

Old Testament scholar, Sandra Richter, asserts that a thoughtful and careful reading of Deuteronomy reveals an amazing consistency by Yahweh regarding His expectations of Israel as "tenants" in Canaan,[1] when it comes to Creation care. Among them are attentive and compassionate protection of their livestock, a yearlong rest for the soil, and crop rotation. Even their animals were granted a sabbath each week! Richter calculated the annual cost to the average Jewish household for obeying a single injunction of Yahweh's that they were not to "muzzle the ox when he is threshing the grain."[2] This command's full force is buried from our sight, because we have no idea what subsistence farming is like. Essentially, Yahweh is requiring His people to care for their beasts in ways that are immensely costly to themselves. And this was to be done despite the yield. It wasn't an ancient form of profit-sharing for the animals. It was to be the norm. In fact, we are told in Scripture that how one treated his animals reflected his spirituality:

> Whoever is righteous has regard for the life of his beast, but the mercy of the wicked is cruel. **–Proverbs 12:10**

Yahweh also expected His people to deal differently than their pagan neighbors in their hunting practices. A mother *and* its eggs, if found together, could not both be taken. And, that wasn't all. Yahweh forbade the Jews from destroying fruit-bearing trees of their enemies, when besieging a city. This was in direct contrast to the military tactics of their neighboring enemies, the Egyptians and Assyrians. Fruit devastation was the surest way to destroy the economy of an enemy. The psychological effect of witnessing the destruction of trees that were in your family for centuries was a profound weapon in itself. Yahweh forbade it. Please don't jump ship here, and think I'm merely promoting being "green."

1 The content for this section is from: Sandra Richter, *Environmental Law in Deuteronomy: One Lens on a Biblical Theology of Creation Care.* Bulletin for Biblical Research 20.3 (2010) 355–376

2 Deuteronomy 25:4

Instead, I'm simply trying to call us back to a theology of Creation that is rooted in Scripture instead of convenience or conventionality. If we are Creationists in the truest sense of the word—that God is the source of everything that has breath, and that which doesn't, that exists alone or comes from itself—then to embrace or incarnate any view of Creation that does not honor and obey the Creator, is sin. In fact, for you and me to live in such a way is to *spoil* shalom. I am also trying to help us ease our way into an understanding of what's really happening when humanity misuses and abuses Creation. It's much, much bigger and more serious for us than it is for industry, because we know The Story. We know what Creation was, what it's become, and what it will be again. To live inconsistently with that knowledge is willful rebellion.

Christians, of all people, should have been *leading* the way in what has now become America's latest cultural barometer. Everybody's in the race to be "green," or at least wants to be see that way. Do I really need to know how much post-consumer waste is in the paper napkin handed to me? Truthfully, if I really wanted to be "green," I should have brought my own cloth napkin. And predictably, now that it's become red-white-and-blue to be green, the Church has jumped on board. We should *own* this issue, not copy it! Over forty years ago, Francis Schaeffer, a prophet everyone wanted to read but no one wanted to heed, penned *Pollution And The Death of Man: A Christian View of Ecology.* I'll never forget reading it. I was a new believer *and* an environmental research chemist. He was arguing for Christians to take the lead on this issue, based on our *theology*, not our pocketbooks. And, of special interest to us, he linked Creation care to redemption:

> On the basis of the fact that there is going to be total redemption in the future, not only of man but of all creation, the Christian who believes the Bible should be the man who—with God's help and in the power of the Holy Spirit—is treating nature now in the direction of the way nature will be then. It will not now be perfect, but there should be something substantial or we have missed our calling. God's calling to the Christian now, and to the Christian community, in the area of nature (just as it is in the area of personal Christian living in true spirituality) is that we should exhibit a substantial healing here and now, between man and nature and nature and itself, as far as Christians can bring it to pass.[1]

Schaeffer, nearly half century ago, made a passionate plea to the Church to have an expansive understanding of redemption. One that was large enough to include everything in life that wasn't the way it was supposed to be. And Creation, God's "very good" Creation, is part of that redemption. The Church didn't pay attention to Schaeffer in the 1970's because it was too busy paying attention to itself. But, I think those who will populate the Church of the twenty-first century, the "next Christians," as one author dubs them, are longing for an expansive doctrine of redemption.[2] One that has room for everything that's

---

1 Francis Schaeffer, *Pollution And The Death of Man: A Christian View of Ecology.* (Wheaton, IL: Tyndale House Publishers, 1970), 39-40.

2 Gabe Lyons, *The Next Christians: The Good News About the End of Christian America.* New York: Doubleday Religion, 2010.

broken. A redemption—a restoration of shalom—in the words of the popular Christmas Carol, *Joy to the World*, which extends "as far as the curse is found."[1]

When Paul says God has a *"plan for the fullness of time, to unite in him all things, things in heaven and things on earth,"* we need to know he means by "all things". At the end of The Story, when God Himself, speaking from the throne in Scene 3 of Act V, says *"Behold, I make all things new,"*[2] we need to know what He means by "all things".I suspect that by this point, you and I are agreed that the *absence* of shalom is owed to the *presence* of sin, and "all things" must refer to everything that sin has infected. This means "all things" is everything from which shalom has been banished. Therefore, "all things" *is* all things. It's no coincidence, that in the final moments of The Story, near the end of Scene 3, a city representing the entire Story of redemption descends from heaven to the earth. Its name is Jeru-shalom, "vision of peace." The Story concludes with the passing away of the "former things," and the restoration of shalom. That means the loss of shalom and its restoration to the glory of God, *is* The Story. The restoration of shalom *is* "the point"!

Coming Full Circle

Thus, the Abrahamic mission, the "blessing of the nations," the restoration of shalom, is also the mission of every adopted, abrahamic, alien, apprentice, ambassador, advocate. It means those of us who've been restored to shalom with God, who are beneficiaries of His grace, have also been enlisted to be agents of His redemption. It smacks of either ignorance (that *can* be remedied) or rebellion that any who've been restored to shalom with God would refuse to be agents of its restoration in all the areas where it is missing. The spoiling of shalom *is* sin, but so is hindering or refusing its restoration. Regarding the final question, *"What's my place?"* this is our "place," because *this* is the "point." This is the dramatic Story into which we've been drawn, if we are believers (or invited into, if we're not). To be a Story-dweller is to be a shalom-restorer. It is the purpose of my justification, and the responsibility of my adoption. My peace with God becomes the starting point for me to be a restorer of peace as a child of God. This is what he meant when Jesus said, *"Blessed are the peace [shalom]-makers, for they shall be called sons of God."*[3] Proclaiming to people that God has made a way for them to be restored to shalom with Him, and that He has a place for them in His shalom-restoring enterprise, is the "good news," the gospel. The *"God loves you and has a wonderful plan for your life"* version is an embarrassment by comparison. The gospel has always been centrifugal, moving out from

---

1 Interestingly, this hymn by Isaac Watts, is a song about Jesus's return, not his birth. How it became a Christmas carol is beyond me. Ironic, isn't it, that we've confused a glorious hymn extolling the restoration of shalom into a seasonal melody sung while we're thinking of a babe in a manger? The chorus at the end of the first stanza, "Let heaven and nature sing," comes much closer to a biblical understanding of Scene 3 than most modern praise choruses.

2 cf. Revelation 21:5.

3 cf. Matthew 5:9.

ourselves, instead of inward:

> For if we are beside ourselves, it is for God; if we are in our right mind, it is for you. For the love of Christ controls us, because we have concluded this: that one has died for all, therefore all have died; and *he died for all, that those who live might no longer live for themselves but for him* who for their sake died and was raised.
> –2 Corinthians 5:13–15

"Not living for ourselves, but for him who for our sake died and was raised," Jesus called "losing" our lives for his sake and the gospel.[1] It is the captivation of our hearts by the Spirit of God for the work of shalom. Its arms reach around every facet of Creation that has been vandalized by sin, and no longer is the way it's supposed to be. It means for those who understand *who* they are, and The Story that explains *why* they are, the possibilities for participating in the restoration of shalom, the *what* of mission, are as expansive as the reach of sin. And, God assures us that in the process we too will be transformed. The gradual entrance of shalom into the areas of our own lives that thirst for it, is the simultaneous fruit of us seeking to be agents of shalom to others and to the rest of Creation. Or to put it more theologically, my own sanctification is a byproduct of the fulfillment of the Abrahamic mission, not the result of focus on myself. My own spirituality, at the end of the day, is inseparably bound to the restoration of shalom:

> But seek the welfare [*shalom*] of the city where I have sent you into exile, and pray to the LORD on its behalf, for in its welfare [*shalom*]you will find your welfare [*shalom*].
> –Jeremiah 29:7

Those of us in His Story are at vastly different stages of our own. Some of us are at the beginning of life's longest chapter. Marriage, first career, and raising a family, the typical concentric circles of life, are beginning to work their way outward. The opportunities for restoring shalom in the midst of these circles are nearly endless. If it contributes to the restoration of shalom, it is the will of God. If it brings the message of reconciliation, it is the will of God. Discard the notion that life is a blueprint, and can be easily ruined by failing to be attentive. Life is an adventure with God in the restoration of shalom. A dangerous adventure, but an adventure nonetheless. And, If you are abandoned to that vision, He promises to correct your misjudgments along the way. Whether it's providing healthcare to orphans and widows in rural Guatemala, designing green cars in metro California, fighting sex-trafficking in Cambodia, raising the literacy rates in a neighborhood school, mentoring in urban and suburban America, or serving as the First Lady of one of America's most influential Christian colleges, there's a place for it in God's shalom-restoring enterprise. In know, because I've seen it in action. I have former students doing all the above.

One Point - Many Possibilities

We are called to live as restorers of shalom wherever we are and whatever we are doing. God expects us to raise children with a deep understanding not only

1 Mark 8:35.

that things are not the way they're supposed to be, and why, but also to see their role in reversing Eden's folly. Or in the vocabulary of this book, kids who are equipped with a keen sense of identity, purpose, and mission from childhood. And, as in all true apprenticeship programs, they should acquire this at home by watching their parents. In an era when many Christian parents are frantically trying to raise their children to be able to "compete" in the twenty-first century, I believe God is calling us to embrace a different twenty-first century vision. The one He inaugurated with a wandering Aramean twenty-one centuries *before* Christ—the Abrahamic mission. I also believe, as I said in the Introduction, God is calling His new chosen people to intently look backward in order to properly look forward. And now, like then, the temptation is to refuse:

> Thus says the LORD: "Stand by the roads, and look, and ask for the ancient paths, where the good way is; and walk in it, and find rest for your souls. But they said, 'We will not walk in it.'" –Jeremiah 6:16

Christian homes are to be the watersheds from which shalom-restorers should flow. Other complimentary institutions should have the same vision. Christian day schools and home-schooling parents are in unique positions to incorporate a vision of shalomic restoration into the fabric of their educational models. I would go so far as to say that any educational curricula that fails to instill an understanding of The Story, and equip children to find their place in it, is sub-Christian in the truest sense of the word. Upon close examination, some are merely Christianized versions of a CYOA, in which success is measured by ACT scores and college placement, instead of the restoration of shalom. As someone who spent nearly three decades teaching in two of the best Christian schools in America, I am acutely aware of the need to put an expansive understanding of redemption at the center of a school's mission. Unfortunately, I am also acquainted with the reluctance to do so. In tuition-based schools, the pressure is enormous to produce athletes and scholars, competitive in every way the government run schools deem the norm. Seeking to interject an ideology as comprehensive as what I've outlined in this book, is unrealistic. It would be comparable to asking Christian schools to put their ship in a different sea, not merely change its course. For two years, I directed a spiritual "startup" called the Office of Christian Outreach at the Christian school where I taught Bible. During my two-year tenure in that office, I was surprised and overwhelmed at the effect pairing high school students with shalom-restoring enterprises in our city had on their spiritual lives. We had built partnerships with a multitude of ministries and NGO's in our city, all which, whether they realized it or not, were in the shalom-restoring business. Crisis pregnancy centers, urban ministries, special needs programs, tutoring, reading initiatives, and Habitat for Humanity were among the partnerships. Many students found their own souls awakening as they stepped into face-to-face, life-to-life ministry to people in need. For some of them, their entire world tilted, resulting in reordered career plans and different college majors. Why? What was happening to these students? Most social scientists would tell us it would have been age-appropriate for them to be self-centered. It turns out, however, these excursions in the world where shalom was absent, were the closest thing our Christian school launched for a Bible "lab." And, all activities were "after hours," like homework!

Students saw firsthand, that things were *not* as they're supposed to be. When you've become attached to an urban child through tutoring her math, and then discover you're the only person on the planet she has confided in that she was raped by a cousin, you *really* know things aren't the way they're supposed to be. When you spend your Saturdays working with an organization that uses horses to assist special needs kids develop motor skills, you also realize things aren't the way they're supposed to be. When you have a wallpapered ceiling you are trying to paint fall in while removing the wallpaper (because it was the only thing holding it up), you realize things aren't the way they're supposed to be. And when faces and names are associated with these vandalizations of shalom, you find yourself being drawn in as part of the solution. And best of all, when you engage yourself in bringing life and healing (aka shalom) into the places where it is missing, you discover a deep sense of joy that comes from doing what you were called to do. And, as we know, fulfillment comes from doing what you were *designed* to do as an image-bearer of God. At one point, we had nearly 20 kids, driving 50 miles round-trip a week to tutor at the urban Christian school where my son was teaching. Upperclassmen were taking freshmen who couldn't drive yet. It was a thrilling chapter in my life, and I think for the life of the school too. Unfortunately, when I returned full time to the classroom, the office was closed and never reopened. That was nine years ago. Students no longer show up to tutor, except during the summer.

Home-schooling parents are in the best possible place to do shalom-restoration, *and* weave it into the fabric of their children's souls. A typical home school curriculum can be completed before 1 p.m. each day, leaving a significant amount of time each week for extracurricular supplements. Often, these take the form of field trips, ballet, band, and sports. I have always been amazed at the quality of education that can be delivered in a home school environment done properly. Some of the smartest children I've met are products of this educational model. The 2007 Scripps National Spelling Bee champion was a home school prodigy. He was also an accomplished pianist, martial artist, and "mathalete."[1] But, I have been equally disappointed by the failure of *Christian* homeschooling parents to utilize a portion of this "extracurricular" time for shalom restoration. It would not only assist their children in finding their place in The Story, it would aid in their socialization, character education, and might even lead to an innovative vision for raising the standard of living in a developing country!

The larger, non-religious culture is beginning to show signs of an awakening conscience in the arena of social justice.[2] One of my oldest and dearest

1 http://www.lifesitenews.com/news/archive/ldn/2007/jun/07060102

2 See: http://www.forbes.com/sites/ciocentral/2012/03/18/giving-back-how-every-startup-can-be-philanthropic/

friends was recently presented with the prestigious James Beard Humanitarian Of The Year Award for his work in relieving hunger in America. His vision, "The Taste of the NFL," a one-night, high cost, one-of-a-kind-restaurant in Super Bowl cities, has raised over $10 million dollars for food banks throughout the U.S.[1] If you ask him why, he'll tell you because it's the "right thing to do." That's another way of saying the way it is, *isn't* the way it's supposed to be. He lives in Minneapolis and was one of the first persons to call me after Alabama's devastating and deadly tornados to ask, "What can I do?" Food for those who found themselves homeless was soon on trucks headed our way. It will be an unnecessary travesty if we believers find ourselves playing catchup on shalom-restoration like we're currently trying to do with the "green" movement. It both diminishes and discredits the gospel, when Christianity *appears* to be mimicking the secular culture, when in fact we're simply trying to catch up to it by doing what we're supposed to be doing continually. Actually appearing to be "followers" on issues when we should have been leaders, is dishonoring to God and to The Story.

The restoration of shalom should also be a litmus test for churches when it comes to setting budgets, implementing curricula and programs, and forging theologies of church growth. Rock-climbing walls and Family Fitness Centers *could* easily be tools of shalom restoration. But, most aren't. Until the restoration of shalom is understood as a divine imperative and therefore a key Christian virtue and ecclesiastical value, our Adamic residue will pull our money and our time back to ourselves and our agendas. But, in cases where the restoration of shalom, in all its variegated beauty, is understood and embraced, churches will discover they are valued in the communities where they work and worship. And, their members will find purpose and joy in their service. It is also possible that the fastest growing group in America, the "Nones," who have no affiliation with church, nor any desire to do so, may experience a nudge back.

Purpose comes from following design. And design, when it is applied to living, is known as plot. When we become Story-dwellers instead of Story-tellers, life goes from black and white to 3-D color. That's known as adventure. Life, as it turns out, though you're *not* choosing your *own* adventure, is an adventure nonetheless. And, there is much liberty in "choosing," I think, regarding *our* place in *His* adventure. But, there's still some tempting distractions from, and distortions to The Story that need to be exposed before you and me part ways.

---

1 See: http://www.jamesbeard.org/awards/search/Taste+of+the+NFL?

The Real World of Warcraft

There are some industries that are in the shalom-restoration business whether they know it or not. Our twin daughters have given their lives to one of them. Healthcare, that oft-maligned and politically-hijacked cauldron of dissent and complaint, also happens to be populated by people of deep compassion, relentless patience, and immeasurable service. Of course it's also characterized by arrogant, calloused, and avaricious pirates and merchants, many of whom have the personality of a Coke machine. Anyone who's had more than a single stay in a hospital knows this. But, I will bet that each of you reading this has memories of at least one nurse whose face and kindness, not to mention their ability to speak to you about medical issues in English, escorted you in that wheelchair to the exit. Heather and Havilah are those kinds of nurses. Stories abound, saturated with hilarity, of situations involving nameless patients (wouldn't want a HIPPA violation here), and the ubiquitous laughter generator in our family—feces. We've laughed till we've cried. But, more often than not, the stories Jill and I hear from our daughters, especially Heather who's an ICU nurse, involve wrenching tales of pain, suffering, and loneliness. "The girls," as we have always called them, have received letters from patients—some copies sent to the hospital administration as well—praising them for their care. Heather, who's in her seventh year as a hospital nurse, has *never* had a patient die on her watch. She told me once, she feels like God has given her "the gift of life." She actually had a patient *tell* her those very words, when she started her 12-hour shift one morning. People recognize shalom when they receive it and when they see it. Even though they may have no idea what to call it.

But, for those in the business of doling it out, it can become a wearisome task over time. Genuine love, the fruit of the Spirit that energizes shalom-giving, is costly. Immensely so. It cost Yahweh His son, and it cost Jesus his life. And it will cost any of us who choose to abandon our lives to become part of The Story. The girls' most difficult days are those when they are caring for marginally ill people, whose egos and felt needs far outstrip their medical condition. Or worse, family members of patients who demand to be treated like they were at a Five-Star hotel, while sitting watching TV. The expectation is that the nursing staff does all the menial tasks for their loved one that they could do themselves. I mean, wouldn't *you* get up and pour it, if your mother wanted some more water? They've actually had patients like this hit them, and cuss them out, all because they wouldn't turn their marginally unnecessary hospital stay into a Make-A-Wish fulfillment.

Ministry, the restoration of shalom, is a lot like healthcare. In fact, I would put ministry and healthcare at a tie for third place as America's most *under*-appreciated, yet often totally fulfilling vocations. (Right behind parenting and teaching.) The difference is, when people quit teaching because they've burned out, they don't stop learning. And when parents hit a wall with a difficult child, they don't change his name. But, when people burn out in ministry, which happens frequently, it often attacks their entire outlook, especially towards God. They become cynical, critical, and negative. Sadly, I have to admit that I have looked into that chasm more than once in the past 40 years. And, I'd be less than honest if I claimed that some of the residue of burnout, which attaches comfortably to the residue of Adam, isn't still with me. I smell its foul odor from time to time, especially when I'm exhausted. And ministry, real ministry, shalom-restoring ministry, is *always* exhausting. It has to be, because of why it exists in the first place.

If I've done my job, and God has unleashed His power in answer to the prayers that have surrounded this book, some of you have gotten a glimpse of just how enormous, how gorgeous, how positively amazing this Story really is. It may have restored hope to some of you who were about to give up on the whole notion of Jesus or church. Others of you may have discovered a unifying center from which to construct a vision of life and ministry. Some of you may have had to take your theology to the woodshed for a long conversation. If you've been moved at all while reading these pages, then it is also likely that some of you are going to seek to incarnate a few ideas into the sacred space called *your life*. It is never, *ever*, too late. I want to do all I can to insure that you are able to go the distance; that you finish the race; that you don't burn out. As I seek to draw this book to a close, you will need to consider some things. Four of them, to be exact. They are very important questions that you must have clarified and answered prior to embarking on a shalom-restoring life of any kind.

Question 1: *What is my model?*

It's been said that in an insane world, sane people eventually conclude that *they* are insane. In the arena of Christian discipleship, this becomes a vital axiom when it comes to going the distance, and finishing well, without regret or shame. It means that if you and I do not have people of shared values and vision in our lives, we will slowly but surely conclude that our zeal is misplaced or at least misappropriated. We will allow our convictions to soften, and slowly accommodate ourselves to the prevailing mood among believers around us. In short, we'll become the "tourist" Christian we examined in Chapter 7. But like senility, *we* won't see it or know it. And part of the reason we won't is that we will be surrounded by a host of other "tourists," rather than a few Story-driven believers, in which we collectively remind ourselves of *who* we are, *why* we're here, and *what* we're to be about until Scene 3 appears. Sanity, after all, is living in a manner that corresponds with what's real. For us, that means sanity is owning an identity, a purpose, and a mission that are rooted firmly in The Story. In short, we need a mental *model* that consistently reminds us where we are at all times. A sort of reality check. Something that will always make sense of what we're seeing and experiencing, providing hope and direction. It needs to be deeply theological at its core. But, the theology must be instrumental, not consequential. It will likely be more unconscious than conscious, unless I'm around other "sane" people and we begin to talk about life. It will also typically be *un*systematic because it involves the world of people who tend to be that way! And, if left unattended, it may deteriorate, or worse, be hijacked. Yet, it operates at the deep motivational levels of our lives. So, unlike a worldview, which may or may not have anything to do with how one actually *lives,* this does. As Christians, we all need one. I think Paul alluded to something like this when he admonished us to "set our minds on things above, where Christ is seated." And he did so in the context of how to live in Scene 2, waiting for Scene 3.[1] If there isn't an "Adventure" we are *supposed* to choose, we'll simply Choose Our Own Adventure.

The CYOA gene in our Adamic residue is dominant, like brown eyes. It trumps pretty much everything, especially among believers unfamiliar with The Story. As a result, in a biblically illiterate Church, which characterizes a growing percentage of American Christianity, "Christian" versions of a CYOA have sprung up and spread like Bermuda grass. Counterfeit mental models of what the "Christian life" is, and what it should look like, abound. Being incestuous by nature, a variety of step-cousins exist as well. But there a two that have the most traction in America. We've flown over these at high altitude earlier, but I need for us to revisit them one last time. (**Note to Self:** whenever we find ourselves talking and thinking in terms of the "Christian life" instead of The Story, we're in danger of going insane.)

The first CYOA-Christian Edition, is *"Living in Scene 2 – Longing For Scene 3."* Although there are varieties of this edition, the best known one has been present since the nineteenth century. Recently, it was popularized and given near viral status by the 16-book, *Left Behind* series, complete with movies and video games. Theological argumentation aside, the most unfortunate, yet inevitable byproduct of this neutered version of The Story is what it does to the psyche of the believer. It puts his *body* here, because Scene 2 is where he lives,

---

1 cf. Colossians 3:1-2.

but his mind and heart "there," in Scene 3, the *end* of The Story. This CYOA hijacks the "trailer" Scene 3 provides, and twists it into something pointing to the *future*, instead of a source of hope in the *present*. As we've said, "trailers" are always for the present, not the future. Predictive prophecy's place in The Story is to be the ground of hope in the midst of grueling shalom-restoring ministry *prior* to the end. God understands this. When someone's gaze is directed away from the present, it is unlikely that there will be much passion or interest in restoring shalom here and now. And to complicate matters (typically in this scenario), the gospel is reduced to getting people "saved" to avoid the coming wrath, which will be poured out on those who've been "left behind." This CYOA-Christian Edition essentially cuts the heart out of mission, by taking the restoration of shalom completely out of the picture. It is portrayed as a carrot of sorts, dangling at the end of Scene 3.

The second model is the CYOA-Christian Edition, *"Living Gratefully in Scene 2."* This perversion of The Story rewrites the script so that Yahweh has a supporting role, but humanity is the star. We are told that He wants it this way. This is the tourist version of The Story. No shalom here because there's no mission here. There's also no purpose because there's no plot. This is pure, unadulterated, CYOA, but dressed up and ready for church. Health and wealth theology has its own version of it. Upon close examination, we discover God works for *us*. It transforms the adoption aspect of identity into an excuse for excess and privilege instead of submission and responsibility. Books like, *Your Best Life Now* make no excuses about where a Christian's real focus should be. Humanity—not the glory of God and the restoration of all things—is at the center of the gospel. Gratitude becomes the banner and banter for this counterfeit. Listen carefully, and you'll hear plenty of "I thank the Lord's" being pronounced. As if God is pleased by what we've done to His Story by putting ourselves into it, like a proud father watching his son play ball! "Getting *saved*" in this model is important, because it's all about "getting *in*." Going out, giving away, giving up aren't on the agenda because they're not in the script. I suspect that the reason this CYOA is so popular, is that it focuses on the present only. And, Scene 2 is the one part of The Story for which we have absolutely no handbook. Remember, Scene 2 is Spirit-led improvisation. This CYOA is improvisation too, just without the Spirit.

I realize this sounds cynical and critical. It is. But, I think it's better to come from me than Jay Leno. Plus, we're talking about The Story here, not baptismal modes or tithing! Folks *died* in the Old Testament for getting this wrong. In fact, folks died in the New Testament for this very thing, turning the gospel into a means for personal advancement.[1]

---

[1] The story of the couple, Ananias and Sapphira in Acts 5:1-15 is an excellent example of this. They lied in front of the church regarding a gift they had made, hoping to make an impression on the people gathered. They turned the spotlight on themselves, and God took them out. Tough love you might call it, but God was just getting this "church" thing off the ground, and it was already being hijacked. The CYOA gene was alive and well in Jerusalem. It is especially noteworthy that church growth exploded after the Story was rescued and put back in place.

I've saved the best for last. Seriously. We must have a model that is big enough to accommodate the entire Story, provide answers to life as we see it, and instill hope and perseverance for shalom restoration. And, I do *not* believe this one is a CYOA. In fact, it is more likely the Choose The One Adventure. It's *"Living in Scene 2-Longing for Scene 3, but Driven by Acts II and IV."* This is an expansive and highly nuanced model; not just a long name. It is a biblical literacy based model and therefore demands a firsthand, constantly maturing understanding of The Story. It requires a mature appreciation for sin and sees *it* as an explanation for what we see around us that isn't the way it's supposed to be. It values people because they are image-bearers, not because of what they believe, or how they behave. It champions the centrality of the death, resurrection, and ascension of Jesus Christ as the essential and instrumental turning point in The Story. It engenders responsibility for the restoration of shalom as the birthright and mission of every adopted and justified son of Adam and daughter of Eve. And it values the hope provided by Scene 3, but refuses to focus on the future to the neglect of the present.

This model embodies a realistic optimism regarding the substantial restoration of shalom in every area of life, while reserving its full flowering in the life to come. It sees all of life through the pages of the One Story of the One God and His plan for the fullness of time to unite all things in him, things in heaven and things on earth. This model is the raging torrent of grace we spoke of in Chapter 15. And it flows only in this life, on this earth. When I was in college, a recreational beverage company had a popular slogan, "You only go around once in life, grab for all the gusto you can." They had the first part right, but the second part backwards. When we step into the One Story of the One God, the gusto grabs us.

Question 2: *What Is My Mission?*

For those of us living in the U.S., there's a thousand variations of the same song floating around when it comes to the notion of "mission." Its textbook title is the "American Dream," but it shows up under a host of aliases. "Miss America," "The World's Sexiest Man," "American Idol," (insert a noun here) Hall of Fame," "(insert a name here), CEO," GPA (insert a number here), etc. Surely not evil aspirations, but all the result of pursuing *desire* within the circumference of a promise that if you want it bad enough, you can get it. The ideology fueling this desire has been quaintly called the "American Dream," a sort of modern version of "Rome" being an idea more than a place. The American Dream is the offspring of the union of capitalism and democracy. Liberty and free enterprise create wide highways to success and wealth. It's nearly the Fourth of July as I'm writing this, nestled away in a cabin overlooking the Tennessee River Valley. And there are lots of regal flags flying along the roads up to where I'm holding out. Two kinds of flags. One that is red-white-and-blue, with lots of stars and stripes. The other bears the same colors, but not the same history. My kids' first exposure to it was on the roof of a car called The General Lee on the 1980's TV show, *The Dukes of Hazzard*. We are territorial and patriotic creatures, us Americans. And, lest I am accused of being *un*patriotic for what follows, let me say that I'm both proud *and* grateful to be an American. After seeing AK-47s and dogs on Guatemalan soldiers at the airport, and teenage "escorts" with sawed-off shotguns as guards on Coke trucks in the mountains, I felt safe returning to American soil. The 18 year-olds with military-issue rifles walking around Jerusalem was also unnerving. When I got back to the States, I felt like Dorothy in the *Wizard of Oz*, "There's *no* place like home." Jill and I regularly have dinner with my brother and sister-in-law. Watching the debilitating effect of 40-year old shrapnel floating around in his body from Vietnam, is a constant reminder of the debt I owe to those who serve in places I'll never have to see.

But, the One Story doesn't have a country or an economic system. It claims no favorites. God doesn't take "sides," except for His own. This is probably best illustrated in the classic story of Joshua preparing to enter Canaan with the Israelite army. The night before the invasion, an angel appears to him. I've always gotten a little amused thinking of what it must have been like to be an angel in biblical times. Every time you show up to tell someone something, they lose it! They fall on their faces, or lose their ability to talk, and are always being told, "stand up, it's just me." Joshua's no different. He marches up and asks him whose side he's on; is it Israel or the enemy? Good question to ask the night before engagement. The angel says "I'm on *Yahweh's* side, who's side are *you* on?"[1] Joshua falls down on his face.

The point here for us, is that as Christians, we must separate the American Dream from The Story. They have nothing in common. The Story can *speak* to the American Dream. And it does. But, the idea that if you want it, you can achieve it, and if you get it, you can keep it, is not biblical. If God *wants* you to have it, you'll get it. But, you might not get to keep it. He might have given it to you to give to someone else as a necessary ingredient in the restoration of shalom. Sometimes, if you want it, He might not want you to have it, *or* want it. Paul wanted a physical ailment removed from his body. He prayed, begging God to take it away. Remember this is *Paul* here, not you or me. God said "No, you keep it. You will need it." Turns out it was a shalomic gift to make sure Paul's Adamic residue stays in its cage.[2] On one occasion, much like many modern children, Moses tried to negotiate with Yahweh to have his punishment reduced so he could go into the Promised Land. Yahweh, surely in a more godly way than this, told him to "shut up."[3] So, if you and I want something, well, we better figure out why and for what. And then, we need to ask ourselves, "How does this fit into The Story?" The Story has no place for the American Dream, or

---

1 cf. Joshua 5:13-15; It wasn't *quite* like that, but the point the angel was making is the same.
2 cf. 2 Corinthians 12:7-10.
3 cf. Deuteronomy 3:25-26.

the Israeli Dream, or the Italian Dream, or any Dream that's not affiliated with the restoration of shalom and the demolition of the "former things." God is still passionate about us striving to find our role in His Story, instead of figuring out creative ways to squeeze Him into our dream or our story. Maybe that's why David Platt, one of the most passionate young men I know, added this subtitle to *Radical*, his NY Times best seller: *Taking Back Your Faith from the American Dream*. All our dreams, if they really are a product *of* The Story, will naturally fold back *into* The Story. They will ultimately contribute to the restoration of shalom.

The second option, since we've retired the American Dream as an option for those of us who know our part in The Story, is the mission of the restoration of shalom. But, I need to add a small but important addendum to what we've already come to see. It takes us back to the beginning of our journey in these pages. Just as following desire turned out to be Adamic instead of Abrahamic, so too, surrendering oneself to the mission of shalomic restoration is Abrahamic, instead of Adamic. But, it's also something monumental because of all the ground we've covered to get arrive at this place. Giving myself to the restoration of shalom is following *design*. It's living in a way that is consistent with how I was made. It's resembling the One whose damaged image I bear, but whose image is being renewed in me, as Paul says, "from one degree of glory to another."[1] And because fulfillment comes from following design, involvement in the restoration of shalom is the path to personal fulfillment. It all converges here. Identity, design, plot, purpose, and mission. This, is the "point."

Question 3: *What Is My Metaphor?*

For years, I have taught that the sport of running cross-country captures many of the qualities necessary to live the "Christian life." Having a son who helped lead his school to its first male State Championship in any sport surely biased my choice. But, I believed it is a suitable metaphor. In a cross-country race, everyone starts, fewer finish, and those who run fastest don't always take first place. Mental strategy outweighs physical stamina. Training is grueling. You run alone, but your results affect the team. The illustrative comparisons seemed endless. It has served me well for many years, and I am still a firm believer in the need to own a metaphor for the journey of faith. It needs to be one that holds together under the pressure and pain that life this side of Scene 3 entails for each of us. Especially, for those in The Story. While Scripture also employs the metaphor of a race,[2] I think under scrutiny you will discover that although it surely illumines aspects of the journey, it's not the best one to use for life in Scene 2. And like our discussion on the question of "What's my model?" this question also has some popular but anemic contenders.

One is what I can only call, "Fellowship and Worship." Because I am a con-

----

1 cf. 2 Corinthians 3:17-18.

2 cf. 1 Corinthians 9:24-27; Hebrews 12:1.

ference speaker as well as a Bible teacher, I am often asked to address audiences of varying ages across a wide spectrum of venues. One fairly constant item, when it involves conferences of people under forty, is the "praise and worship" segment. Characteristically, it is relatively long, tends to be hymn-less, and is biased towards the present over the past. It is led by a "praise team," and usually features a drummer, though an occasional djimbe ("jimbay") will appear. During these times of worship, it is not uncommon to see men as well as women, with exalted hands, or prostrate on the floor. Some will be quietly worshipping through dance off to one side. I am often quite moved by this time at a conference, if it's done well and doesn't become a dorm room showcase. But, I also have ears and eyes trained to process what others don't know I'm hearing or seeing (a skill developed from years in the classroom), so I'm also curious and attentive to what many of these same people are doing the rest of the weekend. The lunchroom, hallways, greenways, and lounges serve as enormous data servers for me. What I have noticed is that some who worship with reverence don't really behave that way the rest of the weekend. I'm not suggesting they're pretending to worship, but I have to wonder if they have made the connection between genuine worship and The Story.

In the days of ancient Israel's decline, God sent in His servants, the Assyrians, to destroy the Northern Kingdom, its capital city of Samaria, and distribute the ten tribes who lived there throughout the Assyrian Empire. Population displacement was their preferred way of ensuring a permanent conquest. The people who repopulated what was left of Israel, eventually intermarried with the remaining Jews. The result of these unions became known as the Samaritans. The pagan immigrants also brought with them their idols and their worship. What happened during this time has enormous relevance for the praise and worship movement in the Church today. It also speaks to the "Fellowship and Worship" metaphor.

> Even while these people were worshiping the LORD, they were serving their idols. To this day their children and grandchildren continue to do as their fathers did.
> –2 Kings 17:41, NIV

The sobering principle here is that whom you're worshipping may not be whom you are serving. And, in our case, "serving" has to do with submission to The Story, which is the restoration of shalom. This means that unless worship results in mission; it's not worship at all. It is not possible to draw near to the heart of Yahweh, which is what true worship is, and not come away with something of His passion. And the passion of Yahweh, from the very beginning of The Story, was the restoration of shalom. The movement *back* to the way things are supposed to be, the passing away of the "former things." Substantially in this life, and permanently in the next. True worship will draw those who enter it, into that passion.

This becomes of utmost importance to me because when you read carefully the part of Scene 3, where God announces that He is "making all things new," and the "former things are passing away," you'll discover it is in the context of tears, death, mourning, crying out, and weeping passing away as well. The reason these "former things" are passing away, is that sin no longer exists. Sin is gone in Scene 3, and along with it, all the foul fruit that it bore. The pain from rape, hunger, racism, adultery, sickness, mental illness, and all expressions of shalomic absence, are gone. This is glorious. But, there's another thing that is also missing in eternity. Ministry. There is no need for ministry in eternity because there is no sin.

This is why this metaphor is not only insufficient; it is dangerous. I sometimes fear that the energetic rising generation may spend too much time doing what it will be doing forever—fellowship and worship. Meanwhile, they may miss the one thing they *cannot* do forever—ministry. True worship should lead to service, and service leads to The Story. And, The Story is all about ministry and mission, the restoration of shalom.

A second metaphor, one that comes closer to the truth, is what I call, "Fellowship in War." This metaphor has a more sober assessment of the difficulty associated with following Christ. It portrays the believer engaged in battle as a soldier or a warrior. Paul employs this metaphor at the end of his letter to the Ephesians. But, even this metaphor can prove to be too weak, if it's combined with any of the CYOA versions of the faith. What can happen is that the "war" metaphor diminishes to a romantic *idea* about war, instead of one that is realistic. If you've seen the movie, *The Princess Bride,* you've got a great illustration of this type of "Fellowship in War" metaphor. There's danger, fighting, romance, good, and evil. Satan plays with our minds from time to time (Vizinni's battle of the wits with Westley), but in the end, evil is vanquished, and everyone gets to ride off on their own white horse. I love the movie, but a romantic comedy is the wrong metaphor for the life of a believer in Scene 2.

I think a better illustration for the metaphor, "Fellowship in War," is the scene in the cinema version 0f Tolkien's, *The Two Towers,* known as the Battle for Helm's Deep. It has proven true to my own experience for the past 40 years in The Story. The classic dialogue between King Théoden and Aragorn, as they look out at an innumerable enemy host of orcs, goblins, and Uruk-hai sets the stage:

> **Théoden:** A great host, you say?
> **Aragorn:** All Isengard is emptied.
> **Théoden:** How many?
> **Aragorn:** Ten thousand strong at least.
> **Théoden:** [astonished] Ten thousand?
> **Aragorn:** It is an army bred for a single purpose: to destroy the world of men. They will be here by nightfall.
> **Théoden:** Let them come.

And what follows is brutal. There is widespread carnage as the combined forces of Middle Earth seek to do their part to turn back the darkness of Mordor incarnate in the hordes of Isengard. Many do not live to see the sunrise. This, not The *Princess Bride,* is a metaphor of life in Scene 2. I owe this metaphor to my son, Ben. Fighting for the restoration of shalom in the spiritual darkness of inner city Birmingham, via an urban Christian school aptly called, Restoration Academy, has taught him many things about Scene 2. One of them, is that those who seek to turn back the "former things," align themselves as enemies to the King of Former Things, the one Paul calls "the prince of the power of the air." Shalomic restoration is a war in the spiritual realm, not only a struggle in the material world. The one who first stole shalom from the Garden will not sit and idly watch for its return. I know this sounds mystical, or maybe even primitive to any overly rational types. But, it is the inescapable message of Scripture, the only record we have on everything in The Story *except* Scene 2. And there's no reason to assume Satan's in the break room during this Scene. And, because it's a war, there *will* be casualties. There *will* be traitors and deserters. There *will* be injuries, and even "friendly fire." Some of us will not live to see the White Horse arrive. Some of us will die. That is already happening around the globe to many brothers and sisters who are serving in The Story elsewhere. Martyrdom is not a word limited to an entry in Wikipedia about first century Christianity. It is a twenty-first century reality. And, as painful as it is to say, martyrdom fits within the boundaries of this metaphor. Those of us privileged to be living in safer regions of Scene 2, still need to accept the fact that we are in The Story's equivalent of the Battle For Helm's Deep. And we need to keep that before us as we engage in mission. And, we do not give way to fear.

Within this metaphor, there is also room for an informed understanding of suffering in the life of a Story-dweller. In an age of increased longevity, and spacious insight into disease causation, we are tempted to think outside The Story framework. Though medicine and the healing arts are shalomic gifts, suffering and pain will never fade until Scene 3 arrives. This is an important facet in our metaphor of "Fellowship in War," to keep always before us. I have fallen prey to the comforting myth that by being a Story-dweller, Yahweh will spare me some of the pain I see around me; a sort of twisted form of spiritual favoritism, I suppose. Thinking this way is to take a stroll near the precipice of resentment. I've nearly fallen over its edge more than once, when disease, disappointment, and despair came to call at my front door. The fact that the Author of The Story laid His own Son on an altar of wood, suspended between earth and heaven, is cause to trust Him when prayers go unheeded, darkness persists, and suffering is frequent or even permanent. Peter tells us that Jesus died so we wouldn't *have* to, but he suffered so that we'd know *how* to, *"For to this you have been called, because Christ also suffered for you, leaving you an example, so that you might follow in his steps."*[1]

I want to sensitively and carefully say this, because undoubtedly, many of you have endured or are enduring a seemingly endless season of difficult obedience. But, the fact that there truly *is* a Story means that there is purpose in

1 cf. 1 Peter 2:20–21.

our pain. Surely, some of it is the fire of transforming grace to burn away the Adamic dross that parades as godliness. But, and this can be a source of sweet resolve, some suffering we endure is for people we have yet to meet. Some suffering is the womb out of which shalomic love and compassion are birthed.

> Blessed be the God and Father of our Lord Jesus Christ, the Father of mercies and God of all comfort, *who comforts us in all our affliction, so that we may be able to comfort those who are in any affliction,* with the comfort with which we ourselves are comforted by God.   **–2 Corinthians 1:3–4**

Sometimes, for those of us submerged in The Story, "Fellowship in War" is what Eugene Peterson calls a long obedience in the same direction.[1] It is difficult and disappointing when friends and colleagues become casualties in the war through their own sin or that of others. Hardly a month goes by in which I don't hear of another tale of someone I know being taken out of the fight. Often, it is a moral indiscretion. We are in a war. But, the Apostle John assures us that *"the reason the Son of God appeared was to destroy the works of the devil."*[2] We know how this thing ends. We have Scene 3. So, in the words of Théoden, *"Let them come!"*

Question 4: *What Is My Motive?*

The flattening of the world through technology has happened with such blistering speed, assessment and thoughtful evaluation have given way to the frenzied attempt to "stay current." For many, it's like trying to chase a train. Eventually, you just give up, wave goodbye and let it follow its course. Neil Postman and Sherry Turkle were once lonely voices. Now, they have been joined by so many that it has become a prophetic chorus. We are being warned to be attentive to what's happening *to* us as a result of what's happening *around* us. This is particularly significant to me regarding The Story, and our place in it. The benign rise of social networking sites, like Friendster, MySpace, and Facebook—originally created to help people "connect"—was not designed to be environments where people would prefer to "live." But, that is what they have become for many people. Though there are undoubtedly thousands of graduate-level theses currently in motion on the subject, I am only interested in a single unintended consequence of social networking's meteoric rise to digital ascendancy. And that is the phenomenon of self-promotion.

Without providing a list of sites that provide self-promotion services as examples, suffice it to say that the digital machinery is in place and available to anyone who is interested. You and I can let the whole connected world know what we think and enjoy, whom we know and like, what or who we *don't* like, where we've been or are going, what we're reading and watching, and who we're seeing, or planning to dump (aka "defriend"). Journaling, the ancient art

---

1 Peterson has written a book by this title, and it is a theme that appears repeatedly in his memoir, *The Pastor.*

2 cf. 1 John 3:8.

of thinking privately on paper, has morphed into full public exposure to near strangers. We are becoming a race of serial monologuers instead of curious dialoguers. And, at the end of the day, the disheartening truth is, most of the information we send out points the world back to us. My centripetal self, it seems, now has free exposure to the known universe. And, we'll gladly accept the offer, because our Adamic residue always pushes to the front of the line of recognition. Because everybody has been told that the world wants to "find them" on Facebook, or "follow" them on Twitter, the phenomenon sociologists call the "cult of celebrity" has had its own IPO. It has happened quietly and transparently, but the "self" is now being publicly traded. But, more significantly, this has become the new normal. Hopefully, by this point on our walk together through this book, your dash lights have come on, and you see a message that says, "This is *not* the way it's supposed to be." When you combine this reality with the internal momentum of the gospel to go to the nations, near perfect storm conditions arise within the Church for us to inject ourselves into The Story. And we have.

The modern church is replete with revisionist versions of The Story, thanks to the unannounced marriage of Christian merchandising and the technorati. And self-promotion has been granted sacramental status as we are assaulted on shelves and Kindles by the covers of Christian books, boasting full color photos of the *authors*, purportedly writing to point us to Jesus. Study Bibles abound, with the names of pastors and teachers on the covers, obviously to add credibility, or (less obviously) to increase sales. Prominent Christian leaders encourage us to "Follow Them" on Twitter, apparently believing that the dangers associated with that behavior have been quelled since Paul warned the Corinthians against it in the first century.[1] Preachers download sermons and PowerPoint files from other pastors and preach them as their own. This isn't a slippery slope; it's a dark pit. And, it is one which those who fall in, find themselves climbing out as presenters, instead of prophets. One website selling sermons actually had an article on "How To Use Other People's Sermons With Integrity." Interestingly, I haven't seen similar articles by the AMA on "How To Submit Other's Medical Research With Integrity," or the NEA on "How To Hand-In Your Classmates' Term Paper With Integrity." Even the secular world would never use the word "integrity" in a headline about prophetic pilfering. Our own newspaper, in May of 2007, had an article on the rise of preaching plagiarism entitled, "Thou Shall Not Steal...Unless It's The Sermon." Unfortunately, it appears that Yahweh's

---

1 See 1 Corinthians 1:10-13; 3:2-4); I am not mishandling the Scriptures by making this association. Paul's rebuke to the Corinthians, who were living more like their zip code than beneficiaries of the Abrahamic covenant, was to reject the then modern notion that they had to choose a person to identify with. But, of even greater application here, is the clear implication that genuine godly leaders would *never* approve of such a thing! In fact, Paul, in no uncertain terms lets them know that *he* does not want anyone to "follow" him in that sense. In my opinion, and that's all it is, I think Twitter has no place in the life of a Christian leader, and this is proportionally more relevant in regard to his or her visibility. The cult of celebrity that characterized the Romanized city of Corinth was Paul's target. The principle is unchanged even though the technology has changed. If anything, it's *more* relevant in a global culture, not less.

lament through the voice of Jeremiah, "Woe to the shepherds who steal my words from one another,"[1] has fallen on deaf ears in our day just as it did in his. But, stealing each other's words, or pulpit plagiarism as it's been christened, is not the inevitable stepchild of globalism and the internet, as many claim. It is the unfortunate consequence of having a textbook or handbook perspective on the Bible, to the neglect of its narrative. This is especially true in non-liturgical churches, where for centuries the pulpit has replaced the altar. It's the churches that have enjoyed a long tenure in the primacy of preaching that find themselves scrambling to maintain membership in a flat world. The unintended consequence of worship services constructed so that everything else is a prelude to the sermon, turns preaching into the "main act." And in an entertainment culture, if the "act" isn't good enough, customers will leave and shop for one that is better. Technology, which has served the entertainment industry so well for so long, became a perceived solution. Multiple screens, impressive sound systems, movie clips, even interactive Tweeting during church, have become common place. Like the church of Laodecia that believed nothing was missing from its fellowship and worship, I fear that many twenty-first century churches will soon discover Jesus is "knocking on the door," *outside* the church.[2]

Liturgical churches, however, where the sermon is merely a component in a larger experience shaped by community participation in Eucharist and liturgy, though not immune from the new normal, are not facing the same pressure to bow at the altar of the Great iAm. It comes as no surprise to me that growing numbers of the rising generation are moving away from churches specializing in smoke and mirror worship, complete with plasma screen preachers and celebrity pulpits, to those that value solemnity, reverence, and our ancient roots.[3] In fact, the quality most attractive to those drawn to liturgical churches, is a diminished emphasis on the modern and a connection to the ancient. Sounds rather Abrahamic, doesn't it?

This question of motive in mission is huge, because motives are unseen, and rarely discussed. Maybe that's why they are also often misjudged. Also, we've already seen that deep within each of us, is a craving to be noticed. But, when it comes to The Story, this craving is out of place, because there are no "stars." We would do well to take the counsel of U2 rockstar-prophet, Bono: *"Coolness may help your negotiation with people through the world, maybe, but it's impossible to meet God with sunglasses on."*[4] In other words, we're out of our league when it comes to His place and ours in His Story. It's sort of like if we were the donkey carrying Jesus into Jerusalem on Palm Sunday, we'd want to believe the crowds

---

1 cf. Jeremiah 23:23-32, especially verse 30.

2 cf. Revelation 3:14-20.

3 Cf. http://www.cbn.com/cbnnews/us/2011/December/Anglican-Fever-Youth-Flock-to-New-Denomination-/

4 Bono, and Michka Assayas. *Bono In Conversation with Michka Assayas ; with a Foreword by Bono.* (New York: Riverhead Books, 2005), 53.

were cheering for us! Sadly, if Palm Sunday happened today, the donkey would probably be interviewed on some Christian talk show. Can't you picture it:

Interviewer: *"So, what was it like, carrying the Messiah amidst all that fanfare, with palm branches waving everywhere and people throwing their clothing?"*

Donkey: *"Well first of all, I just want to thank my agent. I mean, of all the donkeys in Jerusalem...and of course I want to thank the Lord. I couldn't have done it without him...."*

Seriously, we are hardwired since Eden to hijack The Story and recast it to feature *us*. This is captured in the title of a recent best-selling Christian book, *It's Your Time: Activate Your Faith, Achieve Your Dreams, Increase in God's Favor.*[1] I hope this doesn't disappoint you, but it's *never* "your" time in His Story. Learning to be content and grateful to simply *be* in The Story, is the greatest need we have during Scene 2.

This tendency of the Adamic residue to reach for notoriety in ministry is real enough for it to be a recurring theme in Scripture. It becomes even more dangerous in an age where one can be notorious globally, and nearly instantly. Paul dismantles the notion that I can be a Story-dweller *and* a "star" simultaneously:

For am I now seeking the approval of man, or of God? Or am I trying to please man? If I were still trying to please man, I would not be a servant of Christ.
–**Galatians 1:10**

But, the most riveting statement about our place in The Story, comes from the lips of one whose role in Act IV was the second most anticipated appearance in the narrative since the fall of Jerusalem to the Babylonians. John the Baptizer stands forever as the epitome of getting it right when it comes to the self and The Story. He had already endured one grueling inquisition by the Jewish authorities on the issues of identity, purpose, and mission. Shortly after, he found himself in a similar dilemma with his own disciples. They were confused about the relationship of Jesus to John, particularly, to whom they should pay the most attention. John summarized his role in The Story with a single statement, *"He must increase, but I must decrease."*[2] John lived out this conviction by pointing all who had followed him to the one he called, "the lamb of God." Make no mistake, John was a hot item in first century Palestine. The hottest, since Jeremiah. His following was significant in size, and his influence wide in scope. Yet, he turned it all over to Jesus. Why? That was his role in The Story. For John, the questions of *"Who am I? Why am I? and What is my place?"* were all answered in the One Story of the One God to unite in him all things, things in heaven and things on earth. Nothing has changed. God has no other plan, because there is no other Story.

1 Joel Olsteen, *It's Your Time : Activate Your Faith, Achieve Your Dreams, and Increase in God's Favor.* New York: Free Press, 2009.

2 John 3:30; The Greek here is significant. The "increasing" of Jesus is a present infinitive, indicating ongoing "increasing." But the "decreasing" is a perfect passive, indicating John is the agent of the decreasing, *not* his circumstances, and he is to be in a state of decrease. In other words, this is John's new role in The Story, and it's permanent.

When I ask Christians, *"What do you want to hear from God on the day that you meet Him?"* their knee-jerk response is to answer by quoting from Jesus' parable of talents: *"Well done, thou good and faithful servant."*[1] I want to hear that too. I suspect you do also. But, what if we have to speak first? What if, when we meet God, it's required that we have the first word, so that He can have the last? What would you say? Keep in mind what you want Him to say in response. What is the only reasonable thing you and I can say to Yahweh that would elicit the response, *"Well done, thou good and faithful servant."*? It can't be profuse thanksgiving for forgiveness, or for His faithful provision. It can't be gratitude for answered prayer, or deliverance from impossible circumstances. It can't be praise for His healing of loved ones, or the salvation of friends. I believe the only reasonable thing we can say, is what Jesus said when he was about to meet the Father, *"I glorified you on earth, having accomplished the work that you gave me to do."*[2]

I began this book with this quote from Gordon Dahl: ·

> "Most middle class Americans tend to worship their work, work at their play, and play at their worship. As a result, their meanings and values are distorted. Their relationships disintegrate faster than they can keep them in repair. Their lifestyles resemble a cast of characters in search of a plot."

There is absolutely no reason why this assessment should ever be made about you. You understand who you are, why you are, and have an expansive understanding of both the vastness and the beauty of The Story. What remains is for you to determine whether you've been trying to find a role for Jesus in your Chart Your Own Adventure, or find your place in His. At the end of the day, this is the only choice you have. And, it's the only one that really matters. Choose well.

....

1 cf. Matthew 25:14-30.

2 John 17:4

Acknowledgments

It is customary, as it should be, that an author acknowledge in no uncertain terms that the book in your hands was not a solo effort. It is no exaggeration to say that without the contributions from a cadre of kind friends and mentors, what you are about to read would still be inside my head.

Our son Ben, who for several years has goaded me to leave something behind for his generation and his own children, besides just cabinets full of notebooks and digital files. His gratitude for this effort is my reward. Ben embodies much of this book, living out the life of a disciple in the inner city with his wife and four children. He also crafted the Discussion Questions at the back of the book. Our middle son, Geoff, is responsible for the interior and cover design. I stand amazed at his ability to simultaneously accomplish multiple tasks demanding Herculean effort. His tenure portfolio as a graphic design professor was due the same week as his design deadlines for this book. And, as usual, he did an outstanding job on both!

My Board, a loyal band of men and women who encouraged me to clear my calendar for most of a spring and summer to give myself to read, research, and write. They also approved my unyielding insistence on self-publishing. Their enthusiastic support was a liberating force in this project. My dear friend and co-belligerent, Dana Thomas, who graciously and speedily created a sanctuary for me at the camp of Kids Across America in Golden, Missouri. Thanks to his kind provision, I lived in total isolation, writing 10 hours a day for two weeks. Part I and II were written there. Hal Threadcraft, a dear brother, provided a week at his cottage on Gorham's Bluff in northern Alabama. I worked another week in isolation, moving my office into his quiet and secluded retreat, where I completed Part III. Doug and Beth Heimburger provided a fourth week in their home in Nashville. While there, I was able to revisit the work I'd done in Missouri and Alabama months earlier. I list all these provisions because most of my life is like living in a food processor. Consequently, solitude, contemplation, and quiet are distant strangers to my daily, production-laden lifestyle. These dear people created quiet space, in which my mind, so full of passionate thoughts and prone to distraction, could find its way to a keyboard. It is no exaggeration to say without these sacred spaces I would never have gotten this done.

I am grateful for the comments, and criticisms provided by scholar-friends whose intellectual pay grades are way above mine. They took time out of already-compacted schedules to read and evaluate the first draft of the manuscript. Among them are Walter Schultz, my spiritual father and oldest kindred friend on earth. His insight into ideas and arguments is matched only by his love for God and His Word. Bill Klein, my friend and New Testament professor in seminary when we both were younger men. He, more than any other, has shaped my desire to teach the Word of God clearly, correctly, and with humility. Lyle Dorsett, a dear brother and friend whose prolific pen is only exceeded by his unvarnished honesty. He helped me clear the landscape of this manuscript of remnants of my own agenda, to open the way to seeing Yeshua more clearly. Lisa Ryken, former student and now First Lady of Wheaton College. She knew me when these ideas were in their infancy, 32 years ago. Her endorsement of them in their adulthood means a great deal to me.

It is no exaggeration to say that without the gracious provision of office space for my ministry, not only would this book never have been born, but Hands of Hur could not exist. Thank you, Darrell. I am also indebted to Steve Antonello for his meticulous eye as proofreader of the final version. Finally, my deep gratitude goes out to a handful of faithful supporters who've invested financially in this book's production. Their generosity is equaled by their desire for anonymity. Thank you.

But, most important—and it always seems to get down to this in most books—I am grateful to my wife, Jill. Her amazing skill as a developmental editor sharpened the message of this book without softening it. She also graciously allowed me to be absent more than any other time in our marriage, to write. But most of all for the innumerable nights we have sat, discussing the ideas that populate these pages. She knew everything that would be in this book before a word found its way to paper. Mostly because it has become the fabric of our lives together for nearly 40 years. In a very real sense, she is an unseen presence on every page.

Bibliography

(**Author's note:** The following list, while certainly not exhaustive, represents the books that have shaped my own thinking in varying degrees. The fruit of many other authors' labor is present in my own writing. Some are cited, and others are not. Some are congruent with my own conclusions and convictions, others are at odds with them. I am not endorsing any of them, only acknowledging that they have provoked thoughtful consideration on the issues raised in this book.)

Bartholomew, Craig G., and Michael W. Goheen. *The Drama of Scripture: Finding Our Place in the Biblical Story*. Grand Rapids, Mich: Baker Academic, 2004.

Bell, Rob. *Love Wins: A Book About Heaven, Hell, and the Fate of Every Person Who Ever Lived*. New York, NY: HarperOne, 2011.

Blomberg, Craig. *Neither Poverty nor Riches: A Biblical Theology of Material Possessions*. Grand Rapids, Mich: Eerdmans, 1999.

Bonhoeffer, Dietrich. *Life Together*. London: SCM, 1954.

Bono, and Michka Assayas. *Bono In Conversation with Michka Assayas ; with a Foreword by Bono*. New York: Riverhead Books, 2005. <http://site. ebrary. com/id/10126237>.

Bradshaw, Timothy. *Grace and Truth in the Secular Age*. Grand Rapids, Mich: W. B. Eerdmans Pub, 1998.

Burke, Trevor J., and Brian S. Rosner. *Paul As Missionary: Identity, Activity, Theology, and Practice*. London: T & T Clark, 2011.

Byers, Andrew J. *Faith Without Illusions: Following Jesus As a Cynic Saint*. Downers Grove, Ill: IVP Books, 2011.

Carr, Nicholas G. *The Shallows: What the Internet Is Doing to Our Brains*. New York: W. W. Norton, 2010.

Carson, D. A. *Becoming Conversant with the Emerging Church: Understanding a Movement and Its Implications*. Grand Rapids, Mich: Zondervan, 2005.

Claiborne, Shane. *The Irresistible Revolution: Living As an Ordinary Radical*. Grand Rapids, Mich: Zondervan, 2006.

Colson, Charles W., and Ellen Santilli Vaughn. *Kingdoms in Conflict*. [New York]: W. Morrow, 1987.

Commission on Children at Risk. *Hardwired to Connect: The New Scientific Case for Authoritative Communities*. New York: Institute for American Values, 2003.

Cope, Landa L. *An Introduction to the Old Testament Template: Rediscovering God's Principles for Discipling Nations*. Seattle, Wash: YWAM Pub, 2011.

Davis, Tom. *Red Letters: Living a Faith That Bleeds*. Colorado Springs, CO: David C. Cook, 2007.

Dillard, Annie. *The Annie Dillard Reader*. New York: HarperCollins Publishers, 1994.

Erickson, Millard J., Paul Kjoss Helseth, and Justin Taylor. *Reclaiming the Center: Confronting Evangelical Accommodation in Postmodern Times*. Wheaton, Ill: Crossway Books, 2004.

Ford, Michael. *Wounded Prophet: A Portrait of Henri J. M. Nouwen.* New York: Doubleday, 1999.

Friedman, Thomas L. *The World Is Flat: A Brief History of the Twenty-First Century.* New York: Farrar, Straus and Giroux, 2005.

Friedman, Thomas L. *Hot, Flat, and Crowded: Why We Need a Green Revolution-- and How It Can Renew America.* New York: Farrar, Straus and Giroux, 2008.

Goldsworthy, Graeme. *According to Plan.* Inter-Varsity, 1991.

Guinness, Os, and John Seel. *No God but God.* Chicago, Ill: Moody Press, 1992.

Hays, J. Daniel. *From Every People and Nation: A Biblical Theology of Race.* Downers Grove, Ill: Inter Varsity Press, 2003.

Hedges, Chris. *Empire of Illusion: The End of Literacy and the Triumph of Spectacle.* New York: Nation Books, 2009.

Hunter, James Davison. *Evangelicalism: The Coming Generation.* Chicago: University of Chicago Press, 1987.

Jackson, Maggie. *Distracted: The Erosion of Attention and the Coming Dark Age.* Amherst, N. Y. : Prometheus Books, 2008.

Johnson, Paul. *Modern Times: The World from the Twenties to the Eighties.* New York: Harper & Row, 1983.

Juhnke, James C., and Dale Schrag. *Anabaptist Visions for the New Millennium: A Search for Identity.* Kitchener, Ont: Pandora Press, 2000.

Keller, Timothy J. *The Prodigal God: Recovering the Heart of the Christian Faith.* New York: Dutton, 2008.

Lanier, Jaron. *You Are Not a Gadget: A Manifesto.* New York: Alfred A. Knopf, 2010.

Lewis, C. S. *The Problem of Pain.* San Francisco: HarperSanFrancisco, 2001.

Lyons, Gabe. *The Next Christians: The Good News About the End of Christian America.* New York: Doubleday Religion, 2010.

Manning, Brennan. *The Ragamuffin Gospel.* Sisters, Or: Multnomah Publishers, 2000.

Mason, Mike. *The Gospel According to Job.* Wheaton, Ill: Crossway Books, 1994.

Mason, Mike. *The Mystery of Marriage.* London: Triangle, 1997.

McLaren, Brian D. *A Generous Othodoxy: Why I Am a Missional, Evangelical, Post/Protestant, Liberal/Conservative, Mystical/Poetic, Biblical, Charismatic/Contemplative, Fundamentalist/ Calvinist, Anabaptist/Anglican, Methodist, Catholic, Green, Incarnational, Depressed-yet-Hopeful, Emergent, Unfinished Christian.* El Cajon, CA: Emergent YS, 2004.

McLuhan, T. C. *Touch the Earth; A Self-Portrait of Indian Existence.* New York: Outerbridge & Dienstfrey; distributed by E.P. Dutton, 1971.

Metaxas, Eric,. *Bonhoeffer: Pastor, Martyr, Prophet, Spy.* Nashville: Thomas Nelson, 2011.

Miller, Donald. *Searching for God Knows What.* Nashville: Nelson Books, 2004.

Olson, C. Gordon. Beyond *Calvinism and Arminianism: An Inductive Mediate Theology of Salvation.* Cedar Knolls, NJ: Global Gospel Publishers, 2002.

Peterson, Eugene H. *The Pastor: A Memoir.* New York: HarperOne, 2011.

Plantinga, Cornelius. *Not the Way It's Supposed to Be: A Breviary of Sin.* Grand Rapids, Mich: Eerdmans, 1995.

Platt, David. *Radical: Taking Back Your Faith from the American Dream.* Colorado Springs, CO: Multnomah Books, 2010.

Postman, Neil. *Amusing Ourselves to Death: Public Discourse in the Age of Show Business.* New York: Penguin Books, 1986.

Postman, Neil. *Technopoly: The Surrender of Culture to Technology.* New York: Knopf, 1992.

Schaeffer, Edith. *Christianity Is Jewish.* Wheaton, Ill: Tyndale House Publishers, 1975.

Schaeffer, Francis A. *Pollution and the Death of Man; The Christian View of Ecology.* Wheaton, Ill: Tyndale House Publishers, 1970.

———. *The Church at the End of the 20th Century.* Downers Grove, Ill: Inter-Varsity Press, 1970.

Schultze, Quentin J. *Habits of the High-Tech Heart: Living Virtuously in the Information Age.* Grand Rapids, Mich: Baker Books, 2002.

Sciacca, Fran. *Generation at Risk: What Legacy Are the Baby-Boomers Leaving Their Kids?* Chicago: Moody Press, 1991.

Shenk, David. *Data Smog: Surviving the Information Glut.* San Francisco, Calif: Harper Edge, 1997.

Shenk, David. *The End of Patience: Cautionary Notes on the Information Revolution.* Bloomington: Indiana University Press, 1999.

Smith, Christian, and Melinda Lundquist Denton. *Soul Searching: The Religious and Spiritual Lives of American Teenagers.* Oxford: Oxford University Press, 2005.

Sweet, Leonard I. *Carpe Mañana: Is Your Church Ready to Seize Tomorrow?* Grand Rapids, Mich: Zondervan, 2001.

Tickle, Phyllis. *The Great Emergence: How Christianity Is Changing and Why.* Grand Rapids, Mich: Baker Books, 2008.

Toqueville, Alexis de. *Democracy in America.* Cambridge: Sever & Francis, 1863.

Tozer, A. W. *The Knowledge of the Holy: The Attributes of God, Their Meaning in the Christian Life.* New York: Harper & Row, 1961.

Turkle, Sherry. *Alone Together: Why We Expect More From Technology And Less From Each Other.* New York: Basic Books, 2011.

Twenge, Jean M. *Generation Me: Why Today's Young Americans Are More Confident, Assertive, Entitled—and More Miserable Than Ever Before.* New York: Free Press, 2006.

Twenge, Jean M., and W. Keith Campbell. *The Narcissism Epidemic: Living in the Age of Entitlement.* New York: Free Press, 2009.

Wangerin, Walter. *The Book of God: The Bible As a Novel.* Grand Rapids, Mich: Zondervan, 1996.

Wangerin, Walter. *Paul: A Novel.* Grand Rapids, Mich: Zondervan Pub. House, 2000.

Wangerin, Walter. *Jesus: A Novel.* Grand Rapids, Mich: Zondervan, 2005.

Webber, Robert. *Ancient-Future Faith: Rethinking Evangelicalism for a Postmodern World.* Grand Rapids, Mich: Baker Books, 1999.

Webber, Robert. *The Younger Evangelicals: Facing the Challenges of the New World.* Grand Rapids, Mich: Baker Books, 2002.

Willard, Dallas. *The Divine Conspiracy: Rediscovering Our Hidden Life in God.* San Francisco: HarperSanFrancisco, 1998.

Wolterstorff, Nicholas, Clarence W. Joldersma, and Gloria Goris Stronks. *Educating for Shalom: Essays on Christian Higher Education.* Grand Rapids, Mich: W. B. Eerdmans Pub. Co, 2004.

Wright, Christopher J. H. *The Mission of God: Unlocking the Bible's Grand Narrative.* Downers Grove, Ill: IVP Academic, 2006.

Wright, Christopher J. H. *The Mission of God's People: A Biblical Theology of the Church's Mission.* Grand Rapids, Mich: Zondervan, 2010.

Wright, N. T. *Surprised by Hope: Rethinking Heaven, the Resurrection, and the Mission of the Church.* New York: HarperOne, 2008.

Wright, N. T. *Simply Jesus: Who He Was, What He Did, Why It Matters.* New York: HarperOne, 2011.

Reflective Questions
For Individuals or Groups

The following pages are intended to provide the opportunity to engage the content of *So, What's Your Point?* on a more personal and practical level. They are equally suited for private reflection, and group discussion.

Chapter 1 – We're In Middle Earth, Not Kansas

Questions

1. Which shift within the spiritual landscape of our country over the last several years surprised you the most and why?

2. Fran states that much of the prophetic and critical voice of our society is coming from the unbelieving world as opposed to the church. Why is that? What should that tell us about ourselves?

3. Fran also states that we are becoming increasingly selfish and less rational as a society at large. What do you see are the primary culprits for this moral and intellectual deterioration?

Application

Take an honest assessment of your own time use each day, particularly as it relates to use of "virtual" community. Ask the Lord to help you identify an area where you can reduce your time consumption with that medium. Ask a friend if they would be willing to hold you accountable—to check on how you are doing each week.

Chapter 2 – Pushing Koheleth's Chain

Questions

1. "Disillusion is the child of illusion." What are some of the illusions that we as believers latch onto that leads to disillusion? Give some specific examples.

2. Why is an illusory understanding of the gospel or of Christ Himself so dangerous to our faith?

3. Why do you believe so many Christians purchase books pertaining to find their purpose, discovering meaning, and achieving fulfillment? What does this tell us about ourselves?

Application

Before diving into part 2 take some time to list your top-seven descriptors for yourself if someone were to stop and ask, "who are you?

Chapter 4 – The Adamic Rung

Questions

1. Why is it important that our "Adamic residue" should be the first rung on our Identity Ladder?

2. How should it help us relate to unbelievers when we consider that we have a shared Adamic residue?

3. Fran states that like Adam a) there's a part of us that loves sin, b) we tend to hide our sin and c) we usually blame others when we sin. Do you agree with these three points? If so, where do you see examples of this pattern in our culture? Where do you see it in the church?

Application

In your devotional time this week ask the Lord to identify an aspect of your Adamic residue that you have either defended, hidden, or blamed on others. Confess that sin and repent. If reconciliation needs to be pursued with someone else—do it.

Chapter 5 – The Adopted Rung

Questions

1. Fran states that our adoption in Christ is both "thrilling" and "chilling." What does he mean by this?

2. When we share our testimony with others how can we erroneously focus all of it on ourselves? How do we keep the focus on Christ?

3. Fran says, "Humility" is the inevitable consequence of truly understanding adoption." What does he mean by this? How does pride defeat the fact that we've properly understood adoption?

4. Is it possible to declare to others that we're adopted by Christ but not embrace the responsibilities that come with being a part of His family? How have you seen yourself living responsibly? Explain.

Application

Take an opportunity this week to share what you've learned regarding adoption. Seek a way to share or re-express your testimony with someone in your family or group, using the adoption language. Or prayerfully look for an opportunity to share your testimony with an unbeliever and ask the Lord to help you share it in a way that only He gets the glory.

Chapter 6 – The Abrahamic Rung

Questions

1. What are the dangers of compartmentalizing our study and understanding of Scripture into three stories as opposed to seeing it as one Story?

2. Why is it important to know and understand that we are children of Abraham if we are Christians?

3. Beyond the "who" and the "how" of election, what is so crucial about understanding the "why" of election?

4. How does God's initial call to Abraham to be a blessing to the nations fill your own life with a sense of meaning and purpose? How might that impact your future?

Application

Thank God that he extended the Abrahamic blessing to both Jews and Gentiles alike. Then ask him to show you specific ways to use your life as a blessing to those around you.

Chapter 7 – The Alien Rung

Questions

1. How is an absence of faith exhibited when we despise the role God has called us to play in His story?

2. Why do we place such an emphasis on Jesus' command to "come" and so little emphasis on His command to "go?" How has this impacted you, personally?

3. What are the primary "tourist traps" that can increase our love for the kosmos but not the natives? How do we avoid these traps?

4. What would it look like for you to live a distinct "Alien life" in today's modern American culture?

5. What are the specific and primary ways Aliens can show genuine love and concern for the Natives?

Application

Think of an unbelieving family member, friend or co-worker that you know. Identify up to three specific ways that you can serve or be a blessing to them this week.

Chapter 8 – The Apprentice Rung

Questions

1. How would our lives look different if we embraced the reality that our existence as subjects to a King supersedes the fact that we are citizens in a democracy?

2. What are some of the key distractions even within our spiritual disciplines that keep us from pursuing Christ so that we might actually be more like Him?

3. Which "common law marriage" do you struggle with the most in your own spiritual life and why?

4. What are some key strategies and disciplines that we can develop to help us from making godless decisions?

Application

Take a look at your own plans for the next two or three days. Based on what you learned in this chapter, are any of them "godless"?

Or

Assuming that Christ is who you're seeking to emulate the most, jot down the names of the next top three influencers on your life. Then ask the Lord to help you identify whether or not these men/women are good for you to imitate as an apprentice.

Chapter 9 – The Ambassador Rung

Questions

1. If we understand that we are Ambassadors representing our heavenly King and His heavenly message, how should this affect our daily lives and interactions with Natives?

2. Understanding that we are Ambassadors, how does this affect your view on the gravity of your responsibility to share the gospel?

Application

Pray the Lord would give you a specific opportunity to live out your life as an ambassador and to share something about your faith at least once each day this week.

Chapter 10 – The Advocate Rung

Questions

1. What happens when we view the "poor as a problem to be solved" rather than a "people to be reached?"

2. How does it affect your understanding of Christ's mission on earth when you discover that His first public sermon (Luke 4:18-19) and one of his final recorded statements (Matt. 25:31-46) deals specifically with advocacy for the poor?

3. How does it affect your view of your own life when you discover that your own level of advocacy of the poor will be judged by Christ in the end?

4. Which rung of the Identity Ladder challenged you the most and why? Which rung encouraged you the most and why?

5. In your opinion, what specific ways has "tribalism" disrupted the unity of the American church the most? How do we address and do away with tribalism in our churches?

Application

If you're not already intentionally and regularly involved in some ministry that advocates for the poor and the disenfranchised then do some research in your hometown and find a ministry where you can plug in.

Or

If you're already engaged in such a ministry then recruit a friend or co-worker to start joining you as an advocate.

Chapter 11 – "Plot Hunger"

Questions

1. Fran posits that identity determines purpose and purpose determines meaning. What are the consequences for us of not knowing who we are in the first place?

2. Fran states that God has one central plot to the grand Story of life. Does this excite you or concern you? Why?

3. A competing plot with God's one Story is the "Chart Your Own Adventure" plot line. What are some of the "good adventures" that we as Christ-followers can pursue that are actually distractions from following Christ's plot?

Application

Identify one or two "adventures" in your own life that seem to compete with God's one Story. Prayerfully try to discern if those adventures can be brought into the Story. If they can't pray for the courage and the ability to let those adventures go by the wayside.

Chapters 12 & 13 – Getting The Story Straight & "Working Our Way Backwards"

Questions

1. Why is it important to view the Bible as one grand narrative? What occurs when we don't?

2. How should an understanding that we will spend eternity on a new earth (not heaven) shape the way you live now?

3. Does the false assumption that in eternity, all rewards from Christ will be the same, affect the way you are living? Does anything need to change?

4. Why is it so crucial that we understand and fix our eyes on the "end" of the Story?

Application

In your own prayer life ask the Lord to increasingly expose in your life where you are overemphasizing living for today and not for eternity. Then, discuss this with someone who can hep you make the necessary changes.

Chapter 14 – New Eyes, Not Restored Sight

Questions

1. How does the understanding that God's master story for all of Creation is too lofty for you to comprehend make you feel?

2. What is it about the character of God that gives you great confidence in the Story even though you might be only able to comprehend a small piece of it?

3. Paul required scales to fall from his eyes before he could "see" what God was up to. What are some "scales" in your own eyes that might prevent you from seeing what God is doing?

Application

Ask the Lord to open your eyes to better see and better trust whatHe is doing in the world. Write them down or talk to someone about what you are learning.

Chapter 15 – Epitaphs: A Final Bumper Sticker

Questions

1. What is the difference between placing an emphasis on information and transformation as it relates to maturity in Christ? Why is it important to recognize this difference?

2. Fran states that we must see ourselves as "story-dwellers" as opposed to "story-tellers." What is the danger to our growth as believers if we see ourselves primarily as "story-tellers?"

3. How does understanding our calling into God's bigger Story revolutionize how we can share the gospel with an unbeliever?

Application

Sit down with your spouse, a friend, or accountability partner, and share with them some concrete ways that you hope to use your life, calling and vocation to live more as a "story dweller."

Chapter 16 & 17 – Plot Anemia & "In The Beginning..."

Questions

1. In what ways can we mistakenly live as "story-*quellers*" as opposed to "story-*dwellers?*" What steps can we take to avoid living as "*queller?*"

2. Why do we as believers more often than not have a greater fascination in "foretelling" than "forth-telling?" What does this tell us about ourselves?

3. Fran tells us that "contentment" is finding satisfaction with our role in the Story. How do we cultivate contentment within our role? Are you experiencing this now? If not, what needs to change?

Application

Make a list of ways where you are clearly living as a Story-dweller.

Chapters 18 & 19 – "Intermission" & Looking Back To The Future

Questions

1. Fran urges us to look a the four gospels as Act IV in a larger Story rather than as the start of the New Testament. How will this impact the way you read your Bible?

2. Why is seeing our own personal justification as the center-piece of the gospel so misleading?

3. What happens when we do this? How can we change this?

4. In what ways did both the Pharisees and the Jews look to Jesus to be the center of their own personal stories?

Application

In your own prayers this week, focus some time on asking the Lord to show you specific ways to enter into His Story as a servant. Perhaps begin by committing to read through one of the Gospel accounts to look at the life of Jesus as a servant.

Chapter 20 – Looking Ahead To The Past

Questions

1. Fran says that in this present scene "we haven't got a clue what we're doing." What does he mean by this? How does it make you feel regarding your own life?
2. He says that our certainty without apology or reservation, concerning life and ministry, looks like arrogance to the watching world. In what specific ways have you seen this arrogance displayed by the American church?
3. In what specific ways can our desire to make a contribution to the Story compete with our commitment to the Story itself?

Application

This week ask your spouse to closest friend if (in their opinion) whether or not you've been a good listener when it comes to helping them with their own struggles, fears or concerns. Let them know you want them to be honest with you. Do they feel like you've operated out of a stance of humility or pride? Then ask the Lord to help you respond with increased patience and humility in the days ahead.

Or

Pray for patience and humility as you seek to understand some of the wounds and unexplainable pains in your own life.

Chapter 21 – Milton Got It, Why Can't We?

Questions

1. How does this chapter alter your view of the magnitude of sin's effect on not only you but also on all of creation?
2. How does reducing the gospel to simply declaring man innocent of guilt fail to show the full power of restorative grace?
3. Fran states that sin destroyed our relationship with God, with others, with ourselves and with creation. Of these areas, where have you seen the effects of sin the most and why?
4. Of these areas where do you see the greatest challenges in being a "shalom-restorer?" Why?
5. In what areas would you like to see the Church be a leader in shalom restoring as opposed to following the restorative trends of an unbelieving world?

Application

What are some specific and ongoing ways that you can immerse yourself (and your family if applicable) in being a "shalom-restorer?" Make a list of the possibilities in your own city, working your way outward from your own neighborhood.

Chapter 22 – The Real World of Warcraft

Questions

1. Why is it so tempting to focus on "living in scene two and longing for scene three?" What can we do to prevent that focus from becoming dominant in our lives?

2. What are some intentional steps we can take to prevent the American dream and capitalism from driving our theology and the way we engage the Story?

3. How did you respond to the metaphors of distance running and warfare as descriptors for faithfulness to the Story? Which metaphor did you connect with most and why? Provide some concrete examples from your own life on how that metaphor related.

4. How can social media be used to promote the Story rather than promoting yourself? (This would be an excellent subject to brainstorm with others.)

Application

Take some time to review your application goals from the preceding chapters. Which ones have made an impact on you? Which ones do you need to press into or complete? Who can help you? (Accountability is critical, when it comes to making changes in our lives.)

Jot down 5 specific and achievable ways that you can incorporate this book into your daily living.